DATE DUE			
MAR 1 2 1995			

ALTERNATIVE ALCOTT

AMERICAN WOMEN WRITERS SERIES

Joanne Dobson, Judith Fetterley, and Elaine Showalter, series editors

ALTERNATIVE ALCOTT

LOUISA MAY ALCOTT

Edited and with an Introduction by

ELAINE SHOWALTER

RUTGERS UNIVERSITY PRESS

New Brunswick and London

Second printing, 1989

Copyright © 1988 by Rutgers, The State University
All rights reserved
Manufactured in the United States of America
Diana and Persis is used by permission of the Houghton Library.

Library of Congress Cataloging-in-Publication Data

Alcott, Louisa May, 1832–1888.
Alternative Alcott.

(The American women writers series)
Bibliography: p.
Contents: Hospital sketches—My contraband—
Behind a mask—Happy women—Pysche's art—
The sunny side, from An old-fashioned girl—Work,
a story of experience—How I went out to service—
Transcendental wild oats—Diana and Persis—Jo's
last scrape, from Jo's boys.
I. Showalter, Elaine. II. Title. III. Series.
PS1016.S56 1987 813'.4 87-9744
ISBN 0-8135-1271-9
ISBN 0-8135-1272-7 (pbk.)

British Cataloging-in-Publication information available.

CONTENTS

ACKNOWLEDGMENTS

I owe special thanks in the preparation of this book to Elizabeth Keyser, whose advice about Alcott's manuscripts and texts was invaluable, and who, along with Jan Albergene, first discovered the reversed chapters in *Diana and Persis*. I had expert help too from two Princeton University research assistants; Lynne Rogers tracked down and transcribed many of the texts included here, and Jayne Lewis prepared the notes. Thanks also are due to the Princeton University Faculty Committee on Research in the Humanities and Social Sciences, and to the staff at the Houghton Library at Harvard University. It is always a pleasure to acknowledge the extraordinary editorial support of Leslie Mitchner, and to thank my coeditors in the Rutgers Series, Judith Fetterley and Joanne Dobson.

INTRODUCTION

IN THE late years of her career, pressured by the demands of her readers and her publishers for more work from the pen that had given them the best-selling *Little Women,* Louisa May Alcott taught herself to write with her left hand. Ambidexterity allowed her to keep her desk twice as long, to produce twice as much, in short, to become a doubly efficient writing machine. But Alcott's ambidexterity also appears as a striking physical metaphor for her creativity, the body's correlative for her "double literary life" (Douglas, intro *LW* vii). Modern critics have generally seen her enormous output (at least 270 works in every genre from poetry to tragedy) as divided between conflicting literary impulses. On the genteel, domestic, and moralizing side are Alcott's famous chronicles of the March family—*Little Women* (1868), *Little Men* (1871), and *Jo's Boys* (1886)—as well as the seven other novels and sixteen short-story collections for young people which made her famous as the "children's friend." On the other hand—the left hand?—Alcott inscribed her passion, anger, and satirical wit, producing a series of pseudonymous sensation stories; four novels for adults—*Moods* (1864), *Work* (1873), *A Modern Mephistopheles* (1877), and the unfinished *Diana and Persis* (1879)—; *Transcendental Wild Oats* (1872), a comic memoir of her family's failed communal experiment; and numerous historical and feminist essays.

Introduction

This book brings together many kinds of writing from Louisa May Alcott's left hand, texts that despite their internal differences offer a radical perspective on her work. Both the sensation stories she wrote from "behind a mask" and her feminist novels for adults reveal a woman very different from her celebrated image as either the kindly "Aunt Jo" who preached self-sacrifice, or the self-styled "Ancient Lu" who practiced it in endless support of her family. Instead we see a passionate spinner of feminist plots and counterplots, a writer drawn to "earthquaky" (Cheney 128) and volcanic themes, and a sharp-tongued master of a racy and unladylike American vernacular. Reading the work of this alternative Alcott also leads us back to her domestic romances with a sharper vision of their suppressed radical elements, and helps us understand similar divisions masked by domestic conventions in the writing of other nineteenth-century American women.

The double voice of women's writing has been a central topic in contemporary feminist literary criticism, where it has been analyzed as the product of the daughter's psychic conflict between the cultural legacies and laws of the father and the mother. From the paternal side comes the voice of the rational, realistic, and didactic, defining but also forbidding access to patriarchal cultural authority. From the maternal side comes a more imaginative, disruptive, passionate, and intimate voice, seductive but culturally marginal. Alcott often wrote about such gendered cultural divisions in her fiction, casting realism as masculine, romance as feminine. In an allegorical children's story called "Fancy's Friend" (1868), she describes "Aunt Fiction" as a "graceful picturesque woman, who told stories charmingly, wrote poetry and novels, was much beloved by young folks, and was the friend of some of the most famous people in the world," and "Uncle Fact" as a "grave, decided man" who "knew an immense deal; and was always taking notes of things he saw and heard, to be put in a great encyclopedia he was making. He didn't like romance, loved the truth, and wanted to get to the bottom of everything" (*Aunt Jo's Scrap-Bag* 218).

But if these figures of Fiction and Fact mirrored the values of nineteenth-century American literature, they did not correspond exactly to Alcott's own unusual parents, who mixed and challenged both sex roles and literary roles. The second of four daughters (her sisters Anna, Elizabeth, and May, became the Meg, Beth, and Amy of *Little Women*), Louisa was born on her father's thirty-third birthday, November 29, 1832. Amos Bronson Alcott was one of the eccentric seers of American Transcendentalism, a minor prophet, gadfly, philosopher, and educational reformer admired and often subsidized by more successful contemporaries such as Emerson and Hawthorne. The self-educated son of a poor Connecticut farmer, he had started out as a Yankee peddler, and had risen to directing schools where his progressive and controversial ideas of child development could be put into practice. Within the family, Bronson played an active role in child care, and even baked the family bread. Yet his dreams of achieving spiritual transcendence and human perfection were in continual conflict with his financial obligations as father and husband. "He is quite ready at any moment to abandon his wife and children," Emerson noted at one point, in order "to put any new dream into practice which has bubbled up in the effervescence of discourse" (Whicher, 128). No systematic "Uncle Fact," the visionary but impractical Bronson was both adored and resented by the wife and daughters who had to support the family in the face of his lifelong improvidence. His inability to earn a living became proverbial even among the high-minded and unworldly Transcendentalists; he "possesses no gift for money making," Louisa ruefully noted in her journal (quoted in Stern, intro *Behind a Mask* viii). She took on the roles of the surrogate son and the family breadwinner, as well as that of the dutiful daughter. To a very considerable degree, her identification and rivalry with her father would dominate her whole life.

Abigail May Alcott (Abba), Louisa's mother, was an equally powerful and unusual influence. Abba had been the youngest child in a prominent and politically liberal Boston family, the Mays, who had fought in the Revolution, and supported abolition, prison reform, and philanthropic activism. Well educated, idealistic, and frustrated by the limitations her society placed on women, Abba enthusiastically shared her husband's Romantic and Transcendental ideals of idyllic family life. But with each new hardship and evidence of his inability to plan and provide, she became more cynical about his philosophy and more embittered about women's lot. Forceful and ambitious, she became the decision maker in the marriage, the one who kept the family solvent and together. Nevertheless, she had also internalized nineteenth-century views of female self-sacrifice, and she taught her daughters to repress their anger in the name of duty, as she had struggled with her own hot temper. Both parents thought that the impetuous, strong-willed Louisa took after her mother's side. "Louisa is a true blue May," Abba announced (Bedell, *Alcotts* 74). Throughout her life, Alcott cherished feelings of "fierce, almost primitive simplicity" for her mother, who was, according to the biographer Madelon Bedell, her "twin, her double, her beloved model" (intro *LW* xxxii).

Louisa's early years were marked by a power struggle between the two parents for psychological dominance and authority over their children and for the children's loyalty. Bedell has described Bronson's influence as a "seductive control" (*Alcotts* 89) to which his eldest and favorite daughter Anna meekly succumbed, while the tougher Louisa, her mother's favorite, resisted. Bronson's fascination with child psychology led him to keep lengthy journals describing his three eldest daughters' infancy. Even as a baby, he noted, Louisa had a strong personality, a physical energy and willfulness that he determined to subdue. When Louisa was two and Anna nearly four, Bronson decided to enter the nursery, where Abba, he felt, did not exert enough control, and to establish a firm discipline. He set out to tame stubborn Louisa "down to docility" by an elaborate system of routines, rewards, Socratic interrogations, and punishments (Bedell, intro *LW* xxxi). Opposed to corporal punishment, Bronson usually disciplined the children by withholding affection. The rigid schedule he imposed on the nursery had the children drilled to perform various tasks according to the hour, and he would not tolerate breaks in the routine. Louisa had to sit next to her mother at the dinner table instead of on her lap, go to bed without a light, and give up treats to her sister or to other children in order to learn the "sweetness of self-denial."

Bronson used every ceremonial occasion, such as their joint birthday, to reinforce his critique of Louisa's behavior. On her eighth birthday in 1840, he presented her with a poem: "Two passions strong divide our life,— / Meek, gentle, love, or boisterous strife." These childhood maxims left the naturally ebullient Louisa with permanent feelings of guilt and worthlessness; she could never be gentle, loving or meek enough to please her father, and these were the traits he associated with femininity. No wonder that, as she noted in her journal, birthdays were dismal times to her (Cheney 89). Only "Marmee" seemed to give her unconditional love, sympathy, and support.

Yet Bronson endorsed his daughter's intelligence and imagination, and served as a model of the intellectual life in what she called "this famous land of Emerson, Hawthorne, Thoreau, Alcott, & Co." Her earliest memory, she recalled, was of "playing with books in my father's study—building houses and bridges of the big dictionaries and diaries, looking at pictures, pretending to read, and scribbling on blank pages whenever pen or pencil could be found" (Cheney 27). In a more private way, Abba too was a writer and storyteller. Her stories were "highly romantic" accounts of "the Revolution, of the witchcraft days," while Bronson's were "abstract and allegorical" (Salyer 75). He used every story to teach a moral lesson; on the other hand, Abba stressed ingenuity and imagination and lavished praise on Louisa's literary efforts. As a child, one of Louisa's favorite pastimes was to move her playthings back and forth between her father's study and the nursery where her mother held sway, as if unable to choose between these two powerful precursors.

Bronson's visions, however, determined the shape of Louisa's life until her teens. The family moved frequently, always in a state of financial emergency, to pursue his dreams and enterprises. When his experimental Temple School in Boston collapsed—undermined by reports that he was providing his pupils with sex education in Socratic dialogs about life, and finally destroyed when he took in a black pupil—the Alcotts moved to Concord. The Concord years were Louisa's happiest, even when Bronson left the family for a long sabbatical to England at Emerson's expense. In some respects his absence came as a welcome respite for her from his constant watchful criticism and a chance to enjoy the company of her mother and sisters without competition from his emotional demands on them. The energetic Louisa was allowed to run and to be competitive rather than self-effacing; she recalled that "I always thought I must have been a deer or a horse in some former state, because it was such a joy to run. No boy could be my friend until I had beaten him in a race, and no girl if she refused to climb trees, leap fences, and be a tomboy" (Cheney 20).

Bronson returned from England full of plans for a self-supporting utopian community, and in 1843, when Louisa was eleven, the Alcotts along with six other dedicated members of the Consociate Family set up their commune at Fruitlands. She would later satirize the experiment as "Apple Slump" in *Transcendental Wild Oats* (reprinted here), but the reality was far from comic. The vegetarian Consociates lived on apples, potatoes, bread, and water; the crops failed in their inexperienced hands; the community dwindled and sickened as the harsh winter set in; and for a while the family almost broke up when Charles Lane, the most fanatical ascetic of the group, persuaded Bronson that the utopian ideal required celibacy and renunciation of individual family ties. In the final days of Fruitlands, the despairing Bronson suffered a severe breakdown in which he tried to starve himself to death; Abba rescued the family by appealing to the Mays for support. After 1844, when the Alcotts moved back to Concord, Bronson never again made a serious attempt to provide for them. He led "Conversations" among his Boston disciples, planted gardens and did carpentry at their various houses, carried out lecture tours, and wrote and published unsuccessful volumes of "Orphic Sayings." "I have taken the ship into my own command," Abba wrote to her brother Samuel (Bedell, intro *LW* xxviii).

For Louisa, adolescence was a difficult period. At fourteen, she despaired of ever achieving the docile little womanhood her parents and her society demanded: "I am old for my age and dont care much for girls' things. People think I'm wild and queer; but Mother understands and helps me. . . . I've made so many resolutions, and written sad notes, and cried over my sins, and it doesn't seem to do any good" (Cheney 48). The strenuous boyish activities of her childhood had to be curtailed, and not even Bronson's fanatical vegetarianism could prevent the sexual and emotional turbulence of puberty. "I've never eaten any meat," she noted sadly, "but I'm awfully cross and irritable" (Cheney 54).

Without either formal education or exercise as outlets for her energies, and in the face of the family's continuing poverty, the teenage Louisa lived defiantly in her imagination. She developed a sentimental passion for Emerson, writing him romantic letters she never sent, and hovering outside his house in the moonlight. Many melodramatic fantasies went into writing plays that the sisters performed at home, and both she and Anna dreamed of going on the stage. When she was fifteen, she later recalled, the family decided to "move to Boston and try our fate again after years in the wilderness." Running to her favorite retreat in the woods, Louisa made private vows of success: "I *will* do something by-and-by. Don't care what, teach, sew, act, write, anything to help the family; and I'll be rich and famous and happy before I die, see if I won't!" (Alcott, *Memoir*)

Yet these longings for artistic freedom and fortune had to be totally suppressed in the little house in Boston's South End, where she "felt like a caged sea-gull" as she washed and cooked in the windowless basement kitchen (Alcott, *Memoir*). Her education had always been sketchy and sporadic; among the sisters only May, the youngest, went to the public schools. Now even reading had to be sacrificed; there was "very little time to write or think" (Cheney 62). Her father's censorship of female self-consciousness as selfish and narcissistic conflicted with Alcott's need to explore her own feelings as a young woman and a budding writer. When she was seventeen, Bronson noted disapprovingly that while Anna's journal was "about other people, Louisa's is about herself" (Cheney 60). For several years thereafter she wrote only intermittently in her journal, and her struggle to deny the self shows up as well in her characteristic omission of the first person in both her diary entries and Jo's truncated speech in *Little Women*.

First Abba, who undertook social work among the Irish immigrants in Boston, at a salary of 75 cents a day, and then Louisa, who vowed that she would show that "though an *Alcott,* I *can* support myself" (Cheney 84), became the family breadwinners. Anna too hired herself out as a governess, and Lizzie took over the housework. In 1851, weary of sewing and teaching, and in the spirit of Emersonian self-reliance, Louisa accepted a job as a domestic servant. Her employer, the Honorable James Richardson of Dedham, who had participated in Bronson's "Conversations," had come to the city employment agency run by Abba seeking a companion to his father and sister, and Louisa decided to take the job herself, although, as Abba wrote to her brother, "every sentiment of her being revolted at it" (Saxton 206). In "How I Went Out to Service," published in *The Independent* in June 1874 and reprinted here, Alcott described the experience of drudgery, exploitation, and sexual harassment Madeleine Stern dubs "The Humiliation at Dedham" (*Essays* 52). Although he had promised her light duties in a genteel household, Richardson proved to be a domestic tyrant, almost a caricature of her father, who pursued her with sighs, notes, and poems, and then loaded her down with the dirtiest labor of the house when she rejected his advances. After six weeks, she left, but the story conveys the deep angry sense of women's wrongs which would fuel her sensation fiction.

In spite of all the temporal and psychological pressures against it, writing remained Alcott's main emotional outlet. Whenever she could snatch the time, she gave herself up to a "vortex" of ecstatic creativity in which she felt "neither hunger nor fatigue," but was "perfectly happy and seemed to have no wants" (Cheney 122). Her unquenchable sense of humor allowed her to see the ridiculous aspect of everyday life and, in stories and dramatic recitations performed at private theatricals and club meetings, she mocked pomposity and convention. In 1854, Alcott managed to complete and to publish a collection of fairy tales called *Flower Fables,* written for Emerson's daughter Ellen. The young author presented the book to Abba Alcott "knowing that you will accept it with all its faults (for grandmothers are always kind)" (Cheney 77), and crediting her mother for "whatever beauty or poetry is to be found in my little book." Despite the slightness of her debut, Alcott intended to "pass in time from fairies and fables to men and reality" (Cheney 76–77). In precious minutes saved from her other work, she continued to review books for the newspaper, to "scribble" at her poems and short stories, and to try to get her dramatic farces produced.

Nevertheless, the 1850s were years of hardship and discouragement. At one point in October 1857, Alcott was unable to find work and experienced such despair that she even thought of suicide. It was during this year that she read Elizabeth Gaskell's biography of Charlotte Brontë. *Jane Eyre* had always been one of her favorite novels, and the story of the novelist's tragic life suggested many parallels to her own: "Read Charlotte Brontë's life. A very interesting but sad one. So full of talent; and after working long, just as success, love and happiness come, she dies. Wonder if I shall ever be famous enough for people to care to read my story and struggles. I can't be a C.B., but I may do a little something yet" (Cheney 95). Abba had noted in her journal that the Brontës' "struggle reminded me of my own dear girls" (Elbert, *Hunger* 252), and Alcott must have felt the correspondences that made her family seem like the American Brontës—the sisters drawing and writing together; their melodramas like the Brontës' childhood sagas; the painful decline and death of Lizzie, so like that of Anne Brontë; Anna's terrible homesickness as a governess, like that of Emily Brontë in Brussels.

Lizzie's death in 1858 was a terrible crisis, but Anna's marriage the same year to a neighbor, John Pratt, was almost as hard for Louisa to bear. Anna had been her closest confidante besides her mother, "my one bosom friend and comforter" (Cheney 69), and her wedding signaled the breakup of a sustaining sisterhood. "I'd rather be a free spinster and paddle my own canoe," Louisa wrote; the spectacle of her mother's difficult married life— eight pregnancies in ten years, poverty, and hard work—made her suspicious of marriage in general, and in much of her writing she would defend the option of spinsterhood.

In an 1868 essay called "Happy Women" (reprinted here), Alcott sketched the lives of four contented old maids, putting on her list "all the busy, useful, independent spinsters I know, for liberty is a better husband than love to many of us" (Cheney 197). L., the doctor, is Rhoda Lawrence, a homeopathic physician who treated her for a variety of psychosomatic illnesses; S., the philanthropist, is Hannah Stevenson, the Boston reformer, to whom she dedicated *Hospital Sketches.* Alcott herself appears as the writer A., "who in the course of an unusually varied experience has seen so much of what a wise man has called 'the tragedy of modern married life' that she is afraid to try it. Knowing that for one of a peculiar nature like herself such an experiment would be doubly hazardous, she has obeyed instinct and become a chronic old maid." By "peculiar nature," Alcott probably meant her moodiness, ambition, and hot temper; nevertheless, she had passionate sexual and maternal feelings that she could never entirely repress, and up until her death she would regret the seemingly necessary sacrifice of sexuality and motherhood to work. Contrasting herself to Anna and her children, she wrote, "She is a happy woman! I sell my children, and though they feed me, they don't love me as hers do" (Cheney 195).

In the 1850s, Alcott's journals also reflect the disturbing feelings of rivalry and jealousy generated by the good fortune of her youngest sister, May. The most vivacious, sunny, and independent of the daughters, May had escaped much of the pressure of Bronson's moral surveillance, and had basked in the role of baby in the family. A gifted artist, May grew up determined to design her own life and willing to accept the generosity of others in order to achieve her ends. The guilt-ridden Louisa envied and resented May's capacity for pleasure and ability to put her own needs first. Even in childhood, she had been jealous of the "curly-haired intruder, eight years younger than herself, an irritating child whom she had to care for when she wanted to be free, the little sister whose coming had destroyed her last hopes for a brother. 'I often wish I had a little brother,' she wrote in her diary once, 'but as I have not I shall try to be contented with what I have got'" (Bedell, *Alcotts* 249). Madelon Bedell speculates that Alcott could never forgive May for possessing all the social gifts she herself longed for and lacked: "As if unconsciously to compensate for her obsessive envy of her sister, she began at an early age to take on the role of protector and supporter" to May (250).

In her journal and letters to Anna, Louisa's resentment breaks through as she describes her pleasure at buying May luxuries, while denying herself necessities: "I got a crimson ribbon for a bonnet for May . . . she is so graceful and pretty and loves beauty so much, it is hard for her to be poor and wear other people's ugly things. . . . I have learned not to mind *much* . . ." (Cheney 73–74) In a note often struck, she observes that benefactors were always ready to pay for May's art lessons, while she herself had to struggle alone: "She is a fortunate girl, and always finds someone to help her as she wants to be helped. Wish I could do the same, but suppose as I never do that it is best for me to work and wait and do all for myself" (Ticknor 58).

"Work and wait" became her motto. The best women artists, she tried to persuade herself, were those who were truly unselfish and ultimately womanly self-denial would bring its own reward in an enriched art. In numerous short stories such as "Psyche's Art" (reprinted here), as well as in *Little Women,* Alcott represented suffering, dutifulness, and self-sacrifice as necessary steps toward female artistic success.

Alcott's professional writing life really began after 1862 when she made the daring decision to volunteer as a nurse in a Civil War army hospital. The war had activated many of Alcott's repressed longings for action and adventure, as well as her frustrations with the feminine role: "I've often longed to see a war," she wrote in her journal, "I long to be a man; but as I can't fight I will content myself with working for those who can" (Cheney 127). At last, on her thirtieth birthday, Alcott decided to enlist as an army nurse: "I want new experiences, and am sure to get 'em if I go" (Cheney 140). The age of thirty was a significant threshold for nineteenth-century women, a moment of acknowledgment that the marriageable years were past. Enlistment was a way of declaring herself an independent adult, and a decision to seek out serious material for her writing.

Yet the experience proved far more difficult than she had anticipated. She had expected to serve with other nurses from Massachusetts at the modern Armory Square Hospital, but instead she was assigned to the Union Hotel Hospital, a damp remodeled tavern in Georgetown. Here 189 patients were inefficiently cared for in a dilapidated and poorly heated building by an untrained staff, assisted by convalescent soldiers. Military nursing was a new field for American women. Despite the heroic example of Florence Nightingale, whose *Notes on Nursing* had been published in the United States and who had been commemorated in Longfellow's "The Lady with the Lamp," women were not recruited as hospital nurses until the spring of 1861, when conditions in the Union army hospitals were desperate. Although the work was backbreaking and miserably paid, and the spectacle of suffering much more traumatic than she had anticipated, she was exhilarated by the city of Washington and the challenge of important work: "Though often homesick, heartsick, and worn out, I like it," she wrote in her journal (Cheney 142). But after only six weeks of duty, she caught typhoid fever and was brought home in delirium by her father.

During her convalescence she had strange hallucinations: "The most vivid and enduring was the conviction that I had married a stout, handsome Spaniard, dressed in black velvet, with very soft hands, and a voice that was continually saying, 'Lie still my dear!' This was Mother, I suspect; but with all the comfort I often found in her presence, there was blended an awful fear of the Spanish spouse who was always coming after me, appearing out of closets, in at windows, or threatening me dreadfully all night long. . . . A mob at Baltimore breaking down the door to get me, being hung for a witch, burned, stoned, and otherwise maltreated, were some of my fancies. Also being tempted to join Dr. W. and two of the nurses in worshipping the Devil" (Cheney 146–47).

Alcott's biographers have interpreted these fever dreams, which sound like scenes from the stories of Hawthorne or Poe, as displacements of the sexual anxieties aroused by her intimate contact with male bodies in the hospital. The dreams also suggest her mingled desires toward men and women, black and white; and her confusion of sexual and racial boundaries. Like her mother, Alcott had "Spanish" features—dark hair and olive skin—and among Bronson's eccentric beliefs, bordering on racism, was an attribution of sinister qualities to dark-skinned people. The dream also suggests her rivalry with her father, the "Spanish spouse," whose role she was usurping economically and emotionally. He tells her to "lie still" and spies on her, as Bronson had tried to tame her through supervision and routine. Yet Alcott's erotic feelings toward women, as well as men, may find guilty expression in the dream, which records bisexual desires echoed in her writing (Strickland 108–9). The "soft hands" of the imagined spouse belonged to her mother, who attracted her to an intimate and sensual female world, but also represented "entrapment in the web of Alcott domesticity" (Halttunen, 240). In an interview with the writer Louise Chandler Moulton in 1883, Alcott commented with the candid innocence of a pre-Freudian on her own feelings of bisexuality: "I am more than half-persuaded that I am a man's soul, put by some freak of nature into a woman's body . . . because I have fallen in love in my live with so many pretty girls, and never once the least bit with any man" (Phelps, p. 49). Alcott describes passionate female friendships in *An Old-Fashioned Girl, Work,* and *Diana and Persis.*

Finally, the dream suggests anxieties about the transgressions of writing itself. Alcott's vision of the Baltimore mob referred specifically to the rioters who had stoned the soldiers of the Massachusetts Sixth Regiment as they passed through the city on the way to Washington in April 1861. But in addition, it recalls family legends about witchcraft, stories Abba had told the children about the Salem trials in which a May ancestor had been a repentant judge. As a writer, Alcott had always identified with the witch; in a memoir, she described her imagination as "the caldron" into which every experience entered. As a girl, she wrote a play called "The Witch's Curse," and in "Behind a Mask" her heroine declares, "I am a witch, and one day my disguise will drop away and you will see me as I am, old, ugly, bad, and lost."

The illness took a lifelong toll on Alcott; she never recovered from the poisonous side effects of mercury medication, and permanently lost the stamina and health of her youth. Yet she was able to draw on her war experiences to write about "men and reality" as she had intended. *Hospital Sketches* (1863) was her first literary success; the little volume "never made much money, but it showed me my 'style'"—a mixture of humor, realism, and pathos (Jones xlii). During the next several years, she was finally able to give up other work, developing her literary skills by writing in several different modes. In 1862 she wrote the first of her sensation tales in order to win a hundred-dollar prize offered by *Frank Leslie's Illustrated Newspaper.* "I intend to illuminate the Ledger with a blood and thunder tale as they are easier to 'compoze' & are better paid than moral tales," she wrote a friend (Stern, *Essays* 55). Using the sexually ambiguous pseudonym A. M. Barnard, she published a number of thrillers during the next five years.

In contrast, her much-revised Emersonian novel *Moods* (1864), inscribed to "Mother, my earliest patron, kindest critic, and dearest reader," drew criticism for its frank representation of marriage and divorce. To speak freely of marriage caused trouble, Alcott noted: "My next book shall have no *ideas* in it, only facts, and the people shall be as ordinary as possible; then critics will say it is all right" (Cheney, 166)

In 1865–66, Alcott went to Europe for the first time, not as a journalist, but as the companion to a wealthy young invalid, Anna Weld. The trip might have been a turning point for her; it was her first extended absence from her parents, and she had long dreamed of traveling abroad. Instead she chafed at the restrictions of her job, and often felt lonely, homesick, and bored. The high point of the trip was her meeting in Switzerland with a young Polish musician, Ladislas Wisniewski, who probably was the model for Laurie in *Little Women.* Alcott's defense against sexual attraction and the temptations of marriage, developed during her time as a nurse, was to cast her relationships with men as maternal, and to think of them as "boys" to whom she could safely minister. Since "Laddie" was twelve years younger, she felt secure in expressing her affection for him, and rationalized their friendshp as one of mother and son, indulgently recalling in an essay called "My Boys" (1872) "the frank, fresh affection he gave his 'little mama,' as he insisted on calling the lofty spinster who loved him like half a dozen grandmothers rolled into one." Alcott felt that the age difference allowed her to spend all her time with him, "for my twelve years seniority made our adventures quite proper, and I fearlessly went anywhere on the arm of my big son." Alcott later destroyed her letters about the trip, and we cannot be sure how she felt about Laddie, although in 1873, hearing that he was in need, she sent him $1000. Yet their farewell brought out her feelings of renunciation: "My heart was quite rent within me, and regardless of several prim English ladies, I drew down his tall head and kissed him tenderly, feeling that in this world there were no more meetings for us." ("My Boys")

The trip to Europe was Alcott's farewell to adventure and romance. She returned home in July to Marmee's welcoming arms, but also to new financial obligations and family debts. "Behind a Mask," which she wrote in August 1866, suggests her rage at servitude, and the bitterness with which she faced the prospects of eternal repression and pretense. Her last sensation story, "A Modern Mephistopheles, or The Fatal Love Chase" (1867), was rejected by her publishers as too lurid. A full-length novel about a girl who sells her soul to the devil in exchange for a life of adventure, it powerfully mirrored many of her own temptations, and her fascination with the idea of a female Faust. Alcott never published the story, the manuscript of which is in Houghton Library at Harvard; ten years later she would use the title for a different novel, one that editors and biographers have often confused with her unpublished thriller.

After several years of rising income, Alcott earned $1000 in 1867 and saw a secure future: "I want to realize my dream of supporting the family and being perfectly independent" (Cheney 193). In the interests of this quest for financial stability, she began to make the literary compromises that would plague her for the rest of her career. Early in 1868, she accepted the editorship of a girls' magazine, *Merry's Museum,* to which she contributed stories, poems, and advice under the diminishing pseudonym of "Aunty Wee." She also set out to prepare a new edition of *Hospital Sketches* and her war stories: "By taking out all Biblical allusions, and softening all allusions to rebs, the book may be made 'quite perfect,' I am told. Anything to suit customers" (Cheney 197). Soon after, at the request of her publishers, Roberts Brothers, she set aside her own literary projects to write a "girls' story." *Little Women*—a book she had not particularly wanted to write—ironically made her not only famous, but famous for womanly goodness. Money came pouring in, pilgrims came to see the famous author, and Bronson found new celebrity as the Father of the Little Women.

Despite fame and prosperity, Alcott's maturity found her increasingly "porcupiny," (Cheney 166), sick, and embittered. Celebrity seekers invaded her privacy, and she never felt pride in her work. "When I had youth," she wrote, "I had no money; now I have the money, I have no time; and when I get the time, if I ever do, I shall have no health to enjoy life" (Saxton 359). The demands of her readers for more books like *Little Women* tied her to a particular domestic style she found maddeningly restrictive, while her family's constant needs kept her at the grindstone of literary production. Anna's husband died in 1870, leaving the widow with two small sons; and Louisa rushed back from a European vacation to churn out books for their support.

Yet Alcott's feminist interests entered her work even under the guise of conventional plots; in 1868 she had joined the New England Woman Suffrage Association, and women's rights are an issue in much of her writing in the next decade. *An Old-Fashioned Girl* (1870) and *Little Men* (1871), which continued the story of the March family, presented lively independent girls and described communities that took them seriously. In 1872, Alcott carried the theme further in *Work*, a feminist novel she had begun ten years earlier. Two other novels for girls, *Eight Cousins* (1875) and *Rose in Bloom* (1876), also took a feminist perspective on women's education, dress reform, physical education for girls, and women's work. In the second book, the heroine Rose offers a spirited defense of feminist ideals: "We've got minds and souls as well as hearts; ambition and talents as well as beauty and accomplishments; and we want to live and learn as well as love and be loved. I'm sick of being told that is all a woman is fit for! I won't have anything to do with love until I prove that I am something beside a housekeeper and a baby-tender!" Alcott also published several collections of stories and sketches for her insatiable readers, including the temperance stories of *Silver Pitchers* and six volumes of *Aunt Jo's Scrap-Bag*.

In 1877, eager for a way out of the role of domestic novelist, Alcott published *A Modern Mephistopheles,* another Faustian fantasy, in Roberts Brothers' anonymous No Name Series. As Eugenia Kaledin and Judith Fetterley have suggested, the novel's plot of a writer who sells his soul for

Introduction

fame by publishing poetry that is not his own reflected Alcott's feeling that she had made her own "Faustian pact" of inauthenticity for the sake of financial success (Kaledin 257 and Fetterley, "Impersonating" 1). By the end of the decade, as she nursed Abba through the final illness, the quality of her writing noticeably declined, although the quantity of her production stayed high. *Under the Lilacs* (1878) and *Jack and Jill* (1879) were feeble and moralistic recyclings of her earlier work. Although she had always intended to write the story of her mother's life, she burned many of Abba's diaries after her mother's death instead, perhaps unable to face the realities she had learned to evade after so many years.

From 1873 on, Alcott also was subsidizing May's training as an artist in Europe. Her sister's happy life in Paris in the late 1870s, as a New Woman sharing rooms with a lively group of women artists, must have been a sore trial for Alcott, still the "little woman" and the "old-fashioned girl." While she drudged away in Concord, her more daring sister was continuing, at Alcott's expense, to live out the romantic and feminist adventures she had always imagined for herself. In her journal she called May "cold-hearted" and then struck it out (Saxton 292). In 1877 the thirty-seven-year-old May traveled to England to work on her watercolors. In her London lodging house she met Ernest Nierecker, a Swiss clerk with musical interests, fourteen years younger, who consoled her after her mother's death. On March 24, only two weeks after she had written to her father and sisters announcing her engagement, May and Nierecker were married. While the family publicly rejoiced, the difference in the couple's ages, Nierecker's unstable employment, and the brevity of their acquaintance raised eyebrows in Concord. May's husband was even more her junior than Louisa's Laddie had been—and in that relationship Alcott had pretended to be the grandmother. May's letters to the Alcotts however were both confident and defiant about her intent to continue with her painting and to shape a new life for herself in Europe. "We mean to live our own life free from conventionalities," she wrote; Louisa "must not think my own happiness has made me unmindful of her, for it only draws us nearer. But I have laid out my future life and hope not to swerve from my purpose. I do not mean to be hindered by envious people, or anything to divert me from accomplishing my dream" (Ticknor 267).

At home in Concord, an ailing Louisa once more compared her lot unfavorably to May's: "How different our lives are just now—I so lonely, sad, and sick; she so happy, well and blest. She always had the cream of things and deserved it. My time is yet to come" (Elbert, intro *D & P* 33). She began a novel about two women artists, *Diana and Persis* (reprinted here), which explored the possibilities of combining motherhood and career. But the idyll of May's marriage was brief. Within a year, she died after giving birth to a daughter, Louisa, whom everyone called Lulu. With the consent of the Nierecker family, Alcott decided to raise the child.

Meanwhile, Bronson remained a steady responsibility. In August 1879 Alcott endowed a School of Philosophy for her eighty-year-old father at Concord. While Bronson basked in the attention and acclaim, his daughter, as usual, did all the work: "The town swarms with budding philosophers, and they roost on our steps like hens waiting for corn. Father revels in it, so we keep the hotel going, and try to look as if we liked it. If they were philanthropists, I should enjoy it; but speculation seems a waste of time when there is so much real work crying to be done" (Cheney 321). She had put her own celebrity to work for the women's suffrage movement, writing frequent letters of endorsement for the *Woman's Journal,* attending women's congresses, and leading the campaign for the vote in Concord. While the philosophers roosted and clucked, she "drove about and drummed up women to my suffrage meeting" (Cheney 321), and became the first woman in Concord to register as a voter.

Alcott's last years were devoted to the care of Lulu and her father. Mothering the little girl came as a pleasure and gave meaning to a life which seemed to have lost direction: "I see now why I lived. To care for May's child and not leave Anna all alone" (Saxton 393). Lulu's arrival gave her the excuse for the first time to establish her own home in Boston's Louisville Square. But ill health made it difficult for her to be patient and playful, and severe attacks of vertigo, headaches, dyspepsia, rheumatism, insomnia, and nervous prostration made it impossible for her to write. She unsuccessfully sought help from a variety of quacks, homeopathic physicians, and mind-cure specialists, but never could confront the emotional conflicts that expressed themselves in these physical forms.

During her last years, her literary productivity finally began to decline; *Jo's Boys* had be put aside while she rested. Instead she wrote down in *Lulu's Library* the simple stories she had told her niece: "Old ladies come to this twaddle when they can do nothing else," she told her publisher (Saxton 412). In 1881, having bought the copyright of *Moods* from the publisher for one dollar, she issued a revised and moralistic version of the earlier text, in which the heroine repents of her adulterous longings and goes back to her husband. To the last, Alcott tried to believe that her self-sacrifice would be rewarded, and that any success she had won had come because "my ambition was not for selfish ends but for my dear family." Yet somehow there was never time for the rest, pleasure, and travel she desired. "Shall never live my own life," she wrote bleakly in her journal (Saxton 406).

Jo's Boys, which she finally managed to finish in 1886, completed the saga of the March family, and the real family seemed to follow its literary destiny. After a long decline, Bronson Alcott died on March 4, 1888, and the weary Louisa wondered, "Shall I ever find time to die?" (Saxton 415). Two days later, the slowly accumulating effects of mercury poisoning from her Civil War treatment finally took her life. At their joint funeral, the minister suggested that Bronson had needed his dutiful daughter's help even in heaven.

ALCOTT'S first successful literary work, *Hospital Sketches* (1863), records her experience as a Civil War nurse in the winter of 1862–63. When she turned the sketches, originally written for the Boston antislavery paper *The Commonwealth,* into a book, Alcott added a Dickensian narrative frame, creating the comic persona of Tribulation Periwinkle, a doughty spinster who goes to Washington because she wants something to do, and not because she understands very well where she is going. While she was influenced by Dickens's satirical treatment of the female activists Mrs. Jellyby and Mrs. Pardiggle in *Bleak House* (1852), Alcott's creation of Trib also reflects her perennial difficulty in constructing a serious female narrative voice. In the early 1850s, she had followed the American fashion set by Fanny Fern (Sara P. Willis) and Grace Greenwood (Sara Jane Lippincott) by signing her first newspaper poems with the hyperfeminine pseudonym Flora Fairchild. In Boston, Alcott's pseudonyms included the parodic

Oranthy Bluggage and Minerva Moody, self-mocking names revealing her fear that female intellectualism and strong-mindedness would invite ridicule.

As *Hospital Sketches* develops, however, Alcott abandons much of the defensive satire of her narrator and allows Trib to grow into a serious and eloquent witness. In the beginning, although Trib describes herself as a "women's rights woman" who will not show "unmanly emotion," we see that she is also a naive and sheltered provincial who is unprepared for the emotional shocks she will face. Her trip from Concord to Washington, requiring stopovers in Boston, frequent changes of train, and an overnight boat trip, seems endlessly long, almost like Lucy Snowe's journey in *Villette*. By the time that Trib arrives at Hurly-Burly House, we feel that she has come very far from the illusions of home and that she is almost in a foreign country where there are different standards for female behavior, where, in fact, gender is irrelevant in the face of sickness and death. Trib's voice becomes stronger with each chapter as she enters ever deeper into her own war, ending with her collapse from typhoid. In this sense, Alcott made the narrative not just a description of nursing, but also the story of Trib's passage from innocence to maturity.

Trib's transformation begins in the ramshackle hospital when she must abruptly face forty ambulances bearing the wounded from the slaughter of Fredericksburg. At first she does not have language to describe her experience, especially her contact with men's wounded and vulnerable bodies. At some points, as when she is ordered to strip and wash the wounded men, she becomes virtually speechless: "If she had requested me to shave them all, or dance a hornpipe on the stove-funnel, I should have been less staggered; but to scrub some dozen lords of creation at a moment's notice was really—really—." But she rapidly recovers and finds her own voice.

The center of the book deals with Trib's involvement with wounded and dying men, and her efforts to maintain some emotional distance from them so as not to be overwhelmed by her own pity and grief. As in most situations where she was faced with strong and potentially sexual feelings for men, Alcott compensated by defining her feelings as "motherly affection" and by transforming the soldiers into "big babies," "boys," or "sleepy children." But here this maternal rhetoric conveys pathos, espe-

Introduction

cially in the story of the blacksmith John Sulie, whom Trib must tell that he is going to die. Without the "false pieties" of many Civil War reminiscences (Jones xliii), the deaths are movingly described.

Alcott is at her best in the book when she can vent her indignation. Her most forceful pages give her outraged critique of the mismanagement of the hospital, and of the callousness and indifference of the surgeons. Trib describes herself as "naturally irascible," a human teakettle boiling over with "angry passions," and she gives pungent accounts of offensive scenes and smells, of stewed blackberries looking like "preserved cockroaches." Eugenia Kaledin has noted that Alcott never holds back about "human animosity, which she always depicted with realistic clarity" (Kaledin 252). In contrast to Whitman's "persistently idealized greatheartedness" in his memoir of nursing (Kaledin 252), she does not disguise her own unrepentant hostility to the Confederate soldiers in her care, or conceal her longing to "insinuate a few of his own disagreable knives and scissors" into the insensitive surgeon. Alcott is particularly sharp too on the tests of masculinity to which the sick men are repeatedly subjected, and the sadness of their desperate efforts to conceal their suffering before a woman. Ironically, after Alcott had become famous in the children's book market, her publisher Thomas Niles took *Hospital Sketches* out of the collected edition of her work because he thought its realism would be a "drag on the other books" (Kaledin 260).

Some of the psychological after-effects of Alcott's Georgetown experience are reflected in "My Contraband" (also called "The Brothers"), an abolitionist story set in the Civil War hospital, and first published in the *Atlantic Monthly* in 1863. Here Alcott's narrative persona is Nurse Dane, another courageous spinster; in her novel *Moods,* Alcott would further develop the nurse's character as Faith Dane, a figure of womanly self-reliance. Nurse Dane is put in charge of a wounded Confederate officer, and assigned the help of Bob, a freed mulatto slave who is the soldier's half brother. Racial and class conflict between the two brothers constitutes the main plot of the story, which, however, also has a sexual subtext. While Alcott uses the term "contraband" in its specialized Civil War sense, to mean a slave escaped to Union forces, it also suggests the illegal or illicit, here the nurse's repressed or "contraband" desire for the black hero. In

Introduction

October 1863, Alcott had thought about going to Port Royal on the Sea Islands of South Carolina to teach contrabands who had established a community there, and another story she wrote that year, "M.L.," deals with interracial love between a rich white woman and a handsome octoroon musician. In "My Contraband" she uses an image of sexual and racial division, as one side of Bob's face is deeply scarred, while the other is magnificently handsome in its "Saxon features, Spanish complexion." Alcott writes explicitly of the nurse's admiration of Bob ("I had seen many contrabands, but never one so attractive as this"); yet, because "all colored men are called 'boys,'" this attraction, like those described in *Hospital Sketches,* may be denied or labeled as maternal. At the end of the story, declaring "I'll fight for her till I'm killed," Bob adopts Dane's surname in a kind of marriage. The character of Nurse Dane is another contraband, the independent woman, who vicariously shares the ex-slave's revenge against the white men who have enslaved and betrayed him.

The fantasies of power, rebellion, and revenge which are marginalized in the war stories are more overtly realized in Alcott's sensation fiction. "Behind a Mask" is the most skillful of the tales Alcott published under the pseudonym A. M. Barnard, in her first effort to disguise her gender. "I think my natural ambition is for the lurid style," she told a friend. "I indulge in gorgeous fancies and wish that I dare inscribe them upon my pages and set them before the public" (Stern, intro *Behind a Mask* xxvi) In this tale of female revenge, she drew heavily on her childhood reading of *Jane Eyre,* and on best-selling English sensation novels of the 1860s such as Mary Elizabeth Braddon's *Lady Audley's Secret* (1861) and Wilkie Collins's *Armadale* (1866). Braddon and Collins portray ambitious and passionate governesses, who use their ambiguous position within the family to initiate romantic plots.

The story can be read several ways. On an autobiographical level, Madeleine Stern sees "Behind a Mask" as a "Gothic *roman à clef*" which reveals a great deal about Alcott herself as a dutiful daughter who secretly writes lurid thrillers (Stern, intro *Behind a Mask* xviii). In a feminist sense, Judith Fetterley has described it as Alcott's "most radical text," which "presents an incisive analysis of the economic situation of the white middle-class woman in late nineteenth century society" (Fetterley, "Impersonating" 2). As Fetterley points out, Alcott had come to realize that women's "honest" labor was miserably underpaid; her survival depended on subterfuge and stratagem.

On another level, the story can be seen as a narrative meditation on the possibilities for feminist subversion of patriarchal culture, on the ways for women to express themselves, or at least their power, through role playing. Alcott's heroine, the ex-actress Jean Muir, can never be offstage; she always acts the feminine parts that her society allows her, but acts them with a brilliance that exposes their artifice and emptiness. If women are trapped within feminine scripts of childishness and victimization, Alcott suggests, they can unmask these roles only by deliberately overacting them. Thus Jean's well-timed and carefully staged swoons, raptures, tears, and songs reveal the secret of feminine social and literary pretense. Through this active appropriation, as the French feminist theorist Luce Irigaray has argued, women can "convert a form of subordination into an affirmation, and thus . . . begin to thwart it" (76)

Alcott makes use of the narrative conventions of Victorian sensation fiction, such as theatricals and letters, to underscore her theme of feminine appropriation. Jean participates in an evening of *tableaux vivants,* like those in *Jane Eyre* and *Vanity Fair,* in which she portrays Judith beheading Holofernes after he has raped her. The painting described is clearly the French artist Horace Vernet's "Judith and Holofernes" (1831), a famous nineteenth-century work which had inspired Heine, among others; but the story of Judith had become an icon of the vengeful and castrating woman for nineteenth-century artists. (See Jacobus 116–34 and Dijkstra 376–79). Jean's appropriation of the role gives her an opportunity to flaunt her real desires under cover of yet another exhibition of the feminine. In another reversal, Jean has the men bear her letters to a female accomplice, a sarcastic reversal of patriarchal assumptions that women are bearers of the male word.

Yet finally, as Ann Douglas has noted, the story suggests Alcott's own contradictions and tensions, her fear of aging, her terror of being loved, her self-masking "to avoid confronting the fissures of her self" (Stern, *Essays* 237). Behind the mask of Jean Muir is a member of the "sad sisterhood" Alcott movingly described in her novel of the same period, *Moods:* "Gifted creatures, kindled into fitful brilliance by some inward fire that consumes morning glories in chapter 12, declaring that "frost comes latest to those that bloom the highest." Her gardener-husband seems to exist more to fertilize the ambitious female flower than to complete her. Having given Christie a daughter/flower—Pansy—, David conveniently dies.

By the novel's end, Christie has motherhood, money, and independence; and she has been reunited with Rachel, who turns out to be David's long-lost sister. In a remarkable feminist conclusion, she merges her life with that of a new women's movement, becoming a mediator between ladies and working women. The final illustration shows Christie, Pansy, Hepsey, Mrs. Wilkins, Bella, Mrs. Sterling, and Rachel/Letty, holding hands beneath a wreathed portrait of David in his Civil War uniform and his mounted cap and sword. While the emblems of Civil War hang over them, the women in contrast are "a loving league of sisters, old and young, black and white, rich and poor, each ready to do her part." As Elizabeth Langland points out, Christie's marriage "is part of the total female experience that marks her development and increases her credibility with the working women" (117).

Following *Work,* Alcott went on to write about another experiment in *Transcendental Wild Oats* (1873), her keenest and most assured piece of feminist satire. A comic history of the Fruitlands fiasco, it gives a sharp picture of the commune, from the bust of Socrates to the lunatic fringe of nudists, visionaries, and freeloaders who joined the Consociate family. The essay had been long smouldering, in the notes from Alcott's own Fruitlands diary, and in her earlier plans to write a novel about her father called "The Cost of an Idea." Portraying her father as the well-meaning but innocent Abel Lamb and her mother as the stalwart and heroic Sister Hope, Alcott managed to exonerate Bronson from his share of responsibility in the Fruitlands disaster by putting all the blame on Charles Lane, who becomes the dictatorial misogynist Timon Lion.

Despite its obfuscation of Bronson's role, the story is a brilliant critique of the sexism of male radical ideals. Alcott took many of the letters and speeches directly from the publications of Bronson Alcott and Charles Lane, and adjusted her own satiric language to their overblown rhetoric. From the beginning, she points out, the motives of the men and the women are different. The power-hungry Lion wants to found a new religion in which he can rule, and placid Lamb has a naive but sincere vision of a new Eden; Sister Hope, however, wants only to create a home for her children. Despite their highblown talk of noble labor and "human freedom," the men are either incompetent or hypocritical when it comes to doing the real work of the commune, and it never occurs to them to challenge the sexual division of labor. Sister Hope's sharp questions about household management in the face of the Transcendentalists' severe restrictions, are dismissed as "trivial." Yet she becomes the "good angel" of the family, and its only dependable member.

Alcott exposes the exploitation of women and the dread of female sexuality that lay behind the Consociate family's ascetic program. As Sarah Elbert has noted, the vegetarianism and asceticism of Bronson and Lane was an effort to denigrate women's role as nurturer and comforter. Alcott shows in her story "how food and diet and also domestic labor become concrete vehicles for the expression of sexual conflict" (Elbert, *Hunger* 65, 66). She suspected that the men's insistence on the impurity of the body and their obsession with abstinence and denial of appetite was deeply misogynistic despite its rhetoric of equality. As Sister Hope senses, it is the female body that is being rejected.

Several of Alcott's novels and stories deal with women artists, and with the conflicts between creativity and domesticity. All of these narratives draw to a considerable degree on her own life history, and rewrite her most compelling fantasy: A gifted young woman writer or painter or sculptor or musician is forced by circumstances to devote herself to her needy family. Her art is deepened and improved by the sacrifice. In one version of the story, her final reward is the love of an even more gifted older man, an artist or intellectual, often European. But Alcott also experiments with the idea that women artists might form their own loving communities in which they could all dedicate themselves to their work without losing companionship and affection.

In an early story called "A Modern Cinderella" (1860), based on her sister Anna's courtship by John Pratt, Alcott portrays herself as the scribbling sister Di, who must give up her books and take over the cooking when the Cinderella sister falls sick: "Di was better all her days for the tribulations and trials of that time; for she drowned her idle fancies in her washtub, made burnt offerings of selfishness and pride, and learned the worth of self-denial as she sang with a happy voice among the pots and kettles of her conquered realm." With a new "motive for her art," Di resolves to turn her "books and pen to some account."

In 1868, the same year that she wrote *Little Women,* Alcott tried out another version of what we may call her masterplot. The sculptor Psyche Dean in "Psyche's Art" has many parallels with Jo March, discovering that when she abandons her art studies to take care of her family and to nurse her invalid sister, she discovers a "newly found power" of aesthetic imagination. While the story is generally formulaic and sentimental, it also represents Alcott's resistance to the narrative conventions of domestic fiction. In *Little Women,* she felt pressured to marry Jo to the fatherly Professor Bhaer. In "Psyche's Art," however, although the sculptor Paul Gage follows the trail of violets to Psyche's house, discovers her unselfishness in reading her conveniently lost diary, and praises her statue of the dead sister, Alcott leaves the ending open for the reader to decide. For those who can "imagine a world outside of a wedding-ring," she concludes, it will be possible to have an ending in which the hero and heroine do not marry but happily go their separate ways.

There is a more radical speculation on the possibilities for women artists within the novel *An Old-Fashioned Girl* (1870). In a chapter called "The Sunny Side," the excerpt reprinted here, the heroines Polly and Fanny visit several working women who keep house together. Becky and Bess are a sculptor and an engraver who are inseparable friends, almost lovers, although Alcott carefully gives Bess a fiancé. Becky's statue of "the coming woman" is Alcott's most utopian vision of the future: a woman "bigger, lovelier, and more imposing than any we see nowadays," "strong-minded, strong-hearted, strong-souled, and strong-bodied," she will "stand alone and help herself." Like the women of Charlotte Perkins Gilman's *Herland* (1915), the coming woman is both powerful and creative. But another character in the story, the writer Kate King, represents Alcott's defeated feelings about herself in the present; she is "a shabby young woman" who looks "sick, tired, and too early old." At this point, the American woman artist who stood alone and fulfilled could be only one of Alcott's utopian dreams.

In 1879, turning again to her favorite motif, Alcott began "an art novel, with May's romance as its theme," which told the story of two dedicated artist friends separated when one, Persis, goes to Europe to study and then marries. Left unfinished and untitled when May died after childbirth, the four chapters of the novel were first edited and published in 1978 as *Diana & Persis*. In that edition, the editor, Sarah Elbert, transcribed the chapters in the order they are numbered in the manuscript at Harvard University, so that the book ends with Diana's visit to Persis in France. Internal evidence, however, suggests that this chapter ordering is incorrect, and after reexamining the manuscript, I have concluded that the last two chapters have been reversed: Diana *first* visits Persis and her family, and then, with the memory of their happiness in her mind, goes to Rome where she meets a male artist who may offer her a similar choice. Giving the chapters their correct order and going back to the manuscript to correct mistranscriptions, significantly change our interpretation of the novel as well as our sense of Alcott's attitudes toward the combination of love and art in women's lives.

Alcott establishes the theme of the woman artist who denies her womanhood from the beginning. The sculptor Diana is a vestal virgin of art like the goddess for whom she is named. Cold, brilliant, and sexually repressed, she has denied herself all the "pleasures of youth, the honors of sex and beauty, the joys of love, the solaces of home." Alcott compares her to a nun in her cell, whose commitment to art requires severe repression of all other human passions. In contrast, the painter Persis, called Percy in an allusion to Shelley, has a "warm, rich nature" and a "hungry heart." Both are ambitious, but "with Diana success came first, with Percy happiness."

Their work too reflects these differences. Diana, the eagle who soars above all human things, sculpts "calm and beautiful" classic figures in her bare studio "coldly lighted from the north," while Percy paints a throbbing skylark ardent as the "sunshine, life and warmth that filled her own little studio." Their studios are spaces which also metaphorically represent their bodies and the sources of their art. Percy's creativity comes from her female ardor, while Diana's comes only from her "marble heart."

Alcott had written before about the repressed female artist in her sensation story, "A Marble Woman" (1865). The heroine Cecil has been trained by her sculptor-guardian to "repress all natural emotions." He wants her to be as "beautiful and passionless as Psyche." Finally, in a virgin marriage, Cecil turns to opium to calm her desires; she has become a marble goddess, but in the process she has lost her identity. For Alcott, who had become dependent on opiates, and who hid her passionate feelings while she labored for her family, the image of the cold statue represented her own imprisonment.

Persis/May, however, represents a generation of women artists who no longer feel obliged to hide behind a mask, and who are not stifled by ideals of feminine self-sacrifice. Percy's letters in chapter 2 were taken in most details from May Alcott's letters home from Paris, and they give a fascinating picture of life abroad for adventurous female art students in the late nineteenth century. "K's school" was the studio of Krug in the Boulevard Clichy, which May attended and which was "devoted to female students in all branches of art" (Ticknor 138). Here, for a fee of one hundred francs a month, women could draw from the nude, and have their work criticized every week by the painter Carl Müller and the sculptor Carrière Belleuse. "J's great school for men and women" was the Aca-démie Julien, on Passage Panorama, where the painter Tony Robert-Fleury, among others, taught; but here "it was found impossible that women should paint from the living nude models of both sexes, side by side with the Frenchmen" (Ticknor 139–40). Miss Cassal in the novel is a portrait of the American painter Mary Cassatt, who befriended May in Paris; the party at her home is described by May in a letter of November 1876.

Percy's community of women artists in Paris evolves a lifestyle very different from that available to single women in Boston or New York. Housekeeping and cooking are simplified by the availability of prepared food in the Parisian restaurants and markets, and by the sharing of respon-sibilities. The hardworking students are proud of their indifference to fashion; May had written that "shops abound with cheap clothing of all sorts, ready made. Work's also so cheap that a young woman of moderate means can get up a neat and handsome wardrobe for half the sum it costs at home" (Elbert intro D & P 27).

The female community is also free of prudery. In contrast to her sister's discomfort with male bodies in her nursing experience, May had an artist's healthy appreciation of the male nude: "This week we have a perfectly superb model, an Italian of fine rich color, grand physique, and head of a god," she wrote to her mother and sisters, in a letter Alcott used for *Diana and Persis*. In describing the art students, Alcott incorporates May's feminist critique of the tame subjects and styles thought suitable for a "lady's brush," and thus indirectly presents her most explicit critique of nineteenth-century standards for women's writing as well.

Chapter 3 is similarly based on both May's letters and Alcott's feelings about motherhood, marriage, and art. It is June; time has passed, and Percy is married for a year, with a three-month-old daughter, baby Di. Having put her own "marble offspring" in storage, Diana stops en route to Rome where she is to study to see if Percy "can combine art and domestic life harmoniously." Alcott presents the idyll of Percy's family life in the language of romance; it is a "fairy story" that contrasts with the "small, dull world of reality" which Diana has inhabited. Percy is in the full bloom of motherhood, and her adoring husband August not only speaks up in support of woman's right to love and fame, but also does the shopping. Yet in Percy's studio the paint is dry and the easel covered with dust; her "youthful audacity" has been replaced by maternal anxiety. Her casual student meals have given way to more conventional dinners, and her musician husband resembles pictures of Shelley, as if to imply that now he has taken over the role of artist. In addition, Diana's feelings about Percy suggest sexual jealousy as well as fear about artistic dedication. August perceives her as the "fair serpent" who is tempting his Eve, and feels both jealousy and rivalry when she visits them.

But despite these conflicts, there are several foreshadowings in the chapter of the change in Diana's feelings. August gives her a red rose to wear on her nunlike grey dress, and thinks that she "is not all the artist but a woman to be loved as well as admired." Alcott compares Diana to a "chaste goddess" before she has found her own Endymion. We see Percy through Diana's eyes in ways that suggest that Diana's sexual awakening has become the center of the novel. In the freer world of Europe, a woman does not have to choose between love and art, and Diana can allow herself to recognize her own feelings.

In the fourth chapter, Diana's story of love and work takes precedence. Diana goes off to work in Rome, where she meets a celebrated sculptor, Antony Stafford. That his motherless little son is named Nino, like Margaret Fuller's child, suggests how powerfully Fuller's choice to seek fulfillment in her Italian exile had inspired Alcott. It is early spring, and the atmosphere is one of "awakening Nature". Diana's nature too is waking to a sense of longing and loneliness, "a bittersweet regret for something lost or never found."

In many details, the chapter alludes to the well-known lives of a group of American sculptors who had established a colony in Rome. Diana's career strongly resembles that of Harriet Hosmer, the most famous and iconoclastic American woman sculptor of the century. Among her achievements were a number of revisionary statues of female figures such as Medusa and Zenobia; but her greatest financial and critical successes came from her "Puck" and "Saul," the two statues specifically attributed to Diana in the novel. Like Diana, Hosmer had decided not to marry in order to dedicate herself to art. "I am the only faithful worshipper of Celibacy," she wrote, "and her service becomes more fascinating the longer I remain in it. Even if so inclined, an artist has no business to marry. For a man, it may be well enough, but for a woman on whom matrimonial duties and cares weigh more heavily, it is a moral wrong, I think, for she must neglect her profession or her family, becoming neither a good wife and mother nor a good artist" (Rubenstein 79). Diana, however, seems about to prove Hosmer wrong. Stafford has raised his son himself, demonstrating his own capacity for tenderness; he also appreciates the "virile force" of Diana's monumental statue of Saul. Furthermore, she and Nino already look like "mother and child." When Nino kisses her, his touch seems to release sexual desire as well as maternal feelings; "all the pent-up tenderness of her nature seemed to gush out."

Basing their views on the 1978 text, scholars have generally argued that Alcott could not bring herself to envision a happy ending for the married woman artist. Charles Strickland, for example, observes that "this acquaintance with males is only a brief interlude for Diana, and she remains dedicated to the single life. . . . If, indeed, Diana speaks for Louisa, it would appear that she believed an irreconcilable conflict existed between feminism and the family" (Strickland 81–82). Other scholars have noticed that the friendship between Diana and Persis also seems ephemeral in the face of heterosexual love. Nina Auerbach notes that "the fragment ends in this failure of fellowship . . . Alcott has evoked a conflict she cannot resolve" (*Communities* 66).

While we cannot be sure of the way in which Alcott intended to end the novel, the reordering of the chapters strongly suggests that Diana was going to marry her sculptor-hero, become a mother to his little boy, maintain her friendship with Persis, and become a much greater artist because she is no longer starving the sexual and emotional side of her nature. Thus the story of Diana and Persis is not simply Alcott's rewriting of her sister May's life, but also a painful meditation on her own personality and her own choices.

In a chapter of *Jo's Boys* called "Jo's Last Scrape," Alcott summed up her career as the "golden goose whose literary eggs found such an unexpected market." Jo March Bhaer has become a literary celebrity, and describes the justification of her success as the power of making Marmee's last years happy and serene. But Jo's health and temper suffer as she avoids importunate fans and struggles to supply the demand always in the mouths of her voracious young readers: "More stories; more right away!" Unlike Josephine Bhaer, moreover, Alcott did not have a "thoughtful angel" for a husband, or devoted sons who stood guard over her privacy.

Alcott's wry judgment of her alter ego as a "literary nursemaid who provides moral pap for the young" raises some final questions about her literary career. Had she, like Jean Muir, cynically played "little woman" in order to succeed in the terms allowed by her society? Had her "willingness to buy success by catering to middle-class ideals aborted the promise of her art?" (Kaledin 251). Many feminist critics who have looked at Alcott's life have concluded that she gave in to financial pressure, and betrayed her genius.

My own view is far more positive. Alcott habitually underestimated and denigrated her own work. She never entirely got over her awe for the masculine literary community of American Transcendentalist philosophy which her father represented, nor forgave herself for failing to measure up to his moral and intellectual standards. For Alcott, genius—as Martha Saxton shrewdly notes—was a "kind of godly inspiration that she associated with men like her father. She always downplayed her talent and refused to give herself credit for anything other than a drudgelike capacity for labor" (297). She censored and denied her own imagination in order to conform to external and internalized patriarchal expectations of seriousness, duty, and high-mindedness. "To have had Mr. Emerson for an intellectual God all one's life," she once ruefully observed, "is to be invested with a chain armour of propriety. . . . And what would my own good father think of me if I set folks to doing the things I have a longing to see my people do?" (Stern, *Essays* 42).

The masks that proliferate in Alcott's stories represent her own perennial effort to conceal the deeper meanings of her work from herself, as well as from others. Just as *Little Women,* the novel she did not want to write and thought dull, has proved to be "*the* American female myth" (Bedell, intro *LW* xi), the writing Alcott produced in the 1870s, after her great success, included some of her most skilled, important, and feminist contributions: *Work;* the "minor masterpiece" *Transcendental Wild Oats* (Bedell, intro *LW* li), and the unfinished but remarkable *Diana & Persis.* With the recent publication of her letters, and this first anthology of her work, Alcott can now be re-evaluated in terms of her full accomplishments as a novelist and realist.

OTHER WORKS BY LOUISA MAY ALCOTT

Flower Fables. Boston: George W. Briggs & Co., 1855.

"The Lady and the Woman." *Saturday Evening Gazette* 4 Oct. 1856.

Moods. Boston: Loring, 1865. Rev. ed. Boston: Roberts Bros., 1882.

Little Women. Boston: Roberts Bros., 1868.

Little Men: Life at Plumfield with Jo's Boys. Boston: Roberts Bros., 1871.

Aunt Jo's Scrap-Bag: My Boys. Boston: Roberts Bros., 1872.

Shawl-Straps. Boston: Roberts Bros., 1872.

Eight Cousins; or, The Aunt-Hill. Boston: Roberts Bros., 1875.

Rose in Bloom. Boston: Roberts Bros., 1876.

A Modern Mephistopheles. Boston: Roberts Bros., 1877.

Under the Lilacs. Boston: Roberts Bros., 1878.

Jack and Jill: A Village Story. Boston: Roberts Bros., 1880.

Proverb Stories. Boston: Roberts Bros., 1882.

Jo's Boys, and How They Turned Out. Boston: Roberts Bros., 1886.

Lulu's Library. 3 vols. Boston: Roberts Bros., 1886–89.

A Garland for Girls. Boston: Roberts Bros., 1888.

"Memoir of My Childhood." *The Woman's Journal* 19 (26 May 1888): 180.

Behind a Mask: The Unknown Thrillers of Louisa May Alcott. Ed. Madeleine Stern. New York: William Morrow, 1975.

Plots and Counterplots: More Unknown Thrillers of Louisa May Alcott. Ed. Madeleine Stern. New York: William Morrow, 1976.

Diana & Persis. Ed. Sarah Elbert. New York: Arno Press, 1978.

SOURCES AND FURTHER READING

Auerbach, Nina. Afterword to *Little Women.* New York: Bantam, 1983. 461–70.

———. *Communities of Women.* Cambridge, MA: Harvard UP, 1978.

Bedell, Madelon. *The Alcotts: Biography of a Family.* New York: Clarkson N. Potter, 1980.

———. Introduction to *Little Women.* New York: Modern Library, 1983. ix–xlix.

Cheney, Ednah D. *Louisa May Alcott: Her Life, Letters, and Journals.* Boston: Roberts Bros., 1889.

Dahlstrad, Frederick C. *Amos Bronson Alcott: An Intellectual Biography.* London: Associated UP, 1982.

Dijkstra, Bram. *Idols of Perversity: Fantasies of Feminine Evil in Fin-de-Siècle Culture.* New York: Oxford UP, 1986.

Douglas, Ann. Introduction to *Little Women.* New York: NAL, 1983. vii–xxvii.

Douglas, Ann. "Mysteries of Louisa May Alcott." *Critical Essays on Louisa May Alcott.* Ed. Madeleine Stern. Boston: G. K. Hall, 1984. 231–39.

Elbert, Sarah. *A Hunger for Home: Louisa May Alcott and Little Women.* Philadelphia: Temple UP, 1984. Rev. ed. New Brunswick, NJ: Rutgers UP, 1987.

———. Introduction to *Diana & Persis.* New York: Arno, 1978. pp. 7–52.

———. Introduction to *Work: A Story of Experience.* New York: Schocken, 1977. ix–xliv.

Fetterley, Judith. "Impersonating "Little Women": The Radicalism of Alcott's *Behind a Mask.*" *Women's Studies* 10 (1983): 1–14.

———. "Little Women: Alcott's Civil War." *Feminist Studies* 5 (1979): 369–83.

Selected Bibliography

Halttunen, Karen. "The Domestic Drama of Louisa May Alcott." *Feminist Studies* 10 (Summer 1984): 233–54.

Harrison, William Henry. Introduction to *Transcendental Wild Oats*. Harvard: Harvard Common P, 1981. 3–21.

Irigaray, Luce. *This Sex Which Is Not One*. Trans. Catherine Porter. Ithaca: Cornell UP, 1986.

Jacobus, Mary. *Reading Woman*. New York: Columbia UP, 1986.

Jones, Bessie Z. Introduction to *Hospital Sketches*. Cambridge: Harvard UP, 1960. vii–xliv.

Kaledin, Eugenia. "Louisa May Alcott: Success and the Sorrow of Self-Denial." *Women's Studies* 5 (1983): 251–64.

Langland, Elizabeth. "Female Stories of Experience: Alcott's *Little Women* in Light of *Work*." *The Voyage In: Fictions of Female Development*. Ed. Elizabeth Abel, Marianne Hirsch, and Elizabeth Langland. Hanover, NH.: UP of New England, 1983. 112–30.

MacDonald, Ruth K. *Louisa May Alcott*. Boston: Twayne, 1983.

Marsella, Joy. *The Promise of Destiny: Children and Women in the Short Stories of Louisa May Alcott*. Westport, CT: Greenwood, 1983.

Myerson, Joel and Daniel Shealy, eds. *Selected Letters of Louisa May Alcott*. Boston: Little, Brown, 1987.

O'Brien, Sharon. "Tomboyism and Adolescent Conflict: Three Nineteenth-Century Case Studies." *Woman's Being, Woman's Place: Female Identity and Vocation in American History*. Ed. Mary Kelley. Boston: G. K. Hall, 1979. 351–72.

Phelps, Elizabeth Stuart, ed. *Our Famous Women* (1883). Repr. Freeport, NY: Books for Libraries Press.

Rubenstein, Charlotte Streifer. *American Women Artists*. New York: Avon, 1982.

Salyer, Sanford. *Marmee: The Mother of Little Women*. Norman: U of Oklahoma P, 1949.

Saxton, Martha. *Louisa May: A Modern Biography*. New York: Avon, 1978.

Stern, Madeleine, ed. *Critical Essays on Louisa May Alcott*. Boston: G. K. Hall, 1984.

———. Introduction to *Behind a Mask*. New York: William Morrow, 1975. vii–xxxiii.

————. Introduction to *Plots and Counterplots*. New York: William Morrow, 1976.

Strickland, Charles. *Victorian Domesticity: Families in the Life and Art of Louisa May Alcott*. U of Alabama P, 1985.

Ticknor, Caroline. *May Alcott: A Memoir*. Boston: Little, 1928.

Whicher, Stephen E., ed. *Selections from Ralph Waldo Emerson*. Boston: Houghton Mifflin, 1960.

Yellin, Jean Fagan. "From *Success* to *Experience*: Louisa May Alcott's *Work*." *Massachusetts Review* 21 (1980): 527–39.

Young, Elizabeth. "'Gorgeous Fancies': Louisa May Alcott, the Female Gothic, and Nineteenth-Century Women Readers." Honors Thesis, Harvard and Radcliffe Colleges, 1985.

A NOTE ON THE TEXT

THE TEXTS in this anthology were compiled from manuscripts, journals, and editions of Alcott's work at the Baker Library, Dartmouth College; Miriam Holden Collection, Firestone Library, Princeton University; the Houghton Library, Harvard University; and the New York Public Library. Complete bibliographical information is as follows:

Hospital Sketches. Boston: James Redpath, 1863.
"My Contraband," in *Hospital Sketches and Camp and Fireside Stories.* Boston: Roberts Bros., 1869.
Behind a Mask. The Flag of Our Union 21, nos. 41, 42, 43, 44 (13, 20, 27 Oct. and 3 Nov. 1866).
"Happy Women." *The New York Ledger* 24, no. 7 (11 Apr. 1868).
Psyche's Art. Boston: Loring, 1868.
"The Sunny Side" from *An Old-Fashioned Girl.* Boston: Roberts Bros., 1870.
"How I Went Out to Service." *The Independent* 26, no. 1331 (4 June 1874).
Work: A Story of Experience. Boston: Roberts Bros., 1873.
Transcendental Wild Oats. The Woman's Journal 5, no. 8 (21 Feb. 1874).
Diana and Persis. From manuscript, "An untitled romance," Alcott Papers 59M–309 (21), Houghton Library, Harvard University.
"Jo's Last Scrape." *Jo's Boys.* Boston: Roberts Bros., 1886.

ALTERNATIVE ALCOTT

HOSPITAL SKETCHES

OBTAINING SUPPLIES

"I WANT something to do."

This remark being addressed to the world in general, no one in particular felt it their duty to reply; so I repeated it to the smaller world about me, received the following suggestions, and settled the matter by answering my own inquiry, as people are apt to do when very much in earnest.

"Write a book," quoth the author of my being.

"Don't know enough, sir. First live, then write."

"Try teaching again," suggested mother.

"No thank you, ma'am, ten years of that is enough."

"Take a husband like my Darby, and fulfill your mission," said sister Joan, home on a visit.

"Can't afford expensive luxuries, Mrs. Coobiddy."

"Turn actress, and immortalize your name," said sister Vashti, striking an attitude.

"I won't."

"Go nurse the soldiers," said my young brother, Tom, panting for "the tented field."

"I will!"

So far, very good. Here was the will—now for the way. At first sight not a foot of it appeared, but that didn't matter, for the Periwinkles are a hopeful race; their crest is an anchor, with three cock-a-doodles crowing atop. They all wear rose-colored spectacles, and are lineal descendants of the inventor of aerial architecture. An hour's conversation on the subject set the whole family in a blaze of enthusiasm. A model hospital was erected, and each member had accepted an honorable post therein. The paternal P. was chaplain, the maternal P. was matron, and all the youthful P.s filled the pod of futurity with achievements whose brilliancy eclipsed the glories of the present and the past. Arriving at this satisfactory conclusion, the meeting adjourned, and the fact that Miss Tribulation was available as army nurse went abroad on the wings of the wind.

In a few days a townswoman heard of my desire, approved of it, and brought about an interview with one of the sisterhood which I wished to join, who was at home on a furlough, and able and willing to satisfy all inquiries. A morning chat with Miss General S.—we hear no end of Mrs. Generals, why not a Miss?—produced three results: I felt that I could do the work, was offered a place, and accepted it, promising not to desert, but stand ready to march on Washington at an hour's notice.[1]

A few days were necessary for the letter containing my request and recommendation to reach headquarters, and another, containing my commission, to return; therefore no time was to be lost; and heartily thanking my pair of friends, I tore home through the December slush as if the rebels were after me, and like many another recruit, burst in upon my family with the announcement—

"I've enlisted!"

An impressive silence followed. Tom, the irrepressible, broke it with a slap on the shoulder and the graceful compliment—

"Old Trib, you're a trump!"

"Thank you; then I'll *take* something:" which I did, in the shape of dinner, reeling off my news at the rate of three dozen words to a mouthful; and as everyone else talked equally fast, and all together, the scene was most inspiring.

As boys going to sea immediately become nautical in speech, walk as if they already had their "sea legs" on, and shiver their timbers on all possible occasions, so I turned military at once, called my dinner my rations, saluted all new comers, and ordered a dress parade that very afternoon. Having reviewed every rag I possessed, I detailed some for picket duty while airing over the fence; some to the sanitary influences of the wash-tub; others to mount guard in the trunk; while the weak and wounded went to the Work-basket Hospital, to be made ready for active service again. To this squad I devoted myself for a week; but all was done, and I had time to get powerfully impatient before the letter came. It did arrive however, and brought a disappointment along with its good will and friendliness, for it told me that the place in the Armory Hospital that I supposed I was to take, was already filled, and a much less desirable one at Hurly-burly House was offered instead.

"That's just your luck, Trib. I'll tote your trunk up garret for you again; for of course you won't go," Tom remarked, with the disdainful pity which small boys affect when they get into their teens. I was wavering in my secret soul, but that settled the matter, and I crushed him on the spot with martial brevity—

"It is now one; I shall march at six."

I have a confused recollection of spending the afternoon in pervading the house like an executive whirlwind, with my family swarming after me, all working, talking, prophesying and lamenting, while I packed my "go-abroady" possessions, tumbled the rest into two big boxes, danced on the lids till they shut, and gave them in charge, with the direction,—

"If I never come back, make a bonfire of them."

Then I choked down a cup of tea, generously salted instead of sugared, by some agitated relative, shouldered my knapsack—it was only a traveling bag, but do let me preserve the unities—hugged my family three times all round without a vestige of unmanly emotion, till a certain dear old lady broke down upon my neck, with a despairing sort of wail—

"Oh, my dear, my dear, how can I let you go?"

"I'll stay if you say so, mother."

"But I don't; go, and the Lord will take care of you."

Much of the Roman matron's courage had gone into the Yankee matron's composition, and, in spite of her tears, she would have sent ten sons to the war, had she possessed them, as freely as she sent one daughter, smiling and flapping on the door-step till I vanished, though the eyes that followed me were very dim, and the handkerchief she waved was very wet.

My transit from The Gables to the village depot was a funny mixture of good wishes and good byes, mud-puddles and shopping. A December twilight is not the most cheering time to enter upon a somewhat perilous enterprise, and, but for the presence of Vashti and neighbor Thorn, I fear that I might have added a drop of the briny to the native moisture of—

"The town I left behind me;"

though I'd no thought of giving out: oh, bless you, no! When the engine screeched "Here we are," I clutched my escort in a fervent embrace, and skipped into the car with as blithe a farewell as if going on a bridal tour— though I believe brides don't usuallly wear cavernous black bonnets and fuzzy brown coats, with a hair-brush, a pair of rubbers, two books, and a bag of ginger-bread distorting the pockets of the same. If I thought that any one would believe it, I'd boldly state that I slept from C. to B., which would simplify matters immensely; but as I know they wouldn't, I'll confess that the head under the funereal coal-hod fermented with all manner of high thoughts and heroic purposes "to do or die,"—perhaps both; and the heart under the fuzzy brown coat felt very tender with the memory of the dear old lady, probably sobbing over her army socks and the loss of her topsy-turvy Trib. At this juncture I took the veil, and what I did behind it is nobody's business; but I maintain that the soldier who cries when his mother says "Good bye," is the boy to fight best, and die bravest, when the time comes, or go back to her better than he went.

Till nine o'clock I trotted about the city streets, doing those last errands which no woman would even go to heaven without attempting, if she could. Then I went to my usual refuge, and, fully intending to keep awake, as a sort of vigil appropriate to the occasion, fell fast asleep and dreamed propitious dreams till my rosy-faced cousin waked me with a kiss.

A bright day smiled upon my enterprise, and at ten I reported myself to my General, received last instructions and no end of the sympathetic encouragement which women give, in look, touch, and tone more effectually than in words. The next step was to get a free pass to Washington, for I'd no desire to waste my substance on railroad companies when "the boys" needed even a spinster's mite. A friend of mine had procured such a pass, and I was bent on doing likewise, though I had to face the president of the railroad to accomplish it. I'm a bashful individual, though I can't get any one to believe it; so it cost me a great effort to poke about the Worcester depot till the right door appeared, then walk into a room containing several gentlemen, and blunder out my request in a high state of stammer and blush. Nothing could have been more courteous than this dreaded President, but it was evident that I had made as absurd a demand as if I had asked for the nose off his respectable face. He referred me to the Governor at the State House, and I backed out, leaving him no doubt to regret that such mild maniacs were left at large. Here was a Scylla and Charybdis business: as if a President wasn't trying enough, without the Governor of Massachusetts and the hub of the hub piled on top of that. "I never can do it," thought I. "Tom will hoot at you if you don't," whispered the inconvenient little voice that is always goading people to the performance of disagreeable duties, and always appeals to the most effective agent to produce the proper result. The idea of allowing any boy that ever wore a felt basin and a shoddy jacket with a microscopic tail, to crow over me, was preposterous, so giving myself a mental slap for such faintheartedness, I streamed away across the Common, wondering if I ought to say "your Honor," or simply "Sir," and decided upon the latter, fortifying myself with recollections of an evening in a charming green library, where I beheld the Governor placidly consuming oysters, and laughing as if Massachusetts was a myth, and he had no heavier burden on his shoulders than his host's handsome hands.

Like an energetic fly in a very large cobweb, I struggled through the State House, getting into all the wrong rooms and none of the right, till I turned desperate, and went into one, resolving not to come out till I'd made somebody hear and answer me. I suspect that of all the wrong places I had blundered into, this was the most so. But I didn't care; and, though the apartment was full of soldiers, surgeons, starers, and spittoons, I cornered a perfectly incapable person, and proceeded to pump for information with the following result:

"Was the Governor anywhere about?"

No, he wasn't.

"Could he tell me where to look?"

No, he couldn't.

"Did he know anything about free passes?"

No, he didn't.

"Was there any one there of whom I could inquire?"

Not a person.

"Did he know of any place where information could be obtained?"
Not a place.

"Could he throw the smallest gleam of light upon the matter, in
any way?"

Not a ray.

I am naturally irascible, and if I could have shaken this negative
gentleman vigorously, the relief would have been immense. The prejudices
of society forbidding this mode of redress, I merely glowered at him; and,
before my wrath found vent in words, my General appeared, having seen
me from an opposite window, and come to know what I was about. At her
command the languid gentleman woke up, and troubled himself to remember that Major or Sergeant or something Mc K. knew all about the
tickets, and his office was in Milk Street. I perked up instanter, and then, as
if the exertion was too much for him, what did this animated wet blanket
do but add—

"I think Mc K. may have left Milk Street, now, and I don't know
where he has gone."

"Never mind; the new comers will know where he has moved to, my
dear, so don't be discouraged; and if you don't succeed, come to me, and
we will see what to do next," said my General.

I blessed her in a fervent manner and a cool hall, fluttered round the
corner, and bore down upon Milk Street, bent on discovering Mc K. if such
a being was to be found. He wasn't, and the ignorance of the neighborhood
was really pitiable. Nobody knew anything, and after tumbling over
bundles of leather, bumping against big boxes, being nearly annihilated by
descending bales, and sworn at by aggravated truckmen, I finally elicited
the advice to look for Mc K. in Haymarket Square. Who my informant was
I've really forgotten; for, having hailed several busy gentlemen, some one of
them fabricated this delusive quietus for the perturbed spirit, who instantly departed to the sequestered locality he named. If I had been in
search of th Koh-i-noor diamond I should have been as likely to find it
there as any vestige of Mc K. I stared at signs, inquired in shops, invaded an
eating house, visited the recruiting tent in the middle of the Square, made
myself a nuisance generally, and accumulated mud enough to retard another Nile. All in vain: and I mournfully turned my face toward the
General's, feeling that I should be forced to enrich the railroad company

after all; when, suddenly, I beheld that admirable young man, brother-in-law Darby Coobiddy, Esq. I arrested him with a burst of news, and wants, and woes, which caused his manly countenance to lose its usual repose.

"Oh, my dear boy, I'm going to Washington at five, and I can't find the free ticket man, and there won't be time to see Joan, and I'm so tired and cross I don't know what to do; and will you help me, like a cherub as you are?"

"Oh, yes, of course. I know a fellow who will set us right," responded Darby, mildly excited, and darting into some kind of an office, held counsel with an invisible angel, who sent him out radiant. "All serene. I've got him. I'll see you through the business, and then get Joan from the Dove Cote in time to see you off."

I'm a woman's rights woman, and if any man had offered help in the morning, I should have condescendingly refused it, sure that I could do everything as well, if not better, myself. My strong-mindedness had rather abated since then, and I was now quite ready to be a "timid trembler," if necessary. Dear me! how easily Darby did it all: he just asked one question, received an answer, tucked me under his arm, and in ten minutes I stood in the presence of Mc K., the Desired.

"Now my troubles are over," thought I, and as usual was direfully mistaken.

"You will have to get a pass from Dr. H., in Temple Place,[2] before I can give you a pass, madam," answered Mc K., as blandly as if he wasn't carrying desolation to my soul. Oh, indeed! why didn't he send me to Dorchester Heights, India Wharf, or Bunker Hill Monument, and done with it? Here I was, after a morning's tramp, down in some place about Dock Square, and was told to step to Temple Place. Nor was that all; he might as well have asked me to catch a humming-bird, toast a salamander, or call on the man in the moon, as find a Doctor at home at the busiest hour of the day. It was a blow; but weariness had extinguished enthusiasm, and resignation clothed me as a garment. I sent Darby for Joan, and doggedly paddled off, feeling that mud was my native element, and quite sure that the evening papers would announce the appearance of the Wandering Jew, in feminine habiliments.

"Is Dr. H. in?"

"No, mum, he aint."

Of course he wasn't; I knew that before I asked: and, considering it all in the light of a hollow mockery, added:

"When will he probably return?"

If the damsel had said, "ten to-night," I should have felt a grim satisfaction, in the fulfillment of my own dark prophecy; but she said, "At two, mum;" and I felt it a personal insult.

"I'll call, then. Tell him my business is important:" with which mysteriously delivered message I departed, hoping that I left her consumed with curiosity; for mud rendered me an object of interest.

By way of resting myself, I crossed the Common, for the third time, bespoke the carriage, got some lunch, packed my purchases, smoothed my plumage, and was back again, as the clock struck two. The Doctor hadn't come yet; and I was morally certain that he would not, till, having waited till the last minute, I was driven to buy a ticket, and, five minutes after the irrevocable deed was done, he would be at my service, with all manner of helpful documents and directions. Everything goes by contraries with me; so, having made up my mind to be disappointed, of course I wasn't; for, presently, in walked Dr. H., and no sooner had he heard my errand, and glanced at my credentials, than he said, with the most engaging readiness:

"I will give you the order, with pleasure, madam."

Words cannot express how soothing and delightful it was to find, at last, somebody who could do what I wanted, without sending me from Dan to Beersheba, for a dozen other bodies to do something else first. Peace descended, like oil, upon the ruffled waters of my being, as I sat listening to the busy scratch of his pen; and, when he turned about, giving me not only the order, but a paper of directions wherewith to smooth away all difficulties between Boston and Washington, I felt as did poor Christian when the Evangelist gave him the scroll, on the safe side of the Slough of Despond. I've no doubt many dismal nurses have inflicted themselves upon the worthy gentleman since then; but I am sure none have been more kindly helped, or are more grateful, than T. P.; for that short interview added another to the many pleasant associations that already surround his name.

Feeling myself no longer a "Martha Struggles," but a comfortable young woman, with plain sailing before her, and the worst of the voyage well over, I once more presented myself to the valuable Mc K. The order was read, and certain printed papers, necessary to be filled out, were given a young gentleman—no, I prefer to say Boy, with a scornful emphasis upon the word, as the only means of revenge now left me. This Boy, instead of doing his duty with the diligence so charming in the young, loitered and lounged, in a manner which proved his education to have been sadly neglected in the—

"How doth the little busy bee,"

direction. He stared at me, gaped out of the window, ate peanuts, and gossiped with his neighbors—Boys, like himself, and all penned in a row, like colts at a Cattle Show. I don't imagine he knew the anguish he was inflicting; for it was nearly three, the train left at five, and I had my ticket to get, my dinner to eat, my blessed sister to see, and the depot to reach, if I didn't die of apoplexy. Meanwhile, Patience certainly had her perfect work that day, and I hope she enjoyed the job more than I did. Having waited some twenty minutes, it pleased this reprehensible Boy to make varous marks and blots on my documents, toss them to a venerable creature of sixteen, who delivered them to me with such paternal directions, that it only needed a pat on the head and an encouraging—"Now run home to your Ma, little girl, and mind the crossings, my dear," to make the illusion quite perfect.

Why I was sent to a steamboat office for car tickets, is not for me to say, though I went as meekly as I should have gone to the Probate Court, if sent. A fat, easy gentleman gave me several bits of paper, with coupons attached, with a warning not to separate them, which instantly inspired me with a yearning to pluck them apart, and see what came of it. But, remembering through what fear and tribulation I had obtained them, I curbed Satan's promptings, and, clutching my prize, as if it were my pass to the Elysian Fields, I hurried home. Dinner was rapidly consumed; Joan enlightened, comforted, and kissed; the dearest of apple-faced cousins hugged; the kindest of apple-faced cousins' fathers subjected to the same process; and I mounted the ambulance, baggage-wagon, or anything you please but hack, and drove away, too tired to feel excited, sorry, or glad.

II

A FORWARD MOVEMENT

AS travellers like to give their own impressions of a journey, though every inch of the way may have been described a half dozen times before, I add some of the notes made by the way, hoping that they will amuse the reader, and convince the skeptical that such a being as Nurse Periwinkle does exist, that she really did go to Washington, and that these Sketches are not romance.

New York Train—Seven P.M.—Spinning along to take the boat at New London. Very comfortable; munch gingerbread, and Mrs. C.'s fine pear, which deserves honorable mention, because my first loneliness was comforted by it, and pleasant recollections of both kindly sender and bearer. Look much at Dr. H.'s paper of directions—put my tickets in every conceivable place, that they may be get-at-able, and finish by losing them entirely. Suffer agonies till a compassionate neighbor pokes them out of a crack with his pen-knife. Put them in the inmost corner of my purse, that in the deepest recesses of my pocket, pile a collection of miscellaneous articles atop, and pin up the whole. Just get composed, feeling that I've done my best to keep them safely, when the Conductor appears, and I'm forced to rout them all out again, exposing my precautions, and getting into a flutter at keeping the man waiting. Finally, fasten them on the seat before me, and keep one eye steadily upon the yellow torments, till I forget all about them, in chat with the gentleman who shares my seat. Having heard complaints of the absurd way in which American women become images of petrified propriety, if addressed by strangers, when traveling alone, the inborn perversity of my nature causes me to assume an entirely opposite style of deportment; and, finding my companion hails from Little Athens, is acquainted with several of my three hundred and sixty-five cousins, and in every way a respectable and respectful member of society, I put my bashfulness in my pocket, and plunge into a long conversation on the war, the weather, music, Carlyle, skating, genius, hoops, and the immortality of the soul.

Ten, P.M.—Very sleepy. Nothing to be seen outside, but darkness made visible; nothing inside but every variety of bunch into which the human form can be twisted, rolled, or "massed," as Miss Prescott says of her jewels.[3] Every man's legs sprawl drowsily, every woman's head (but mine), nods, till it finally settles on somebody's shoulder, a new proof of the truth of the everlasting oak and vine simile; children fret; lovers whisper; old folks snore, and somebody privately imbibes brandy, when the lamps go out. The penetrating perfume rouses the multitude, causing some to start up, like war horses at the smell of powder. When the lamps are relighted, every one laughs, sniffs, and looks inquiringly at his neighbor— every one but a stout gentleman, who, with well-gloved hands folded upon his broad-cloth rotundity, sleeps on impressively. Had he been innocent, he would have waked up; for, to slumber in that babe-like manner, with a car full of giggling, staring, sniffing humanity, was simply preposterous. Public suspicion was down upon him at once. I doubt if the appearance of a flat black bottle with a label would have settled the matter more effectually than did the over dignified and profound repose of this short-sighted being. His moral neck-cloth, virtuous boots, and pious attitude availed him nothing, and it was well he kept his eyes shut, for "Humbug!" twinkled at him from every window-pane, brass nail and human eye around him.

Eleven, P.M.—In the boat "City of Boston," escorted thither by my car acquaintance, and deposited in the cabin. Trying to look as if the greater portion of my life had been passed on board boats, but painfully conscious that I don't know the first thing; so sit bolt upright, and stare about me till I hear one lady say to another—"We must secure our berths at once;" whereupon I dart at one, and, while leisurely taking off my cloak, wait to discover what the second move may be. Several ladies draw the curtains that hang in a semi-circle before each nest—instantly I whisk mine smartly together, and then peep out to see what next. Gradually, on hooks above the blue and yellow drapery, appear the coats and bonnets of my neighbors, while their boots and shoes, in every imaginable attitude, assert themselves below, as if their owners had committed suicide in a body. A violent creaking, scrambling, and fussing, causes the fact that people are going regularly to bed to dawn upon my mind. Of course they are! and so am I—but pause at the seventh pin, remembering that, as I was born to be drowned, an eligible opportunity now presents itself; and, having twice escaped a watery grave, the third immersion will certainly extinguish my vital spark. The boat is new, but if it ever intends to blow up, spring a leak, catch afire, or be run into, it will do the deed tonight, because I'm here to fulfill my destiny. With tragic calmness I resign myself, replace my pins, lash my purse and papers together, with my handkerchief, examine the saving circumference of my hoop, and look about me for any means of deliverance when the moist moment shall arrive; for I've no intention of folding my hands and bubbling to death without an energetic splashing first. Barrels, hen-coops, portable settees, and life-preservers do not adorn the cabin, as they should; and, roving wildly to and fro, my eye sees no ray of hope till it falls upon a plump old lady, devoutly reading in the cabin Bible, and a voluminous night-cap. I remember that, at the swimming school, fat girls always floated best, and in an instant my plan is laid. At the first alarm I firmly attach myself to the plump lady, and cling to her through fire and water; for I feel that my old enemy, the cramp, will seize me by the foot, if I attempt to swim; and, though I can hardly expect to reach Jersey City with myself and my baggage in as good condition as I hoped, I might manage to get picked up by holding to my fat friend; if not it will be a comfort to feel that I've made an effort and shall die in good society. Poor dear woman! how little she dreamed, as she read and rocked, with her cap in a high state of starch, and her feet comfortably cooking at the register, what fell designs were hovering about her, and how intently a small but determined eye watched her, till it suddenly closed.

Sleep got the better of fear to such an extent that my boots appeared to gape, and my bonnet nodded on its peg, before I gave in. Having piled my cloak, bag, rubbers, books and umbrella on the lower shelf, I drowsily swarmed onto the upper one, tumbling down a few times, and excoriating the knobby portions of my frame in the act. A very brief nap on the upper roost was enough to set me gasping as if a dozen feather beds and the whole boat were laid over me. Out I turned; and, after a series of convulsions, which caused my neighbor to ask if I wanted the stewardess, I managed to get my luggage up and myself down. But even in the lower berth, my rest was not unbroken, for various articles kept dropping off the little shelf at the bottom of the bed, and every time I flew up, thinking my hour had come, I bumped my head severely against the little shelf at the top, evidently put there for that express purpose. At last, after listening to the swash of the waves outside, wondering if the machinery usually creaked in that way, and watching a knot-hole in the side of my berth, sure that death would creep in there as soon as I took my eye from it, I dropped asleep, and dreamed of muffins.

Five, A.M.—On deck, trying to wake up and enjoy an east wind and a morning fog, and a twilight sort of view of something on the shore. Rapidly achieve my purpose, and do enjoy every moment, as we go rushing through the Sound, with steamboats passing up and down, lights dancing on the shore, mist wreaths slowly furling off, and a pale pink sky above us, as the sun comes up.

Seven, A.M.—In the cars, at Jersey City. Much fuss with tickets, which one man scribbles over, another snips, and a third "makes note on." Partake of refreshment, in the gloom of a very large and dirty depot. Think that my sandwiches would be more relishing without so strong a flavor of napkin, and my gingerbread more easy of consumption if it had not been pulverized by being sat upon. People act as if early travelling didn't agree with them. Children scream and scamper; men smoke and growl; women shiver and fret; porters swear; great truck horses pace up and down with loads of baggage; and every one seems to get into the wrong car, and come tumbling out again. One man, with three children, a dog, a bird-cage, and several bundles, puts himself and his possessions into every possible place where a man, three children, dog, bird-cage and bundles could be got, and is satisfied with none of them. I follow their movements, with an interest that is really exhausting, and, as they vanish, hope for rest, but don't get it. A strong-minded woman, with a tumbler in her hand, and no cloak or shawl on, comes rushing through the car, talking loudly to a small porter, who lugs a folding bed after her, and looks as if life were a burden to him.

"You promised to have it ready. It is not ready. It must be a car with a water jar, the windows must be shut, the fire must be kept up, the blinds must be down. No, this won't do. I shall go through the whole train, and suit myself, for you promised to have it ready. It is not ready," &c., all through again, like a hand-organ. She haunted the cars, the depot, the office and baggage-room, with her bed, her tumbler, and her tongue, till the train started; and a sense of fervent gratitude filled my soul, when I found that she and her unknown invalid were not to share our car.

Philadelphia.—An old place, full of Dutch women, in "bellus top" bonnets, selling vegetables, in long, open markets. Every one seems to be scrubbing their white steps. All the houses look like tidy jails, with their outside shutters. Several have crape on the door-handles, and many have flags flying from roof or balcony. Few men appear, and the women seem to do the business, which, perhaps, accounts for its being so well done. Pass fine buildings, but don't know what they are. Would like to stop and see my native city; for, having left it at the tender age of two, my recollections are not vivid.

Baltimore.—A big, dirty, shippy, shiftless place, full of goats, geese, colored people, and coal, at least the part of it I see. Pass near the spot where the riot took place, and feel as if I should enjoy throwing a stone at somebody, hard.[4] Find a guard at the ferry, the depot, and here and there, along the road. A camp whitens one hill-side, and a cavalry training school, or whatever it should be called, is a very interesting sight, with quantities of horses and riders galloping, marching, leaping, and skirmishing, over all manner of break-neck places. A party of English people get in—the men, with sandy hair and red whiskers, all trimmed alike, to a hair; rough grey coats, very rosy, clean faces, and a fine, full way of speaking, which is particularly agreeable, after our slip-shod American gabble. The two ladies wear funny velvet fur-trimmed hoods; are done up, like compact bundles, in tartan shawls; and look as if bent on seeing everything thoroughly. The devotion of one elderly John Bull to his red-nosed spouse was really beautiful to behold. She was plain and cross, and fussy and stupid, but J. B., Esq., read no papers when she was awake, turned no cold shoulder when she wished to sleep, and cheerfully said, "Yes, me dear," to every wish or want the wife of his bosom expressed. I quite warmed to the excellent man, and asked a question or two, as the only means of expressing my good will. He answered very civilly, but evidently hadn't been used to being addressed by strange women in public conveyances; and Mrs. B. fixed her green eyes upon me, as if she thought me a forward huzzy, or whatever is good English for a presuming young woman. The pair left their friends before we reached Washington; and the last I saw of them was a vision of a large plaid lady, stalking grimly away, on the arm of a rosy, stout gentleman, loaded with rugs, bags, and books, but still devoted, still smiling, and waving a hearty "Fare ye well! We'll meet ye at Willard's on Chusday."

Soon after their departure we had an accident; for no long journey in America would be complete without one. A coupling iron broke; and, after leaving the last car behind us, we waited for it to come up, which it did, with a crash that knocked every one forward on their faces, and caused several old ladies to screech dismally. Hats flew off, bonnets were flattened, the stove skipped, the lamps fell down, the water jar turned a somersault, and the wheel just over which I sat received some damage. Of course, it became necessary for all the men to get out, and stand about in everybody's way, while repairs were made; and for the women to wrestle their heads out of the windows, asking ninety-nine foolish questions to one sensible one. A few wise females seized this favorable moment to better their seats, well knowing that few men can face the wooden stare with which they regard the former possessors of the places they have invaded.

The country through which we passed did not seem so very unlike that which I had left, except that it was more level and less wintry. In summer time the wide fields would have shown me new sights, and the way-side hedges blossomed with new flowers; now, everything was sere and sodden, and a general air of shiftlessness prevailed, which would have caused a New England farmer much disgust, and a strong desire to "buckle to," and "right up" things. Dreary little houses, with chimneys built outside, with clay and rough sticks piled crosswise, as we used to build cob towers, stood in barren looking fields, with cow, pig, or mule lounging about the door. We often passed colored people, looking as if they had come out of a picture book, or off the stage, but not at all the sort of people I'd been accustomed to see at the North.

Way-side encampments made the fields and lanes gay with blue coats and the glitter of buttons. Military washes flapped and fluttered on the fences; pots were steaming in the open air; all sorts of tableaux seen through the openings of tents, and everywhere the boys threw up their caps and cut capers as we passed.

Washington.—It was dark when we arrived; and, but for the presence of another friendly gentleman, I should have yielded myself a helpless prey to the first overpowering hackman, who insisted that I wanted to go just where I didn't. Putting me into the conveyance I belonged in, my escort added to the obligation by pointing out the objects of interest which we passed in our long drive. Though I'd often been told that Washington was a spacious place, its visible magnitude quite took my breath away, and of course I quoted Randolph's expression, "a city of magnificent distances," as I suppose every one does when they see it.[5] The Capitol was so like the pictures that hang opposite the staring Father of his Country, in boarding-houses and hotels, that it did not impress me, except to recall the time when I was sure that Cinderella went to housekeeping in just such a place, after she had married the inflammable Prince; though, even at that early period, I had my doubts as to the wisdom of a match whose foundation was of glass.

The White House was lighted up, and carriages were rolling in and out of the great gate. I stared hard at the famous East Room, and would have like a peep through the crack of the door. My old gentleman was indefatigable in his attentions, and I said "Splendid!" to everything he pointed out, though I suspect I often admired the wrong place, and missed the right. Pennsylvania Avenue, with its bustle, lights, music, and military, made me feel as if I'd crossed the water and landed somewhere in Carnival time. Coming to less noticeable parts of the city, my companion fell silent, and I meditated upon the perfection which Art had attained in America—having just passed a bronze statue of some hero, who looked like a black Methodist minister, in a cocked hat, above the waist, and tipsy squire below; while his horse stood like an opera dancer, on one leg, in a high, but somewhat remarkable wind, which blew his mane one way and his massive tail the other.[6]

"Hurly-burly House, ma'am!" called a voice, startling me from my reverie, as we stopped before a great pile of buildings, with a flag flying before it, sentinels at the door, and a very trying quantity of men lounging about. My heart beat rather faster than usual, and it suddenly struck me that I was very far from home; but I descended with dignity, wondering whether I should be stopped for want of a countersign, and forced to pass the night in the street. Marching boldly up the steps, I found that no form was necessary, for the men fell back, the guard touched their caps, a boy opened the door, and, as it closed behind me, I felt that I was fairly started, and Nurse Periwinkle's Mission was begun.

III

A DAY

"*THEY'VE* come! they've come! hurry up, ladies—you're wanted."

"Who have come? the rebels?"

This sudden summons in the gray dawn was somewhat startling to a three days' nurse like myself, and, as the thundering knock came at our door, I sprang up in my bed, prepared

> "To gird my woman's form,
> And on the ramparts die,"

if necessary, but my room-mate took it more coolly, and, as she began a rapid toilet, answered my bewildered question,—

"Bless you, no child; it's the wounded from Fredericksburg; forty ambulances are at the door, and we shall have our hands full in fifteen minutes."

"What shall we have to do?"

"Wash, dress, feed, warm and nurse them for the next three months, I dare say. Eighty beds are ready, and we were getting impatient for the men to come. Now you will begin to see hospital life in earnest, for you won't probably find time to sit down all day, and may think yourself fortunate if you get to bed by midnight. Come to me in the ball-room when you are ready; the worst cases are always carried there, and I shall need your help."

So saying, the energetic little woman twirled her hair into a button at the back of her head, in a "cleared for action" sort of style, and vanished, wrestling her way into a feminine kind of pea-jacket as she went.

I am free to confess that I had a realizing sense of the fact that my hospital bed was not a bed of roses just then, or the prospect before me one of unmingled rapture. My three days' experiences had begun with a death, and, owing to the defalcation of another nurse, a somewhat abrupt plunge into the superintendence of a ward containing forty beds, where I spent my shining hours washing faces, serving rations, giving medicine, and sitting in a very hard chair, with pneumonia on one side, diptheria on the other, five typhoids on the opposite, and a dozen dilapidated patriots, hopping, lying, and lounging about, all staring more or less at the new "nuss," who suffered untold agonies, but concealed them under as matronly an aspect as a spinster could assume, and blundered through her trying labors with a Spartan firmness, which I hope they appreciated, but am afraid they didn't. Having a taste for "ghastliness," I had rather longed for the wounded to arrive, for rheumatism wasn't heroic, neither was liver complaint, or measles; even fever had lost its charms since "bathing burning brows" had been used up in romances, real and ideal; but when I peeped into the dusky street lined with what I at first had innocently called market carts, now unloading their sad freight at our door, I recalled sundry reminiscences I had heard from nurses of longer standing, my ardor experienced a sudden chill, and I indulged in a most unpatriotic wish that I was safe at home again, with a quiet day before me, and no necessity for being hustled up, as if I were a hen and had only to hop off my roost, give my plumage a peck, and be ready for action. A second bang at the door sent this recreant desire to the right about, as a little woolly head popped in, and Joey, (a six years' old contraband), announced—

"Miss Blank is jes' wild fer ye, and says fly round right away. They's comin' in, I tell yer, heaps on 'em—one was took out dead, and I see him,—ky! warn't he a goner!"

With which cheerful intelligence the imp scuttled away, singing like a blackbird, and I followed, feeling that Richard was *not* himself again, and wouldn't be for a long time to come.

The first thing I met was a regiment of the vilest odors that ever assaulted the human nose, and took it by storm. Cologne, with its seven and seventy evil savors, was a posy-bed to it; and the worst of this affliction was, every one had assured me that it was a chronic weakness of all hospitals, and I must bear it. I did, armed with lavender water, with which I so besprinkled myself and premises, that, like my friend, Sairy, I was soon known among my patients as "the nurse with the bottle."[7] Having been run over by three excited surgeons, bumped against by migratory coal-hods, water-pails, and small boys; nearly scalded by an avalanche of newly-filled tea-pots, and hopelessly entangled in a knot of colored sisters coming to wash, I progressed by slow stages up stairs and down, till the main hall was reached, and I paused to take breath and a survey. There they were! "our brave boys," as the papers justly call them, for cowards could hardly have been so riddled with shot and shell, so torn and shattered, nor have borne suffering for which we have no name, with an uncomplaining fortitude, which made one glad to cherish each as a brother. In they came, some on stretchers, some in men's arms, some feebly staggering along propped on rude crutches, and one lay stark and still with covered face, as a comrade gave his name to be recorded before they carried him away to the dead house. All was hurry and confusion; the hall was full of these wrecks of humanity, for the most exhausted could not reach a bed till duly ticketed and registered; the walls were lined with rows of such as could sit, the floor covered with the more disabled, the steps and doorways filled with helpers and lookers on; the sound of many feet and voices made that usually quiet hour as noisy as noon; and, in the midst of it all, the matron's motherly face brought more comfort to many a poor soul, than the cordial draughts she administered, or the cheery words that welcomed all, making of the hospital a home.

The sight of several stretchers, each with its legless, armless, or desperately wounded occupant, entering my ward, admonished me that I was there to work, not to wonder or weep; so I corked up my feelings, and returned to the path of duty, which was rather "a hard road to travel" just then. The house had been a hotel before hospitals were needed, and many of the doors still bore their old names; some not so inappropriate as might be imagined, for my ward was in truth a *ball-room,* if gun-shot wounds could christen it. Forty beds were prepared, many already tenanted by tired men who fell down anywhere, and drowsed till the smell of food roused them. Round the great stove was gathered the dreariest group I ever saw—ragged, gaunt and pale, mud to the knees, with bloody bandages untouched since put on days before; many bundled up in blankets, coats being lost or useless; and all wearing that disheartened look which proclaimed defeat, more plainly than any telegram of the Burnside blunder.[8] I pitied them so much, I dared not speak to them, though, remembering all they had been through since the route at Fredericksburg, I yearned to serve the dreariest of them all. Presently, Miss Blank tore me from my refuge behind piles of one-sleeved shirts, odd socks, bandages and lint; put basin, sponge, towels, and a block of brown soap into my hands, with these appalling directions:

"Come, my dear, begin to wash as fast as you can. Tell them to take off socks, coats and shirts, scrub them well, put on clean shirts, and the attendants will finish them off, and lay them in bed."

If she had requested me to shave them all, or dance a horn-pipe on the stove funnel, I should have been less staggered; but to scrub some dozen lords of creation at a moment's notice, was really—really—. However, there was no time for nonsense, and, having resolved when I came to do everything I was bid, I drowned my scruples in my washbowl, clutched my soap manfully, and, assuming a businesslike air, made a dab at the first dirty specimen I saw, bent on performing my task *vi et armis*[9] if necessary. I chanced to light on a withered old Irishman, wounded in the head, which caused that portion of his frame to be tastefully laid out like a garden, the bandages being the walks, his hair the shrubbery. He was so overpowered by the honor of having a lady wash him, as he expressed it, that he did nothing but roll up his eyes, and bless me, in an irresistible style which was too much for my sense of the ludicrous; so we laughed together, and when I knelt down to take off his shoes, he "flopped" also and wouldn't hear of my touching "them dirty craters. May your bed above be aisy darlin', for the day's work ye are doon!—Woosh! there ye are, an bedad, it's hard tellin' which is the dirtiest, the fut or the shoe." It was; and if he hadn't been to the fore, I should have gone on pulling, under the impression that the "fut" was a boot, for trousers, socks, shoes and legs were a mass of mud. This comical tableau produced a general grin, at which propitious beginning I took heart and scrubbed away like any tidy parent on a Saturday night. Some of them took the performance like sleepy children, leaning their tired heads against me as I worked, others looked grimly scandalized, and several of the roughest colored like bashful girls. One wore a soiled little bag about his neck, and, as I moved it, to bathe his wounded breast, I said,

"Your talisman didn't save you, did it?"

"Well, I reckon it did, marm, for that shot would a gone a couple of inches deeper but for my old mammy's camphor bag," answered the cheerful philosopher.

Another, with a gun-shot wound through the cheek, asked for a looking-glass, and when I brought one, regarded his swollen face with a dolorous expression, as he muttered—

"I vow to gosh, that's too bad! I warn't a bad looking chap before, and now I'm done for; won't there be a thunderin' scar? and what on earth will Josephine Skinner say?"

He looked up at me with his one eye so appealingly, that I controlled my risibles, and assured him that if Josephine was a girl of sense, she would admire the honorable scar, as a lasting proof that he had faced the enemy, for all women thought a wound the best decoration a brave soldier could wear. I hope Miss Skinner verified the good opinion I so rashly expressed of her, but I shall never know.

The next scrubbee was a nice looking lad, with a curly brown mane, and a budding trace of gingerbread over the lip, which he called his beard, and defended stoutly, when the barber jocosely suggested its immolation. He lay on a bed, with one leg gone, and the right arm so shattered that it must evidently follow; yet the little Sergeant was as merry as if his afflictions were not worth lamenting over, and when a drop or two of salt water mingled with my suds at the sight of this strong young body, so marred and and maimed, the boy looked up, with a brave smile, though there was a little quiver of the lips, as he said,

"Now don't you fret yourself about me, miss; I'm first rate here, for it's nuts to lie still on this bed, after knocking about in those confounded ambulances, that shake what there is left of a fellow to jelly. I never was in one of these places before, and think this cleaning up a jolly thing for us, though I'm afraid it isn't for you ladies."

"Is this your first battle, Sergeant?"

"No, miss; I've been in six scrimmages, and never got a scratch till this last one; but it's done the business pretty thoroughly for me, I should say. Lord! what a scramble there'll be for arms and legs, when we old boys come out of our graves, on the Judgment Day: wonder if we shall get our own again? If we do, my leg will have to tramp from Fredericksburg, my arm from here, I suppose, and meet my body, wherever it may be."

The fancy seemed to tickle him mightily, for he laughed blithely, and so did I; which, no doubt, caused the new nurse to be regarded as a light-minded sinner by the Chaplain, who roamed vaguely about, informing the men that they were all worms, corrupt of heart, with perishable bodies, and souls only to be saved by a diligent perusal of certain tracts, and other equally cheering bits of spiritual consolation, when spirituous ditto would have been preferred.

"I say, Mrs.!" called a voice behind me; and, turning, I saw a rough Michigander, with an arm blown off at the shoulder, and two or three bullets still in him—as he afterwards mentioned, as carelessly as if gentlemen were in the habit of carrying such trifles about with them. I went to him, and, while administering a dose of soap and water, he whispered, irefully:

"That red-headed devil, over yonder, is a reb, damn him! You'll agree to that, I'll bet? He's got shet of a foot, or he'd a cut like the rest of the lot. Don't you wash him, nor feed him, but jest let him holler till he's tired. It's a blasted shame to fetch them fellers in here, along side of us; and so I'll tell the chap that bosses this concern; cuss me if I don't."

I regret to say that I did not deliver a moral sermon upon the duty of forgiving our enemies, and the sin of profanity, then and there; but, being a red-hot Abolitionist, stared fixedly at the tall rebel, who was a copperhead, in every sense of the word, and privately resolved to put soap in his eyes, rub his nose the wrong way, and excoriate his cuticle generally, if I had the washing of him.

My amiable intentions, however, were frustrated; for, when I approached, with as Christian an expression as my principles would allow, and asked the question—"Shall I try to make you more comfortable, sir?" all I got for my pains was a gruff—

"No; I'll do it myself."

"Here's your Southern chivalry, with a witness," thought I, dumping the basin down before him, thereby quenching a strong desire to give him a summary baptism, in return for his ungraciousness; for my angry passions rose, at this rebuff, in a way that would have scandalized good Dr. Watts. He was a disappointment in all respects, (the rebel, not the blessed Doctor,) for he was neither fiendish, romantic, pathetic, or anything interesting; but a long, fat man, with a head like a burning bush, and a perfectly expressionless face: so I could hate him without the slightest drawback, and ignored his existence from that day forth. One redeeming trait he certainly did possess, as the floor speedily testified; for his ablutions were so vigorously performed, that his bed soon stood like an isolated island, in a sea of soap-suds, and he resembled a dripping merman, suffering from the loss of a fin. If cleanliness is a near neighbor to godliness, then was the big rebel the godliest man in my ward that day.

Having done up our human wash, and laid it out to dry, the second syllable of our version of the word war-fare was enacted with much success. Great trays of bread, meat, soup and coffee appeared; and both nurses and attendants turned waiters, serving bountiful rations to all who could eat. I can call my pinafore to testify to my good will in the work, for in ten minutes it was reduced to a perambulating bill of fare, presenting samples of all the refreshments going or gone. It was a lively scene; the long room lined with rows of beds, each filled by an occupant, whom water, shears, and clean raiment, had transformed from a dismal ragamuffin into a recumbent hero, with a cropped head. To and fro rushed matrons, maids, and convalescent "boys," skirmishing with knives and forks; retreating with empty plates; marching and counter-marching, with unvaried success, while the clash of busy spoons made most inspiring music for the charge of our Light Brigade:

> "Beds to the front of them,
> Beds to the right of them,
> Beds to the left of them,
>   Nobody blundered.
> Beamed at by hungry souls,
> Screamed at with brimming bowls,
> Steamed at by army rolls,
>   Buttered and sundered.

With coffee not cannon plied,
Each must be satisfied,
Whether they lived or died;
All the men wondered."

Very welcome seemed the generous meal, after a week of suffering, exposure, and short commons; soon the brown faces began to smile,
as food, warmth, and rest, did their pleasant work; and the grateful
"Thankee's" were followed by more graphic accounts of the battle and
retreat, than any paid reporter could have given us. Curious contrasts of
the tragic and comic met one everywhere; and some touching as well as
ludicrous episodes, might have been recorded that day. A six foot New
Hampshire man, with a leg broken and perforated by a piece of shell, so
large that, had I not seen the wound, I should have regarded the story as a
Munchausenism, beckoned me to come and help him, as he could not sit
up, and both his bed and beard were getting plentifully anointed with
soup. As I fed my big nestling with corresponding mouthfuls, I asked him
how he felt during the battle.

"Well, 'twas my fust, you see, so I ain't ashamed to say I was a trifle
flustered in the beginnin', there was such an all-fired racket; for ef there's
anything I do spleen agin, it's noise. But when my mate, Eph Sylvester,
caved, with a bullet through his head, I got mad, and pitched in, licketty
cut. Our part of the fight didn't last long; so a lot of us larked round
Fredericksburg, and give some of them houses a pretty consid'able of a
rummage, till we was ordered out of the mess. Some of our fellows cut like
time; but I warn't a-goin to run for nobody; and, fust thing I knew, a shell
bust, right in front of us, and I keeled over, feeling' as if I was blowed
higher'n a kite. I sung out, and the boys come back for me, double quick;
but the way they chucked me over them fences was a caution, I tell you.
Next day I was most as black as that darkey yonder, lickin' plates on the
sly. This is bully coffee, ain't it? Give us another pull at it, and I'll be
obleeged to you."

I did; and, as the last gulp subsided, he said, with a rub of his old
handkerchief over eyes as well as mouth:

"Look a here; I've got a pair of earbobs and a handkercher pin I'm a
goin' to give you, if you'll have them; for you're the very moral o' Lizy

Sylvester, poor Eph's wife: that's why I signalled you to come over here. They ain't much, I guess, but they'll do to memorize the rebs by."

Burrowing under his pillow, he produced a little bundle of what he called "truck," and gallantly presented me with a pair of earrings, each representing a cluster of corpulent grapes, and the pin a basket of astonishing fruit, the whole large and coppery enough for a small warming-pan. Feeling delicate about depriving him of such valuable relics, I accepted the earrings alone, and was obliged to depart, somewhat abruptly, when my friend stuck the warming-pan in the bosom of his night-gown, viewing it with much complacency, and perhaps, some tender memory, in that rough heart of his, for the comrade he had lost.

Observing that the man next him had left his meal untouched, I offered the same service I had performed for his neighbor, but he shook his head.

"Thank you, ma'am; I don't think I'll ever eat again, for I'm shot in the stomach. But I'd like a drink of water, if you aint too busy.

I rushed away, but the water-pails were gone to be refilled, and it was some time before they reappeared. I did not forget my patient patient, meanwhile, and, with the first mugful, hurried back to him. He seemed asleep; but something in the tired white face caused me to listen at his lips for a breath. None came. I touched his forehead; it was cold: and then I knew that, while he waited, a better nurse than I had given him a cooler draught, and healed him with a touch. I laid the sheet over the quiet sleeper, whom no noise could now disturb; and, half an hour later, the bed was empty. It seemed a poor requital for all he had sacrificed and suffered,—that hospital bed, lonely even in a crowd; for there was no familiar face for him to look his last upon; no friendly voice to say, Good bye; no hand to lead him gently down into the Valley of the Shadow; and he vanished, like a drop in that red sea upon whose shores so many women stand lamenting. For a moment I felt bitterly indignant at this seeming carelessness of the value of life, the sanctity of death; then consoled myself with the thought that, when the great muster roll was called, these nameless men might be promoted above many whose tall monuments record the barren honors they have won.

All having eaten, drank, and rested, the surgeons began their rounds; and I took my first lesson in the art of dressing wounds. It wasn't a festive scene, by any means; for Dr. P., whose Aid I constituted myself, fell to work with a vigor which soon convinced me that I was a weaker vessel, though nothing would have induced me to confess it then. He had served in the Crimea, and seemed to regard a dilapidated body very much as I should have regarded a damaged garment; and, turning up his cuffs, whipped out a very unpleasant looking housewife, cutting, sawing, patching and piecing, with the enthusiasm of an accomplished surgical seamstress; explaining the process, in scientific terms, to the patient, meantime; which, of course, was immensely cheering and comfortable. There was an uncanny sort of fascination in watching him, as he peered and probed into the mechanism of those wonderful bodies, whose mysteries he understood so well. The more intricate the wound, the better he liked it. A poor private, with both legs off, and shot through the lungs, possessed more attractions for him than a dozen generals, slightly scratched in some "masterly retreat;" and had any one appeared in small pieces, requesting to be put together again, he would have considered it a special dispensation.

The amputations were reserved till the morrow, and the merciful magic of ether was not thought necessary that day, so the poor souls had to bear their pains as best they might. It is all very well to talk of the patience of woman; and far be it from me to pluck that feather from her cap, for, heaven knows, she isn't allowed to wear many; but the patient endurance of these men, under trials of the flesh, was truly wonderful; their fortitude seemed contagious, and scarcely a cry escaped them, though I often longed to groan for them, when pride kept their white lips shut, while great drops stood upon their foreheads, and the bed shook with the irrepressible tremor of their tortured bodies. One or two Irishmen anathematized the doctors with the frankness of their nation, and ordered the Virgin to stand by them, as if she had been the wedded Biddy to whom they could administer the poker, if she didn't; but, as a general thing, the work went on in silence, broken only by some quiet request for roller, instruments, or plaster, a sigh from the patient, or a sympathizing murmur from the nurse.

It was long past noon before these repairs were even partially made; and, having got the bodies of my boys into something like order, the next task was to minister to their minds, by writing letters to the anxious souls at home; answering questions, reading papers, taking possession of money and valuables; for the eighth commandment was reduced to a very fragmentary condition, both by the blacks and whites, who ornamented our hospital with their presence. Pocket books, purses, miniatures, and watches, were sealed up, labelled, and handed over to the matron, till such times as the owners thereof were ready to depart homeward or campward again. The letters dictated to me, and revised by me, that afternoon, would have made an excellent chapter for some future history of the war; for, like that which Thackeray's "Ensign Spooney"[10] wrote his mother just before Waterloo, they were "full of affection, pluck, and bad spelling;" nearly all giving lively accounts of the battle, and ending with a somewhat sudden plunge from patriotism to provender, desiring "Marm," "Mary Ann," or "Aunt Peters," to send along some pies, pickles, sweet stuff, and apples, "to yourn in haste," Joe, Sam, or Ned, as the case might be.

My little Sergeant insisted on trying to scribble something with his left hand, and patiently accomplished some half dozen lines of hieroglyphics, which he gave me to fold and direct, with a boyish blush, that rendered a glimpse of "My Dearest Jane," unnecessary, to assure me that the heroic lad had been more successful in the service of Commander-in-Chief Cupid than that of Gen. Mars; and a charming little romance blossomed instanter in Nurse Periwinkle's romantic fancy, though no further confidences were made that day, for Sergeant fell asleep, and, judging from his tranquil face, visited his absent sweetheart in the pleasant land of dreams.

At five o'clock a great bell rang, and the attendants flew, not to arms, but to their trays, to bring up supper, when a second uproar announced that it was ready. The new comers woke at the sound; and I presently discovered that it took a very bad wound to incapacitate the defenders of the faith for the consumption of their rations; the amount that some of them sequestered was amazing; but when I suggested the probability of a famine hereafter, to the matron, that motherly lady cried out: "Bless their hearts, why shouldn't they eat? It's their only amusement; so fill every one, and, if there's not enough ready to-night, I'll lend my share to the Lord by giving it to the boys." And, whipping up her coffee-pot and plate of toast, she gladdened the eyes and stomachs of two or three dissatisfied heroes, by serving them with a liberal hand; and I haven't the slightest doubt that, having cast her bread upon the waters, it came back buttered, as another large-hearted old lady was wont to say.

Then came the doctor's evening visit; the administration of medi-
cines; washing feverish faces; smoothing tumbled beds; wetting wounds;
singing lullabies; and preparations for the night. By eleven, the last labor of
love was done; the last "good night" spoken; and, if any needed a reward
for that day's work, they surely received it, in the silent eloquence of those
long lines of faces, showing pale and peaceful glances that lighted us to bed,
where rest, the sweetest, made our pillows soft, while Night and Nature
took our places, filling that great house of pain with the healing miracles of
Sleep, and his diviner brother, Death.

IV

A NIGHT

BEING fond of the night side of nature, I was soon promoted to the post of night nurse, with every facility for indulging in my favorite pastime of "owling." My colleague, a black-eyed widow, relieved me at dawn, we two taking care of the ward, between us, like the immortal Sairy and Betsey,[11] "turn and turn about." I usually found my boys in the jolliest state of mind their condition allowed; for it was a known fact that Nurse Periwinkle objected to blue devils, and entertained a belief that he who laughed most was surest of recovery. At the beginning of my reign, dumps and dismals prevailed; the nurses looked anxious and tired, the men gloomy or sad; and a general "Hark!-from-the-tombs-a-doleful-sound" style of conversation seemed to be the fashion: a state of things which caused one coming from a merry, social New England town, to feel as if she had got into an exhausted receiver; and the instinct of self-preservation, to say nothing of a philanthropic desire to serve the race, caused a speedy change in Ward No. 1.

More flattering than the most gracefully turned compliment, more grateful than the most admiring glance, was the sight of those rows of faces, all strange to me a little while ago, now lighting up, with smiles of welcome, as I came among them, enjoying that moment heartily, with a womanly pride in their regard, a motherly affection for them all. The evenings were spent in reading aloud, writing letters, waiting on and amusing the men, going the rounds with Dr. P., as he made his second daily survey, dressing my dozen wounds afresh, giving last doses, and making them cozy for the long hours to come, till the nine o'clock bell rang, the gas was turned down, the day nurses went off duty, the night watch came on, and my nocturnal adventure began.

My ward was now divided into three rooms; and, under favor of the matron, I had managed to sort out the patients in such a way that I had what I called, "my duty room," my "pleasure room," and my "pathetic room," and worked for each in a different way. One, I visited, armed with a dressing tray, full of rollers, plasters, and pins; another, with books, flowers, games, and gossip; a third, with teapots, lullabies, consolation, and, sometimes, a shroud.

Wherever the sickest or most helpless man chanced to be, there I held my watch, often visiting the other rooms, to see that the general watchman of the ward did his duty by the fires and the wounds, the latter needing constant wetting. Not only on this account did I meander, but also to get fresher air than the close rooms afforded; for, owing to the stupidity of that mysterious "somebody" who does all the damage in the world, the windows had been carefully nailed down above, and the lower sashes could only be raised in the mildest weather, for the men lay just below. I had suggested a summary smashing of a few panes here and there, when frequent appeals to headquarters had proved unavailing, and daily orders to lazy attendants had come to nothing. No one seconded the motion, however, and the nails were far beyond my reach; for, though belonging to the sisterhood of "ministering angels," I had no wings, and might as well have asked for Jacob's ladder, as a pair of steps, in that charitable chaos.

One of the harmless ghosts who bore me company during the haunted hours, was Dan, the watchman, whom I regarded with a certain awe; for, though so much together, I never fairly saw his face, and, but for his legs, should never have recognized him, as we seldom met by day. These legs were remarkable, as was his whole figure, for his body was short, rotund, and done up in a big jacket, and muffler; his beard hid the lower part of his face, his hat-brim the upper; and all I ever discovered was a pair of sleepy eyes, and a very mild voice. But the legs!—very long, very thin, very crooked and feeble, looking like grey sausages in their tight coverings, without a ray of pegtopishness about them, and finished off with a pair of expansive, green cloth shoes, very like Chinese junks, with the sails down. This figure, gliding noiselessly about the dimly lighted rooms, was strongly suggestive of the spirit of a beer barrel mounted on cork-screws, haunting the old hotel in search of its lost mates, emptied and staved in long ago.

Another goblin who frequently appeared to me, was the attendant of the pathetic room, who, being a faithful soul, was often up to tend two or three men, weak and wandering as babies, after the fever had gone. The amiable creature beguiled the watches of the night by brewing jorums of a fearful beverage, which he called coffee, and insisted on sharing with me; coming in with a great bowl of something like mud soup, scalding hot, guiltless of cream, rich in an all-pervading flavor of molasses, scorch and tin pot. Such an amount of good will and neighborly kindness also went into the mess, that I never could find the heart to refuse, but always received it with thanks, sipped it with hypocritical relish while he remained, and whipped it into the slop-jar the instant he departed, thereby gratifying him, securing one rousing laugh in the doziest hour of the night, and no one was the worse for the transaction but the pigs. Whether they were "cut off untimely in their sins," or not, I carefully abstained from inquiring.

It was a strange life—asleep half the day, exploring Washington the other half, and all night hovering, like a massive cherubim, in a red rigolette [12] over the slumbering sons of man. I liked it, and found many things to amuse, instruct, and interest me. The snores alone were quite a study, varying from the mild sniff to the stentorian snort, which startled the echoes and hoisted the performer erect to accuse his neighbor of the deed, magnanimously forgive him, and, wrapping the drapery of his couch about him, lie down to vocal slumber. After listening for a week to this band of wind instruments, I indulged in the belief that I could recognize each by the snore alone, and was tempted to join the chorus by breaking out with John Brown's favorite hymn:

"Blow ye the trumpet, blow!"

I would have given much to have possessed the art of sketching, for many of the faces became wonderfully interesting when unconscious. Some grew stern and grim, the men evidently dreaming of war, as they gave orders, groaned over their wounds, or damned the rebels vigorously; some grew sad and infinitely pathetic, as if the pain borne silently all day, revenged itself by now betraying what the man's pride had concealed so well. Often the roughest grew young and pleasant when sleep smoothed the hard lines away, letting the real nature assert itself; many almost seemed to speak, and I learned to know these men better by night than through any intercourse by day. Sometimes they disappointed me, for faces that looked merry and good in the light, grew bad and sly when the shadows came; and though they made no confidences in words, I read their lives, leaving them to wonder at the change of manner this midnight magic wrought in their nurse. A few talked busily; one drummer boy sang sweetly, though no persuasions could win a note from him by day; and several depended on being told what they had talked of in the morning. Even my constitutionals in the chilly halls, possessed a certain charm, for the house was never still. Sentinels tramped round it all night long, their muskets glittering in the wintry moonlight as they walked, or stood before the doors, straight and silent, as figures of stone, causing one to conjure up romantic visions of guarded forts, sudden surprises, and daring deeds; for in these war times the hum drum life of Yankeedom has vanished, and the most prosaic feel some thrill of that excitement which stirs the nation's heart, and makes its capital a camp of hospitals. Wandering up and down these lower halls, I often heard cries from above, steps hurrying to and fro, saw surgeons passing up, or men coming down carrying a stretcher, where lay a long white figure, whose face was shrouded and whose fight was done. Sometimes I stopped to watch the passers in the street, the moonlight shining on the spire opposite, or the gleam of some vessel floating, like a white-winged sea-gull, down the broad Potomac, whose fullest flow can never wash away the red stain of the land.

The night whose events I have a fancy to record, opened with a little comedy, and closed with a great tragedy; for a virtuous and useful life untimely ended is always tragical to those who see not as God sees. My headquarters were beside the bed of a New Jersey boy, crazed by the horrors of that dreadful Saturday. A slight wound in the knee brought him there; but his mind had suffered more than his body; some string of that delicate machine was over strained, and, for days, he had been reliving, in imagination, the scenes he could not forget, till his distress broke out in incoherent ravings, pitiful to hear. As I sat by him, endeavoring to soothe his poor distracted brain by the constant touch of wet hands over his hot forehead, he lay cheering his comrades on, hurrying them back, then counting them as they fell around him, often clutching my arm, to drag me from the vicinity of a bursting shell, or covering up his head to screen himself from a shower of shot; his face brilliant with fever; his eyes restless; his head never still; every muscle strained and rigid; while an incessant stream of defiant shouts, whispered warnings, and broken laments, poured from his lips with that forceful bewilderment which makes such wanderings so hard to overhear.

It was past eleven, and my patient was slowly wearying himself into fitful intervals of quietude, when, in one of these pauses, a curious sound arrested my attention. Looking over my shoulder, I saw a one-legged phantom hopping nimbly down the room; and, going to meet it, recognized a certain Pennsylvania gentleman, whose wound-fever had taken a turn for the worse, and, depriving him of the few wits a drunken campaign had left him, set him literally tripping on the light, fantastic toe "toward home," as he blandly informed me, touching the military cap which formed a striking contrast to the severe simplicity of the rest of his decidedly *undress* uniform. When sane, the least movement produced a roar of pain or a volley of oaths; but the departure of reason seemed to have wrought an agreeable change, both in the man and his manners; for, balancing himself on one leg, like a meditative stork, he plunged into an animated discussion of the war, the President, lager beer, and Enfield rifles, regardless of any suggestions of mine as to the propriety of returning to bed, lest he be court-martialed for desertion.

Anything more supremely ridiculous can hardly be imagined than this figure, scantily draped in white, its one foot covered with a big blue sock, a dingy cap set rakingly askew on its shaven head, and placid satisfaction beaming in its broad red face, as it flourished a mug in one hand, an old boot in the other, calling them canteen and knapsack, while it skipped and fluttered in the most unearthly fashion. What to do with the creature I didn't know; Dan was absent, and if I went to find him, the perambulator might festoon himself out of the window, set his toga on fire, or do some of his neighbors a mischief. The attendant of the room was sleeping like a near relative of the celebrated Seven [13] and nothing short of pins would rouse him; for he had been out that day, and whiskey asserted its supremacy in balmy whiffs. Still declaiming, in a fine flow of eloquence, the demented gentleman hopped on, blind and deaf to my graspings and entreaties; and I was about to slam the door in his face, and run for help, when a second and saner phantom, "all in white," came to the rescue, in the likeness of a big Prussian, who spoke no English, but divined the crisis, and put an end to it, by bundling the lively monoped into his bed, like a baby, with an authoritative command to "stay put," which received added weight from being delivered in an odd conglomeration of French and German, accompanied by warning wags of a head decorated with a yellow cotton night cap, rendered most imposing by a tassel like a bell-pull. Rather exhausted by his excursion, the member from Pennsylvania subsided; and, after an irrepressible laugh together, my Prussian ally and myself were returning to our places, when the echo of a sob caused us to glance along the beds. It came from one in the corner—such a little bed!—and such a tearful little face looked up at us, as we stopped beside it! The twelve years old drummer boy was not singing now, but sobbing, with a manly effort all the while to stifle the distressful sounds that would break out.

"What is it, Teddy?" I asked, as he rubbed the tears away, and checked himself in the middle of a great sob to answer plaintively:

"I've got a chill, ma'am, but I ain't cryin' for that, 'cause I'm used to it. I dreamed Kit was here, and when I waked up he wasn't, and I couldn't help it, then."

The boy came in with the rest, and the man who was taken dead from the ambulance was the Kit he mourned. Well he might; for, when the wounded were brought from Fredericksburg, the child lay in one of the camps thereabout, and this good friend, though sorely hurt himself, would not leave him to the exposure and neglect of such a time and place; but, wrapping him in his own blanket, carried him in his arms to the transport, tended him during the passage, and only yielded up his charge when Death met him at the door of the hospital which promised care and comfort for the boy. For ten days, Teddy had shivered or burned with fever and ague, pining the while for Kit, and refusing to be comforted, because he had not been able to thank him for the generous protection, which, perhaps, had cost the giver's life. The vivid dream had wrung the childish heart with a fresh pang, and when I tried the solace fitted for his years, the remorseful fear that haunted him found vent in a fresh burst of tears, as he looked at the wasted hands I was endeavoring to warm:

"Oh! if I'd only been as thin when Kit carried me as I am now, maybe he wouldn't have died; but I was heavy, he was hurt worser than we knew, and so it killed him; and I didn't see him, to say good bye."

This thought had troubled him in secret; and my assurances that his friend would probably have died at all events, hardly assuaged the bitterness of his regretful grief.

At this juncture, the delirious man began to shout; the one-legged rose up in his bed, as if preparing for another dart; Teddy bewailed himself more piteously than before: and if ever a woman was at her wit's end, that distracted female was Nurse Periwinkle, during the space of two or three minutes, as she vibrated between the three beds, like an agitated pendulum. Like a most opportune reinforcement, Dan, the bandy, appeared, and devoted himself to the lively party, leaving me free to return to my post; for the Prussian, with a nod and a smile, took the lad away to his own bed, and lulled him to sleep with a soothing murmur, like a mammoth humble bee. I liked that in Fritz, and if he ever wondered afterward at the dainties which sometimes found their way into his rations, or the extra comforts of his bed, he might have found a solution of the mystery in sundry persons' knowledge of the fatherly action of that night.

Hardly was I settled again, when the inevitable bowl appeared, and its bearer delivered a message I had expected, yet dreaded to receive:

"John is going, ma'am, and wants to see you, if you can come."

"The moment this boy is asleep; tell him so, and let me know if I am in danger of being too late."

My Ganymede departed, and while I quieted poor Shaw, I thought of John. He came in a day or two after the others; and, one evening, when I entered my "pathetic room," I found a lately emptied bed occupied by a large, fair man, with a fine face, and the serenest eyes I ever met. One of the earlier comers had often spoke of a friend, who had remained behind, that those apparently worse wounded than himself might reach a shelter first. It seemed a David and Jonathan sort of friendship. The man fretted for his mate, and was never tired of praising John—his courage, sobriety, self-denial, and unfailing kindliness of heart; always winding up with: "He's an out an' out fine feller, ma'am; you see if he aint."

I had some curiosity to behold this piece of excellence, and when he came, watched him for a night or two, before I made friends with him; for, to tell the truth, I was a little afraid of the stately looking man, whose bed had to be lengthened to accommodate his commanding stature; who seldom spoke, uttered no complaint, asked no sympathy, but tranquilly observed what went on about him; and, as he lay high upon his pillows, no picture of dying statesman or warrior was ever fuller of real dignity than this Virginia blacksmith. A most attractive face he had, framed in brown hair and beard, comely featured and full of vigor, as yet unsubdued by pain; thoughtful and often beautifully mild while watching the afflictions of others, as if entirely forgetful of his own. His mouth was grave and firm, with plenty of will and courage in its lines, but a smile could make it as sweet as any woman's; and his eyes were child's eyes, looking one fairly in the face, with a clear, straightforward glance, which promised well for such as placed their faith in him. He seemed to cling to life, as if it were rich in duties and delights, and he had learned the secret of content. The only time I saw his composure disturbed, was when my surgeon brought another to examine John, who scrutinized their faces with an anxious look, asking of the elder: "Do you think I shall pull through, sir?" "I hope so, my man." And, as the two passed on, John's eye still followed them, with an intentness which would have won a clearer answer from them, had they seen it. A momentary shadow flitted over his face; then came the usual serenity, as if, in that brief eclipse, he had acknowledged the existence of some hard possibility, and, asking nothing yet hoping all things, left the issue in God's hands, with that submission which is true piety.

The next night, as I went my rounds with Dr. P., I happened to ask which man in the room probably suffered most; and, to my great surprise, he glanced at John:

"Every breath he draws is like a stab; for the ball pierced the left lung, broke a rib, and did no end of damage here and there; so the poor lad can find neither forgetfulness nor ease, because he must lie on his wounded back or suffocate. It will be a hard struggle, and a long one, for he possesses great vitality; but even his temperate life can't save him; I wish it could."

"You don't mean he must die, Doctor?"

"Bless you, there's not the slightest hope for him; and you'd better tell him so before long; women have a way of doing such things comfortably, so I leave it to you. He won't last more than a day or two, at furthest."

I could have sat down on the spot and cried heartily, if I had not learned the wisdom of bottling up one's tears for leisure moments. Such an end seemed very hard for such a man, when half a dozen worn out, worthless bodies round him, were gathering up the remnants of wasted lives, to linger on for years perhaps, burdens to others, daily reproaches to themselves. The army needed men like John, earnest, brave, and faithful; fighting for liberty and justice with both heart and hand, true soldiers of the Lord. I could not give him up so soon, or think with any patience of so excellent a nature robbed of its fulfillment, and blundered into eternity by the rashness or stupidity of those at whose hands so many lives may be required. It was an easy thing for Dr. P. to say: "Tell him he must die," but a cruelly hard thing to do, and by no means as "comfortable" as he politely suggested. I had not the heart to do it then, and privately indulged the hope that some change for the better might take place, in spite of gloomy prophesies; so, rendering my task unnecessary. A few minutes later, as I came in again, with fresh rollers, I saw John sitting erect, with no one to support him, while the surgeon dressed his back. I had never hitherto seen it done; for, having simpler wounds to attend to, and knowing the fidelity of the attendant, I had left John to him, thinking it might be more agreeable and safe; for both strength and experience were needed in his case. I had forgotten that the strong man might long for the gentler tendance of a woman's hands, the sympathetic magnetism of a woman's presence, as well as the feebler souls about him. The Doctor's words caused me to reproach myself with neglect, not of any real duty perhaps, but of those little cares and kindnesses that solace homesick spirits, and make the heavy hours pass easier. John looked lonely and forsaken just then, as he sat with bent head, hands folded on his knee, and no outward sign of suffering, till, looking nearer, I saw great tears roll down and drop upon the floor. It was a new sight there; for, though I had seen many suffer, some swore, some groaned, most endured silently, but none wept. Yet it did not seem weak, only very touching, and straightway my fear vanished, my heart opened wide and took him in, as, gathering the bent head in my arms, as freely as if he had been a little child, I said, "Let me help you bear it, John."

Never, on any human countenance, have I seen so swift and beautiful a look of gratitude, surprise and comfort, as that which answered me more eloquently than the whispered—

"Thank you, ma'am, this is right good! this is what I wanted!"

"Then why not ask for it before?"

"I didn't like to be a trouble; you seemed so busy, and I could manage to get on alone."

"You shall not want it any more, John."

Nor did he; for now I understood the wistful look that sometimes followed me, as I went out, after a brief pause beside his bed, or merely a passing nod, while busied with those who seemed to need me more than he, because more urgent in their demands; now I knew that to him, as to so many, I was the poor substitute for mother, wife, or sister, and in his eyes no stranger, but a friend who hitherto had seemed neglectful; for, in his modesty, he had never guessed the truth. This was changed now; and, through the tedious operation of probing, bathing, and dressing his wounds, he leaned against me, holding my hand fast, and, if pain wrung further tears from him, no one saw them fall but me. When he was laid down again, I hovered about him, in a remorseful state of mind that would not let me rest, till I had bathed his face, brushed his "bonny brown hair," set all things smooth about him, and laid a knot of heath and heliotrope on his clean pillow. While doing this, he watched me with the satisfied expression I so liked to see; and when I offered the little nosegay, held it carefully in his great hand, smoothed a ruffled leaf or two, surveyed and smelt it with an air of genuine delight, and lay contentedly regarding the glimmer of the sunshine on the green. Although the manliest man among my forty, he said, "Yes, ma'am," like a little boy; received suggestions for his comfort with the quick smile that brightened his whole face; and now and then, as I stood tidying the table by his bed, I felt him softly touch my gown, as if to assure himself that I was there. Anything more natural and frank I never saw, and found this brave John as bashful as brave, yet full of excellencies and fine aspirations, which, having no power to express themselves in words, seemed to have bloomed into his character and made him what he was.

After that night, an hour of each evening that remained to him was devoted to his ease or pleasure. He could not talk much, for breath was precious, and he spoke in whispers; but from occasional conversations, I gleaned scraps of private history which only added to the affection and respect I felt for him. Once he asked me to write a letter, and as I settled pen and paper, I said, with an irrepressible glimmer of feminine curiosity, "Shall it be addressed to wife, or mother, John?"

"Neither, ma'am; I've got no wife, and will write to mother myself when I get better. Did you think I was married because of this?" he asked, touching a plain ring he wore, and often turned thoughtfully on his finger when he lay alone.

"Partly that, but more from a settled sort of look you have, a look which young men seldom get until they marry."

"I don't know that; but I'm not so very young, ma'am, thirty in May, and have been what you might call settled this ten years; for mother's a widow, I'm the oldest child she has, and it wouldn't do for me to marry until Lizzy has a home of her own, and Laurie's learned his trade; for we're not rich, and I must be father to the children and husband to the dear old woman, if I can."

"No doubt but you are both, John; yet how came you to go to war, if you felt so? Wasn't enlisting as bad as marrying?"

"No, ma'am, not as I see it, for one is helping my neighbor, the other pleasing myself. I went because I couldn't help it. I didn't want the glory or the pay; I wanted the right thing done, and people kept saying the men who were in earnest ought to fight. I was in earnest, the Lord knows! but I held off as long as I could, not knowing which was my duty; mother saw the case, gave me her ring to keep me steady, and said 'Go:' so I went."

A short story and a simple one, but the man and the mother were portrayed better than pages of fine writing could have done it.

"Do you ever regret that you came, when you lie here suffering so much?"

"Never, ma'am; I haven't helped a great deal, but I've shown I was willing to give my life, and perhaps I've got to; but I don't blame anybody, and if it was to do over again, I'd do it. I'm a little sorry I wasn't wounded in front; it looks cowardly to be hit in the back, but I obeyed orders, and it don't matter in the end, I know."

Poor John! it did not matter now, except that a shot in front might have spared the long agony in store for him. He seemed to read the thought that troubled me, as he spoke so hopefully when there was no hope, for he suddenly added:

"This is my first battle; do they think it's going to be my last?"

"I'm afraid they do, John."

It was the hardest question I had ever been called upon to answer; doubly hard with those clear eyes fixed on mine, forcing a truthful answer by their own truth. He seemed a little startled at first, pondered over the fateful fact a moment then shook his head, with a glance at the broad chest and muscular limbs stretched out before him:

"I'm not afraid, but it's difficult to believe all at once. I'm so strong it don't seem possible for such a little wound to kill me."

Merry Mercutio's dying words glanced through my memory as he spoke: "'Tis not so deep as a well, nor so wide as a church door, but 'tis enough." And John would have said the same could he have seen the ominous black holes between his shoulders, he never had; and, seeing the ghastly sights about him, could not believe his own wound more fatal than these, for all the suffering it caused him.

"Shall I write to your mother, now?" I asked, thinking that these sudden tidings might change all plans and purposes; but they did not; for the man received the order of the Divine Commander to march with the same unquestioning obedience with which the soldier had received that of the human one, doubtless remembering that the first led him to life, and the last to death.

"No, ma'am; to Laurie just the same; he'll break it to her best, and I'll add a line to her myself when you get done."

So I wrote the letter which he dictated, finding it better than any I had sent; for, though here and there a little ungrammatical or inelegant, each sentence came to me briefly worded, but most expressive; full of excellent counsel to the boy, tenderly bequeathing "mother and Lizzie" to his care, and bidding him good bye in words the sadder for their simplicity. He added a few lines, with steady hand, and, as I sealed it, said, with a patient sort of sigh, "I hope the answer will come in time for me to see it;" then, turning away his face, laid the flowers against his lips, as if to hide some quiver of emotion at the thought of such a sudden sundering of all the dear home ties.

These things had happened two days before; now John was dying, and the letter had not come. I had been summoned to many death beds in my life, but to none that made my heart ache as it did then, since my mother called me to watch the departure of a spirit akin to this in its gentleness and patient strength. As I went in, John stretched out both hands:

"I knew you'd come! I guess I'm moving on, ma'am."

He was; and so rapidly that, even while he spoke, over his face I saw the grey veil falling that no human hand can lift. I sat down by him, wiped the drops from his forehead, stirred the air about him with the slow wave of a fan, and waited to help him die. He stood in sore need of help—and I could do so little; for, as the doctor had foretold, the strong body rebelled against death, and fought every inch of the way, forcing him to draw each breath with a spasm, and clench his hands with an imploring look, as if he asked, "How long must I endure this, and be still!" For hours he suffered dumbly, without a moment's respite, or a moment's murmuring; his limbs grew cold, his face damp, his lips white, and, again and again, he tore the covering off his breast, as if the lightest weight added to his agony; yet through it all, his eyes never lost their perfect serenity, and the man's soul seemed to sit therein, undaunted by the ills that vexed his flesh.

One by one, the men woke, and round the room appeared a circle of pale faces and watchful eyes, full of awe and pity; for, though a stranger, John was beloved by all. Each man there had wondered at his patience, respected his piety, admired his fortitude, and now lamented his hard death; for the influence of an upright nature had made itself deeply felt, even in one little week. Presently, the Jonathan who so loved this comely David, came creeping from his bed for a last look and word. The kind soul was full of trouble, as the choke in his voice, the grasp of his hand, betrayed; but there were no tears, and the farewell of the friends was the more touching for its brevity.

"Old boy, how are you?" faltered the one.

"Most through, thank heaven!" whispered the other.

"Can I say or do anything for you anywheres?"

"Take my things home, and tell them that I did my best."

"I will! I will!"

"Good bye, Ned."

"Good bye, John, good bye!"

They kissed each other, tenderly as women, and so parted, for poor Ned could not stay to see his comrade die. For a little while, there was no sound in the room but the drip of water, from a stump or two, and John's distressful gasps, as he slowly breathed his life away. I thought him nearly gone, and had just laid down the fan, believing its help to be no longer needed, when suddenly he rose up in his bed, and cried out with a bitter cry that broke the silence, sharply startling every one with its agonized appeal:

"For God's sake, give me air!"

It was the only cry pain or death had wrung from him, the only boon he had asked; and none of us could grant it, for all the airs that blew were useless now. Dan flung up the window. The first red streak of dawn was warming the grey east, a herald of the coming sun; John saw it, and with the love of light which lingers in us to the end, seemed to read in it a sign of hope of help, for, over his whole face there broke that mysterious expression, brighter than any smile, which often comes to eyes that look their last. He laid himself gently down; and, stretching out his strong right arm, as if to grasp and bring the blessed air to his lips in a fuller flow, lapsed into a merciful unconsciousness, which assured us that for him suffering was forever past. He died then; for, though the heavy breaths still tore their way up for a little longer, they were but the waves of an ebbing tide that beat unfelt against the wreck, which an immortal voyager had deserted with a smile. He never spoke again, but to the end held my hand close, so close that when he was asleep at last, I could not draw it away. Dan helped me, warning me as he did so that it was unsafe for dead and living flesh to lie so long together; but though my hand was strangely cold and stiff, and four white marks remained across its back, even when warmth and color had returned elsewhere, I could not but be glad that, through its touch, the presence of human sympathy, perhaps, had lightened that hard hour.

When they had made him ready for the grave, John lay in state for half an hour, a thing which seldom happened in that busy place; but a universal sentiment of reverence and affection seemed to fill the hearts of all who had known or heard of him; and when the rumor of his death went through the house, always astir, many came to see him, and I felt a tender sort of pride in my lost patient; for he looked a most heroic figure, lying there stately and still as the statue of some young knight asleep upon his tomb. The lovely expression which so often beautifies dead faces, soon replaced the marks of pain, and I longed for those who loved him best to see him when half an hour's acquaintance with Death had made them friends. As we stood looking at him, the ward master handed me a letter, saying it had been forgotten the night before. It was John's letter, come just an hour too late to gladden the eyes that had longed and looked for it so eagerly: yet he had it; for, after I had cut some brown locks for his mother, and taken off the ring to send her, telling how well the talisman had done its work, I kissed this good son for her sake, and laid the letter in his hand, still folded as when I drew my own away, feeling that its place was there, and making myself happy with the thought, that, even in his solitary place in the "Government Lot," he would not be without some token of love which makes life beautiful and outlives death. Then I left him, glad to have known so genuine a man, and carrying with me an enduring memory of the brave Virginia blacksmith, as he lay serenely waiting for the dawn of that long day which knows no night.

V

OFF DUTY

"*MY DEAR GIRL*, we shall have you sick in your bed, unless you keep yourself warm and quiet for a few days. Widow Wadman can take care of the ward alone, now the men are so comfortable, and have her vacation when you are about again. Now do be prudent in time, and don't let me have to add a Periwinkle to my bouquet of patients."

This advice was delivered, in a paternal manner, by the youngest surgeon in the hospital, a kind-hearted little gentleman, who seemed to consider me a frail young blossom, that needed much cherishing, instead of a tough old spinster, who had been knocking about the world for thirty years. At the time I write of, he discovered me sitting on the stairs, with a nice cloud of unwholesome steam rising from the washroom; a party of January breezes disporting themselves in the halls; and perfumes, by no means from "Araby the blest," keeping them company; while I enjoyed a fit of coughing, which caused my head to spin in a way that made the application of a cool banister both necessary and agreeable, as I waited for the frolicsome wind to restore the breath I'd lost; cheering myself, meantime, with a secret conviction that pneumonia was waiting for me round the corner. This piece of advice had been offered by several persons for a week, and refused by me with the obstinacy with which my sex is so richly gifted. But the last few hours had developed several surprising internal and external phenomena, which impressed upon me the fact that if I didn't make a masterly retreat very soon, I should tumble down somewhere, and have to be borne ignominiously from the field. My head felt like a cannon ball; my feet had a tendency to cleave to the floor; the walls at times undulated in a most disagreeable manner; people looked unnaturally big; and the "very bottles on the mankle shelf" appeared to dance derisively before my eyes. Taking these things into consideration, while blinking stupidly at Dr. Z., I resolved to retire gracefully, if I must; so, with a valedictory to my boys, a private lecture to Mrs. Wadman, and a fervent wish that I could take off my body and work in my soul, I mournfully ascended to my apartment, and Nurse P. was reported off duty.

For the benefit of any ardent damsel whose patriotic fancy may have surrounded hospital life with a halo of charms, I will briefly describe the bower to which I retired, in a somewhat ruinous condition. It was well ventilated, for five panes of glass had suffered compound fractures, which all the surgeons and nurses had failed to heal; the two windows were draped with sheets, the church hospital opposite being a brick and mortar Argus, and the female mind cherishing a prejudice in favor of retiracy during the night-capped periods of existence. A bare floor supported two narrow iron beds, spread with thin mattresses like plasters, furnished with pillows in the last stages of consumption. In a fire place, guiltless of shovel, tongs, andirons, or grate, burned a log, inch by inch, being too long to go on all at once; so, while the fire blazed away at one end, I did the same at the other, as I tripped over it a dozen times a day, and flew up to poke it a dozen times at night. A mirror (let us be elegant!) of the dimensions of a muffin, and about as reflective, hung over a tin basin, blue pitcher, and a brace of yellow mugs. Two invalid tables, ditto chairs, wandered here and there, and the closet contained a varied collection of bonnets, bottles, bags, boots, bread and butter, boxes and bugs. The closet was a regular Blue Beard cupboard to me; I always opened it with fear and trembling, owing to rats, and shut it in anguish of spirit; for time and space were not to be had, and chaos reigned along with the rats. Our chimney-piece was decorated with a flat-iron, a Bible, a candle minus stick, a lavender bottle, a new tin pan, so brilliant that it served nicely for a pier-glass, and such of the portly black bugs as preferred a warmer climate than the rubbish hole afforded. Two arks, commonly called trunks, lurked behind the door, containing the worldly goods of the twain who laughed and cried, slept and scrambled, in this refuge; while from the white-washed walls above either bed, looked down the pictured faces of those whose memory can make for us—

"One little room an everywhere."

For a day or two I managed to appear at meals; for the human grub must eat till the butterfly is ready to break loose, and no one had time to come up two flights while it was possible for me to come down. Far be it from me to add another affliction or reproach to that enduring man, the steward; for, compared with his predecessor, he was a horn of plenty; but—I put it to any candid mind—is not the following bill of fare susceptible of improvement, without plunging the nation madly into debt? The three meals were "pretty much of a muchness," and consisted of beef, evidently put down for the men of '76; pork, just in from the street; army bread, composed of saw-dust and saleratus; butter, salt as if churned by Lot's wife; stewed blackberries, so much like preserved cockroaches, that only those devoid of imagination could partake thereof with relish; coffee, mild and muddy; tea, three dried huckleberry leaves to a quart of water— flavored with lime—also animated and unconscious of any approach to clearness. Variety being the spice of life, a small pinch of the article would have been appreciated by the hungry, hard-working sisterhood, one of whom, though accustomed to plain fare, soon found herself reduced to bread and water; having an inborn repugnance to the fat of the land, and the salt of the earth.

Another peculiarity of these hospital meals was the rapidity with which the edibles vanished, and the impossibility of getting a drop or crumb after the usual time. At the first ring of the bell, a general stampede took place; some twenty hungry souls rushed to the dining-room, swept over the table like a swarm of locusts, and left no fragment for any tardy creature who arrived fifteen minutes late. Thinking it of more importance that the patients should be well and comfortably fed, I took my time about my own meals for the first day or two after I came, but was speedily enlightened by Isaac, the black waiter who bore with me a few times, and then informed me, looking as stern as fate:

"I say, mam, ef you comes so late you can't have no vittles,—'cause I'm 'bleeged fer ter git things ready fer de doctors 'mazin' spry arter you nusses and folks is done. De gen'lemen don't kere fer ter wait, no more does I; so you jes' please ter come at de time, and dere won't be no frettin' nowheres."

It was a new sensation to stand looking at a full table, painfully conscious of one of the vacuums which Nature abhors, and receive orders to right about face, without partaking of the nourishment which your inner woman clamorously demanded. The doctors always fared better than we; and for a moment a desperate impulse prompted me to give them a hint, by walking off with the mutton, or confiscating the pie. But Ike's eye was on me, and, to my shame be it spoken, I walked meekly away; went dinnerless that day, and that evening went to market, laying in a small stock of crackers, cheese and apples, that my boys might not be neglected, nor myself obliged to bolt solid and liquid dyspepsias, or starve. This plan would have succeeded admirably had not the evil star under which I was born, been in the ascendant during that month, and cast its malign influences even into my "'umble" larder; for the rats had their dessert off my cheese, the bugs set up housekeeping in my cracker-bag, and the apples like all worldly riches, took to themselves wings and flew away; whither no man could tell, though certain black imps might have thrown light upon the matter, had not the plaintiff in the case been loth to add another to the many trials of long-suffering Africa. After this failure I resigned myself to fate, and, remembering that bread was called the staff of life, leaned pretty exclusively upon it; but it proved a broken reed, and I came to the ground after a few weeks of prison fare, varied by an occasional potato or surreptitious sip of milk.

Very soon after leaving the care of my ward, I discovered that I had no appetite, and cut the bread and butter interests almost entirely, trying the exercise and sun cure instead. Flattering myself that I had plenty of time, and could see all that was to be seen, so far as a lone lorn female could venture in a city, one-half of whose male population seemed to be taking the other half to the guard-house,—every morning I took a brisk run in one direction or another; for the January days were as mild as Spring. A rollicking north wind and occasional snow storm would have been more to my taste, for the one would have braced and refreshed tired body and soul, the other have purified the air, and spread a clean coverlid over the bed, wherein the capital of these United States appeared to be dozing pretty soundly just then.

One of these trips was to the Armory Hospital, the neatness, comfort, and convenience of which makes it an honor to its presiding genius, and arouses all the covetous propensities of such nurses as came from other hospitals to visit it.

The long, clean, warm, and airy wards, built barrack-fashion, with the nurse's room at the end, were fully appreciated by Nurse Periwinkle, whose ward and private bower were cold, dirty, inconvenient, up stairs and down stairs, and in everybody's chamber. At the Armory, in ward K, I found a cheery, bright-eyed, white-aproned little lady, reading at her post near the stove; matting under her feet; a draft of fresh air flowing in above her head; a table full of trays, glasses, and such matters, on one side, a large, well-stocked medicine chest on the other; and all her duty seemed to be going about now and then to give doses, issue orders, which well-trained attendants executed, and pet, advise, or comfort Tom, Dick, or Harry, as she found best. As I watched the proceedings, I recalled my own tribulations, and contrasted the two hospitals in a way that would have caused my summary dismissal, could it have been reported at headquarters. Here, order, method, common sense and liberality reigned and ruled, in a style that did one's heart good to see; at the Hurly-burly Hotel, disorder, discomfort, bad management, and no visible head, reduced things to a condition which I despair of describing. The circumlocution fashion prevailed, forms and fusses tormented our souls, and unnecessary strictnss in one place was counter-balanced by unpardonable laxity in another. Here is a sample: I am dressing Sam Dammer's shoulder; and, having cleansed the wound, look about for some strips of adhesive plaster to hold on the little square of wet linen which is to cover the gunshot wound; the case is not in the tray; Frank, the sleepy, half-sick attendant, knows nothing of it; we rummage high and low; Sam is tired, and fumes; Frank dawdles and yawns; the men advise and laugh at the flurry; I feel like a boiling tea-kettle, with the lid ready to fly off and damage somebody.

"Go and borrow some from the next ward, and spend the rest of the day in finding ours," I finally command. A pause; then Frank scuffles back with the message: "Miss Peppercorn ain't got none, and says you ain't no business to lose your own duds and go borrowin' other folkses." I say nothing, for fear of saying too much, but fly to the surgery. Mr. Toddypestle informs me that I can't have anything without an order from the surgeon of my ward. Great heavens! where is he? and away I rush, up and down, here and there, till at last I find him, in a state of bliss over a complicated amputation, in the fourth story. I make my demand; he answers: "In five minutes," and works away, with his head upside down, as he ties an artery, saws a bone, or does a little needle-work, with a visible relish and very sanguinary pair of hands. The five minutes grow to fifteen, and Frank appears, with the remark that, "Dammer wants to know what in thunder you are keeping him there with his finger on a wet rag for?" Dr. P. tears himself away long enough to scribble the order, with which I plunge downward to the surgery again, find the door locked, and, while hammering away on it, am told that two friends are waiting to see me in the hall. The matron being away, her parlor is locked, and there is no where to see my guests but in my own room, and no time to enjoy them till the plaster is found. I settle this matter, and circulate through the house to find Toddypestle, who has no right to leave the surgery till night. He is discovered in the dead house, smoking a cigar, and very much the worse for his researches among the spirituous preparations that fill the surgery shelves. He is inclined to be gallant, and puts the finishing blow to the fire of my wrath; for the tea-kettle lid flies off, and driving him before me to his post, I fling down the order, take what I choose; and, leaving the absurd incapable kissing his hand to me, depart, feeling as Grandma Riglesty is reported to have done, when she vainly sought for chips, in Bimleck Jackwood's "chifless paster." [14]

I find Dammer a well acted charade of his own name, and, just as I get him done, struggling the while with a burning desire to clap an adhesive strip across his mouth, full of heaven-defying oaths, Frank takes up his boot to put it on, and exclaims:

"I'm blest ef here ain't that case now! I recollect seeing it pitch in this mornin', but forgot all about it, till my heel went smash inter it. Here, ma'am, ketch hold on it, and give the boys a sheet on't all round, 'gainst it tumbles inter t'other boot next time yer want it."

If a look could annihilate, Francis Saucebox would have ceased to exist, but it couldn't; therefore, he yet lives, to aggravate some unhappy woman's soul, and wax fat in some equally congenial situation.

Now, while I'm freeing my mind, I should like to enter my protest against employing convalescents as attendants, instead of strong, properly trained, and cheerful men. How it may be in other places I cannot say; but here it was a source of constant trouble and confusion, these feeble, ignorant men trying to sweep, scrub, lift, and wait upon their sicker comrades. One, with a diseased heart, was expected to run up and down stairs, carry heavy trays, and move helpless men; he tried it, and grew rapidly worse than when he first came: and, when he was ordered out to march away to the convalescent hospital, fell, in a sort of fit, before he turned the corner, and was brought back to die. Another, hurt by a fall from his horse, endeavored to do his duty, but failed entirely, and the wrath of the ward master fell upon the nurse, who must either scrub the rooms herself, or take the lecture; for the boy looked stout and well, and the master never happened to see him turn white with pain, or hear him groan in his sleep when an involuntary motion strained his poor back. Constant complaints were being made of incompetent attendants, and some dozen women did double duty, and then were blamed for breaking down. If any hospital director fancies this a good and economical arrangement, allow one used up nurse to tell him it isn't, and beg him to spare the sisterhood, who sometimes, in their sympathy, forget that they are mortal, and run the risk of being made immortal, sooner than is agreeable to their partial friends.

Another of my few rambles took me to the Senate Chamber, hoping to hear and see if this large machine was run any better than some small ones I knew of. I was too late, and found the Speaker's chair occupied by a colored gentleman of ten; while two others were "on their legs," having a hot debate on the cornball question, as they gathered the waste paper strewn about the floor into bags; and several white members played leap-frog over the desks, a much wholesomer relaxation than some of the older Senators indulge in, I fancy. Finding the coast clear, I likewise gambolled up and down, from gallery to gallery; sat in Sumner's chair, and cudgelled an imaginary Brooks within an inch of his life; examined Wilson's books in the coolest possible manner;[15] warmed my feet at one of the national registers; read people's names on scattered envelopes, and pocketed a castaway autograph or two; watched the somewhat unparliamentary proceedings going on about me, and wondered who in the world all the sedate gentlemen were, who kept popping out of odd doors here and there, like respectable Jacks-in-the-box. Then I wandered over the "palatial residence" of Mrs. Columbia, and examined its many beauties, though I can't say I thought her a tidy housekeeper, and didn't admire her taste in pictures,[16] for the eye of this humble individual soon wearied of expiring patriots, who all appeared to be quitting their earthly tabernacles in convulsious, ruffled shirts, and a whirl of torn banners, bomb shells, and buff and blue arms and legs. The statuary also was massive and concrete, but rather wearying to examine; for the colossal ladies and gentlemen, carried no cards of introduction in face or figure; so, whether the meditative party in a kilt, with well-developed legs, shoes like army slippers, and a ponderous nose, was Columbus, Cato, or Cockelorum Tibby, the tragedian, was more than I could tell. Several robust ladies attracted me, as I felt particularly "wimbly" myself, as old country women say; but which was America and which Pocahontas was a mystery, for all affected much looseness of costume, dishevelment of hair, swords, arrows, lances, scales, and other ornaments quite *passé* with damsels of our day, whose effigies should go down to posterity armed with fans, crochet needles, riding whips, and parasols, with here and there one holding pen or pencil, rolling-pin or broom. The statue of Liberty I recognized at once, for it had no pedestal as yet, but stood flat in the mud, with Young America most symbolically making dirt pies, and chip forts, in its shadow. But high above the squabbling little throng and their petty plans, the sun shone full on Liberty's broad forehead, and, in her hand, some summer bird had built its nest. I accepted the good omen then, and, on the first of January, the Emancipation Act gave the statue a nobler and more enduring pedestal than any marble or granite ever carved and quarried by human hands.[17]

One trip to Georgetown Heights, where cedars sighed overhead, dead leaves rustled underfoot, pleasant paths led up and down, and a brook wound like a silver snake by the blackened ruins of some French Minister's house, through the poor gardens of the black washerwomen who congregated there, and, passing the cemetery with a murmurous lullaby, rolled away to pay its little tribute to the river. This breezy run was the last I took;

for, on the morrow, came rain and wind: and confinement soon proved a powerful reinforcement to the enemy, who was quietly preparing to spring a mine, and blow me five hundred miles from the position I had taken in what I called my Chickahominy Swamp.

Shut up in my room, with no voice, spirits, or books, that week was not a holiday, by any means. Finding meals a humbug, I stopped away altogether, trusting that if this sparrow was of any worth, the Lord would not let it fall to the ground. Like a flock of friendly ravens, my sister nurses fed me, not only with food for the body, but kind words for the mind; and soon, from being half starved, I found myself so beteaed an betoasted, petted and served, that I was quite "in the lap of luxury," in spite of cough, headache, a painful consciousness of my pleura, and a realizing sense of bones in the human frame. From the pleasant house on the hill, the home in the heart of Washington, and the Willard caravansary, came friends new and old, with bottles, baskets, carriages and invitations for the invalid; and daily our Florence Nightingale climbed the steep stairs, stealing a moment from her busy life, to watch over the stranger, of whom she was as thoughtfully tender as any mother. Long may she wave! Whatever others may think or say, Nurse Periwinkle is forever grateful; and among her relics of that Washington defeat, none is more valued than the little book which appeared on her pillow, one dreary day; for the D. D. written in it means to her far more than Doctor of Divinity.[18]

Being forbidden to meddle with fleshly arms and legs, I solaced myself by mending cotton ones, and, as I sat sewing at my window, watched the moving panorama that passed below; amusing myself with taking notes of the most striking figures in it. Long trains of army wagons kept up a perpetual rumble from morning till night; ambulances rattled to and fro with busy surgeons, nurses taking an airing, or convalescents going in parties to be fitted to artificial limbs. Strings of sorry looking horses passed, saying as plainly as dumb creatures could, "Why, in a city full of them, is there no *horse*pital for us?" Often a cart came by, with several rough coffins in it, and no mourners following; barouches, with invalid officers rolled round the corner, and carriage loads of pretty children, with black coachmen, footmen, and maids. The women who took their walks abroad, were so extinguished in three story bonnets, with overhanging balconies of flowers, that their charms were obscured; and all I can say of them is, that they dressed in the worse possible taste, and walked like ducks.

The men did the picturesque, and did it so well that Washington looked like a mammoth masquerade. Spanish hats, scarlet lined riding cloaks, swords and sashes, high boots and bright spurs, beards and mustaches, which made plain faces comely, and comely faces heroic; these vanities of the flesh transformed our butchers, bakers, and candlestick makers into gallant riders of gaily caparisoned horses, much handsomer than themselves; and dozens of such figures were constantly prancing by, with private prickings of spurs, for the benefit of the perambulating flower-bed. Some of these gentlemen affected painfully tight uniforms, and little caps, kept on by some new law of gravitation, as they covered only the bridge of the nose, yet never fell off; the men looked like stuffed fowls, and rode as if the safety of the nation depended on their speed alone. The fattest, greyest officers dressed most, and ambled statelily along, with orderlies behind, trying to look as if they didn't know the stout party in front, and doing much caracoling on their own account.

The mules were my especial delight; and an hour's study of a constant succession of them introduced me to many of their characteristics; for six of these odd little beasts drew each army wagon, and went hopping like frogs through the stream of mud that gently rolled along the street. The coquettish mule had small feet, a nicely trimmed tassel of a tail, perked up ears, and seemed much given to little tosses of the head, affected skips and prances; and, if he wore the bells, or were bedizzened with a bit of finery, put on as many airs as any belle. The moral mule was a stout, hardworking creature, always tugging with all his might; often pulling away after the rest had stopped, laboring under the conscientious delusion that food for the entire army depended upon his private exertions. I respected this style of mule; and, had I possessed a juicy cabbage, would have pressed it upon him, with thanks for his excellent example. The historical mule was a melo-dramatic quadruped, prone to startling humanity by erratic leaps, and wild plunges, much shaking of his stubborn head, and lashing out of his vicious heels; now and then falling, flat, and apparently dying *à la* Forrest: a gasp—a squirm—a flop, and so on, till the street was well blocked up, the drivers all swearing like demons in bad hats, and the chief actor's circulation decidedly quickened by every variety of kick, cuff, jerk and haul. When the last breath seemed to have left his body, and "Doctors were in vain," a sudden resurrection took place; and if ever a mule laughed with scornful triumph, that was the beast, as he leisurely rose, gave a comfortable shake; and, calmly regarding the excited crowd seemed to say—"A hit! a decided hit! for the stupidest of animals has bamboozled a dozen men. Now, then! what are *you* stopping the way for?" The pathetic mule was, perhaps, the most interesting of all; for, though he always seemed to be the smallest, thinnest, weakest of the six, the postillion, with big boots, long-tailed coat, and heavy whip, was sure to bestride this one, who struggled feebly along, head down, coat muddy and rough, eye spiritless and sad, his very tail a mortified stump, and the whole beast a picture of meek misery, fit to touch a heart of stone. The jovial mule was a roly poly, happy-go-lucky little piece of horse-flesh, taking everything easily, from cudgeling to caressing; strolling along with a roguish twinkle of the eye, and, if the thing were possible, would have had his hands in his pockets, and whistled as he went. If there ever chanced to be an apple core, a stray turnip, or wisp of hay, in the gutter, this Mark Tapley[19] was sure to find it, and none of his mates seemed to begrudge him his bite. I suspected this fellow was the peacemaker, confidant and friend of all the others, for he had a sort of "Cheer-up,-old-boy,-I'll-pull-you-through" look, which was exceedingly engaging.

Pigs also possessed attractions for me, never having had an opportunity of observing their graces of mind and manner till I came to Washington, whose porcine citizens appeared to enjoy a larger liberty than many of its human ones. Stout, sedate looking pigs, hurried by each morning to their places of business, with a preoccupied air, and sonorous greeting to their friends. Genteel pigs, with an extra curl to their tails, promenaded in pairs, lunching here and there, like gentlemen of leisure. Rowdy pigs pushed the passers by off the side walk; tipsy pigs hiccoughed their version of "We wont go home till morning," from the gutter; and delicate young pigs tripped daintily through the mud, as if, like "Mrs. Peerybingle,"[20] they plumed themselves upon their ankles, and kept themselves particularly neat in point of stockings. Maternal pigs, with their interesting families, strolled by in the sun; and often the pink, babylike squealers lay down for a nap, with a trust in Providence worthy of human imitation.

But more interesting than officers, ladies, mules, or pigs, were my colored brothers and sisters, because so unlike the respectable members of society I'd known in moral Boston.

Here was the genuine article—no, not the genuine article at all, we must go to Africa for that—but the sort of creatures generations of slavery have made them: obsequious, trickish, lazy and ignorant, yet kind-hearted, merry-tempered, quick to feel and accept the least token of the brotherly love which is slowly teaching the white hand to grasp the black, in this great struggle for the liberty of both the races.

Having been warned not to be too rampant on the subject of slavery, as secesh principles flourished even under the respectable nose of Father Abraham, I had endeavored to walk discreetly, and curb my unruly member; looking about me with all my eyes, the while, and saving up the result of my observations for future use. I had not been there a week, before the neglected, devil-may care expression in many of the faces about me, seemed an urgent appeal to leave nursing white bodies, and take some care for these black souls. Much as the lazy boys and saucy girls tormented me, I liked them, and found that any show of interest or friendliness brought out the better traits which live in the most degraded and forsaken of us all. I liked their cheerfulness, for the dreariest old hag, who scrubbed all day in that pestilential steam, gossiped and grinned all the way out, when night set her free from drudgery. The girls romped with their dusky sweethearts, or tossed their babies, with the tender pride that makes mother-love a beautifier to the homeliest face. The men and boys sang and whistled all day long; and often, as I held my watch, the silence of the night was sweetly broken by some chorus from the street, full of real melody, whether the song was of heaven, or of hoe-cakes; and, as I listened, I felt that we never should doubt nor despair concerning a race which, through such griefs and wrongs, still clings to this good gift, and seems to solace with it the patient hearts that wait and watch and hope until the end.

I expected to have to defend myself from accusations of a prejudice against color; but was surprised to find things just the other way, and daily shocked some neighbor by treating the blacks as I did the whites. The men *would* swear at the "darkies," would put two *g*s into negro, and scoff at the idea of any good coming from such trash. The nurses were willing to be served by the colored people, but seldom thanked them, never praised, and scarcely recognized them in the street; whereat the blood of two generations of abolitionists waxed hot in my veins, and, at the first opportunity, proclaimed itself, and asserted the right of free speech as doggedly as the irrepressible Folsom herself.[21]

Happening to catch up a funny little black baby, who was toddling about the nurses' kitchen, one day, when I went down to make a mess for some of my men, a Virginia woman standing by elevated her most prominent features, with a sniff of disapprobation, exclaiming:

"Gracious, Miss P.! how can you? I've been here six months, and never so much as touched the little toad with a poker."

"More shame for you, ma'am," responded Miss P.; and, with the natural perversity of a Yankee, followed up the blow by kissing "the toad," with ardor. His face was providentially as clean and shiny as if his mamma had just polished it up with a corner of her apron and a drop from the tea-kettle spout, like old Aunt Chloe.[22] This rash act, and the anti-slavery lecture that followed, while one hand stirred gruel for sick America, and the other hugged baby Africa, did not produce the cheering result which I fondly expected; for my comrade henceforth regarded me as a dangerous fanatic, and my protegé nearly came to his death by insisting on swarming up stairs to my room, on all occasions, and being walked on like a little black spider.

I waited for New Year's day with more eagerness than I had ever known before; and, though it brought me no gift, I felt rich in the act of justice so tardily performed toward some of those about me.[23] As the bells rung midnight, I electrified my room-mate by dancing out of bed, throwing up the window, and flapping my handkerchief, with a feeble cheer, in answer to the shout of a group of colored men in the street below. All night they tooted and tramped, fired crackers, sung "Glory, Hallelujah," and took comfort, poor souls! in their own way. The sky was clear, the moon shone benignly, a mild wind blew across the river, and all good omens seemed to usher in the dawn of the day whose noontide cannot now be long in coming. If the colored people had taken hands and danced around the White House, with a few cheers for the much abused gentleman who has immortalized himself by one just act, no President could have had a finer levee, or one to be prouder of.

While these sights and sounds were going on without, curious scenes were passing within, and I was learning that one of the best methods of fitting oneself to be a nurse in a hospial, is to be a patient there; for then only can one wholly realize what the men suffer and sigh for; how acts of kindness touch and win; how much or little we are to those about us; and for the first time really see that in coming there we have taken our lives in our hands, and may have to pay dearly for a brief experience. Every one was very kind; the attendants of my ward often came up to report progress, to fill my wood-box, or bring messages and presents from my boys. The nurses took many steps with those tired feet of theirs, and several came each evening, to chat over my fire and make things cosy for the night. The doctors paid daily visits, tapped at my lungs to see if pneumonia was within, left doses without names, and went away, leaving me as ignorant, and much more uncomfortable than when they came. Hours began to get confused; people looked odd; queer faces haunted the room, and the nights were one long fight with weariness and pain. Letters from home grew anxious; the doctors lifted their eyebrows, and nodded ominously; friends said "Don't stay," and an internal rebellion seconded the advice; but the three months were not out, and the idea of giving up so soon was proclaiming defeat before I was fairly routed; so to all "Don't stays" I opposed "I wills," till, one fine morning, a grey-headed gentlemen rose like a welcome ghost on my hearth; and, at the sight of him, my resolution melted away, my heart turned traitor to my boys, and, when he said, "Come home," I answered, "Yes, father;" and so ended my career as an army nurse.

I never shall regret the going, though a sharp tussle with typhoid, ten dollars, and a wig, are all the visible results of the experiment; for one may live and learn much in a month. A good fit of illness proves the value of health; real danger tries one's mettle; and self-sacrifice sweetens character. Let no one who sincerely desires to help the work on in this way, delay going through any fear; for the worth of life lies in the experiences that fill it, and this is one which cannot be forgotten. All that is best and bravest in the hearts of men and women, comes out in scenes like these; and, though a hospital is a rough school, its lessons are both stern and salutary; and the humblest of pupils there, in proportion to his faithfulness, learns a deeper faith in God and in himself. I, for one, would return tomorrow, on the "up-again,-and-take-another" principle, if I could; for the amount of pleasure and profit I got out of that month compensates for all after pangs; and, though a sadly womanish feeling, I take some satisfaction in the thought that, if I could not lay my head on the altar of my country, I have my hair; and that is more than handsome Helen did for her dead husband, when she sacrificed only the ends of her ringlets on his urn. Therefore, I close this little chapter of hospital experiences, with the regret that they were no better worth recording; and add the poetical gem with which I console myself for the untimely demise of "Nurse Periwinkle:"

> Oh, lay her in a little pit,
> With a marble stone to cover it;
> And carve thereon a gruel spoon,
> To show a "nuss" has died too soon.

VI

A POSTSCRIPT

MY DEAR S.:—As inquiries like your own have come to me from various friendly readers of the Sketches, I will answer them *en masse,* and in printed form, as a sort of postscript to what has gone before. One of these questions was, "Are there no services by hospital death-beds, or on Sundays?"

In most Hospitals I hope there are; in ours, the men died, and were carried away, with as little ceremony as on a battlefield. The first event of this kind which I witnessed was so very brief, and bare of anything like reverence, sorrow, or pious consolation, that I heartily agreed with the bluntly expressed opinion of a Maine man lying next his comrade, who died with no visible help near him, but a compassionate woman and a tender-hearted Irishman, who dropped upon his knees, and told his beads, with Catholic fervor, for the good of his Protestant brother's parting soul:

"If, after gettin' all the hard knocks, we are left to die this way, with nothing but a Paddy's prayers to help us, I guess Christians are rather scarce round Washington."

I thought so too; but though Miss Blank, one of my mates, anxious that souls should be ministered to, as well as bodies, spoke more than once to the Chaplain, nothing ever came of it. Unlike another Shepherd,[24] whose earnest piety weekly purified the Senate Chamber, this man did not feed as well as fold his flock, nor make himself a human symbol of the Divine Samaritan, who never passes by on the other side.

I have since learned that our non-committal Chaplain had been a Professor, in some Southern College; and, though he maintained that he had no secesh proclivities, I can testify that he seceded from his ministerial duties, I may say, skedaddled; for, being one of his own words, it is as appropriate as inelegant. He read Emerson, quoted Carlyle, and tried to be a Chaplain; but judging from his success, I am afraid he still hankered after the hominy pots of Rebeldom.

Occasionally, on a Sunday afternoon, such of the nurses, officers, attendants, and patients as could avail themselves of it, were gathered in the Ball Room, for an hour's service, of which the singing was the better part. To me it seemed that if ever strong, wise, and loving words were needed, it was then; if ever mortal man had living texts before his eyes to illustrate and illuminate his thought, it was there; and if ever hearts were prompted to devoutest self-abnegation, it was in the work which brought us to anything but a Chapel of Ease. But some spiritual paralysis seemed to have befallen our pastor; for, though many faces turned toward him, full of the dumb hunger that often comes to men when suffering or danger brings them nearer to the heart of things, they were offered the chaff of divinity, and its wheat was left for less needy gleaners, who knew where to look. Even the fine old Bible stories, which may be made as lifelike as any history of our day, by a vivid fancy and pictorial diction, were robbed of all their charms by dry explanations and literal applications, instead of being useful and pleasant lessons to those men, whom weakness had rendered as docile as children in a father's hands.

I watched the listless countenances all about me, while a mild Daniel was moralizing in a den of utterly uninteresting lions; while Shadrach, Meshech, and Abednego were leisurely passing through the fiery furnace, where, I sadly feared, some of us sincerely wished they had remained as permanencies; while the Temple of Solomon was laboriously erected, with minute descriptions of the process, and any quantity of bells and pome-granates on the raiment of the priests. Listless they were at the beginning, and listless at the end; but the instant some stirring old hymn was given out, sleepy eyes brightened, lounging figures sat erect, and many a poor lad rose up in his bed, or stretched an eager hand for the book, while all broke out with a heartiness that proved that somewhere at the core of even the most abandoned, there still glowed some remnant of the native piety that flows in music from the heart of every little child. Even the big rebel joined, and boomed away in a thunderous bass, singing—

"Salvation! let the echoes fly,"

as energetically as if he felt the need of a speedy execution of the command.

That was the pleasantest moment of the hour, for then it seemed a homelike and happy spot; the groups of men looking over one another's shoulders as they sang; the few silent figures in the beds: here and there a woman noiselessly performing some necessary duty, and singing as she worked; while in the arm chair standing in the midst, I placed, for my own satisfaction, the imaginary likeness of a certain faithful pastor who took all outcasts by the hand, smote the devil in whatever guise he came, and comforted the indigent in spirit with the best wisdom of a great and tender heart, which still speaks to us from its Italian grave.[25] With that addition, my picture was complete; and I often longed to take a veritable sketch of a Hospital Sunday, for, despite its drawbacks, consisting of continued labor, the want of proper books, the barren preaching that bore no fruit, this day was never like the other six.

True to their home training, our New England boys did their best to make it what it should be. With many, there was much reading of Testaments, humming over of favorite hymns, and looking at such books as I could cull from a miscellaneous library. Some lay idle, slept, or gossiped; yet, when I came to them for a quiet evening chat, they often talked freely and well of themselves; would blunder out some timid hope that their troubles might "do 'em good, and keep 'em stiddy;" would choke a little, as they said good night, and turned their faces to the wall to think of mother, wife, or home, these human ties seeming to be the most vital religion which they yet knew. I observed that some of them did not wear their caps on this day, though at other times they clung to them like Quakers; wearing them in bed, putting them on to read the paper, eat an apple, or write a letter, as if, like a new sort of Samson, their strength lay, not in their hair, but in their hats. Many read no novels, swore less, were more silent, orderly, and cheerful, as if the Lord were an invisible Wardmaster, who went his rounds but once a week, and must find all things at their best. I liked all this in the poor, rough boys, and could have found it in my heart to put down sponge and tea-pot, and preach a little sermon then and there, while homesickness and pain had made these natures soft, that some good seed might be cast therein, to blossom and bear fruit here or hereafter.

Regarding the admission of friends to nurse their sick, I can only say, it was not allowed at Hurly-burly House; though one indomitable parent took my ward by storm, and held her position, in spite of doctors, matron, and Nurse Periwinkle. Though it was against the rules, though the culprit was an acid, frost-bitten female, though the young man would have done quite as well without her anxious fussiness, and the whole room-full been much more comfortable, there was something so irresistible in this per-sistent devotion, that no one had the heart to oust her from her post. She slept on the floor, without uttering a complaint; bore jokes somewhat of the rudest; fared scantily, though her basket was daily filled with luxuries for her boy; and tended that petulant personage with a never-failing patience beautiful to see.

I feel a glow of moral rectitude in saying this of her; for, though a perfect pelican to her young, she pecked and cackled (I don't know that pelicans usually express their emotions in that manner,) most obstreper-ously, when others invaded her premises; and led me a weary life, with "George's tea-rusks," "George's foot-bath," "George's measles," and "George's mother;" till, after a sharp passage of arms and tongues with the matron, she wrathfully packed up her rusks, her son, and herself, and departed, in an ambulance, scolding to the very last.

This is the comic side of the matter. The serious one is harder to describe; for the presence, however brief, of relations and friends by the bedsides of the dead or dying, is always a trial to the bystanders. They are not near enough to know how best to comfort, yet too near to turn their backs upon the sorrow that finds its only solace in listening to recitals of last words, breathed into nurse's ears, or receiving the tender legacies of love and longing bequeathed through them.

To me, the saddest sight I saw in that sad place, was the spectacle of a grey-haired father, sitting hour after hour by his son, dying from the poison of his wound. The old father, hale and hearty; the young son, past all help, though one could scarcely believe it; for the subtle fever, burning his strength away, flushed his cheeks with color, filled his eyes with lustre, and lent a mournful mockery of health to face and figure, making the poor lad comelier in death than in life. His bed was not in my ward; but I was often in and out, and, for a day or two, the pair were much together, saying little, but looking much. The old man tried to busy himself with book or pen, that his presence might not be a burden; and once when he sat writing, to the anxious mother at home, doubtless, I saw the son's eyes fixed upon his face, with a look of mingled resignation and regret, as if endeavoring to teach himself to say cheerfully the long good bye. And again, when the son slept, the father watched him, as he had himself been watched; and though no feature of his grave countenance changed, the rough hand, smoothing the lock of hair upon the pillow, the bowed attitude of the grey head, were more pathetic than the loudest lamentations. The son died; and the father took home the pale relic of the life he gave, offering a little money to the nurse, as the only visible return it was in his power to make her; for, though very grateful, he was poor. Of course, she did not take it, but found a richer compensation in the old man's earnest declaration:

"My boy couldn't have been better cared for if he'd been at home; and God will reward you for it, though I can't."

My own experiences of this sort began when my first man died. He had scarcely been removed, when his wife came in. Her eye went straight to the well-known bed; it was empty; and feeling, yet not believing the hard truth, she cried out, with a look I never shall forget:

"Why, where's Emanuel?"

I had never seen her before, did not know her relationship to the man whom I had only nursed for a day, and was about to tell her he was gone, when McGee, the tender-hearted Irishman before mentioned, brushed by me with a cheerful—"It's shifted to a better bed he is, Mrs. Connel. Come out, dear, till I show ye;" and, taking her gently by the arm, he led her to the matron, who broke the heavy tidings to the wife, and comforted the widow.

Another day, running up to my room for a breath of fresh air and a five minutes' rest after a disagreeable task, I found a stout young woman sitting on my bed, wearing the miserable look which I had learned to know by that time. Seeing her, reminded me that I had heard of some one's dying in the night, and his sister's arriving in the morning. This must be she, I thought. I pitied her with all my heart. What could I say or do? Words always seem impertinent at such times; I did not know the man; the woman was neither interesting in herself nor graceful in her grief; yet, having known a sister's sorrow myself, I could not leave her alone with her trouble in that strange place, without a word. So, feeling heart-sick, home-sick, and not knowing what else to do, I just put my arms about her, and began to cry in a very helpless but hearty way; for, as I seldom indulge in this moist luxury, I like to enjoy it with all my might, when I do.

It so happened I could not have done a better thing; for, though not a word was spoken, each felt the other's sympathy; and, in the silence, our handkerchiefs were more eloquent than words. She soon sobbed herself quiet; and, leaving her on my bed, I went back to work, feeling much refreshed by the shower, though I'd forgotten to rest, and had washed my face instead of my hands. I mention this successful experiment as a receipt proved and approved, for the use of any nurse who may find herself called upon to minister to these wounds of the heart. They will find it more efficacious than cups of tea, smelling-bottles, psalms, or sermons; for a friendly touch and a companionable cry, unite the consolations of all the rest for womankind; and, if genuine, will be found a sovereign cure for the first sharp pang so many suffer in these heavy times.

I am gratified to find that my little Sergeant has found favor in several quarters, and gladly respond to sundry calls for news of him, though my personal knowledge ended five months ago. Next to my good John—I hope the grass is green above him, far away there in Virginia!—I placed the Sergeant on my list of worthy boys; and many a jovial chat have I enjoyed with the merry-hearted lad, who had a fancy for fun, when his poor arm was dressed. While Dr. P. poked and strapped, I brushed the remains of the Sergeant's brown mane—shorn sorely against his will—and gossiped with all my might, the boy making odd faces, exclamations, and appeals, when nerves got the better of nonsense, as they sometimes did:

"I'd rather laugh than cry, when I must sing out anyhow, so just say that bit from Dickens again, please, and I'll stand it like a man." He did; for "Mrs. Cluppins," "Chadband," and "Sam Weller," always helped him through; thereby causing me to lay another offering of love and admiration on the shrine of the god of my idolatry, though he does wear too much jewelry and talk slang.[26]

The Sergeant also originated, I believe, the fashion of calling his neighbors by their afflictions instead of their names; and I was rather taken aback by hearing them bandy remarks of this sort, with perfect good humor and much enjoyment of the new game.

"Hallo, old Fits is off again!" "How are you, Rheumatiz?" "Will you trade apples, Ribs?" "I say, Miss P., may I give Typus a drink of this?" "Look here, No Toes, lend us a stamp, there's a good feller," etc. He himself was christened "Baby B.," because he tended his arm on a little pillow, and called it his infant.

Very fussy about his grub was Sergeant B., and much trotting of attendants was necessary when he partook of nourishment. Anything more irresistibly wheedlesome I never saw, and constantly found myself indulging him, like the most weak-minded parent, merely for the pleasure of seeing his brown eyes twinkle, his merry mouth break into a smile, and his one hand execute a jaunty little salute that was entirely captivating. I am afraid that Nurse P. damaged her dignity, frolicking with this persuasive young gentleman, though done for his well-being. But "boys will be boys," is perfectly applicable to the case; for, in spite of years, sex, and the "prunes-and-prisms" doctrine laid down for our use, I have a fellow feeling for lads, and always owed Fate a grudge because I wasn't a lord of creation instead of a lady.

Since I left, I have heard, from a reliable source, that my Sergeant has gone home; therefore, the small romance that budded the first day I saw him, has blossomed into its second chapter; and I now imagine "dearest Jane" filling my place, tending the wounds I tended, brushing the curly jungle I brushed, loving the excellent little youth I loved, and eventually walking altarward, with the Sergeant stumping gallantly at her side. If she doesn't do all this, and no end more, I'll never forgive her; and sincerely pray to the guardian saint of lovers, that "Baby B." may prosper in his wooing, and his name be long in the land.

One of the lively episodes of hospital life, is the frequent marching away of such as are well enough to rejoin their regiments, or betake themselves to some convalescent camp. The ward master comes to the door of each room that is to be thinned, reads off a list of names, bids their owners look sharp and be ready when called for; and, as he vanishes, the rooms fall into an indescribable state of topsy-turvyness, as the boys begin to black their boots, brighten spurs, if they have them, overhaul knapsacks, make presents; are fitted out with needfuls, and—well, why not?—kissed sometimes, as they say, good bye; for in all human probability we shall never meet again, and a woman's heart yearns over anything that has clung to her for help and comfort. I never liked these breakings-up of my little household; though my short stay showed me but three. I was immensely gratified by the hand shakes I got, for their somewhat painful cordiality assured me that I had not tried in vain. The big Prussian rumbled out his unintelligible *adieux,* with a grateful face and a premonitory smooth of his yellow moustache, but got no farther, for some one else stepped up, with a large brown hand extended, and this recommendation of our very faulty establishment:

"We're off, ma'am, and I'm powerful sorry, for I'd no idea a 'orspittle was such a jolly place. Hope I'll git another ball somewheres easy, so I'll come back, and be took care on again. Mean, ain't it?"

I didn't think so, but the doctrine of inglorious ease was not the right one to preach up, so I tried to look shocked, failed signally, and consoled myself by giving him the fat pincushion he had admired as the "cutest little machine agoin." Then they fell into line in front of the house, looking rather wan and feeble, some of them, but trying to step out smartly and march in good order, though half the knapsacks were carried by the guard, and several leaned on sticks instead of shouldering guns. All looked up and smiled, or waved their hands and touched their caps, as they passed under our windows down the long street, and so away, some to their homes in this world, and some to that in the next; and, for the rest of the day, I felt like Rachel mourning for her children, when I saw the empty beds and missed the familiar faces.

You ask if nurses are obliged to witness amputations and such matters, as a part of their duty? I think not, unless they wish; for the patient is under the effects of ether, and needs no care but such as the surgeons can best give. Our work begins afterward, when the poor soul comes to himself, sick, faint, and wandering; full of strange pains and confused visions, of disagreeable sensations and sights. Then we must sooth and sustain, tend and watch; preaching and practicing patience, till sleep and time have restored courage and self-control.

I witnessed several operations; for the height of my ambition was to go to the front after a battle, and feeling that the sooner I inured myself to trying sights, the more useful I should be. Several of my mates shrunk from such things; for though the spirit was wholly willing, the flesh was inconveniently weak. One funereal lady came to try her powers as a nurse; but, a brief conversation eliciting the facts that she fainted at the sight of blood, was afraid to watch alone, couldn't possibly take care of delirious persons, was nervous about infections, and unable to bear much fatigue, she was mildly dismissed. I hope she found her sphere, but fancy a comfortable bandbox on a high shelf would best meet the requirements of her case.

Dr. Z. suggested that I should witness a dissection; but I never accepted his invitations, thinking that my nerves belonged to the living, not to the dead, and I had better finish my education as a nurse before I began that of a surgeon. But I never met the little man skipping through the hall, with oddly shaped cases in his hand, and an absorbed expression of countenance, without being sure that a select party of surgeons were at work in the dead house, which idea was a rather trying one, when I knew the subject was some person whom I had nursed and cared for.

But this must not lead any one to suppose that the surgeons were willfully hard or cruel, though one of them remorsefully confided to me that he feared his profession blunted his sensibilities, and, perhaps, rendered him indifferent to the sight of pain.

I am inclined to think that in some cases it does; for, though a capital surgeon and a kindly man, Dr. P., through long acquaintance with many of the ills flesh is heir to, had acquired a somewhat trying habit of regarding a man and his wound as separate institutions, and seemed rather annoyed that the former should express any opinion upon the latter, or claim any right in it, while under his care. He had a way of twitching off a bandage, and giving a limb a comprehensive sort of clutch, which, though no doubt entirely scientific, was rather startling than soothing, and highly objectionable as a means of preparing nerves for any fresh trial. He also expected the patient to assist in small operations, as he considered them, and to restrain all demonstrations during the process.

"Here, my man, just hold it this way, while I look into it a bit," he said one day to Fitz G., putting a wounded arm into the keeping of a sound one, and proceeding to poke about among bits of bone and visible muscles, in a red and black chasm made by some infernal machine of the shot or shell description. Poor Fitz held on like grim Death, ashamed to show fear before a woman, till it grew more than he could bear in silence; and, after a few smothered groans, he looked at me imploringly, as if he said, "I wouldn't, ma'am, if I could help it," and fainted quietly away.

Dr. P. looked up, gave a compassionate sort of cluck, and poked away more busily than ever, with a nod at me and a brief—"Never mind; be so good as to hold this till I finish."

I obeyed, cherishing the while a strong desire to insinuate a few of his own disagreeable knives and scissors into him, and see how he liked it. A very disrespectful and ridiculous fancy, of course; for he was doing all that could be done, and the arm prospered finely in his hands. But the human mind is prone to prejudice; and, though a personable man, speaking French like a born "Parley voo," and whipping off legs like an animated guillotine, I must confess to a sense of relief when he was ordered elsewhere; and suspect that several of the men would have faced a rebel battery with less trepidation than they did Dr. P., when he came briskly in on his morning round.

As if to give us the pleasures of contrast, Dr. Z. succeeded him, who, I think, suffered more in giving pain than did his patients in enduring it; for he often paused to ask: "Do I hurt you?" and, seeing his solicitude, the boys invariably answered: "Not much; go ahead, Doctor," though the lips that uttered this amiable fib might be white with pain as they spoke. Over the dressing of some of the wounds, we used to carry on conversations upon subjects foreign to the work in hand, that the patient might forget himself in the charms of our discourse. Christmas eve was spent in this way; the Doctor strapping the little Sergeant's arm, I holding the lamp, while all three laughed and talked, as if anywhere but in a hospital ward; except when the chat was broken by a long-drawn "Oh!" from "Baby B.," an abrupt request from the Doctor to "Hold the lamp a little higher, please," or an encouraging, "Most through, Sergeant," from Nurse P.

The chief Surgeon, Dr O., I was told, refused the higher salary, greater honor, and less labor, of an appointment to the Officer's Hospital, round the corner, that he might serve the poor fellows at Hurly-burly House, or go to the front, working there day and night, among the horrors that succeed the glories of a battle. I liked that so much, that the quiet, brown-eyed Doctor was my especial admiration; and when my own turn came, had more faith in him than in all the rest put together, although he did advise me to go home, and authorize the consumption of blue pills.

Speaking of the surgeons reminds me that, having found all manner of fault, it becomes me to celebrate the redeeming feature of Hurly-burly House. I had been prepared by the accounts of others, to expect much humiliation of spirit from the surgeons, and to be treated by them like a door-mat, a worm, or any other meek and lowly article, whose mission it is to be put down and walked upon; nurses being considered as mere servants, receiving the lowest pay, and, it's my private opinion, doing the hardest work of any part of the army, except the mules. Great, therefore, was my surprise, when I found myself treated with the utmost courtesy and kindness. Very soon my carefully prepared meekness was laid upon the shelf; and, going from one extreme to the other, I more than once expressed a difference of opinion regarding sundry messes it was my painful duty to administer.

As eight of us nurses chanced to be off duty at once, we had an excellent opportunity of trying the virtues of these gentlemen; and I am bound to say they stood the test admirably, as far as my personal observation went. Dr. O's stethoscope was unremitting in its attentions; Dr. S. brought his buttons into my room twice a day, with the regularity of a medical clock; while Dr. Z. filled my table with neat little bottles, which I never emptied, prescribed Browning, bedewed me with Cologne, and kept my fire going, as if, like the candles in St. Peter's, it must never be permitted to die out. Waking, one cold night, with the certainty that my last spark had pined away and died, and consequently hours of coughing were in store for me, I was much amazed to see a ruddy light dancing on the wall, a jolly blaze roaring up the chimney, and, down upon his knees before it, Dr. Z., whittling shavings. I ought to have risen up and thanked him on the spot; but, knowing that he was one of those who liked to do good by stealth, I only peeped at him as if he were a friendly ghost; till, having made things as cozy as the most motherly of nurses could have done, he crept away, leaving me to feel, as somebody says, "as if angels were a watching of me in my sleep;" though that species of wild fowl do not usually descend in broadcloth and glasses. I afterwards discovered that he split the wood himself on that cool January midnight, and went about making or mending fires for the poor old ladies in their dismal dens; thus causing himself to be felt—a bright and shining light in more ways than one. I never thanked him as I ought; therefore, I publicly make a note of it, and further aggravate that modest M.D. by saying that if this was not being the best of doctors and the gentlest of gentlemen, I shall be happy to see any improvement upon it.[27]

To such as wish to know where these scenes took place, I must respectfully decline to answer; for Hurly-burly House has ceased to exist as a hospital; so let it rest, with all its sins upon its head,—perhaps I should say chimney top. When the nurses felt ill, the doctors departed and the patients got well, I believe the concern gently faded from existence, or was merged into some other and better establishment, where I hope the washing of three hundred sick people is done out of the house, the food is eatable, and mortal women are not expected to possess an angelic exemption from all wants, and the endurance of truck horses.

Since the appearance of these hasty Sketches, I have heard from several of my comrades at the Hospital; and their approval assures me that I have not let sympathy and fancy run away with me, as that lively team is apt to do when harnessed to a pen. As no two persons see the same thing with the same eyes, my view of hospital life must be taken through my glass, and held for what it is worth. Certainly, nothing was set down in malice, and to the serious-minded party who objected to a tone of levity in some portions of the Sketches, I can only say that it is a part of my religion to look well after the cheerfulnesses of life, and let the dismals shift for themselves; believing, with good Sir Thomas More, that it is wise to "be merrie in God."

The next hospital I enter will, I hope, be one for the colored regiments, as they seem to be proving their right to the admiration and kind offices of their white relations, who owe them so large a debt, a little part of which I shall be so proud to pay.

Yours,

    With a firm faith

      In the good time coming,

        TRIBULATION PERIWINKLE.

MY CONTRABAND

DOCTOR FRANCK came in as I sat sewing up the rents in an old shirt, that Tom might go tidily to his grave. New shirts were needed for living, and there was no wife or mother to "dress him handsome when he went to meet the Lord," as one woman said, describing the fine funeral she had pinched herself to give her son.

"Miss Dane, I'm in a quandary," began the Doctor, with that expression of countenance which says as plainly as words, "I want to ask a favor, but I wish you'd save me the trouble."

"Can I help you out of it?"

"Faith! I don't like to propose it, but you certainly can, if you please."

"Then name it, I beg."

"You see a Reb has just been brought in crazy with typhoid; a bad case every way; a drunken, rascally little captain somebody took the trouble to capture, but whom nobody wants to take the trouble to cure. The wards are full, the ladies worked to death, and willing to be for our own boys, but rather slow to risk their lives for a Reb. Now, you've had the fever, you like queer patients, your mate will see to your ward for a while, and I will find you a good attendant. The fellow won't last long, I fancy; but he can't die without some sort of care, you know. I've put him in the fourth story of the west wing, away from the rest. It is airy, quiet, and comfortable there. I'm on that ward, and will do my best for you in every way. Now, then, will you go?"

74

My Contraband

"Of course I will, out of perversity, if not common charity; for some of these people think that because I'm an abolitionist I am also a heathen, and I should rather like to show them that, though I cannot quite love my enemies, I am willing to take care of them."

"Very good; I thought you'd go; and speaking of abolition reminds me that you can have a contraband for servant, if you like. It is that fine mulatto fellow who was found burying his rebel master after the fight, and, being badly cut over the head, our boys brought him along. Will you have him?"

"By all means,—for I'll stand to my guns on that point, as on the other; these black boys are far more faithful and handy than some of the white scamps given me to serve, instead of being served by. But is this man well enough?"

"Yes, for that sort of work, and I think you'll like him. He must have been a handsome fellow before he got his face slashed; not much darker than myself; his master's son, I dare say, and the white blood makes him rather high and haughty about some things. He was in a bad way when he came in, but vowed he'd die in the street rather than turn in with the black fellows below; so I put him up in the west wing, to be out of the way, and he's seen to the captain all the morning. When can you go up?"

"As soon as Tom is laid out, Skinner moved, Haywood washed, Marble dressed, Charley rubbed, Downs taken up, Upham laid down, and the whole forty fed."

We both laughed, though the Doctor was on his way to the dead-house and I held a shroud on my lap. But in a hospital one learns that cheerfulness is one's salvation; for, in an atmosphere of suffering and death, heaviness of heart would soon paralyze usefulness of hand, if the blessed gift of smiles had been denied us.

In an hour I took possession of my new charge, finding a dissipated-looking boy of nineteen or twenty raving in the solitary little room, with no one near him but the contraband in the room adjoining. Feeling decidedly more interest in the black man than in the white, yet remembering the Doctor's hint of his being "high and haughty," I glanced furtively at him as I scattered chloride of lime about the room to purify the air, and settled matters to suit myself. I had seen many contrabands, but never one so attractive as this. All colored men are called "boys," even if their heads are white; this boy was five-and-twenty at least, strong-limbed and manly, and had the look of one who never had been cowed by abuse or worn with oppressive labor. He sat on his bed doing nothing; no book, no pipe, no pen or paper anywhere appeared, yet anything less indolent or listless than his attitude and expression I never saw. Erect he sat, with a hand on either knee, and eyes fixed on the bare wall opposite, so rapt in some absorbing thought as to be unconscious of my presence, though the door stood wide open and my movements were by no means noiseless. His face was half averted, but I instantly approved the Doctor's taste, for the profile which I saw possessed all the attributes of comeliness belonging to his mixed race. He was more quadroon than mulatto, with Saxon features, Spanish complexion darkened by exposure, color in lips and cheek, waving hair, and an eye full of the passionate melancholy which in such men always seems to utter a mute protest against the broken law that doomed them at their birth. What could he be thinking of? The sick boy cursed and raved, I rustled to and fro, steps passed the door, bells rang, and the steady rumble of army-wagons came up from the street, still he never stirred. I had seen colored people in what they call "the black sulks," when, for days, they neither smiled nor spoke, and scarcely ate. But this was something more than that; for the man was not dully brooding over some small grievance; he seemed to see an all-absorbing fact or fancy recorded on the wall, which was a blank to me. I wondered if it were some deep wrong or sorrow, kept alive by memory and impotent regret; if he mourned for the dead master to whom he had been faithful to the end; or if the liberty now his were robbed of half its sweetness by the knowledge that some one near and dear to him still languished in the hell from which he had escaped. My heart quite warmed to him at that idea; I wanted to know and comfort him; and, following the impulse of the moment, I went in and touched him on the shoulder.

In an instant the man vanished and the slave appeared. Freedom was too new a boon to have wrought its blessed changes yet; and as he started up, with his hand at his temple, and an obsequious "Yes, Missis," any romance that had gathered round him fled away, leaving the saddest of all sad facts in living guise before me. Not only did the manhood seem to die out of him, but the comeliness that first attracted me; for, as he turned, I saw the ghastly wound that had laid open cheek and forehead. Being partly healed, it was no longer bandaged, but held together with strips of that transparent plaster which I never see without a shiver, and swift recollections of the scenes with which it is associated in my mind. Part of his black hair had been shorn away, and one eye was nearly closed; pain so distorted, and the cruel sabre-cut so marred that portion of his face, that, when I saw it, I felt as if a fine medal had been suddenly reversed, showing me a far more striking type of human suffering and wrong than Michael Angelo's bronze prisoner. By one of those inexplicable processes that often teach us how little we understand ourselves, my purpose was suddenly changed; and, though I went in to offer comfort as a friend, I merely gave an order as a mistress.

"Will you open these windows? this man needs more air."

He obeyed at once, and, as he slowly urged up the unruly sash, the handsome profile was again turned toward me, and again I was possessed by my first impression so strongly that I involuntarily said,—

"Thank you."

Perhaps it was fancy, but I thought that in the look of mingled surprise and something like reproach which he gave me, there was also a trace of grateful pleasure. But he said, in that tone of spiritless humility these poor souls learn so soon,—

"I isn't a white man, Missis, I'se a contraband."

"Yes, I know it; but a contraband is a free man, and I heartily congratulate you."

He liked that; his face shone, he squared his shoulders, lifted his head, and looked me full in the eye with a brisk,—

"Thank ye, Missis; anything more to do fer yer?"

"Doctor Franck thought you would help me with this man, as there are many patients and few nurses or attendants. Have you had the fever?"

"No, Missis."

"They should have thought of that when they put him here; wounds and fevers should not be together. I'll try to get you moved."

He laughed a sudden laugh: if he had been a white man, I should have called it scornful; as he was a few shades darker than myself, I suppose it must be considered an insolent, or at least an unmannerly one.

"It don't matter, Missis. I'd rather be up here with the fever than down with those niggers; and there isn't no other place fer me."

Poor fellow! that was true. No ward in all the hospital would take him in to lie side by side with the most miserable white wreck there. Like the bat in Æsop's fable, he belonged to neither race; and the pride of one and the helplessness of the other, kept him hovering alone in the twilight a great sin has brought to overshadow the whole land.

"You shall stay, then; for I would far rather have you than my lazy Jack. But are you well and strong enough?"

"I guess I'll do, Missis."

He spoke with a passive sort of acquiescence,—as if it did not much matter if he were not able, and no one would particularly rejoice if he were.

"Yes, I think you will. By what name shall I call you?"

"Bob, Missis."

Every woman has her pet whim; one of mine was to teach the men self-respect by treating them respectfully. Tom, Dick, and Harry would pass, when lads rejoiced in those familiar abbreviations; but to address men often old enough to be my father in that style did not suit my old-fashioned ideas of propriety. This "Bob" would never do; I should have found it as easy to call the chaplain "Gus" as my tragical-looking contraband by a title so strongly associated with the tail of a kite.

"What is your other name?" I asked. "I like to call my attendants by their last names rather than by their first."

"I'se got no other, Missis; we has our masters' names, or do without. Mine's dead, and I won't have anything of his 'bout me."

"Well, I'll call you Robert, then, and you may fill this pitcher for me, if you will be so kind."

He went; but, through all the tame obedience years of servitude had taught him, I could see that the proud spirit his father gave him was not yet subdued, for the look and gesture with which he repudiated his master's name were a more effective declaration of independence than any Fourth-of-July orator could have prepared.

We spent a curious week together. Robert seldom left his room, except upon my errands; and I was a prisoner all day, often all night, by the bedside of the rebel. The fever burned itself rapidly away, for there seemed little vitality to feed it in the feeble frame of this old young man, whose life had been none of the most righteous, judging from the revelations made by his unconscious lips; since more than once Robert authoritatively silenced him, when my gentler hushings were of no avail, and blasphemous wanderings or ribald camp-songs made my checks burn and Robert's face assume an aspect of disgust. The captain was the gentleman in the world's eye, but the contraband was the gentleman in mine;——I was a fanatic, and that accounts for such depravity of taste, I hope. I never asked Robert of himself, feeling that somewhere there was a spot still too sore to bear the lightest touch; but, from his language, manner, and intelligence, I inferred that his color had procured for him the few advantages within the reach of a quick-witted, kindly-treated slave. Silent, grave, and thoughtful, but most serviceable, was my contraband; glad of the books I brought him, faithful in the performance of the duties I assigned to him, grateful for the friendliness I could not but feel and show toward him. Often I longed to ask what purpose was so visibly altering his aspect with such daily deepening gloom. But I never dared, and no one else had either time or desire to pry into the past of this specimen of one branch of the chivalrous "F.F.Vs." [1]

On the seventh night, Dr. Franck suggested that it would be well for some one, besides the general watchman of the ward, to be with the captain, as it might be his last. Although the greater part of the two preceding nights had been spent there, of course I offered to remain,——for there is a strange fascination in these scenes, which renders one careless of fatigue and unconscious of fear until the crisis is past.

"Give him water as long as he can drink, and if he drops into a natural sleep, it may save him. I'll look in at midnight, when some change will probably take place. Nothing but sleep or a miracle will keep him now. Good-night."

Away went the Doctor; and, devouring a whole mouthful of grapes, I lowered the lamp, wet the captain's head, and sat down on a hard stool to begin my watch. The captain lay with his hot, haggard face turned toward me, filling the air with his poisonous breath, and feebly muttering, with lips and tongue so parched that the sanest speech would have been difficult to understand. Robert was stretched on his bed in the inner room, the door of which stood ajar, that a fresh draught from his open window might carry the fever-fumes away through mine. I could just see a long, dark figure, with the lighter outline of a face, and, having little else to do just then, I fell to thinking of this curious contraband, who evidently prized his freedom highly, yet seemed in no haste to enjoy it. Dr. Franck had offered to send him on to safer quarters, but he had said, "No, thank yer, sir, not yet," and then had gone away to fall into one of those black moods of his, which began to disturb me, because I had no power to lighten them. As I sat listening to the clocks from the steeples all about us, I amused myself with planning Robert's future, as I often did my own, and had dealt out to him a generous hand of trumps wherewith to play this game of life which hitherto had gone so cruelly against him, when a harsh choked voice called,—

"Lucy!"

It was the captain, and some new terror seemed to have gifted him with momentary strength.

"Yes, here's Lucy," I answered, hoping that by following the fancy I might quiet him,—for his face was damp with the clammy moisture, and his frame shaken with the nervous tremor that so often precedes death. His dull eye fixed upon me, dilating with a bewildered look of incredulity and wrath, till he broke out fiercely,—

"That's a lie! she's dead,—and so's Bob, damn him!"

Finding speech a failure, I began to sing the quiet tune that had often soothed delirium like this; but hardly had the line,—

"See gentle patience smile on pain,"

passed my lips, when he clutched me by the wrist, whispering like one in mortal fear,—

"Hush! she used to sing that way to Bob, but she never would to me. I swore I'd whip the devil out of her, and I did; but you know before she cut her throat she said she'd haunt me, and there she is!"

He pointed behind me with an aspect of such pale dismay, that I involuntarily glanced over my shoulder and started as if I had seen a veritable ghost; for, peering from the gloom of that inner room, I saw a shadowy face, with dark hair all about it, and a glimpse of scarlet at the throat. An instant showed me that it was only Robert leaning from his bed's foot, wrapped in a gray army-blanket, with his red shirt just visible above it, and his long hair disordered by sleep. But what a strange expression was on his face! The unmarred side was toward me, fixed and motionless as when I first observed it,—less absorbed now, but more intent. His eye glittered, his lips were apart like one who listened with every sense, and his whole aspect reminded me of a hound to which some wind had brought the scent of unsuspected prey.

"Do you know him, Robert? Does he mean you?"

"Laws, no, Missis; they all own half-a-dozen Bobs: but hearin' my name woke me; that's all."

He spoke quite naturally, and lay down again, while I returned to my charge, thinking that this paroxysm was probably his last. But by another hour I perceived a hopeful change; for the tremor had subsided, the cold dew was gone, his breathing was more regular, and Sleep, the healer, had descended to save or take him gently away. Doctor Franck looked in at midnight, bade me keep all cool and quiet, and not fail to administer a certain draught as soon as the captain woke. Very much relieved, I laid my head on my arms, uncomfortably folded on the little table, and fancied I was about to perform one of the feats which practice renders possible,— "sleeping with one eye open," as we say: a half-and-half doze, for all senses sleep but that of hearing; the faintest murmur, sigh, or motion will break it, and give one back one's wits much brightened by the brief permission to "stand at ease." On this night the experiment was a failure, for previous vigils, confinement, and much care had rendered naps a dangerous indulgence. Having roused half-a-dozen times in an hour to find all quiet, I dropped my heavy head on my arms, and, drowsily resolving to look up again in fifteen minutes, fell fast asleep.

The striking of a deep-voiced clock awoke me with a start. "That is one," thought I; but, to my dismay, two more strokes followed, and in remorseful haste I sprang up to see what harm my long oblivion had done. A strong hand put me back into my seat, and held me there. It was Robert. The instant my eye met his my heart began to beat, and all along my nerves tingled that electric flash which foretells a danger that we cannot see. He was very pale, his mouth grim, and both eyes full of sombre fire; for even the wounded one was open now, all the more sinister for the deep scar above and below. But his touch was steady, his voice quiet, as he said,—

"Sit still, Missis; I won't hurt yer, nor scare yer, ef I can help it, but yer waked too soon."

"Let me go, Robert,—the captain is stirring,—I must give him something."

"No, Missis, yer can't stir an inch. Look here!"

Holding me with one hand, with the other he took up the glass in which I had left the draught, and showed me it was empty.

"Has he taken it?" I asked, more and more bewildered.

"I flung it out o' winder, Missis; he'll have to do without."

"But why, Robert? why did you do it?"

"'Kase I hate him!"

Impossible to doubt the truth of that; his whole face showed it, as he spoke through his set teeth, and launched a fiery glance at the unconscious captain. I could only hold my breath and stare blankly at him, wondering what mad act was coming next. I suppose I shook and turned white, as women have a foolish habit of doing when sudden danger daunts them; for Robert released my arm, sat down upon the bedside just in front of me, and said, with the ominous quietude that made me cold to see and hear,—

"Don't yer be frightened, Missis; don't try to run away, fer the door's locked and the key in my pocket; don't yer cry out, fer yer'd have to scream a long while, with my hand on yer mouth, 'efore yer was heard. Be still, an' I'll tell yer what I'm gwine to do."

"Lord help us! he has taken the fever in some sudden, violent way, and is out of his head. I must humor him till some one comes"; in pursuance of which swift determination, I tried to say, quite composedly,—

"I will be still and hear you; but open the window. Why did you shut it?"

"I'm sorry I can't do it, Missis; but yer'd jump out, or call, if I did, an' I'm not ready yet. I shut it to make yer sleep, an' heat would do it quicker'n anything else I could do."

The captain moved, and feebly muttered "Water!" Instinctively I rose to give it to him, but the heavy hand came down upon my shoulder, and in the same decided tone Robert said,—

"The water went with the physic; let him call."

"Do let me go to him! he'll die without care!"

"I mean he shall;—don't yer meddle, if yer please, Missis."

In spite of his quiet tone and respectful manner, I saw murder in his eyes, and turned faint with fear; yet the fear excited me, and, hardly knowing what I did, I seized the hands that had seized me, crying,—

"No, no; you shall not kill him! It is base to hurt a helpless man. Why do you hate him? He is not your master."

"He's my brother."

I felt that answer from head to foot, and seemed to fathom what was coming, with a prescience vague, but unmistakable. One appeal was left to me, and I made it.

"Robert, tell me what it means? Do not commit a crime and make me accessory to it. There is a better way of righting wrong than by violence;—let me help you find it."

My voice trembled as I spoke, and I heard the frightened flutter of my heart; so did he, and if any little act of mine had ever won affection or respect from him, the memory of it served me then. He looked down, and seemed to put some question to himself; whatever it was, the answer was in my favor, for when his eyes rose again, they were gloomy, but not desperate.

"I *will* tell yer, Missis; but mind, this makes no difference; the boy is mine. I'll give the Lord a chance to take him fust: if He don't, I shall."

"Oh, no! remember he is your brother."

An unwise speech; I felt it as it passed my lips, for a black frown gathered on Robert's face, and his strong hands closed with an ugly sort of grip. But he did not touch the poor soul gasping there behind him, and seemed content to let the slow suffocation of that stifling room end his frail life.

"I'm not like to forgit dat, Missis, when I've been thinkin' of it all this week. I knew him when they fetched him in, an' would 'a' done it long 'fore this, but I wanted to ask where Lucy was; he knows,—he told to-night,—an' now he's done for."

"Who is Lucy?" I asked hurriedly, intent on keeping his mind busy with any thought but murder.

With one of the swift transitions of a mixed temperament like this, at my question Robert's deep eyes filled, the clenched hands were spread before his face, and all I heard were the broken words,—

"My wife,—he took her—"

In that instant every thought of fear was swallowed up in burning indignation for the wrong, and a perfect passion of pity for the desperate man so tempted to avenge an injury for which there seemed no redress but this. He was no longer slave or contraband, no drop of black blood marred him in my sight, but an infinite compassion yearned to save, to help, to comfort him. Words seemed so powerless I offered none, only put my hand on his poor head, wounded, homeless, bowed down with grief for which I had no cure, and softly smoothed the long, neglected hair, pitifully wondering the while where was the wife who must have loved this tender-hearted man so well.

The captain moaned again, and faintly whispered, "Air!" but I never stirred. God forgive me! just then I hated him as only a woman thinking of a sister woman's wrong could hate. Robert looked up; his eyes were dry again, his mouth grim. I saw that, said, "Tell me more," and he did; for sympathy is a gift the poorest may give, the proudest stoop to receive.

"Yer see, Missis, his father,—I might say ours, ef I warn't ashamed of both of 'em,—his father died two years ago, an' left us all to Marster Ned,—that's him here, eighteen then. He always hated me, I looked so like old Marster: he don't,—only the light skin an' hair. Old Marster was kind to all of us, me 'specially, an' bought Lucy off the next plantation down there in South Carolina, when he found I liked her. I married her, all I could; it warn't much, but we was true to one another till Marster Ned come home a year after an' made hell fer both of us. He sent my old mother to be used up in his rice-swamp in Georgy; he found me with my pretty Lucy, an' though young Miss cried, an' I prayed to him on my knees, an' Lucy run away, he wouldn't have no mercy; he brought her back, an'—took her."

"Oh, what did you do?" I cried, hot with helpless pain and passion.

How the man's outraged heart sent the blood flaming up into his face and deepened the tones of his impetuous voice, as he stretched his arm across the bed, saying, with a terribly expressive gesture,—

"I half murdered him, an' to-night I'll finish."

"Yes, yes—but go on now; what came next?"

He gave me a look that showed no white man could have felt a deeper degradation in remembering and confessing these last acts of brotherly oppression.

"They whipped me till I couldn't stand, an' then they sold me further South. Yer thought I was a white man once,—look here!"

With a sudden wrench he tore the shirt from neck to waist, and on his strong, brown shoulders showed me furrows deeply ploughed, wounds which, though healed, were ghastlier to me than any in that house. I could not speak to him, and, with the pathetic dignity a great grief lends the humblest sufferer, he ended his brief tragedy by simply saying,—

"That's all, Missis. I'se never seen her since, an' now I never shall in this world,—maybe not in t'other."

"But, Robert, why think her dead? The captain was wandering when he said those sad things; perhaps he will retract them when he is sane. Don't despair; don't give up yet."

"No, Missis, I 'spect he's right; she was too proud to bear that long. It's like her to kill herself. I told her to, if there was no other way; an' she always minded me, Lucy did. My poor girl! Oh, it warn't right! No, by God, it warn't!"

As the memory of this bitter wrong, this double bereavement, burned in his sore heart, the devil that lurks in every strong man's blood leaped up; he put his hand upon his brother's throat, and, watching the white face before him, muttered low between his teeth,—

"I'm lettin' him go too easy; there's no pain in this; we a'n't even yet. I wish he knew me. Marster Ned! it's Bob; where's Lucy?"

From the captain's lips there came a long faint sigh, and nothing but a flutter of the eyelids showed that he still lived. A strange stillness filled the room as the elder brother held the younger's life suspended in his hand, while wavering between a dim hope and a deadly hate. In the whirl of thoughts that went on in my brain, only one was clear enough to act upon. I must prevent murder, if I could,—but how? What could I do up there alone, locked in with a dying man and a lunatic?—for any mind yielded utterly to any unrighteous impulse is mad while the impulse rules it. Strength I had not, nor much courage, neither time nor will for stratagem, and chance only could bring me help before it was too late. But one weapon I possesed,—a tongue,—often a woman's best defence; and sympathy, stronger than fear, gave me power to use it. What I said Heaven only knows, but surely Heaven helped me; words burned on my lips, tears streamed from my eyes, and some good angel prompted me to use the one name that had power to arrest my hearer's hand and touch his heart. For at that moment I heartily believed that Lucy lived, and this earnest faith roused in him a like belief.

He listened with the lowering look of one in whom brute instinct was sovereign for the time,—a look that makes the noblest countenance base. He was but a man,—a poor, untaught, outcast, outraged man. Life had few joys for him; the world offered him no honors, no success, no home, no love. What future would this crime mar? and why should he deny himself that sweet, yet bitter morsel called revenge? How many white men, with all New England's freedom, culture, Christianity, would not have felt as he felt then? Should I have reproached him for a human anguish, a human longing for redress, all now left him from the ruin of his few poor hopes? Who had taught him that self-control, self-sacrifice, are attributes that make men masters of the earth, and lift them nearer heaven? Should I have urged the beauty of forgiveness, the duty of devout submission? He had no religion, for he was no saintly "Uncle Tom," and Slavery's black shadow seemed to darken all the world to him, and shut out God. Should I have warned him of penalties, of judgments, and the potency of law? What did he know of justice, or the mercy that should temper that stern virtue, when every law, human and divine, had been broken on his hearthstone? Should I have tried to touch him by appeals to filial duty, to brotherly love? How had his appeals been answered? What memories had father and brother stored up in his heart to plead for either now? No,—all these influences, these associations, would have proved worse than useless, had I been calm enough to try them. I was not; but instinct, subtler than reason, showed me the one safe clue by which to lead this troubled soul from the labyrinth in which it groped and nearly fell. When I paused, breathless, Robert turned to me, asking, as if human assurances could strengthen his faith in Divine Omnipotence,—

"Do you believe, if I let Marster Ned live, the Lord will give me back my Lucy?"

"As surely as there is a Lord, you will find her here or in the beautiful hereafter, where there is no black or white, no master and no slave."

He took his hand from his brother's throat, lifted his eyes from my face to the wintry sky beyond, as if searching for that blessed country, happier even than the happy North. Alas, it was the darkest hour before the dawn!—there was no star above, no light below but the pale glimmer of the lamp that showed the brother who had made him desolate. Like a blind man who believes there is a sun, yet cannot see it, he shook his head, let his arms drop nervelessly upon his knees, and sat there dumbly asking that question which many a soul whose faith is firmer fixed than his has asked in hours less dark than this,—"Where is God?" I saw the tide had turned, and strenuously tried to keep this rudderless life-boat from slipping back into the whirlpool wherein it had been so nearly lost.

"I have listened to you, Robert; now hear me, and heed what I say, because my heart is full of pity for you, full of hope for your future, and a desire to help you now. I want you to go away from here, from the temptation of this place, and the sad thoughts that haunt it. You have conquered yourself once, and I honor you for it, because, the harder the battle, the more glorious the victory; but it is safer to put a greater distance between you and this man. I will write you letters, give you money, and send you to good old Massachusetts to begin your new life a freeman,— yes, and a happy man; for when the captain is himself again, I will learn where Lucy is, and move heaven and earth to find and give her back to you. Will you do this, Robert?"

Slowly, very slowly, the answer came; for the purpose of a week, perhaps a year, was hard to relinquish in an hour.

"Yes, Missis, I will."

"Good! Now you are the man I thought you, and I'll work for you with all my heart. You need sleep, my poor fellow; go, and try to forget. The captain is alive, and as yet you are spared that sin. No, don't look there; I'll care for him. Come, Robert, for Lucy's sake."

Thank Heaven for the immortality of love! for when all other means of salvation failed, a spark of this vital fire softened the man's iron will, until a woman's hand could bend it. He let me take from him the key, let me draw him gently away, and lead him to the solitude which now was the most healing balm I could bestow. Once in his little room, he fell down on his bed and lay there, as if spent with the sharpest conflict of his life. I slipped the bolt across his door, and unlocked my own, flung up the window, steadied myself with a breath of air, then rushed to Doctor Franck. He came; and till dawn we worked together, saving one brother's life, and taking earnest thought how best to secure the other's liberty. When the sun came up as blithely as if it shone only upon happy homes, the Doctor went to Robert. For an hour I heard the murmur of their voices; once I caught the sound of heavy sobs, and for a time a reverent hush, as if in the silence that good man were ministering to soul as well as body. When he departed he took Robert with him, pausing to tell me he should get him off as soon as possible, but not before we met again.

Nothing more was seen of them all day; another surgeon came to see the captain, and another attendant came to fill the empty place. I tried to rest, but could not, with the thought of poor Lucy tugging at my heart, and was soon back at my post again, anxiously hoping that my contraband had not been too hastily spirited away. Just as night fell there came a tap, and, opening, I saw Robert literally "clothed, and in his right mind." The Doctor had replaced the ragged suit with tidy garments, and no trace of the tempestuous night remained but deeper lines upon the forehead, and the docile look of a repentant child. He did not cross the threshold, did not offer me his hand,—only took off his cap, saying, with a traitorous falter in his voice,—

"God bless yer, Missis! I'm gwine."

I put out both my hands, and held his fast.

"Good-by, Robert! Keep up good heart, and when I come home to Massachusetts we'll meet in a happier place than this. Are you quite ready, quite comfortable for your journey?"

"Yes, Missis, yes; the Doctor's fixed everything! I'se gwine with a friend of his; my papers are all right, an' I'm as happy as I can be till I find"—

He stopped there; then went on, with a glance into the room,—

"I'm glad I didn't do it, an' I thank yer, Missis, fer hinderin' me—thank yer hearty; but I'm afraid I hate him jest the same."

Of course he did; and so did I; for these faulty hearts of ours cannot turn perfect in a night, but need frost and fire, wind and rain, to ripen and make them ready for the great harvest-home. Wishing to divert his mind, I put my poor mite into his hand, and, remembering the magic of a certain little book, I gave him mine, on whose dark cover whitely shone the Virgin Mother and the Child, the grand history of whose life the book contained. The money went into Robert's pocket with a grateful murmur, the book into his bosom, with a long look and a tremulous—

"I never saw *my* baby, Missis."

I broke down then; and though my eyes were too dim to see, I felt the touch of lips upon my hands, heard the sound of departing feet, and knew my contraband was gone.

When one feels an intense dislike, the less one says about the subject of it the better; therefore I shall merely record that the captain lived,—in time was exchanged; and that, whoever the other party was, I am convinced the Government got the best of the bargain. But long before this occurred, I had fulfilled my promise to Robert; for as soon as my patient recovered strength of memory enough to make his answer trustworthy, I asked, without any circumlocution,—

"Captain Fairfax, where is Lucy?"

And too feeble to be angry, surprised, or insincere, he straightway answered,—

"Dead, Miss Dane."

"And she killed herself when you sold Bob?"

"How the devil did you know that?" he muttered, with an expression half-remorseful, half-amazed; but I was satisfied, and said no more.

Of course this went to Robert, waiting far away there in a lonely home,—waiting, working, hoping for his Lucy. It almost broke my heart to do it; but delay was weak, deceit was wicked; so I sent the heavy tidings, and very soon the answer came,— only three lines; but I felt that the sustaining power of the man's life was gone.

"I tort I'd never see her any more; I'm glad to know she's out of trouble. I thank yer, Missis; an' if they let us, I'll fight fer yer till I'm killed, which I hope will be 'fore long."

Six months later he had his wish, and kept his word.

Every one knows the story of the attack on Fort Wagner[2]; but we should not tire yet of recalling how our Fifty-Fourth, spent with three sleepless nights, a day's fast, and a march under the July sun, stormed the fort as night fell, facing death in many shapes, following their brave leaders through a fiery rain of shot and shell, fighting valiantly for "God and Governor Andrew,"—how the regiment that went into action seven hundred strong, came out having had nearly half its number captured, killed, or wounded, leaving their young commander to be buried, like a chief of earlier times, with his body-guard around him, faithful to the death. Surely, the insult turns to honor, and the wide grave needs no monument but the heroism that consecrates it in our sight; surely, the hearts that held him nearest, see through their tears a noble victory in the seeming sad defeat; and surely, God's benediction was bestowed, when this loyal soul answered, as Death called the roll, "Lord, here am I, with the brothers Thou hast given me!"

The future must show how well that fight was fought; for though Fort Wagner once defied us, public prejudice is down; and through the cannon-smoke of that black night, the manhood of the colored race shines before many eyes that would not see, rings in many ears that would not hear, wins many hearts that would not hitherto believe.

When the news came that we were needed, there was none so glad as I to leave teaching contrabands, the new work I had taken up, and go to nurse "our boys," as my dusky flock so proudly called the wounded of the Fifty-Fourth. Feeling more satisfaction, as I assumed my big apron and turned up my cuffs, than if dressing for the President's levee, I fell to work in Hospital No. 10 at Beaufort. The scene was most familiar, and yet strange; for only dark faces looked up at me from the pallets so thickly laid along the floor, and I missed the sharp accent of my Yankee boys in the slower, softer voices calling cheerily to one another, or answering my questions with a stout, "We'll never give it up, Missis, till the last Reb's dead," or, "If our people's free, we can afford to die."

Passing from bed to bed, intent on making one pair of hands do the work of three, at least, I gradually washed, fed, and bandaged my way down the long line of sable heroes, and coming to the very last, found that he was my contraband. So old, so worn, so deathly weak and wan, I never should have known him but for the deep scar on his cheek. That side lay uppermost, and caught my eye at once; but even then I doubted, such an awful change had come upon him, when, turning to the ticket just above his head, I saw the name, "Robert Dane." That both assured and touched me, for, remembering that he had no name, I knew that he had taken mine. I longed for him to speak to me, to tell how he had fared since I lost sight of him, and let me perform some little service for him in return for many he had done for me; but he seemed asleep; and as I stood re-living that strange night again, a bright lad, who lay next him softly waving an old fan across both beds, looked up and said,—

"I guess you know him, Missis?"

"You are right. Do you?"

"As much as any one was able to, Missis."

"Why do you say 'was,' as if the man were dead and gone?"

"I s'pose because I know he'll have to go. He's got a bad jab in the breast, an' is bleedin' inside, the Doctor says. He don't suffer any, only gets weaker 'n' weaker every minute. I've been fannin' him this long while, an' he's talked a little; but he don't know me now, so he's most gone, I guess."

There was so much sorrow and affection in the boy's face, that I remembered something, and asked, with redoubled interest,—

"Are you the one that brought him off? I was told about a boy who nearly lost his life in saving that of his mate."

I dare say the young fellow blushed, as any modest lad might have done; I could not see it, but I heard the chuckle of satisfaction that escaped him, as he glanced from his shattered arm and bandaged side to the pale figure opposite.

"Lord, Missis, that's nothin'; we boys always stan' by one another, an' I warn't goin' to leave him to be tormented any more by them cussed Rebs. He's been a slave once, though he don't look half so much like it as me, an' I was born in Boston."

He did not; for the speaker was as black as the ace of spades,—being a sturdy specimen, the knave of clubs would perhaps be a fitter representative,—but the dark freeman looked at the white slave with the pitiful, yet puzzled expression I have so often seen on the faces of our wisest men, when this tangled question of Slavery presented itself, asking to be cut or patiently undone.

"Tell me what you know of this man; for, even if he were awake, he is too weak to talk."

"I never saw him till I joined the regiment, an' no one 'peared to have got much out of him. He was a shut-up sort of feller, an' didn't seem to care for anything but gettin' at the Rebs. Some say he was the fust man of us that enlisted; I know he fretted till we were off, an' when we pitched into Old Wagner, he fought like the devil."

"Were you with him when he was wounded? How was it?"

"Yes, Missis. There was somethin' queer about it; for he 'peared to know the chap that killed him, an' the chap knew him. I don't dare to ask, but I rather guess one owned the other some time; for, when they clinched, the chap sung out, 'Bob!' an' Dane, 'Marster Ned!'—then they went at it."

I sat down suddenly, for the old anger and compassion struggled in my heart, and I both longed and feared to hear what was to follow.

"You see, when the Colonel,—Lord keep an' send him back to us!—it a'n't certain yet, you know, Missis, though it's two days ago we lost him,—well, when the Colonel shouted, 'Rush on, boys, rush on!' Dane tore away as if he was goin' to take the fort alone; I was next him, an' kept close as we went through the ditch an' up the wall. Hi! warn't that a rusher!" and the boy flung up his well arm with a whoop, as if the mere memory of that stirring moment came over him in a gust of irrepressible excitement.

"Were you afraid?" I said, asking the question women often put, and receiving the answer they seldom fail to get.

"No, Missis!"—emphasis on the "Missis"—"I never thought of anything but the damn' Rebs, that scalp, slash, an' cut our ears off, when they git us. I was bound to let daylight into one of 'em at least, an' I did. Hope he liked it!"

"It is evident that you did. Now go on about Robert, for I should be at work."

"He was one of the fust up; I was just behind, an' though the whole thing happened in a minute, I remember how it was, for all I was yellin' an' knockin' round like mad. Just where we were, some sort of an officer was wavin' his sword an' cheerin' on his men; Dane saw him by a big flash that come by; he flung away his gun, give a leap, an' went at that feller as if he was Jeff, Beauregard, an' Lee, all in one. I scrabbled after as quick as I could, but was only up in time to see him git the sword straight through him an' drop into the ditch. You needn't ask what I did next, Missis, for I don't quite know myself; all I'm clear about is, that I managed somehow to pitch that Reb into the fort as dead as Moses, git hold of Dane, an' bring him off. Poor old feller! we said we went in to live or die; he said he went in to die, an' he's done it."

I had been intently watching the excited speaker; but as he regretfully added those last words I turned again, and Robert's eyes met mine,— those melancholy eyes, so full of an intelligence that proved he had heard, remembered, and reflected with that preternatural power which often outlives all other faculties. He knew me, yet gave no greeting; was glad to see a woman's face, yet had no smile wherewith to welcome it; felt that he was dying, yet uttered no farewell. He was too far across the river to return or linger now; departing thought, strength, breath, were spent in one grateful look, one murmur of submission to the last pang he could ever feel. His lips moved, and, bending to them, a whisper chilled my cheek, as it shaped the broken words,—

"I'd 'a' done it,—but it's better so,—I'm satisfied."

Ah! well he might be,—for, as he turned his face from the shadow of the life that was, the sunshine of the life to be touched it with a beautiful content, and in the drawing of a breath my contraband found wife and home, eternal liberty and God.

BEHIND A MASK;
OR,
A WOMAN'S POWER

JEAN MUIR

✗✗✗✗✗

"*HAS* she come?"

"No, Mamma, not yet."

"I wish it were well over. The thought of it worries and excites me. A cushion for my back, Bella."

And poor, peevish Mrs. Coventry sank into an easy chair with a nervous sigh and the air of a martyr, while her pretty daughter hovered about her with affectionate solicitude.

"Who are they talking of, Lucia?" asked the languid young man lounging on a couch near his cousin, who bent over her tapestry work with a happy smile on her usually haughty face.

"The new governess, Miss Muir. Shall I tell you about her?"

"No, thank you. I have an inveterate aversion to the whole tribe. I've often thanked heaven that I had but one sister, and she a spoiled child, so that I have escaped the infliction of a governess so long."

"How will you bear it now?" asked Lucia.

"Leave the house while she is in it."

"No, you won't. You're too lazy, Gerald," called out a younger and more energetic man, from the recess where he stood teasing his dogs.

"I'll give her a three days' trial; if she proves endurable I shall not disturb myself; if, as I am sure, she is a bore, I'm off anywhere, anywhere out of her way."

"I beg you won't talk in that depressing manner, boys. I dread the coming of a stranger more than you possibly can, but Bella *must* not be neglected; so I have nerved myself to endure this woman, and Lucia is good enough to say she will attend to her after tonight."

"Don't be troubled, Mamma. She is a nice person, I dare say, and when once we are used to her, I've no doubt we shall be glad to have her, it's so dull here just now. Lady Sydney said she was a quiet, accomplished, amiable girl, who needed a home, and would be a help to poor stupid me, so try to like her for my sake."

"I will, dear, but isn't it getting late? I do hope nothing has happened. Did you tell them to send a carriage to the station for her, Gerald?"

"I forgot it. But it's not far, it won't hurt her to walk" was the languid reply.

"It was indolence, not forgetfulness, I know. I'm very sorry; she will think it so rude to leave her to find her way so late. Do go and see to it, Ned."

"Too late, Bella, the train was in some time ago. Give your orders to me next time, Mother, and I'll see that they are obeyed," said Edward.

"Ned is just at an age to make a fool of himself for any girl who comes in his way. Have a care of the governess, Lucia, or she will bewitch him."

Gerald spoke in a satirical whisper, but his brother heard him and answered with a good-humored laugh.

"I wish there was any hope of your making a fool of yourself in that way, old fellow. Set me a good example, and I promise to follow it. As for the governess, she is a woman, and should be treated with common civility. I should say a little extra kindness wouldn't be amiss, either, because she is poor, and a stranger."

"That is my dear, good-hearted Ned! We'll stand by poor little Muir, won't we?" And running to her brother, Bella stood on tiptoe to offer him a kiss which he could not refuse, for the rosy lips were pursed up invitingly, and the bright eyes full of sisterly affection.

"I do hope she has come, for, when I make an effort to see anyone, I hate to make it in vain. Punctuality is *such* a virtue, and I know this woman hasn't got it, for she promised to be here at seven, and now it is long after," began Mrs. Coventry, in an injured tone.

Before she could get breath for another complaint, the clock struck seven and the doorbell rang.

"There she is!" cried Bella, and turned toward the door as if to go and meet the newcomer.

But Lucia arrested her, saying authoritatively, "Stay here, child. It is her place to come to you, not yours to go to her."

"Miss Muir," announced a servant, and a little black-robed figure stood in the doorway. For an instant no one stirred, and the governess had time to see and be seen before a word was uttered. All looked at her, and she cast on the household group a keen glance that impressed them curiously; then her eyes fell, and bowing slightly she walked in. Edward came forward and received her with the frank cordiality which nothing could daunt or chill.

"Mother, this is the lady whom you expected. Miss Muir, allow me to apologize for our apparent neglect in not sending for you. There was a mistake about the carriage, or, rather, the lazy fellow to whom the order was given forgot it. Bella, come here."

"Thank you, no apology is needed. I did not expect to be sent for." And the governess meekly sat down without lifting her eyes.

"I am glad to see you. Let me take your things," said Bella, rather shyly, for Gerald, still lounging, watched the fireside group with languid interest, and Lucia never stirred. Mrs. Coventry took a second survey and began:

"You were punctual, Miss Muir, which pleases me. I'm a sad invalid, as Lady Sydney told you, I hope; so that Miss Coventry's lessons will be directed by my niece, and you will go to her for directions, as she knows what I wish. You will excuse me if I ask you a few questions, for Lady Sydney's note was very brief, and I left everything to her judgment."

"Ask anything you like, madam," answered the soft, sad voice.

"You are Scotch, I believe."

"Yes, madam."

"Are your parents living?"

"I have not a relation in the world."

"Dear me, how sad! Do you mind telling me your age?"

"Nineteen." And a smile passed over Miss Muir's lips, as she folded her hands with an air of resignation, for the catechism was evidently to be a long one.

"So young! Lady Sydney mentioned five-and-twenty, I think, didn't she, Bella?

"No, Mamma, she only said she thought so. Don't ask such questions. It's not pleasant before us all," whispered Bella.

A quick, grateful glance shone on her from the suddenly lifted eyes of Miss Muir, as she said quietly, "I wish I was thirty, but, as I am not, I do my best to look and seem old."

Of course, every one looked at her then, and all felt a touch of pity at the sight of the pale-faced girl in her plain black dress, with no ornament but a little silver cross at her throat. Small, thin, and colorless she was, with yellow hair, gray eyes, and sharply cut, irregular, but very expressive features. Poverty seemed to have set its bond stamp upon her, and life to have had for her more frost than sunshine. But something in the lines of the mouth betrayed strength, and the clear, low voice had a curious mixture of command and entreaty in its varying tones. Not an attractive woman, yet not an ordinary one; and, as she sat there with her delicate hands lying in her lap, her head bent, and a bitter look on her thin face, she was more interesting than many a blithe and blooming girl. Bella's heart warmed to her at once, and she drew her seat nearer, while Edward went back to his dogs that his presence might not embarrass her.

"You have been ill, I think," continued Mrs. Coventry, who considered this fact the most interesting of all she had heard concerning the governess.

"Yes, madam, I left the hospital only a week ago."

"Are you quite sure it is safe to begin teaching so soon?"

"I have no time to lose, and shall soon gain strength here in the country, if you care to keep me."

"And you are fitted to teach music, French, and drawing?"

"I shall endeavor to prove that I am."

"Be kind enough to go and play an air or two. I can judge by your touch; I used to play finely when a girl."

Miss Muir rose, looked about her for the instrument, and seeing it at the other end of the room went toward it, passing Gerald and Lucia as if she did not see them. Bella followed, and in a moment forgot everything in admiration. Miss Muir played like one who loved music and was perfect mistress of her art. She charmed them all by the magic of this spell; even indolent Gerald sat up to listen, and Lucia put down her needle, while Ned watched the slender white fingers as they flew, and wondered at the strength and skill which they possessed.

"Please sing," pleaded Bella, as a brilliant overture ended.

With the same meek obedience Miss Muir complied, and began a little Scotch melody, so sweet, so sad, that the girl's eyes filled, and Mrs. Coventry looked for one of her many pocket-handkerchiefs. But suddenly the music ceased, for, with a vain attempt to support herself, the singer slid from her seat and lay before the startled listeners, as white and rigid as if struck with death. Edward caught her up, and, ordering his brother off the couch, laid her there, while Bella chafed her hands, and her mother rang for her maid. Lucia bathed the poor girl's temples, and Gerald, with unwonted energy, brought a glass of wine. Soon Miss Muir's lips trembled, she sighed, then murmured, tenderly, with a pretty Scotch accent, as if wandering in the past, "Bide wi' me, Mither, I'm sae sick an sad here all alone."

"Take a sip of this, and it will do you good, my dear," said Mrs. Coventry, quite touched by the plaintive words.

The strange voice seemed to recall her. She sat up, looked about her, a little wildly, for a moment, then collected herself and said, with a pathetic look and tone, "Pardon me. I have been on my feet all day, and, in my eagerness to keep my appointment, I forgot to eat since morning. I'm better now; shall I finish the song?"

"By no means. Come and have some tea," said Bella, full of pity and remorse.

"Scene first, very well done," whispered Gerald to his cousin.

Miss Muir was just before them, apparently listening to Mrs. Coventry's remarks upon fainting fits; but she heard, and looked over her shoulders with a gesture like Rachel. Her eyes were gray, but at that instant they seemed black with some strong emotion of anger, pride, or defiance. A curious smile passed over her face as she bowed, and said in her penetrating voice, "Thanks. The last scene shall be still better."

Young Coventry was a cool, indolent man, seldom conscious of any emotion, any passion, pleasurable or otherwise; but at the look, the tone of the governess, he experienced a new sensation, indefinable, yet strong. He colored and, for the first time in his life, looked abashed. Lucia saw it, and hated Miss Muir with a sudden hatred; for, in all the years she had passed with her cousin, no look or word of hers had possessed such power. Coventry was himself again in an instant, with no trace of that passing change, but a look of interest in his usually dreamy eyes, and a touch of anger in his sarcastic voice.

"What a melodramatic young lady! I shall go tomorrow."

Lucia laughed, and was well pleased when he sauntered away to bring her a cup of tea from the table where a little scene was just taking place. Mrs. Coventry had sunk into her chair again, exhausted by the flurry of the fainting fit. Bella was busied about her; and Edward, eager to feed the pale governess, was awkwardly trying to make the tea, after a beseeching glance at his cousin which she did not choose to answer. As he upset the caddy and uttered a despairing exclamation, Miss Muir quietly took her place behind the urn, saying with a smile, and a shy glance at the young man, "Allow me to assume my duty at once, and serve you all. I understand the art of making people comfortable in this way. The scoop, please. I can gather this up quite well alone, if you will tell me how your mother likes her tea."

Edward pulled a chair to the table and made merry over his mishaps, while Miss Muir performed her little task with a skill and grace that made it pleasant to watch her. Coventry lingered a moment after she had given him a steaming cup, to observe her more nearly, while he asked a question or two of his brother. She took no more notice of him than if he had been a statue, and in the middle of the one remark he addressed to her, she rose to take the sugar basin to Mrs. Coventry, who was quite won by the modest, domestic graces of the new governess.

"Really, my dear, you are a treasure; I haven't tasted such tea since my poor maid Ellis died. Bella never makes it good, and Miss Lucia always forgets the cream. Whatever you do you seem to do well, and that is *such* a comfort."

"Let me always do this for you, then. It will be a pleasure, madam."

Behind a Mask

And Miss Muir came back to her seat with a faint color in her cheek which improved her much.

"My brother asked if young Sydney was at home when you left," said Edward, for Gerald would not take the trouble to repeat the question.

Miss Muir fixed her eyes on Coventry, and answered with a slight tremor of the lips, "No, he left home some weeks ago."

The young man went back to his cousin, saying, as he threw himself down beside her, "I shall not go tomorrow, but wait till the three days are out."

"Why?" demanded Lucia.

Lowering his voice he said, with a significant nod toward the governess, "Because I have a fancy that she is at the bottom of Sydney's mystery. He's not been himself lately, and now he is gone without a word. I rather like romances in real life, if they are not too long, or difficult to read."

"Do you think her pretty?"

"Far from it, a most uncanny little specimen."

"Then why fancy Sydney loves her?"

"He is an oddity, and likes sensations and things of that sort."

"What do you mean, Gerald?"

"Get the Muir to look at you, as she did at me, and you will understand. Will you have another cup, Juno?"

"Yes, please." She liked to have him wait upon her, for he did it to no other woman except his mother.

Before he could slowly rise, Miss Muir glided to them with another cup on the salver; and, as Lucia took it with a cold nod, the girl said under her breath, "I think it honest to tell you that I possess a quick ear, and cannot help hearing what is said anywhere in the room. What you say of me is of no consequence, but you may speak of things which you prefer I should not hear; therefore, allow me to warn you." And she was gone again as noiselessly as she came.

"How do you like that?" whispered Coventry, as his cousin sat looking after the girl, with a disturbed expression.

"What an uncomfortable creature to have in the house! I am very sorry I urged her coming, for your mother has taken a fancy to her, and it will be hard to get rid of her," said Lucia, half angry, half amused.

"Hush, she hears every word you say. I know it by the expression of her face, for Ned is talking about horses, and she looks as haughty as ever you did, and that is saying much. Faith, this is getting interesting."

"Hark, she is speaking; I want to hear," and Lucia laid her hand on her cousin's lips. He kissed it, and then idly amused himself with turning the rings to and fro on the slender fingers.

"I have been in France several years, madam, but my friend died and I came back to be with Lady Sydney, till—" Muir paused an instant, then added, slowly, "till I fell ill. It was a contagious fever, so I went of my own accord to the hospital, not wishing to endanger her."

"Very right, but are you sure there is no danger of infection now?" asked Mrs. Coventry anxiously.

"None, I assure you. I have been well for some time, but did not leave because I preferred to stay there, than to return to Lady Sydney."

"No quarrel, I hope? No trouble of any kind?"

"No quarrel, but—well, why not? You have a right to know, and I will not make a foolish mystery out of a very simple thing. As your family, only, is present, I may tell the truth. I did not go back on the young gentleman's account. Please ask no more."

"Ah, I see. Quite prudent and proper, Miss Muir. I shall never allude to it again. Thank you for your frankness. Bella, you will be careful not to mention this to your young friends; girls gossip sadly, and it would annoy Lady Sydney beyond everything to have this talked of."

"Very neighborly of Lady S. to send the dangerous young lady here, where there are *two* young gentlemen to be captivated. I wonder why she didn't keep Sydney after she had caught him," murmured Coventry to his cousin.

"Because she had the utmost contempt for a titled fool." Miss Muir dropped the words almost into his ear, as she bent to take her shawl from the sofa corner.

"How the deuce did she get there?" ejaculated Coventry, looking as if he had received another sensation. "She has spirit, though, and upon my word I pity Sydney, if he did try to dazzle her, for he must have got a splendid dismissal."

"Come and play billiards. You promised, and I hold you to your word," said Lucia, rising with decision, for Gerald was showing too much interest in another to suit Miss Beaufort.

"I am, as ever, your most devoted. My mother is a charming woman, but I find our evening parties slightly dull, when only my own family are present. Good night, Mamma." He shook hands with his mother, whose pride and idol he was, and, with a comprehensive nod to the others, strolled after his cousin.

"Now they are gone we can be quite cozy, and talk over things, for I don't mind Ned any more than I do his dogs," said Bella, settling herself on her mother's footstool.

"I merely wish to say, Miss Muir, that my daughter has never had a governess and is sadly backward for a girl of sixteen. I want you to pass the mornings with her, and get her on as rapidly as possible. In the afternoon you will walk or drive with her, and in the evening sit with us here, if you like, or amuse yourself as you please. While in the country we are very quiet, for I cannot bear much company, and when my sons want gaiety, they go away for it. Miss Beaufort oversees the servants, and takes my place as far as possible. I am very delicate and keep my room till evening, except for an airing at noon. We will try each other for a month, and I hope we shall get on quite comfortably together."

"I shall do my best, madam."

One would not have believed that the meek spiritless voice which uttered these words was the same that had startled Coventry a few minutes before, nor that the pale, patient face could ever have kindled with such sudden fire as that which looked over Miss Muir's shoulder when she answered her young host's speech.

Edward thought within himself, Poor little woman! She has had a hard life. We will try and make it easier while she is here; and began his charitable work by suggesting that she might be tired. She acknowledged she was, and Bella led her away to a bright, cozy room, where with a pretty little speech and a good-night kiss she left her.

When alone Miss Muir's conduct was decidedly peculiar. Her first act was to clench her hands and mutter between her teeth, with passionate force, "I'll not fail again if there is power in a woman's wit and will!" She stood a moment motionless, with an expression of almost fierce disdain on her face, then shook her clenched hand as if menacing some unseen enemy. Next she laughed, and shrugged her shoulders with a true French shrug, saying low to herself, "Yes, the last scene *shall* be better than the first. *Mon dieu,* how tired and hungry I am!"

Kneeling before the one small trunk which held her worldly posses-sions, she opened it, drew out a flask, and mixed a glass of some ardent cordial, which she seemed to enjoy extremely as she sat on the carpet, musing, while her quick eyes examined every corner of the room.

"Not bad! It will be a good field for me to work in, and the harder the task the better I shall like it. *Merci,* old friend. You put heart and courage into me when nothing else will. Come, the curtain is down, so I may be myself for a few hours, if actresses ever are themselves."

Still sitting on the floor she unbound and removed the long abundant braids from her head, wiped the pink from her face, took out several pearly teeth, and slipping off her dress appeared herself indeed, a haggard, worn, and moody woman of thirty at least. The metamorphosis was wonderful, but the disguise was more in the expression she assumed than in any art of costume or false adornment. Now she was alone, and her mobile features settled into their natural expression, weary, hard, bitter. She had been lovely once, happy, innocent, and tender; but nothing of all this remained to the gloomy woman who leaned there brooding over some wrong, or loss, or disappointment which had darkened all her life. For an hour she sat so, sometimes playing absently with the scanty locks that hung about her face, sometimes lifting the glass to her lips as if the fiery draught warmed her cold blood; and once she half uncovered her breast to eye with a terrible glance the scar of a newly healed wound. At last she rose and crept to bed, like one worn out with weariness and mental pain.

A GOOD BEGINNING

ONLY the housemaids were astir when Miss Muir left her room next morning and quietly found her way into the garden. As she walked, apparently intent upon the flowers, her quick eye scrutinized the fine old house and its picturesque surroundings.

"Not bad," she said to herself, adding, as she passed into the adjoining park, "but the other may be better, and I will have the best."

Walking rapidly, she came out at length upon the wide green lawn which lay before the ancient hall where Sir John Coventry lived in solitary splendor. A stately old place, rich in oaks, well-kept shrubberies, gay gardens, sunny terraces, carved gables, spacious rooms, liveried servants, and every luxury befitting the ancestral home of a rich and honorable race. Miss Muir's eyes brightened as she looked, her step grew firmer, her carriage prouder, and a smile broke over her face; the smile of one well pleased at the prospect of the success of some cherished hope. Suddenly her whole air changed, she pushed back her hat, clasped her hands loosely before her, and seemed absorbed in girlish admiration of the fair scene that could not fail to charm any beauty-loving eye. The cause of this rapid change soon appeared. A hale, handsome man, between fifty and sixty, came through the little gate leading to the park, and, seeing the young stranger, paused to examine her. He had only time for a glance, however; she seemed conscious of his presence in a moment, turned with a startled look, uttered an exclamation of surprise, and looked as if hesitating whether to speak or run away. Gallant Sir John took off his hat and said, with an old-fashioned courtesy which became him well, "I beg your pardon for disturbing you, young lady. Allow me to atone for it by inviting you to walk where you will, and gather what flowers you like. I see you love them, so pray make free with those about you."

With a charming air of maidenly timidity and artlessness, Miss Muir replied, "Oh, thank you, sir! But it is I who should ask pardon for trespassing. I never should have dared if I had not known that Sir John was absent. I always wanted to see this fine old place, and ran over the first thing, to satisfy myself."

"And *are* you satisfied?" he asked, with a smile.

"More than satisfied—I'm charmed; for it is the most beautiful spot I ever saw, and I've seen many famous seats, both at home and abroad," she answered enthusiastically.

"The Hall is much flattered, and so would its master be if he heard you," began the gentleman, with an odd expression.

"I should not praise it to him—at least, not as freely as I have to you, sir," said the girl, with eyes still turned away.

"Why not?" asked her companion, looking much amused.

"I should be afraid. Not that I dread Sir John; but I've heard so many beautiful and noble things about him, and respect him so highly, that I should not dare to say much, lest he should see how I admire and—"

"And what, young lady? Finish, if you please."

"I was going to say, love him. I will say it, for he is an old man, and one cannot help loving virtue and bravery."

Miss Muir looked very earnest and pretty as she spoke, standing there with the sunshine glinting on her yellow hair, delicate face, and downcast eyes. Sir John was not a vain man, but he found it pleasant to hear himself commended by this unknown girl, and felt redoubled curiosity to learn who she was. Too well bred to ask, or to abash her by avowing what she seemed unconscious of, he left both discoveries to chance; and when she turned, as if to retrace her steps, he offered her the handful of hothouse flowers which he held, saying, with a gallant bow, "In Sir John's name let me give you my little nosegay, with thanks for your good opinion, which, I assure you, is not entirely deserved, for I know him well."

Miss Muir looked up quickly, eyed him an instant, then dropped her eyes, and, coloring deeply, stammered out, "I did not know—I beg your pardon—you are too kind, Sir John."

He laughed like a boy, asking, mischievously, "Why call me Sir John? How do you know that I am not the gardener or the butler?"

"I did not see your face before, and no one but yourself would say that any praise was undeserved," murmured Miss Muir, still overcome with girlish confusion.

"Well, well, we will let that pass, and the next time you come we will be properly introduced. Bella always brings her friends to the Hall, for I am fond of young people."

"I am not a friend. I am only Miss Coventry's governess." And Miss Muir dropped a meek curtsy. A slight change passed over Sir John's manner. Few would have perceived it, but Miss Muir felt it at once, and bit her lips with an angry feeling at her heart. With a curious air of pride, mingled with respect, she accepted the still offered bouquet, returned Sir John's parting bow, and tripped away, leaving the old gentleman to wonder where Mrs. Coventry found such a piquant little governess.

"That is done, and very well for a beginning," she said to herself as she approached the house.

In a green paddock close by fed a fine horse, who lifted up his head and eyed her inquiringly, like one who expected a greeting. Following a sudden impulse, she entered the paddock and, pulling a handful of clover, invited the creature to come and eat. This was evidently a new proceeding on the part of a lady, and the horse careered about as if bent on frightening the newcomer away.

"I see," she said aloud, laughing to herself. "I am not your master, and you rebel. Nevertheless, I'll conquer you, my fine brute."

Seating herself in the grass, she began to pull daisies, singing idly the while, as if unconscious of the spirited prancings of the horse. Presently he drew nearer, sniffing curiously and eyeing her with surprise. She took no notice, but plaited the daisies and sang on as if he was not there. This seemed to pique the petted creature, for, slowly approaching, he came at length so close that he could smell her little foot and nibble at her dress. Then she offered the clover, uttering caressing words and making soothing sounds, till by degrees and with much coquetting, the horse permitted her to stroke his glossy neck and smooth his mane.

It was a pretty sight—the slender figure in the grass, the high-spirited horse bending his proud head to her hand. Edward Coventry, who had watched the scene, found it impossible to restrain himself any longer and, leaping the wall, came to join the group, saying, with mingled admiration and wonder in countenance and voice, "Good morning, Miss Muir. If I had not seen your skill and courage proved before my eyes, I should be alarmed for your safety. Hector is a wild, wayward beast, and has damaged more than one groom who tried to conquer him."

"Good morning, Mr. Coventry. Don't tell tales of this noble creature, who has not deceived my faith in him. Your grooms did not know how to win his heart, and so subdue his spirit without breaking it."

Miss Muir rose as she spoke, and stood with her hand on Hector's neck while he ate the grass which she had gathered in the skirt of her dress.

"You have the secret, and Hector is your subject now, though heretofore he has rejected all friends but his master. Will you give him his morning feast? I always bring him bread and play with him before breakfast."

"Then you are not jealous?" And she looked up at him with eyes so bright and beautiful in expression that the young man wondered he had not observed them before.

"Not I. Pet him as much as you will; it will do him good. He is a solitary fellow, for he scorns his own kind and lives alone, like his master," he added, half to himself.

"Alone, with such a happy home, Mr. Coventry?" And a softly compassionate glance stole from the bright eyes.

"That was an ungrateful speech, and I retract it for Bella's sake. Younger sons have no position but such as they can make for themselves, you know, and I've had no chance yet."

"Younger sons! I thought—I beg pardon." And Miss Muir paused, as if remembering that she had no right to question.

Edward smiled and answered frankly, "Nay, don't mind me. You thought I was the heir, perhaps. Whom did you take my brother for last night?"

"For some guest who admired Miss Beaufort. I did not hear his name, nor observe him enough to discover who he was. I saw only your kind mother, your charming little sister, and—"

She stopped there, with a half-shy, half-grateful look at the young man which finished the sentence better than any words. He was still a boy, in spite of his one-and-twenty years, and a little color came into his brown cheek as the eloquent eyes met his and fell before them.

"Yes, Bella is a capital girl, and one can't help loving her. I know you'll get her on, for, really, she is the most delightful little dunce. My mother's ill health and Bella's devotion to her have prevented our attending to her education before. Next winter, when we go to town, she is to come out, and must be prepared for that great event, you know," he said, choosing a safe subject.

"I shall do my best. And that reminds me that I should report myself to her, instead of enjoying myself here. When one has been ill and shut up a long time, the country is so lovely one is apt to forget duty for pleasure. Please remind me if I am negligent, Mr. Coventry."

"That name belongs to Gerald. I'm only Mr. Ned here," he said as they walked toward the house, while Hector followed to the wall and sent a sonorous farewell after them.

Bella came running to meet them, and greeted Miss Muir as if she had made up her mind to like her heartily. "What a lovely bouquet you have got! I never can arrange flowers prettily, which vexes me, for Mamma is so fond of them and cannot go out herself. You have charming taste," she said, examining the graceful posy which Miss Muir had much improved by adding feathery grasses, delicate ferns, and fragrant wild flowers to Sir John's exotics.

Putting them into Bella's hand, she said, in a winning way, "Take them to your mother, then, and ask her if I may have the pleasure of making her a daily nosegay; for I should find real delight in doing it, if it would please her."

"How kind you are! Of course it would please her. I'll take them to her while the dew is still on them." And away flew Bella, eager to give both the flowers and the pretty message to the poor invalid.

Edward stopped to speak to the gardener, and Miss Muir went up the steps alone. The long hall was lined with portraits, and pacing slowly down it she examined them with interest. One caught her eye, and, pausing before it, she scrutinized it carefully. A young, beautiful, but very haughty female face. Miss Muir suspected at once who it was, and gave a decided nod, as if she saw and caught at some unexpected chance. A soft rustle behind her made her look around, and, seeing Lucia, she bowed, half turned, as if for another glance at the picture, and said, as if involuntarily, "How beautiful it is! May I ask if it is an ancestor, Miss Beaufort?"

"It is the likeness of my mother" was the reply, given with a softened voice and eyes that looked up tenderly.

"Ah, I might have known, from the resemblance, but I scarcely saw you last night. Excuse my freedom, but Lady Sydney treated me as a friend, and I forget my position. Allow me."

As she spoke, Miss Muir stooped to return the handkerchief which had fallen from Lucia's hand, and did so with a humble mien which touched the other's heart; for, though a proud, it was also a very generous one.

"Thank you. Are you better, this morning?" she said, graciously. And having received an affirmative reply, she added, as she walked on, "I will show you to the breakfast room, as Bella is not here. It is a very informal meal with us, for my aunt is never down and my cousins are very irregular in their hours. You can always have yours when you like, without waiting for us, if you are an early riser."

Bella and Edward appeared before the others were seated, and Miss Muir quietly ate her breakfast, feeling well satisfied with her hour's work. Ned recounted her exploit with Hector, Bella delivered her mother's thanks for the flowers, and Lucia more than once recalled, with pardonable vanity, that the governess had compared her to her lovely mother, expressing by a look as much admiration for the living likeness as for the painted one. All kindly did their best to make the pale girl feel at home, and their cordial manner seemed to warm and draw her out; for soon she put off her sad, meek air and entertained them with gay anecdotes of her life in Paris, her travels in Russia when governess in Prince Jermadoff's family, and all manner of witty stories that kept them interested and merry long after the meal was over. In the middle of an absorbing adventure, Coventry came in, nodded lazily, lifted his brows, as if surprised at seeing the governess there, and began his breakfast as if the ennui of another day had already taken possession of him. Miss Muir stopped short, and no entreaties could induce her to go on.

"Another time I will finish it, if you like. Now Miss Bella and I should be at our books." And she left the room, followed by her pupil, taking no notice of the young master of the house, beyond a graceful bow in answer to his careless nod.

"Merciful creature! she goes when I come, and does not make life unendurable by moping about before my eyes. Does she belong to the moral, the melancholy, the romantic, or the dashing class, Ned?" said Gerald, lounging over his coffee as he did over everything he attempted.

"To none of them; she is a capital little woman. I wish you had seen her tame Hector this morning." And Edward repeated his story.

"Not a bad move on her part," said Coventry in reply. "She must be an observing as well as an energetic young person, to discover your chief weakness and attack it so soon. First tame the horse, and then the master. It will be amusing to watch the game, only I shall be under the painful necessity of checkmating you both, if it gets serious."

"You needn't exert yourself, old fellow, on my account. If I was not above thinking ill of an inoffensive girl, I should say you were the prize best worth winning, and advise you to take care of your own heart, if you've got one, which I rather doubt."

"I often doubt it, myself; but I fancy the little Scotchwoman will not be able to satisfy either of us upon that point. How does your highness like her?" asked Coventry of his cousin, who sat near him.

"Better than I thought I should. She is well bred, unassuming, and very entertaining when she likes. She has told us some of the wittiest stories I've heard for a long time. Didn't our laughter wake you?" replied Lucia.

"Yes. Now atone for it by amusing me with a repetition of these witty tales."

"That is impossible; her accent and manner are half the charm," said Ned. "I wish you had kept away ten minutes longer, for your appearance spoilt the best story of all."

"Why didn't she go on?" asked Coventry, with a ray of curiosity.

"You forgot that she overheard us last night, and must feel that you consider her a bore. She has pride, and no woman forgets speeches like those you made," answered Lucia.

"Or forgives them, either, I believe. Well, I must be resigned to languish under her displeasure then. On Sydney's account I take a slight interest in her; not that I expect to learn anything from her, for a woman with a mouth like that never confides or confesses anything. But I have a fancy to see what captivated him; for captivated he was, beyond a doubt, and by no lady whom he met in society. Did you ever hear anything of it, Ned?" asked Gerald.

"I'm not fond of scandal or gossip, and never listen to either." With which remark Edward left the room.

Lucia was called out by the housekeeper a moment after, and Coventry left to the society most wearisome to him, namely his own. As he entered, he had caught a part of the story which Miss Muir had been telling, and it had excited his curiosity so much that he found himself wondering what the end could be and wishing that he might hear it.

What the deuce did she run away for, when I came in? he thought. If she *is* amusing, she must make herself useful; for it's intensely dull, I own, here, in spite of Lucia. Hey, what's that?

It was a rich, sweet voice, singing a brilliant Italian air, and singing it with an expression that made the music doubly delicious. Stepping out of the French window, Coventry strolled along the sunny terrace, enjoying the song with the relish of a connoisseur. Others followed, and still he walked and listened, forgetful of weariness or time. As one exquisite air ended, he involuntarily applauded. Miss Muir's face appeared for an instant, then vanished, and no more music followed, though Coventry lingered, hoping to hear the voice again. For music was the one thing of which he never wearied, and neither Lucia nor Bella possessed skill enough to charm him. For an hour he loitered on the terrace or the lawn, basking in the sunshine, too indolent to seek occupation or society. At length Bella came out, hat in hand, and nearly stumbled over her brother, who lay on the grass.

"You lazy man, have you been dawdling here all this time?" she said, looking down at him.

"No, I've been very busy. Come and tell me how you've got on with the little dragon."

"Can't stop. She bade me take a run after my French, so that I might be ready for my drawing, and so I must."

"It's too warm to run. Sit down and amuse your deserted brother, who has had no society but bees and lizards for an hour."

He drew her down as he spoke, and Bella obeyed; for, in spite of his indolence, he was one to whom all submitted without dreaming of refusal.

"What have you been doing? Muddling your poor little brains with all manner of elegant rubbish?"

"No, I've been enjoying myself immensely. Jean is *so* interesting, so kind and clever. She didn't bore me with stupid grammar, but just talked to me in such pretty French that I got on capitally, and like it as I never expected to, after Lucia's dull way of teaching it."

"What did you talk about?"

"Oh, all manner of things. She asked questions, and I answered, and she corrected me."

"Questions about our affairs, I suppose?"

"Not one. She don't care two sous for us or our affairs. I thought she might like to know what sort of people we were, so I told her about Papa's sudden death, Uncle John, and you, and Ned; but in the midst of it she said, in her quiet way, 'You are getting too confidential, my dear. It is not best to talk too freely of one's affairs to strangers. Let us speak of something else.'"

"What were you talking of when she said that, Bell?"

"You."

"Ah, then no wonder she was bored."

"She was tired of my chatter, and didn't hear half I said; for she was busy sketching something for me to copy, and thinking of something more interesting than the Coventrys."

"How do you know?"

"By the expression of her face. Did you like her music, Gerald?"

"Yes. Was she angry when I clapped?"

"She looked surprised, then rather proud, and shut the piano at once, though I begged her to go on. Isn't Jean a pretty name?"

"Not bad; but why don't you call her Miss Muir?"

"She begged me not. She hates it, and loves to be called Jean, alone. I've imagined such a nice little romance about her, and someday I shall tell her, for I'm sure she has had a love trouble."

"Don't get such nonsense into your head, but follow Miss Muir's well-bred example and don't be curious about other people's affairs. Ask her to sing tonight; it amuses me."

"She won't come down, I think. We've planned to read and work in my boudoir, which is to be our study now. Mamma will stay in her room, so you and Lucia can have the drawing room all to yourselves."

"Thank you. What will Ned do?"

"He will amuse Mamma, he says. Dear old Ned! I wish you'd stir about and get him his commission. He is so impatient to be doing something and yet so proud he won't ask again, after you have neglected it so many times and refused Uncle's help."

"I'll attend to it very soon; don't worry me, child. He will do very well for a time, quietly here with us."

"You always say that, yet you know he chafes and is unhappy at being dependent on you. Mamma and I don't mind; but he is a man, and it frets him. He said he'd take matters into his own hands soon, and then you may be sorry you were so slow in helping him."

"Miss Muir is looking out of the window. You'd better go and take your run, else she will scold."

"Not she. I'm not a bit afraid of her, she's so gentle and sweet. I'm fond of her already. You'll get as brown as Ned, lying here in the sun. By the way, Miss Muir agrees with me in thinking him handsomer than you."

"I admire her taste and quite agree with her."

"She said he was manly, and that was more attractive than beauty in a man. She does express things so nicely. Now I'm off." And away danced Bella, humming the burden of Miss Muir's sweetest song.

" 'Energy is more attractive than beauty in a man.' She is right, but how the deuce *can* a man be energetic, with nothing to expend his energies upon?" mused Coventry, with his hat over his eyes.

A few moments later, the sweep of a dress caught his ear. Without stirring, a sidelong glance showed him Miss Muir coming across the terrace, as if to join Bella. Two stone steps led down to the lawn. He lay near them, and Miss Muir did not see him till close upon him. She started and slipped on the last step, recovered herself, and glided on, with a glance of unmistakable contempt as she passed the recumbent figure of the apparent sleeper. Several things in Bella's report had nettled him, but this look made him angry, though he would not own it, even to himself.

"Gerald, come here, quick!" presently called Bella, from the rustic seat where she stood beside her governess, who sat with her hand over her face as if in pain.

Gathering himself up, Coventry slowly obeyed, but involuntarily quickened his pace as he heard Miss Muir say, "Don't call him; *he* can do nothing'" for the emphasis on the word "he" was very significant.

"What is it, Bella?" he asked, looking rather wider awake than usual.

"You startled Miss Muir and made her turn her ankle. Now help her to the house, for she is in great pain; and don't lie there anymore to frighten people like a snake in the grass," said his sister petulantly.

"I beg your pardon. Will you allow me?" And Coventry offered his arm.

Miss Muir looked up with the expression which annoyed him and answered coldly, "Thank you, Miss Bella will do as well."

"Permit me to doubt that." And with a gesture too decided to be resisted, Coventry drew her arm through his and led her into the house. She submitted quietly, said the pain would soon be over, and when settled on the couch in Bella's room dismissed him with the briefest thanks. Considering the unwonted exertion he had made, he thought she might have been a little more grateful, and went away to Lucia, who always brightened when he came.

No more was seen of Miss Muir till teatime; for now, while the family were in retirement, they dined early and saw no company. The governess had excused herself at dinner, but came down in the evening a little paler than usual and with a slight limp in her gait. Sir John was there, talking with his nephew, and they merely acknowledged her presence by the sort of bow which gentlemen bestow on governesses. As she slowly made her way to her place behind the urn, Coventry said to his brother, "Take her a footstool, and ask her how she is, Ned." Then, as if necessary to account for his politeness to his uncle, he explained how he was the cause of the accident.

"Yes, yes. I understand. Rather a nice little person, I fancy. Not exactly a beauty, but accomplished and well bred, which is better for one of her class."

"Some tea, Sir John?" said a soft voice at his elbow, and there was Miss Muir, offering cups to the gentlemen.

"Thank you, thank you," said Sir John, sincerely hoping she had overheard him.

As Coventry took his, he said graciously, "You are very forgiving,

Miss Muir, to wait upon me, after I have caused you so much pain."

"It is my duty, sir" was her reply, in a tone which plainly said, "but not my pleasure." And she returned to her place, to smile, and chat, and be charming, with Bella and her brother.

Lucia, hovering near her uncle and Gerald, kept them to herself, but was disturbed to find that their eyes often wandered to the cheerful group about the table, and that their attention seemed distracted by the frequent bursts of laughter and fragments of animated conversation which reached them. In the midst of an account of a tragic affair which she endeavored to make as interesting and pathetic as possible, Sir John burst into a hearty laugh, which betrayed that he had been listening to a livelier story than her own. Much annoyed, she said hastily, "I knew it would be so! Bella has no idea of the proper manner in which to treat a governess. She and Ned will forget the difference of rank and spoil that person for her work. She is inclined to be presumptuous already, and if my aunt won't trouble herself to give Miss Muir a hint in time, I shall."

"Wait till she has finished that story, I beg of you," said Coventry, for Sir John was already off.

"If you find that nonsense so entertaining, why don't you follow Uncle's example? I don't need you."

"Thank you. I will." And Lucia was deserted.

But Miss Muir had ended and, beckoning to Bella, left the room, as if quite unconscious of the honor conferred upon her or the dullness she left behind her. Ned went up to his mother, Gerald returned to make his peace with Lucia, and, bidding them good-night, Sir John turned homeward. Strolling along the terrace, he came to the lighted window of Bella's study, and wishing to say a word to her, he half pushed aside the curtain and looked in. A pleasant little scene. Bella working busily, and near her in a low chair, with the light falling on her fair hair and delicate profile, sat Miss Muir, reading aloud. "Novels!" thought Sir John, and smiled at them for a pair of romantic girls. But pausing to listen a moment before he spoke, he found it was no novel, but history, read with a fluency which made every fact interesting, every sketch of character memorable, by the dramatic effect given to it. Sir John was fond of history, and failing eyesight often curtailed his favorite amusement. He had tried readers, but none suited him, and he had given up the plan. Now as he listened, he thought how pleasantly the smoothly flowing voice would wile away his evenings, and he envied Bella her new acquisition.

A bell rang, and Bella sprang up, saying, "Wait for me a minute. I must run to Mamma, and then we will go on with this charming prince." Away she went, and Sir John was about to retire as quietly as he came, when Miss Muir's peculiar behavior arrested him for an instant. Dropping the book, she threw her arms across the table, laid her head down upon them, and broke into a passion of tears, like one who could bear restraint no longer. Shocked and amazed, Sir John stole away; but all that night the kindhearted gentleman puzzled his brains with conjectures about his niece's interesting young governess, quite unconscious that she intended he should do so.

III

PASSION AND PIQUE

🦋🦋🦋🦋🦋🦋

FOR several weeks the most monotonous tranquillity seemed to reign at Coventry House, and yet, unseen, unsuspected, a storm was gathering. The arrival of Miss Muir seemed to produce a change in everyone, though no one could have explained how or why. Nothing could be more unobtrusive and retiring than her manners. She was devoted to Bella, who soon adored her, and was only happy when in her society. She ministered in many ways to Mrs. Coventry's comfort, and that lady declared there never was such a nurse. She amused, interested and won Edward with her wit and womanly sympathy. She made Lucia respect and envy her for her accomplishments, and piqued indolent Gerald by her persistent avoidance of him, while Sir John was charmed with her respectful deference and the graceful little attentions she paid him in a frank and artless way, very winning to the lonely old man. The very servants liked her; and instead of being, what most governesses are, a forlorn creature hovering between superiors and inferiors, Jean Muir was the life of the house, and the friend of all but two.

Lucia disliked her, and Coventry distrusted her; neither could exactly say why, and neither owned the feeling, even to themselves. Both watched her covertly yet found no shortcoming anywhere. Meek, modest, faithful, and invariably sweet-tempered—they could complain of nothing and wondered at their own doubts, though they could not banish them.

It soon came to pass that the family was divided, or rather that two members were left very much to themselves. Pleading timidity, Jean Muir kept much in Bella's study and soon made it such a pleasant little nook that Ned and his mother, and often Sir John, came in to enjoy the music, reading, or cheerful chat which made the evenings so gay. Lucia at first was only too glad to have her cousin to herself, and he too lazy to care what went on about him. But presently he wearied of her society, for she was not a brilliant girl, and possessed few of those winning arts which charm a man and steal into his heart. Rumors of the merrymakings that went on reached him and made him curious to share them; echoes of fine music went sounding through the house, as he lounged about the empty drawing room; and peals of laughter reached him while listening to Lucia's grave discourse.

She soon discovered that her society had lost its charm, and the more eagerly she tried to please him, the more signally she failed. Before long Coventry fell into a habit of strolling out upon the terrace of an evening, and amusing himself by passing and repassing the window of Bella's room, catching glimpses of what was going on and reporting the result of his observations to Lucia, who was too proud to ask admission to the happy circle or to seem to desire it.

"I shall go to London tomorrow, Lucia," Gerald said one evening, as he came back from what he called "a survey," looking very much annoyed.

"To London?" exclaimed his cousin, surprised.

"Yes, I must bestir myself and get Ned his commission, or it will be all over with him."

"How do you mean?"

"He is falling in love as fast as it is possible for a boy to do it. That girl has bewitched him, and he will make a fool of himself very soon, unless I put a stop to it."

"I was afraid she would attempt a flirtation. These persons always do, they are such a mischief-making race."

"Ah, but there you are wrong, as far as little Muir is concerned. She does not flirt, and Ned has too much sense and spirit to be caught by a silly coquette. She treats him like an elder sister, and mingles the most attractive friendliness with a quiet dignity that captivates the boy. I've been watching them, and there he is, devouring her with his eyes, while she reads a fascinating novel in the most fascinating style. Bella and Mamma are absorbed in the tale, and see nothing; but Ned makes himself the hero, Miss Muir the heroine, and lives the love scene with all the ardor of a man whose heart has just waked up. Poor lad! Poor lad!"

Lucia looked at her cousin, amazed by the energy with which he spoke, the anxiety in his usually listless face. The change became him, for it showed what he might be, making one regret still more what he was. Before she could speak, he was gone again, to return presently, laughing, yet looking a little angry.

"What now?" she asked.

"'Listeners never hear any good of themselves' is the truest of proverbs. I stopped a moment to look at Ned, and heard the following flattering remarks. Mamma is gone, and Ned was asking little Muir to sing that delicious barcarole she gave us the other evening.

"'Not now, not here,' she said.

"'Why not? You sang it in the drawing room readily enough,' said Ned, imploringly.

"'That is a very different thing,' and she looked at him with a little shake of the head, for he was folding his hands and doing the passionate pathetic.

"'Come and sing it there then,' said innocent Bella. 'Gerald likes your voice so much, and complains that you will never sing to him.'

"'He never asks me,' said Muir, with an odd smile.

"'He is too lazy, but he wants to hear you.'

"'When he asks me, I will sing—if I feel like it.' And she shrugged her shoulders with a provoking gesture of indifference.

"'But it amuses him, and he gets so bored down here,' began stupid little Bella. 'Don't be shy or proud, Jean, but come and entertain the poor old fellow.'

"'No, thank you. I engaged to teach Miss Coventry, not to amuse Mr. Coventry' was all the answer she got.

"'You amuse Ned, why not Gerald? Are you afraid of him?' asked Bella.

"Miss Muir laughed, such a scornful laugh, and said, in that peculiar tone of hers, 'I cannot fancy anyone being *afraid* of your elder brother.'

"'I am, very often, and so would you be, if you ever saw him angry.' And Bella looked as if I'd beaten her.

"'Does he ever wake up enough to be angry?' asked that girl, with an air of surprise. Here Ned broke into a fit of laughter, and they are at it now, I fancy, by the sound."

"Their foolish gossip is not worth getting excited about, but I certainly would send Ned away. It's no use trying to get rid of 'that girl,' as you say, for my aunt is as deluded about her as Ned and Bella, and she really does get the child along splendidly. Dispatch Ned, and then she can do no harm," said Lucia, watching Coventry's altered face as he stood in the moonlight, just outside the window where she sat.

"Have you no fears for me?" he asked smiling, as if ashamed of his momentary petulance.

"No, have you for yourself?" And a shade of anxiety passed over her face.

"I defy the Scotch witch to enchant me, except with her music," he added, moving down the terrace again, for Jean was singing like a nightingale.

As the song ended, he put aside the curtain, and said, abruptly, "Has anyone any commands for London? I am going there tomorrow."

"A pleasant trip to you," said Ned carelessly, though usually his brother's movements interested him extremely.

"I want quantities of things, but I must ask Mamma first." And Bella began to make a list.

"May I trouble you with a letter, Mr. Coventry?"

Jean Muir turned around on the music stool and looked at him with the cold keen glance which always puzzled him.

He bowed, saying, as if to them all, "I shall be off by the early train, so you must give me your orders tonight."

"Then come away, Ned, and leave Jean to write her letter."

And Bella took her reluctant brother from the room.

"I will give you the letter in the morning," said Miss Muir, with a curious quiver in her voice, and the look of one who forcibly suppressed some strong emotion.

"As you please." And Coventry went back to Lucia, wondering who Miss Muir was going to write to. He said nothing to his brother of the purpose which took him to town, lest a word should produce the catastrophe which he hoped to prevent; and Ned, who now lived in a sort of dream, seemed to forget Gerald's existence altogether.

With unwonted energy Coventry was astir seven next morning. Lucia gave him his breakfast, and as he left the room to order the carriage, Miss Muir came gliding downstairs, very pale and heavy-eyed (with a sleepless, tearful night, he thought) and, putting a delicate little letter into his hand, said hurriedly, "Please leave this at Lady Sydney's, and if you see her, say 'I have remembered.'"

Her peculiar manner and peculiar message struck him. His eye involuntarily glanced at the address of the letter and read young Sydney's name. Then, conscious of his mistake, he thrust it into his pocket with a hasty "Good morning," and left Miss Muir standing with one hand pressed on her heart, the other half extended as if to recall the letter.

All the way to London, Coventry found it impossible to forget the almost tragical expression of the girl's face, and it haunted him through the bustle of two busy days. Ned's affair was put in the way of being speedily accomplished, Bella's commissions were executed, his mother's pet delicacies provided for her, and a gift for Lucia, whom the family had given him for his future mate, as he was too lazy to choose for himself.

Jean Muir's letter he had not delivered, for Lady Sydney was in the country and her townhouse closed. Curious to see how she would receive his tidings, he went quietly in on his arrival at home. Everyone had dispersed to dress for dinner except Miss Muir, who was in the garden, the servant said.

"Very well; I have a message for her"; and, turning, the "young master," as they called him, went to seek her. In a remote corner he saw her sitting alone, buried in thought. As his step roused her, a look of surprise, followed by one of satisfaction, passed over her face, and, rising, she beckoned to him with an almost eager gesture. Much amazed, he went to her and offered the letter, saying kindly, "I regret that I could not deliver it. Lady Sydney is in the country, and I did not like to post it without your leave. Did I do right?"

"Quite right, thank you very much—it is better so." And with an air of relief, she tore the letter to atoms, and scattered them to the wind.

More amazed than ever, the young man was about to leave her when she said, with a mixture of entreaty and command, "Please stay a moment. I want to speak to you."

He paused, eyeing her with visible surprise, for a sudden color dyed her cheeks, and her lips trembled. Only for a moment, then she was quite self-possessed again. Motioning him to the seat she had left, she remained standing while she said, in a low, rapid tone full of pain and of decision:

"Mr. Coventry, as the head of the house I want to speak to you, rather than to your mother, of a most unhappy affair which has occurred during your absence. My month of probation ends today; your mother wishes me to remain; I, too, wish it sincerely, for I am happy here, but I ought not. Read this, and you will see why."

She put a hastily written note into his hand and watched him intently while he read it. She saw him flush with anger, bite his lips, and knit his brows, then assume his haughtiest look, as he lifted his eyes and said in his most sarcastic tone, "Very well for a beginning. The boy has eloquence. Pity that it should be wasted. May I ask if you have replied to this rhapsody?"

"I have."

"And what follows? He begs you 'to fly with him, to share his fortunes, and be the good angel of his life.' Of course you consent?"

There was no answer, for, standing erect before him, Miss Muir regarded him with an expression of proud patience, like one who expected reproaches, yet was too generous to resent them. Her manner had its effect. Dropping his bitter tone, Coventry asked briefly, "Why do you show me this? What can I do?"

"I show it that you may see how much in earnest 'the boy' is, and how open I desire to be. You can control, advise, and comfort your brother, and help me to see what is my duty."

"You love him?" demanded Coventry bluntly.

"No!" was the quick, decided answer.

"Then why make him love you?"

"I never tried to do it. Your sister will testify that I have endeavored to avoid him as I——" And he finished the sentence with an unconscious tone of pique, "As you have avoided me."

She bowed silently, and he went on:

"I will do you the justice to say that nothing can be more blameless than your conduct toward myself; but why allow Ned to haunt you evening after evening? What could you expect of a romantic boy who had nothing to do but lose his heart to the first attractive woman he met?"

A momentary glisten shone in Jean Muir's steel-blue eyes as the last words left the young man's lips; but it was gone instantly, and her voice was full of reproach, as she said, steadily, impulsively, "If the 'romantic boy' had been allowed to lead the life of a man, as he longed to do, he would have had no time to lose his heart to the first sorrowful girl whom he pitied. Mr. Coventry, the fault is yours. Do not blame your brother, but generously own your mistake and retrieve it in the speediest, kindest manner."

For an instant Gerald sat dumb. Never since his father died had anyone reproved him; seldom in his life had he been blamed. It was a new experience, and the very novelty added to the effect. He saw his fault, regretted it, and admired the brave sincerity of the girl in telling him of it. But he did not know how to deal with the case, and was forced to confess not only past negligence but present incapacity. He was as honorable as he was proud, and with an effort he said frankly, "You are right, Miss Muir. I *am* to blame, yet as soon as I saw the danger, I tried to avert it. My visit to town was on Ned's account; he will have his commission very soon, and then he will be sent out of harm's way. Can I do more?"

"No, it is too late to send him away with a free and happy heart. He must bear his pain as he can, and it may help to make a man of him," she said sadly.

"He'll soon forget," began Coventry, who found the thought of gay Ned suffering an uncomfortable one.

"Yes, thank heaven, that is possible, for men."

Miss Muir pressed her hands together, with a dark expression on her half-averted face. Something in her tone, her manner, touched Coventry; he fancied that some old wound bled, some bitter memory awoke at the approach of a new lover. He was young, heart-whole, and romantic, under all his cool nonchalance of manner. This girl, who he fancied loved his friend and who was beloved by his brother, became an object of interest to him. He pitied her, desired to help her, and regretted his past distrust, as a chivalrous man always regrets injustice to a woman. She was happy here, poor, homeless soul, and she should stay. Bella loved her, his mother took comfort in her, and when Ned was gone, no one's peace would be endangered by her winning ways, her rich accomplishments. These thoughts swept through his mind during a brief pause, and when he spoke, it was to say gently:

"Miss Muir, I thank you for the frankness which must have been painful to you, and I will do my best to be worthy of the confidence which you repose in me. You were both discreet and kind to speak only to me. This thing would have troubled my mother extremely, and have done no good. I shall see Ned, and try and repair my long neglect as promptly as possible. I know you will help me, and in return let me beg of you to remain, for he will soon be gone."

She looked at him with eyes full of tears, and there was no coolness in the voice that answered softly, "You are too kind, but I had better go; it is not wise to stay."

"Why not?"

She colored beautifully, hesitated, then spoke out in the clear, steady voice which was her greatest charm, "If I had known there were sons in this family, I never should have come. Lady Sydney spoke only of your sister, and when I found two gentlemen, I was troubled, because—I am so unfortunate—or rather, people are so kind as to like me more than I deserve. I thought I could stay a month, at least, as your brother spoke of going away, and you were already affianced, but—"

"I am not affianced."

Why he said that, Coventry could not tell, but the words passed his lips hastily and could not be recalled. Jean Muir took the announcement oddly enough. She shrugged her shoulders with an air of extreme annoyance, and said almost rudely, "Then you should be; you will be soon. But that is nothing to me. Miss Beaufort wishes me gone, and I am too proud to remain and become the cause of disunion in a happy family. No, I will go, and go at once."

She turned away impetuously, but Edward's arm detained her, and Edward's voice demanded, tenderly, "Where will you go, my Jean?"

The tender touch and name seemed to rob her of her courage and calmness, for, leaning on her lover, she hid her face and sobbed audibly.

"Now don't make a scene, for heaven's sake," began Coventry impatiently, as his brother eyed him fiercely, divining at once what had passed, for his letter was still in Gerald's hand and Jean's last words had reached her lover's ear.

"Who gave you the right to read that, and to interfere in my affairs?" demanded Edward hotly.

"Miss Muir" was the reply, as Coventry threw away the paper.

"And you add to the insult by ordering her out of the house," cried Ned with increasing wrath.

"On the contrary, I beg her to remain."

"The deuce you do! And why?"

"Because she is useful and happy here, and I am unwilling that your folly should rob her of a home which she likes."

"You are very thoughtful and devoted all at once, but I beg you will not trouble yourself. Jean's happiness and home will be my care now."

"My dear boy, do be reasonable. The thing is impossible. Miss Muir sees it herself; she came to tell me, to ask how best to arrange matters without troubling my mother. I've been to town to attend to your affairs, and you may be off now very soon."

"I have no desire to go. Last month it was the wish of my heart. Now I'll accept nothing from you." And Edward turned moodily away from his brother.

"What folly! Ned, you *must* leave home. It is all arranged and cannot be given up now. A change is what you need, and it will make a man of you. We shall miss you, of course, but you will be where you'll see something of life, and that is better for you than getting into mischief here."

"Are you going away, Jean?" asked Edward, ignoring his brother entirely and bending over the girl, who still hid her face and wept. She did not speak, and Gerald answered for her.

"No, why should she if you are gone?"

"Do you mean to stay?" asked the lover eagerly of Jean.

"I wish to remain, but—" She paused and looked up. Her eyes went from one face to the other, and she added decidedly, "Yes, I must go, it is not wise to stay even when you are gone."

Neither of the young men could have explained why that hurried glance affected them as it did, but each felt conscious of a willful desire to oppose the other. Edward suddenly felt that his brother loved Miss Muir, and was bent on removing her from his way. Gerald had a vague idea that Miss Muir feared to remain on his account, and he longed to show her that he was quite safe. Each felt angry, and each showed it in a different way, one being violent, the other satirical.

"You are right, Jean, this is not the place for you; and you must let me see you in a safer home before I go," said Ned, significantly.

"It strikes me that this will be a particularly safe home when your dangerous self is removed," began Coventry, with an aggravating smile of calm superiority.

"And *I* think that I leave a more dangerous person than myself behind me, as poor Lucia can testify."

"Be careful what you say, Ned, or I shall be forced to remind you that I am master here. Leave Lucia's name out of this disagreeable affair, if you please."

"You *are* master here, but not of me, or my actions, and you have no right to expect obedience or respect, for you inspire neither. Jean, I asked you to go with me secretly; now I ask you openly to share my fortune. In my brother's presence I ask, and *will* have an answer."

He caught her hand impetuously, with a defiant look at Coventry, who still smiled, as if at boy's play, though his eyes were kindling and his face changing with the still, white wrath which is more terrible than any sudden outburst. Miss Muir looked frightened; she shrank away from her passionate young lover, cast an appealing glance at Gerald, and seemed as if she longed to claim his protection yet dared not.

"Speak!" cried Edward, desperately. "Don't look to him, tell me truly, with your own lips, do you, can you love me, Jean?"

"I have told you once. Why pain me by forcing another hard reply," she said pitifully, still shrinking from his grasp and seeming to appeal to his brother.

"You wrote a few lines, but I'll not be satisfied with that. You shall answer; I've seen love in your eyes, heard it in your voice, and I know it is hidden in your heart. You fear to own it; do not hesitate, no one can part us—speak, Jean, and satisfy me."

Drawing her hand decidedly away, she went a step nearer Coventry, and answered, slowly, distinctly, though her lips trembled, and she evidently dreaded the effect of her words, "I will speak, and speak truly. You have seen love in my face; it is in my heart, and I do not hesitate to own it, cruel as it is to force the truth from me, but this love is not for you. Are you satisfied?"

He looked at her with a despairing glance and stretched his hand toward her beseechingly. She seemed to fear a blow, for suddenly she clung to Gerald with a faint cry. The act, the look of fear, the protecting gesture Coventry involuntarily made were too much for Edward, already excited by conflicting passions. In a paroxysm of blind wrath, he caught up a large pruning knife left there by the gardener, and would have dealt his brother a fatal blow had he not warded it off with his arm. The stroke fell, and another might have followed had not Miss Muir with unexpected courage and strength wrested the knife from Edward and flung it into the little pond near by. Coventry dropped down upon the seat, for the blood poured from a deep wound in his arm, showing by its rapid flow that an artery had been severed. Edward stood aghast, for with the blow his fury passed, leaving him overwhelmed with remorse and shame.

Gerald looked up at him, smiled faintly, and said, with no sign of reproach or anger, "Never mind, Ned. Forgive and forget. Lend me a hand to the house, and don't disturb anyone. It's not much, I dare say." But his lips whitened as he spoke, and his strength failed him. Edward sprang to support him, and Miss Muir, forgetting her terrors, proved herself a girl of uncommon skill and courage.

"Quick! Lay him down. Give me your handkerchief, and bring some water," she said, in a tone of quiet command. Poor Ned obeyed and watched her with breathless suspense while she tied the handkerchief tightly around the arm, thrust the handle of his riding whip underneath, and pressed it firmly above the severed artery to stop the dangerous flow of blood.

"Dr. Scott is with your mother, I think. Go and bring him here" was the next order; and Edward darted away, thankful to do anything to ease the terror which possessed him. He was gone some minutes, and while they waited Coventry watched the girl as she knelt beside him, bathing his face with one hand while with the other she held the bandage firmly in its place. She was pale, but quite steady and self-possessed, and her eyes shone with a strange brilliancy as she looked down at him. Once, meeting his look of grateful wonder, she smiled a reassuring smile that made her lovely, and said, in a soft, sweet tone never used to him before, "Be quiet. There is no danger. I will stay by you till help comes."

Help did come speedily, and the doctor's first words were "Who improvised that tourniquet?"

"She did," murmured Coventry.

"Then you may thank her for saving your life. By Jove! It was capitally done"; and the old doctor looked at the girl with as much admiration as curiosity in his face.

"Never mind that. See to the wound, please, while I run for bandages, and salts, and wine."

Miss Muir was gone as she spoke, so fleetly that it was in vain to call her back or catch her. During her brief absence, the story was told by repentant Ned and the wound examined.

"Fortunately I have my case of instruments with me," said the doctor, spreading on the bench a long array of tiny, glittering implements of torture. "Now, Mr. Ned, come here, and hold the arm in that way, while I tie the artery. Hey! That will never do. Don't tremble so, man, look away and hold it steadily."

"I can't!" And poor Ned turned faint and white, not at the sight but with the bitter thought that he had longed to kill his brother.

"I will hold it," and a slender white hand lifted the bare and bloody arm so firmly, steadily, that Coventry sighed a sigh of relief, and Dr. Scott fell to work with an emphatic nod of approval.

It was soon over, and while Edward ran in to bid the servants beware of alarming their mistress, Dr. Scott put up his instruments and Miss Muir used salts, water, and wine so skillfully that Gerald was able to walk to his room, leaning on the old man, while the girl supported the wounded arm, as no sling could be made on the spot. As he entered the chamber, Coventry turned, put out his left hand, and with much feeling in his fine eyes said simply, "Miss Muir, I thank you."

The color came up beautifully in her pale cheeks as she pressed the hand and without a word vanished from the room. Lucia and the housekeeper came bustling in, and there was no lack of attendance on the invalid. He soon wearied of it, and sent them all away but Ned, who remorsefully haunted the chamber, looking like a comely young Cain and feeling like an outcast.

"Come here, lad, and tell me all about it. I was wrong to be domineering. Forgive me, and believe that I care for your happiness more sincerely than for my own."

These frank and friendly words healed the breach between the two brothers and completely conquered Ned. Gladly did he relate his love passages, for no young lover ever tires of that amusement if he has a sympathizing auditor, and Gerald *was* sympathetic now. For an hour did he lie listening patiently to the history of the growth of his brother's passion. Emotion gave the narrator eloquence, and Jean Muir's character was painted in glowing colors. All her unsuspected kindness to those about her was dwelt upon; all her faithful care, her sisterly interest in Bella, her gentle attentions to their mother, her sweet forbearance with Lucia, who plainly showed her dislike, and most of all, her friendly counsel, sympathy, and regard for Ned himself.

"She would make a man of me. She puts strength and courage into me as no one else can. She is unlike any girl I ever saw; there's no sentimentality about her; she is wise, and kind, and sweet. She says what she means, looks you straight in the eye, and is as true as steel. I've tried her, I know her, and—ah, Gerald, I love her so!"

Here the poor lad leaned his face into his hands and sighed a sigh that made his brother's heart ache.

"Upon my soul, Ned, I feel for you; and if there was no obstacle on her part, I'd do my best for you. She loves Sydney, and so there is nothing for it but to bear your fate like a man."

"Are you sure about Sydney? May it not be some one else?" and Ned eyed his brother with a suspicious look.

Coventry told him all he knew and surmised concerning his friend, not forgetting the letter. Edward mused a moment, then seemed relieved, and said frankly, "I'm glad it's Sydney and not you. I can bear it better."

"Me!" ejaculated Gerald, with a laugh.

"Yes, you; I've been tormented lately with a fear that you cared for her, or rather, she for you."

"You jealous young fool! We never see or speak to one another scarcely, so how could we get up a tender interest?"

"What do you lounge about on that terrace for every evening? And why does she get fluttered when your shadow begins to come and go?" demanded Edward.

"I like the music and don't care for the society of the singer, that's why I walk there. The fluttering is all your imagination; Miss Muir isn't a woman to be fluttered by a man's shadow." And Coventry glanced at his useless arm.

"Thank you for that, and for not saying 'little Muir,' as you generally do. Perhaps it was my imagination. But she never makes fun of you now, and so I fancied she might have lost her heart to the 'young master.' Women often do, you know."

"She used to ridicule me, did she?" asked Coventry, taking no notice of the latter part of his brother's speech, which was quite true nevertheless.

"Not exactly, she was too well bred for that. But sometimes when Bella and I joked about you, she'd say something so odd or witty that it was irresistible. You're used to being laughed at, so you don't mind, I know, just among ourselves."

"Not I. Laugh away as much as you like," said Gerald. But he did mind, and wanted exceedingy to know what Miss Muir had said, yet was too proud to ask. He turned restlessly and uttered a sigh of pain.

"I'm talking too much; it's bad for you. Dr. Scott said you must be quiet. Now go to sleep, if you can."

Edward left the bedside but not the room, for he would let no one take his place. Coventry tried to sleep, found it impossible, and after a restless hour called his brother back.

"If the bandage was loosened a bit, it would ease my arm and then I could sleep. Can you do it, Ned?"

"I dare not touch it. The doctor gave orders to leave it till he came in the morning, and I shall only do harm if I try."

"But I tell you it's too tight. My arm is swelling and the pain is intense. It can't be right to leave it so. Dr. Scott dressed it in a hurry and did it too tight. Common sense will tell you that," said Coventry impatiently.

"I'll call Mrs. Morris; she will understand what's best to be done." And Edward moved toward the door, looking anxious.

"Not she, she'll only make a stir and torment me with her chatter. I'll bear it as long as I can, and perhaps Dr. Scott will come tonight. He said he would if possible. Go to your dinner, Ned. I can ring for Neal if I need anything. I shall sleep if I'm alone, perhaps."

Edward reluctantly obeyed, and his brother was left to himself. Little rest did he find, however, for the pain of the wounded arm grew unbearable, and, taking a sudden resolution, he rang for his servant.

"Neal, go to Miss Coventry's study, and if Miss Muir is there, ask her to be kind enough to come to me. I'm in great pain, and she understands wounds better than anyone else in the house."

With much surprise in his face, the man departed and a few moments after the door noiselessly opened and Miss Muir came in. It had been a very warm day, and for the first time she had left off her plain black dress. All in white, with no ornament but her fair hair, and a fragrant posy of violets in her belt, she looked a different woman from the meek, nunlike creature one usually saw about the house. Her face was as altered as her dress, for now a soft color glowed in her cheeks, her eyes smiled shyly, and her lips no longer wore the firm look of one who forcibly repressed every emotion. A fresh, gentle, and charming woman she seemed, and Coventry found the dull room suddenly brightened by her presence. Going straight to him, she said simply, and with a happy, helpful look very comforting to see, "I'm glad you sent for me. What can I do for you?"

He told her, and before the complaint was ended, she began loosening the bandages with the decision of one who understood what was to be done and had faith in herself.

"Ah, that's relief, that's comfort!" ejaculated Coventry, as the last tight fold fell away. "Ned was afraid I should bleed to death if he touched me. What will the doctor say to us?"

"I neither know nor care. I shall say to him that he is a bad surgeon to bind it so closely, and not leave orders to have it untied if necessary. Now I shall make it easy and put you to sleep, for that is what you need. Shall I? May I?"

"I wish you would, if you can."

And while she deftly rearranged the bandages, the young man watched her curiously. Presently he asked, "How came you to know so much about these things?"

"In the hospital where I was ill, I saw much that interested me, and when I got better, I used to sing to the patients sometimes."

"Do you mean to sing to me?" he asked, in the submissive tone men unconsciously adopt when ill and in a woman's care.

"If you like it better than reading aloud in a dreamy tone," she answered, as she tied the last knot.

"I do, much better," he said decidedly.

"You are feverish. I shall wet your forehead, and then you will be quite comfortable." She moved about the room in the quiet way which made it a pleasure to watch her, and, having mingled a little cologne with water, bathed his face as unconcernedly as if he had been a child. Her proceedings not only comforted but amused Coventry, who mentally contrasted her with the stout, beer-drinking matron who had ruled over him in his last illness.

"A clever, kindly little woman," he thought, and felt quite at his ease, she was so perfectly easy herself.

"There, now you look more like yourself," she said with an approving nod as she finished, and smoothed the dark locks off his forehead with a cool, soft hand. Then seating herself in a large chair near by, she began to sing, while tidily rolling up the fresh bandages which had been left for the morning. Coventry lay watching her by the dim light that burned in the room, and she sang on as easily as a bird, a dreamy, low-toned lullaby, which soothed the listener like a spell. Presently, looking up to see the effect of her song, she found the young man wide awake, and regarding her with a curious mixture of pleasure, interest, and admiration.

"Shut your eyes, Mr. Coventry," she said, with a reproving shake of the head, and an odd little smile.

He laughed and obeyed, but could not resist an occasional covert glance from under his lashes at the slender white figure in the great velvet chair. She saw him and frowned.

"You are very disobedient; why won't you sleep?"

"I can't, I want to listen. I'm fond of nightingales."

"Then I shall sing no more, but try something that has never failed yet. Give me your hand, please."

Much amazed, he gave it, and, taking it in both her small ones, she sat down behind the curtain and remained as mute and motionless as a statute. Coventry smiled to himself at first, and wondered which would tire first. But soon a subtle warmth seemed to steal from the soft palms that enclosed his own, his heart beat quicker, his breath grew unequal, and a thousand fancies danced through his brain. He sighed, and said dreamily, as he turned his face toward her, "I like this." And in the act of speaking, seemed to sink into a soft cloud which encompassed him about with an atmosphere of perfect repose. More than this he could not remember, for sleep, deep and dreamless, fell upon him, and when he woke, daylight was shining in between the curtains, his hand lay alone on the coverlet, and his fair-haired enchantress was gone.

IV

A DISCOVERY

FOR several days Coventry was confined to his room, much against his will, though everyone did their best to lighten his irksome captivity. His mother petted him, Bella sang, Lucia read, Edward was devoted, and all the household, with one exception, were eager to serve the young master. Jean Muir never came near him, and Jean Muir alone seemed to possess the power of amusing him. He soon tired of the others, wanted something new; recalled the piquant character of the girl and took a fancy into his head that she would lighten his ennui. After some hesitation, he carelessly spoke of her to Bella, but nothing came of it, for Bella only said Jean was well, and very busy doing something lovely to surprise Mamma with. Edward complained that he never saw her, and Lucia ignored her existence altogether. The only intelligence the invalid received was from the gossip of two housemaids over their work in the next room. From them he learned that the governess had been "scolded" by Miss Beaufort for going to Mr. Coventry's room; that she had taken it very sweetly and kept herself carefully out of the way of both young gentlemen, though it was plain to see that Mr. Ned was dying for her.

Mr. Gerald amused himself by thinking over this gossip, and quite annoyed his sister by his absence of mind.

"Gerald, do you know Ned's comission has come?"

"Very interesting. Read on, Bella."

"You stupid boy! You don't know a word I say," and she put down the book to repeat her news.

"I'm glad of it; now we must get him off as soon as possible—that is, I suppose he will want to be off as soon as possible." And Coventry woke up from his reverie.

"You needn't check yourself, I know all about it. I think Ned was very foolish, and that Miss Muir has behaved beautifully. It's quite impossible, of course, but I wish it wasn't, I do so like to watch lovers. You and Lucia are so cold you are not a bit interesting."

"You'll do me a favor if you'll stop all that nonsense about Lucia and me. We are not lovers, and never shall be, I fancy. At all events, I'm tired of the thing, and wish you and Mamma would let it drop, for the present at least."

"Oh Gerald, you know Mamma has set her heart upon it, that Papa desired it, and poor Lucia loves you so much. How can you speak of dropping what will make us all so happy?"

"It won't make me happy, and I take the liberty of thinking that this is of some importance. I'm not bound in any way, and don't intend to be till I am ready. Now we'll talk about Ned."

Much grieved and surprised, Bella obeyed, and devoted herself to Edward, who very wisely submitted to his fate and prepared to leave home for some months. For a week the house was in a state of excitement about his departure, and everyone but Jean was busied for him. She was scarcely seen; every morning she gave Bella her lessons, every afternoon drove out with Mrs. Coventry, and nearly every evening went up to the Hall to read to Sir John, who found his wish granted without exactly knowing how it had been done.

The day Edward left, he came down from bidding his mother good-bye, looking very pale, for he had lingered in his sister's little room with Miss Muir as long as he dared.

"Good-bye, dear. Be kind to Jean," he whispered as he kissed his sister.

"I will, I will," returned Bella, with tearful eyes.

"Take care of Mamma, and remember Lucia," he said again, as he touched his cousin's beautiful cheek.

"Fear nothing. I will keep them apart," she whispered back, and Coventry heard it.

Edward offered his hand to his brother, saying, significantly, as he looked him in the eye, "I trust you, Gerald."

"You may, Ned."

Then he went, and Coventry tired himself with wondering what Lucia meant. A few days later he understood.

Now Ned is gone, little Muir will appear, I fancy, he said to himself; but "little Muir" did not appear, and seemed to shun him more carefully than she had done her lover. If he went to the drawing room in the evening hoping for music, Lucia alone was there. If he tapped at Bella's door, there was always a pause before she opened it, and no sign of Jean appeared though her voice had been audible when he knocked. If he went to the library, a hasty rustle and the sound of flying feet betrayed that the room was deserted at his approach. In the garden Miss Muir never failed to avoid him, and if by chance they met in hall or breakfast room, she passed him with downcast eyes and the briefest, coldest greeting. All this annoyed him intensely, and the more she eluded him, the more he desired to see her—from a spirit of opposition, he said, nothing more. It fretted and yet it entertained him, and he found a lazy sort of pleasure in thwarting the girl's little maneuvers. His patience gave out at last, and he resolved to know what was the meaning of this peculiar conduct. Having locked and taken away the key of one door in the library, he waited till Miss Muir went in to get a book for his uncle. He had heard her speak to Bella of it, knew that she believed him with his mother, and smiled to himself as he stole after her. She was standing in a chair, reaching up, and he had time to see a slender waist, a pretty foot, before he spoke.

"Can I help you, Miss Muir?"

She started, dropped several books, and turned scarlet, as she said hurriedly, "Thank you, no; I can get the steps."

"My long arm will be less trouble. I've got but one, and that is tired of being idle, so it is very much at your service. What will you have?"

"I—I—you startled me so I've forgotten." And Jean laughed, nervously, as she looked about her as if planning to escape.

"I beg your pardon, wait till you remember, and let me thank you for the enchanted sleep you gave me ten days ago. I've had no chance yet, you've shunned me so pertinaciously."

"Indeed I try not to be rude, but——" She checked herself, and turned her face away, adding, with an accent of pain in her voice, "It is not my fault, Mr. Coventry. I only obey orders."

"Whose orders?" he demanded, still standing so that she could not escape.

"Don't ask; it is one who has a right to command where you are concerned. Be sure that it is kindly meant, though it may seem folly to us. Nay, don't be angry, laugh at it, as I do, and let me run away, please."

She turned, and looked down at him with tears in her eyes, a smile on her lips, and an expression half sad, half arch, which was altogether charming. The frown passed from his face, but he still looked grave and said decidedly, "No one has a right to command in this house but my mother or myself. Was it she who bade you avoid me as if I was a madman or a pest?"

"Ah, don't ask. I promised not to tell, and you would not have me break my word, I know." And still smiling, she regarded him with a look of merry malice which made any other reply unnecessary. It was Lucia, he thought, and disliked his cousin intensely just then. Miss Muir moved as if to step down; he detained her, saying earnestly, yet with a smile, "Do you consider me the master here?"

"Yes," and to the word she gave a sweet, submissive intonation which made it expressive of the respect, regard, and confidence which men find pleasantest when women feel and show it. Unconsciously his face softened, and he looked up at her with a different glance from any he had ever given her before.

"Well, then, will you consent to obey me if I am not tyrannical or unreasonable in my demands?"

"I'll try."

"Good! Now frankly, I want to say that all this sort of thing is very disagreeable to me. It annoys me to be a restraint upon anyone's liberty or comfort, and I beg you will go and come as freely as you like, and not mind Lucia's absurdities. She means well, but hasn't a particle of penetration or tact. Will you promise this?"

"No."

"Why not?"

"It is better as it is, perhaps."

"But you called it folly just now."

"Yes, it seems so, and yet—" She paused, looking both confused and distressed.

Coventry lost patience, and said hastily, "You women are such enigmas I never expect to understand you! Well, I've done my best to make you comfortable, but if you prefer to lead this sort of life, I beg you will do so."

"I *don't* prefer it; it is hateful to me. I like to be myself, to have my liberty, and the confidence of those about me. But I cannot think it kind to disturb the peace of anyone, and so I try to obey. I've promised Bella to remain, but I will go rather than have another scene with Miss Beaufort or with you."

Miss Muir had burst out impetuously, and stood there with a sudden fire in her eyes, sudden warmth and spirit in her face and voice that amazed Coventry. She was angry, hurt, and haughty, and the change only made her more attractive, for not a trace of her former meek self remained. Coventry was electrified, and still more surprised when she added, imperiously, with a gesture as if to put him aside, "Hand me that book and move away. I wish to go."

He obeyed, even offered his hand, but she refused it, stepped lightly down, and went to the door. There she turned, and with the same indignant voice, the same kindling eyes and glowing cheeks, she said rapidly, "I know I have no right to speak in this way. I restrain myself as long as I can, but when I can bear no more, my true self breaks loose, and I defy everything. I am tired of being a cold, calm machine; it is impossible with an ardent nature like mine, and I shall try no longer. I cannot help it if people love me. I don't want their love. I only ask to be left in peace, and why I am tormented so I cannot see. I've neither beauty, money, nor rank, yet every foolish boy mistakes my frank interest for something warmer, and makes me miserable. It is my misfortune. Think of me what you will, but beware of me in time, for against my will I may do you harm."

Almost fiercely she had spoken, and with a warning gesture she hurried from the room, leaving the young man feeling as if a sudden thunder-gust had swept through the house. For several minutes he sat in the chair she left, thinking deeply. Suddenly he rose, went to his sister, and said, in his usual tone of indolent good nature, "Bella, didn't I hear Ned ask you to be kind to Miss Muir?"

"Yes, and I try to be, but she is so odd lately."

"Odd! How do you mean?"

"Why, she is either as calm and cold as a statue, or restless and queer; she cries at night, I know, and sighs sadly when she thinks I don't hear. Something is the matter."

"She frets for Ned perhaps," began Coventry.

"Oh dear, no; it's a great relief to her that he is gone. I'm afraid that she likes someone very much, and someone don't like her. Can it be Mr. Sydney?"

"She called him a 'titled fool' once, but perhaps that didn't mean anything. Did you ever ask her about him?" said Coventry, feeling rather ashamed of his curiosity, yet unable to resist the temptation of questioning unsuspecting Bella.

"Yes, but she only looked at me in her tragical way, and said, so pitifully, 'My little friend, I hope you will never have to pass through the scenes I've passed through, but keep your peace unbroken all your life.' After that I dared say no more. I'm very fond of her, I want to make her happy, but I don't know how. Can you propose anything?"

"I was going to propose that you make her come among us more, now Ned is gone. It must be dull for her, moping about alone. I'm sure it is for me. She is an entertaining little person, and I enjoy her music very much. It's good for Mamma to have gay evenings; so you bestir yourself, and see what you can do for the general good of the family."

"That's all very charming, and I've proposed it more than once, but Lucia spoils all my plans. She is afraid you'll follow Ned's example, and that is so silly."

"Lucia is a—no, I won't say fool, because she has sense enough when she chooses; but I wish you'd just settle things with Mamma, and then Lucia can do nothing but submit," said Gerald angrily.

"I'll try, but she goes up to read to Uncle, you know, and since he has had the gout, she stays later, so I see little of her in the evening. There she goes now. I think she will captivate the old one as well as the young one, she is so devoted."

Coventry looked after her slender black figure, just vanishing through the great gate, and an uncomfortable fancy took possession of him, born of Bella's careless words. He sauntered away, and after eluding his cousin, who seemed looking for him, he turned toward the Hall, saying to himself, I will see what is going on up here. Such things have happened. Uncle is the simplest soul alive, and if the girl is ambitious, she can do what she will with him.

Here a servant came running after him and gave him a letter, which he thrust into his pocket without examining it. When he reached the Hall, he went quietly to his uncle's study. The door was ajar, and looking in, he saw a scene of tranquil comfort, very pleasant to watch. Sir John leaned in his easy chair with one foot on a cushion. He was dressed with his usual care and, in spite of the gout, looked like a handsome, well-preserved old gentleman. He was smiling as he listened, and his eyes rested complacently on Jean Muir, who sat near him reading in her musical voice, while the sunshine glittered on her hair and the soft rose of her cheek. She read well, yet Coventry thought her heart was not in her task, for once when she paused, while Sir John spoke, her eyes had an absent expression, and she leaned her head upon her hand, with an air of patient weariness.

Poor girl! I did her great injustice; she has no thought of captivating the old man, but amuses him from simple kindness. She is tired. I'll put an end to her task; and Coventry entered without knocking.

Sir John received him with an air of polite resignation, Miss Muir with a perfectly expressionless face.

"Mother's love, and how are you today, sir?"

"Comfortable, but dull, so I want you to bring the girls over this evening, to amuse the old gentleman. Mrs. King has got out the antique costumes and trumpery, as I promised Bella she should have them, and tonight we are to have a merrymaking, as we used to do when Ned was here."

"Very well, sir, I'll bring them. We've all been out of sorts since the lad left, and a little jollity will do us good. Are you going back, Miss Muir?" asked Coventry.

"No, I shall keep her to give me my tea and get things ready. Don't read anymore, my dear, but go and amuse yourself with the pictures, or whatever you like," said Sir John; and like a dutiful daughter she obeyed, as if glad to get away.

"That's a very charming girl, Gerald," began Sir John as she left the room. "I'm much interested in her, both on her own account and on her mother's."

"Her mother's! What do you know of her mother?" asked Coventry, much surprised.

"Her mother was Lady Grace Howard, who ran away with a poor Scotch minister twenty years ago. The family cast her off, and she lived and died so obscurely that very little is known of her except that she left an orphan girl at some small French pension. This is the girl, and a fine girl, too. I'm surprised that you did not know this."

"So am I, but it is like her not to tell. She is a strange, proud creature. Lady Howard's daughter! Upon my word, that is a discovery," and Coventry felt his interest in his sister's governess much increased by this fact; for, like all wellborn Englishmen, he valued rank and gentle blood even more than he cared to own.

"She has had a hard life of it, this poor little girl, but she has a brave spirit, and will make her way anywhere," said Sir John admiringly.

"Did Ned know this?" asked Gerald suddenly.

"No, she only told me yesterday. I was looking in the *Peerage* and chanced to speak of the Howards. She forgot herself and called Lady Grace her mother. Then I got the whole story, for the lonely little thing was glad to make a confidant of someone."

"That accounts for her rejection of Sydney and Ned: she knows she is their equal and will not snatch at the rank which is hers by right. No, she's not mercenary or ambitious."

"What do you say?" asked Sir John, for Coventry had spoken more to himself than to his uncle.

"I wonder if Lady Sydney was aware of this?" was all Gerald's answer.

"No, Jean said she did not wish to be pitied, and so told nothing to the mother. I think the son knew, but that was a delicate point, and I asked no questions."

"I shall write to him as soon as I discover his address. We have been so intimate I can venture to make a few inquiries about Miss Muir, and prove the truth of her story."

"Do you mean to say that you doubt it?" demanded Sir John angrily.

"I beg your pardon, Uncle, but I must confess I have an instinctive distrust of that young person. It is unjust, I dare say, yet I cannot banish it."

"Don't annoy me by expressing it, if you please. I have some penetration and experience, and I respect and pity Miss Muir heartily. This dislike of yours may be the cause of her late melancholy, hey, Gerald?" And Sir John looked suspiciously at his nephew.

Anxious to avert the rising storm, Coventry said hastily as he turned away, "I've neither time nor inclination to discuss the matter now, sir, but will be careful not to offend again. I'll take your message to Bella, so goodbye for an hour, Uncle."

And Coventry went his way through the park, thinking within himself, The dear old gentleman is getting fascinated, like poor Ned. How the deuce does the girl do it? Lady Howard's daughter, yet never told us; I don't understand that.

V

HOW THE GIRL DID IT

AT home he found a party of young friends, who hailed with delight the prospect of a revel at the Hall. An hour later, the blithe company trooped into the great saloon, where preparations had already been made for a dramatic evening.

Good Sir John was in his element, for he was never so happy as when his house was full of young people. Several persons were chosen, and in a few moments the curtains were withdrawn from the first of these impromptu tableaux. A swarthy, darkly bearded man lay asleep on a tiger skin, in the shadow of a tent. Oriental arms and drapery surrounded him; an antique silver lamp burned dimly on a table where fruit lay heaped in costly dishes, and wine shone redly in half-emptied goblets. Bending over the sleeper was a woman robed with barbaric splendor. One hand turned back the embroidered sleeve from the arm which held a scimitar; one slender foot in a scarlet sandal was visible under the white tunic; her purple mantle swept down from snowy shoulders; fillets of gold bound her hair, and jewels shone on neck and arms. She was looking over her shoulder toward the entrance of the tent, with a steady yet stealthy look, so effective that for a moment the spectators held their breath, as if they also heard a passing footstep.

"Who is it?" whispered Lucia, for the face was new to her.

"Jean Muir," answered Coventry, with an absorbed look.

"Impossible! She is small and fair," began Lucia, but a hasty "Hush, let me look!" from her cousin silenced her.

Impossible as it seemed, he was right nevertheless; for Jean Muir it was. She had darkened her skin, painted her eyebrows, disposed some wild black locks over her fair hair, and thrown such an intensity of expression into her eyes that they darkened and dilated till they were as fierce as any southern eyes that ever flashed. Hatred, the deepest and bitterest, was written on her sternly beautiful face, courage glowed in her glance, power spoke in the nervous grip of the slender hand that held the weapon, and the indomitable will of the woman was expressed—even the firm pressure of the little foot half hidden in the tiger skin.

"Oh, isn't she splendid?" cried Bella under her breath.

"She looks as if she'd use her sword well when the time comes," said someone admiringly.

"Good night to Holofernes; his fate is certain," added another.

"He is the image of Sydney, with that beard on."

"Doesn't she look as if she really hated him?"

"Perhaps she does."

Coventry uttered the last exclamation, for the two which preceded it suggested an explanation of the marvelous change in Jean. It was not all art: the intense detestation mingled with a savage joy that the object of her hatred was in her power was too perfect to be feigned; and having the key to a part of her story, Coventry felt as if he caught a glimpse of the truth. It was but a glimpse, however, for the curtain dropped before he had half analyzed the significance of that strange face.

"Horrible! I'm glad it's over," said Lucia coldly.

"Magnificent! Encore! Encore!" cried Gerald enthusiastically.

But the scene was over, and no applause could recall the actress. Two or three graceful or gay pictures followed, but Jean was in none, and each lacked the charm which real talent lends to the simplest part.

"Coventry, you are wanted," called a voice. And to everyone's surprise, Coventry went, though heretofore he had always refused to exert himself when handsome actors were in demand.

"What part am I to spoil?" he asked, as he entered the green room, where several excited young gentlemen were costuming and attitudinizing.

"A fugitive cavalier. Put yourself into this suit, and lose no time asking questions. Miss Muir will tell you what to do. She is in the tableau, so no one will mind you," said the manager pro tem, throwing a rich old suit toward Coventry and resuming the painting of a moustache on his own boyish face.

A gallant cavalier was the result of Gerald's hasty toilet, and when he appeared before the ladies a general glance of admiration was bestowed upon him.

"Come along and be placed; Jean is ready on the stage." And Bella ran before him, exclaiming to her governess, "Here he is, quite splendid. Wasn't he good to do it?"

Miss Muir, in the charming prim and puritanical dress of a Roundhead damsel, was arranging some shrubs, but turned suddenly and dropped the green branch she held, as her eye met the glittering figure advancing toward her.

"You!" she said with a troubled look, adding low to Bella, "Why did you ask *him*? I begged you not."

"He is the only handsome man here, and the best actor if he likes. He won't play usually, so make the most of him." And Bella was off to finish powdering her hair for "The Marriage à la Mode."

"I was sent for and I came. Do you prefer some other person?" asked Coventry, at a loss to understand the half-anxious, half-eager expression of the face under the little cap.

It changed to one of mingled annoyance and resignation as she said, "It is too late. Please kneel here, half behind the shrubs; put down your hat, and—allow me—you are too elegant for a fugitive."

As he knelt before her, she disheveled his hair, pulled his lace collar awry, threw away his gloves and sword, and half untied the cloak that hung about his shoulders.

"That is better; your paleness is excellent—nay, don't spoil it. We are to represent the picture which hangs in the Hall. I need tell you no more. Now, Roundheads, place yourselves, and then ring up the curtain."

With a smile, Coventry obeyed her; for the picture was of two lovers, the young cavalier kneeling, with his arm around the waist of the girl, who tries to hide him with her little mantle, and presses his head to her bosom in an ecstasy of fear, as she glances back at the approaching pursuers. Jean hesitated an instant and shrank a little as his hand touched her; she blushed deeply, and her eyes fell before his. Then, as the bell rang, she threw herself into her part with sudden spirit. One arm half covered him with her cloak, the other pillowed his head on the muslin kerchief folded over her bosom, and she looked backward with such terror in her eyes that more than one chivalrous young spectator longed to hurry to the rescue. It lasted but a moment; yet in that moment Coventry experienced another new sensation. Many women had smiled on him, but he had remained heart-whole, cool, and careless, quite unconscious of the power which a woman possesses and knows how to use, for the weal or woe of man. Now, as he knelt there with a soft arm about him, a slender waist yielding to his touch, and a maiden heart throbbing against his cheek, for the first time in his life he felt the indescribable spell of womanhood, and looked the ardent lover to perfection. Just as his face assumed this new and most becoming aspect, the curtain dropped, and clamorous encores recalled him to the fact that Miss Muir was trying to escape from his hold, which had grown painful in its unconscious pressure. He sprang up, half bewildered, and looking as he had never looked before.

"Again! Again!" called Sir John. And the young men who played the Roundheads, eager to share in the applause begged for a repetition in new attitudes.

"A rustle has betrayed you, we have fired and shot the brave girl, and she lies dying, you know. That will be effective; try it, Miss Muir," said one. And with a long breath, Jean complied.

The curtain went up, showing the lover still on his knees, unmindful of the captors who clutched him by the shoulder, for at his feet the girl lay dying. Her head was on his breast, now, her eyes looked full into his, no longer wild with fear, but eloquent with the love which even death could not conquer. The power of those tender eyes thrilled Coventry with a strange delight, and set his heart beating as rapidly as hers had done. She felt his hands tremble, saw the color flash into his cheek, knew that she had touched him at last, and when she rose it was with a sense of triumph which she found it hard to conceal. Others thought it fine acting; Coventry tried to believe so; but Lucia set her teeth, and, as the curtain fell on that second picture, she left her place to hurry behind the scenes, bent on putting an end to such dangerous play. Several actors were complimenting the mimic lovers. Jean took it merrily, but Coventry, in spite of himself, betrayed that he was excited by something deeper than mere gratified vanity.

As Lucia appeared, his manner changed to its usual indifference; but he could not quench the unwonted fire of his eyes, or keep all trace of emotion out of his face, and she saw this with a sharp pang.

"I have come to offer my help. You must be tired, Miss Muir. Can I relieve you?" said Lucia hastily.

"Yes, thank you. I shall be very glad to leave the rest to you, and enjoy them from the front."

So with a sweet smile Jean tripped away, and to Lucia's dismay Coventry followed.

"I want you, Gerald; please stay," she cried.

"I've done my part—no more tragedy for me tonight." And he was gone before she could entreat or command.

There was no help for it; she must stay and do her duty, or expose her jealousy to the quick eyes about her. For a time she bore it; but the sight of her cousin leaning over the chair she had left and chatting with the governess, who now filled it, grew unbearable, and she dispatched a little girl with a message to Miss Muir.

"Please, Miss Beaufort wants you for Queen Bess, as you are the only lady with red hair. Will you come?" whispered the child, quite unconscious of any hidden sting in her words.

"Yes, dear, willingly though I'm not stately enough for Her Majesty, nor handsome enough," said Jean, rising with an untroubled face, though she resented the feminine insult.

"Do you want an Essex? I'm all dressed for it," said Coventry, following to the door with a wistful look.

"No, Miss Beaufort said *you* were not to come. She doesn't want you both together," said the child decidedly.

Jean gave him a significant look, shrugged her shoulders, and went away smiling her odd smile, while Coventry paced up and down the hall in a curious state of unrest, which made him forgetful of everything till the young people came gaily out to supper.

"Come, bonny Prince Charlie, take me down, and play the lover as charmingly as you did an hour ago. I never thought you had so much warmth in you," said Bella, taking his arm and drawing him on against his will.

"Don't be foolish, child. Where is—Lucia?"

Why he checked Jean's name on his lips and substituted another's, he could not tell; but a sudden shyness in speaking of her possessed him, and though he saw her nowhere, he would not ask for her. His cousin came down looking lovely in a classical costume; but Gerald scarcely saw her, and, when the merriment was at its height, he slipped away to discover what had become of Miss Muir.

Alone in the deserted drawing room he found her, and paused to watch her a moment before he spoke; for something in her attitude and face struck him. She was leaning wearily back in the great chair which had served for a throne. Her royal robes were still unchanged, though the crown was off and all her fair hair hung about her shoulders. Excitement and exertion made her brilliant, the rich dress became her wonderfully, and an air of luxurious indolence changed the meek governess into a charming woman. She leaned on the velvet cushions as if she were used to such support; she played with the jewels which had crowned her as carelessly as if she were born to wear them; her attitude was full of negligent grace, and the expression of her face half proud, half pensive, as if her thoughts were bitter-sweet.

One would know she was wellborn to see her now. Poor girl, what a burden a life of dependence must be to a spirit like hers! I wonder what she is thinking of so intently. And Coventry indulged in another look before he spoke.

"Shall I bring you some supper, Miss Muir?"

"Supper!" she ejaculated, with a start. "Who thinks of one's body when one's soul is—" She stopped there, knit her brows, and laughed faintly as she added, "No, thank you. I want nothing but advice, and that I dare not ask of anyone."

"Why not?"

"Because I have no right."

"Everyone has a right to ask help, especially the weak of the strong. Can I help you? Believe me, I most heartily offer my poor services."

"Ah, you forget! This dress, the borrowed splendor of these jewels, the freedom of this gay evening, the romance of the part you played, all blind you to the reality. For a moment I cease to be a servant, and for a moment you treat me as an equal."

It was true; he *had* forgotten. That soft, reproachful glance touched him, his distrust melted under the new charm, and he answered with real feeling in voice and face, "I treat you as an equal because you *are* one; and when I offer help, it is not to my sister's governess alone, but to Lady Howard's daughter."

"Who told you that?" she demanded, sitting erect.

"My uncle. Do not reproach him. It shall go no further, if you forbid it. Are you sorry that I know it?"

"Yes."

"Why?"

"Because I will not be pitied!" And her eyes flashed as she made a half-defiant gesture.

"Then, if I may not pity the hard fate which has befallen an innocent life, may I admire the courage which meets adverse fortune so bravely, and conquers the world by winning the respect and regard of all who see and honor it?"

Miss Muir averted her face, put up her hand, and answered hastily, "No, no, not that! Do not be kind; it destroys the only barrier now left between us. Be cold to me as before, forget what I am, and let me go on my way, unknown, unpitied, and unloved!"

Her voice faltered and failed as the last word was uttered, and she bent her face upon her hand. Something jarred upon Coventry in this speech, and moved him to say, almost rudely, "You need have no fears for me. Lucia will tell you what an iceberg I am."

"Then Lucia would tell me wrong. I have the fatal power of reading character; I know you better than she does, and I see—" There she stopped abruptly.

"What? Tell me and prove your skill," he said eagerly.

Turning, she fixed her eyes on him with a penetrating power that made him shrink as she said slowly, "Under the ice I see fire, and warn you to beware lest it prove a volcano."

For a moment he sat dumb, wondering at the insight of the girl; for she was the first to discover the hidden warmth of a nature too proud to confess its tender impulses, or the ambitions that slept till some potent voice awoke them. The blunt, almost stern manner in which she warned him away from her only made her more attractive; for there was no conceit or arrogance in it, only a foreboding fear emboldened by past suffering to be frank. Suddenly he spoke impetuously:

"You are right! I am not what I seem, and my indolent indifference is but the mask under which I conceal my real self. I could be as passionate, as energetic and aspiring as Ned, if I had any aim in life. I have none, and so I am what you once called me, a thing to pity and despise."

"I never said that!" cried Jean indignantly.

"Not in those words, perhaps; but you looked it and thought it, though you phrased it more mildly. I deserved it, but I shall deserve it no longer. I am beginning to wake from my disgraceful idleness, and long for some work that shall make a man of me. Why do you go? I annoy you with my confessions. Pardon me. They are the first I ever made; they shall be the last."

"No, oh no! I am too much honored by your confidence; but is it wise, is it loyal to tell *me* your hopes and aims? Has not Miss Beaufort the first right to be your confidante?"

Coventry drew back, looking intensely annoyed, for the name recalled much that he would gladly have forgotten in the novel excitement of the hour. Lucia's love, Edward's parting words, his own reserve so strangely thrown aside, so difficult to resume. What he would have said was checked by the sight of a half-open letter which fell from Jean's dress as she moved away. Mechanically he took it up to return it, and, as he did so, he recognized Sydney's handwriting. Jean snatched it from him, turning pale to the lips as she cried, "Did you read it? What did you see? Tell me, tell me, on your honor!"

"On my honor, I saw nothing but this single sentence, 'By the love I bear you, believe what I say.' No more, as I am a gentleman. I know the hand, I guess the purport of the letter, and as a friend of Sydney, I earnestly desire to help you, if I can. Is this the matter upon which you want advice?"

"Yes."

"Then let me give it?"

"You cannot, without knowing all, and it is so hard to tell!"

"Let me guess it, and spare you the pain of telling. May I?" And Coventry waited eagerly for her reply, for the spell was still upon him.

Holding the letter fast, she beckoned him to follow, and glided before him to a secluded little nook, half boudoir, half conservatory. There she paused, stood an instant as if in doubt, then looked up at him with confiding eyes and said decidedly, "I will do it; for, strange as it may seem, you are the only person to whom I *can* speak. You know Sydney, you have discovered that I am an equal, you have offered your help. I accept it; but oh, do not think me unwomanly! Remember how alone I am, how young, and how much I rely upon your sincerity, your sympathy!"

"Speak freely. I am indeed your friend." And Coventry sat down beside her, forgetful of everything but the soft-eyed girl who confided in him so entirely.

Speaking rapidly, Jean went on, "You know that Sydney loved me, that I refused him and went away. But you do not know that his importunities nearly drove me wild, that he threatened to rob me of my only treasure, my good name, and that, in desperation, I tried to kill myself. Yes, mad, wicked as it was, I did long to end the life which was, at best, a burden, and under his persecution had become a torment. You are shocked, yet what I say is the living truth. Lady Sydney will confirm it, the nurses at the hospital will confess that it was not a fever which brought me there; and here, though the external wound is healed, my heart still aches and burns with the shame and indignation which only a proud woman can feel."

She paused and sat with kindling eyes, glowing cheeks, and both hands pressed to her heaving bosom, as if the old insult roused her spirit anew. Coventry said not a word, for surprise, anger, incredulity, and admiration mingled so confusedly in his mind that he forgot to speak, and Jean went on, "That wild act of mine convinced him of my indomitable dislike. He went away, and I believed that this stormy love of his would be cured by absence. It is not, and I live in daily fear of fresh entreaties, renewed persecution. His mother promised not to betray where I had gone, but he found me out and wrote to me. The letter I asked you to take to Lady Sydney was a reply to his, imploring him to leave me in peace. You failed to deliver it, and I was glad, for I thought silence might quench hope. All in vain; this is a more passionate appeal than ever, and he vows he will never desist from his endeavors till I give another man the right to protect me. I *can* do this—I am sorely tempted to do it, but I rebel against the cruelty. I love my freedom, I have no wish to marry at this man's bidding. What can I do? How can I free myself? Be my friend, and help me!"

Tears streamed down her cheeks, sobs choked her words, and she clasped her hands imploringly as she turned toward the young man in all the abandonment of sorrow, fear, and supplication. Coventry found it hard to meet those eloquent eyes and answer calmly, for he had no experience in such scenes and knew not how to play his part. It is this absurd dress and that romantic nonsense which makes me feel so unlike myself, he thought, quite unconscious of the dangerous power which the dusky room, the midsummer warmth and fragrance, the memory of the "romantic nonsense," and, most of all, the presence of a beautiful, afflicted woman had over him. His usual self-possession deserted him, and he could only echo the words which had made the strongest impression upon him:

"You *can* do this, you are tempted to do it. Is Ned the man who can protect you?"

"No" was the soft reply.

"Who then?"

"Do not ask me. A good and honorable man; one who loves me well, and would devote his life to me; one whom once it would have been happiness to marry, but now—"

There her voice ended in a sigh, and all her fair hair fell down about her face, hiding it in a shining veil.

"Why not now? This is a sure and speedy way of ending your distress. Is it impossible?"

In spite of himself, Gerald leaned nearer, took one of the little hands in his, and pressed it as he spoke, urgently, compassionately, nay, almost tenderly. From behind the veil came a heavy sigh, and the brief answer, "It is impossible."

"Why, Jean?"

She flung her hair back with a sudden gesture, drew away her hand, and answered, almost fiercely, "Because I do not love him! Why do you torment me with such questions? I tell you I am in a sore strait and cannot see my way. Shall I deceive the good man, and secure peace at the price of liberty and truth? Or shall I defy Sydney and lead a life of dread? If he menaced my life, I should not fear; but he menaces that which is dearer than life—my good name. A look, a word can tarnish it; a scornful smile, a significant shrug can do me more harm than any blow; for I am a woman—friendless, poor, and at the mercy of his tongue. Ah, better to have died, and so have been saved the bitter pain that has come now!"

She sprang up, clasped her hands over her head, and paced despairingly through the little room, not weeping, but wearing an expression more tragical than tears. Still feeling as if he had suddenly stepped into a romance, yet finding a keen pleasure in the part assigned him, Coventry threw himself into it with spirit, and heartily did his best to console the poor girl who needed help so much. Going to her, he said as impetuously as Ned ever did, "Miss Muir—nay, I will say Jean, if that will comfort you—listen, and rest assured that no harm shall touch you if I can ward it off. You are needlessly alarmed. Indignant you may well be, but, upon my life, I think you wrong Sydney. He is violent, I know, but he is too honorable a man to injure you by a light word, an unjust act. He did but threaten, hoping to soften you. Let me see him, or write to him. He is my friend; he will listen to me. Of that I am sure."

"Be sure of nothing. When a man like Sydney loves and is thwarted in his love, nothing can control his headstrong will. Promise me you will not see or write to him. Much as I fear and despise him, I will submit, rather than any harm should befall you—or your brother. You promise me, Mr. Coventry?"

He hesitated. She clung to his arm with unfeigned solicitude in her eager, pleading face, and he could not resist it.

"I promise; but in return you must promise to let me give what help I can; and, Jean, never say again that you are friendless."

"You are so kind! God bless you for it. But I dare not accept your friendship; *she* will not permit it, and I have no right to mar her peace."

"Who will not permit it?" he demanded hotly.

"Miss Beaufort."

"Hang Miss Beaufort!" exclaimed Coventry, with such energy that Jean broke into a musical laugh, despite her trouble. He joined in it, and, for an instant they stood looking at one another as if the last barrier were down, and they were friends indeed. Jean paused suddenly, with the smile on her lips, the tears still on her cheek, and made a warning gesture. He listened: the sound of feet mingled with calls and laughter proved that they were missed and sought.

"That laugh betrayed us. Stay and meet them. I cannot." And Jean darted out upon the lawn. Coventry followed; for the thought of confronting so many eyes, so many questions, daunted him, and he fled like a coward. The sound of Jean's flying footsteps guided him, and he overtook her just as she paused behind a rose thicket to take breath.

"Fainthearted knight! You should have stayed and covered my retreat. Hark! they are coming! Hide! Hide!" she panted, half in fear, half in merriment, as the gay pursuers rapidly drew nearer.

"Kneel down; the moon is coming out and the glitter of your embroidery will betray you," whispered Jean, as they cowered behind the roses.

"Your arms and hair will betray you. 'Come under my plaiddie,' as the song says." And Coventry tried to make his velvet cloak cover the white shoulders and fair locks.

"We are acting our parts in reality now. How Bella will enjoy the thing when I tell her!" said Jean as the noises died away.

"Do not tell her," whispered Coventry.

"And why not?" she asked, looking up into the face so near her own, with an artless glance.

"Can you not guess why?"

"Ah, you are so proud you cannot bear to be laughed at."

"It is not that. It is because I do not want you to be annoyed by silly tongues; you have enough to pain you without that. I am your friend, now, and I do my best to prove it."

"So kind, so kind! How can I thank you?" murmured Jean. And she involuntarily nestled closer under the cloak that sheltered both.

Neither spoke for a moment, and in the silence the rapid beating of two hearts was heard. To drown the sound, Coventry said softly, "Are you frightened?"

"No, I like it," she answered, as softly, then added abruptly, "But why do we hide? There is nothing to fear. It is late. I must go. You are kneeling on my train. Please rise."

"Why in such haste? This flight and search only adds to the charm of the evening. I'll not get up yet. Will you have a rose, Jean?"

"No, I will not. Let me go, Mr. Coventry, I insist. There has been enough of this folly. You forget yourself."

She spoke imperiously, flung off the cloak, and put him from her. He rose at once, saying, like one waking suddenly from a pleasant dream, "I do indeed forget myself."

Here the sound of voices broke on them, nearer than before. Pointing to a covered walk that led to the house, he said, in his usually cool, calm tone, "Go in that way; I will cover your retreat." And turning, he went to meet the merry hunters.

Half an hour later, when the party broke up, Miss Muir joined them in her usual quiet dress, looking paler, meeker, and sadder than usual. Coventry saw this, though he neither looked at her nor addressed her. Lucia saw it also, and was glad that the dangerous girl had fallen back into her proper place again, for she had suffered much that night. She appropriated her cousin's arm as they went through the park, but he was in one of his taciturn moods, and all her attempts at conversation were in vain. Miss Muir walked alone, singing softly to herself as she followed in the dusk. Was Gerald so silent because he listened to that fitful song? Lucia thought so, and felt her dislike rapidly deepening to hatred.

When the young friends were gone, and the family were exchanging good-nights among themselves, Jean was surprised by Coventry's offering his hand, for he had never done it before, and whispering, as he held it, though Lucia watched him all the while, "I have not given my advice, yet."

"Thanks, I no longer need it. I have decided for myself."

"May I ask how?"

"To brave my enemy."

"Good! But what decided you so suddenly?".

"The finding of a friend." And with a grateful glance she was gone.

VI

ON THE WATCH

"IF you please, Mr. Coventry, did you get the letter last night?" were the first words that greeted the "young master" as he left his room next morning.

"What letter, Dean? I don't remember any," he answered, pausing, for something in the maid's manner struck him as peculiar.

"It came just as you left for the Hall, sir. Benson ran after you with it, as it was marked 'Haste.' Didn't you get it, sir?" asked the woman, anxiously.

"Yes, but upon my life, I forgot all about it till this minute. It's in my other coat, I suppose, if I've not lost it. That absurd masquerading put everything else out of my head." And speaking more to himself than to the maid, Coventry turned back to look for the missing letter.

Dean remained where she was, apparently busy about the arrangement of the curtains at the hall window, but furtively watching meanwhile with a most unwonted air of curiosity.

"Not there, I thought so!" she muttered, as Coventry impatiently thrust his hand into one pocket after another. But as she spoke, an expression of amazement appeared in her face, for suddenly the letter was discovered.

"I'd have sworn it wasn't there! I don't understand it, but she's a deep one, or I'm much deceived." And Dean shook her head like one perplexed, but not convinced.

Coventry uttered an exclamation of satisfaction on glancing at the address and, standing where he was, tore open the letter.

Dear C:

I'm off to Baden. Come and join me, then you'll be out of harm's way; for if you fall in love with J. M. (and you can't escape if you stay where she is), you will incur the trifling inconvenience of having your brains blown out by

Yours truly, F. R. Sydney

"The man is mad!" ejaculated Coventry, staring at the letter while an angry flush rose to his face. "What the deuce does he mean by writing to me in that style? Join him—not I! And as for the threat, I laugh at it. Poor Jean! This headstrong fool seems bent on tormenting her. Well, Dean, what are you waiting for?" he demanded, as if suddenly conscious of her presence.

"Nothing, sir; I only stopped to see if you found the letter. Beg pardon, sir."

And she was moving on when Coventry asked, with a suspicious look, "What made you think it was lost? You seem to take an uncommon interest in my affairs today."

"Oh dear, no, sir. I felt a bit anxious, Benson is so forgetful, and it was me who sent him after you, for I happened to see you go out, so I felt responsible. Being marked that way, I thought it might be important so I asked about it."

"Very well, you can go, Dean. It's all right, you see."

"I'm not so sure of that," muttered the woman, as she curtsied respectfully and went away, looking as if the letter had *not* been found.

Dean was Miss Beaufort's maid, a grave, middle-aged woman with keen eyes and a somewhat grim air. Having been long in the family, she enjoyed all the privileges of a faithful and favorite servant. She loved her young mistress with an almost jealous affection. She watched over her with the vigilant care of a mother and resented any attempt at interference on the part of others. At first she had pitied and liked Jean Muir, then distrusted her, and now heartily hated her, as the cause of the increased indifference of Coventry toward his cousin. Dean knew the depth of Lucia's love, and though no man, in her eyes, was worthy of her mistress, still, having honored him with her regard, Dean felt bound to like him, and the late change in his manner disturbed the maid almost as much as it did the mistress. She watched Jean narrowly, causing that amiable creature much amusement but little annoyance, as yet, for Dean's slow English wit was no match for the subtle mind of the governess. On the preceding night, Dean had been sent up to the Hall with costumes and had there seen something which much disturbed her. She began to speak of it while undressing her mistress, but Lucia, being in an unhappy mood, had so sternly ordered her not to gossip that the tale remained untold, and she was forced to bide her time.

Now I'll see how *she* looks after it; though there's not much to be got out of *her* face, the deceitful hussy, thought Dean, marching down the corridor and knitting her black brows as she went.

"Good morning, Mrs. Dean. I hope you are none the worse for last night's frolic. You had the work and we the play," said a blithe voice behind her; and turning sharply, she confronted Miss Muir. Fresh and smiling, the governess nodded with an air of cordiality which would have been irresistible with anyone but Dean.

"I'm quite well, thank you, miss," she returned coldly, as her keen eye fastened on the girl as if to watch the effect of her words. "I had a good rest when the young ladies and gentlemen were at supper, for while the maids cleaned up, I sat in the 'little anteroom.'"

"Yes, I saw you, and feared you'd take cold. Very glad you didn't. How is Miss Beaufort? She seemed rather poorly last night" was the tranquil reply, as Jean settled the little frills about her delicate wrists. The cool question was a return shot for Dean's hint that she had been where she could oversee the interview between Coventry and Miss Muir.

"She is a bit tired, as any *lady* would be after such an evening. People who are *used* to *play-acting* wouldn't mind it, perhaps, but Miss Beaufort don't enjoy *romps* as much as *some* do."

The emphasis upon certain words made Dean's speech as impertinent as she desired. But Jean only laughed, and as Coventry's step was heard behind them, she ran downstairs, saying blandly, but with a wicked look, "I won't stop to thank you now, lest Mr. Coventry should bid me good-morning, and so increase Miss Beaufort's indisposition."

Dean's eyes flashed as she looked after the girl with a wrathful face, and went her way, saying grimly, "I'll bide my time, but I'll get the better of her yet."

Fancying himself quite removed from "last night's absurdity," yet curious to see how Jean would meet him, Coventry lounged into the breakfast room with his usual air of listless indifference. A languid nod and murmur was all the reply he vouchsafed to the greetings of cousin, sister, and governess as he sat down and took up his paper.

"Have you had a letter from Ned?" asked Bella, looking at the note which her brother still held.

"No" was the brief answer.

"Who then? You look as if you had received bad news."

There was no reply, and, peeping over his arm, Bella caught sight of the seal and exclaimed, in a disappointed tone, "It is the Sydney crest. I don't are about the note now. Men's letters to each other are not interesting."

Miss Muir had been quietly feeding one of Edward's dogs, but at the name she looked up and met Coventry's eyes, coloring so distressfully that he pitied her. Why he should take the trouble to cover her confusion, he did not stop to ask himself, but seeing the curl of Lucia's lip, he suddenly addressed her with an air of displeasure, "Do you know that Dean is getting impertinent? She presumes too much on her age and your indulgence, and forgets her place."

"What has she done?" asked Lucia coldly.

"She troubles herself about my affairs and takes it upon herself to keep Benson in order."

Here Coventry told about the letter and the woman's evident curiosity.

"Poor Dean, she gets no thanks for reminding you of what you had forgotten. Next time she will leave your letters to their fate, and perhaps it will be as well, if they have such a bad effect upon your temper, Gerald."

Lucia spoke calmly, but there was an angry color in her cheek as she rose and left the room. Coventry looked much annoyed, for on Jean's face he detected a faint smile, half pitiful, half satirical, which disturbed him more than his cousin's insinuation. Bella broke the awkward silence by saying, with a sigh, "Poor Ned! I do so long to hear again from him. I thought a letter had come for some of us. Dean said she saw one bearing his writing on the hall table yesterday."

"She seems to have a mania for inspecting letters. I won't allow it. Who was the letter for, Bella?" said Coventry, putting down his paper.

"She wouldn't or couldn't tell, but looked very cross and told me to ask you."

"Very odd! I've had none," began Coventry.

"But I had one several days ago. Will you please read it, and my reply?" And as she spoke, Jean laid two letters before him.

"Certainly not. It would be dishonorable to read what Ned intended for no eyes but your own. You are too scrupulous in one way, and not enough so in another, Miss Muir." And Coventry offered both the letters with an air of grave decision, which could not conceal the interest and surprise he felt.

"You are right. Mr. Edward's note *should* be kept sacred, for in it the poor boy has laid bare his heart to me. But mine I beg you will read, that you may see how well I try to keep my word to you. Oblige me in this, Mr. Coventry; I have a right to ask it of you."

So urgently she spoke, so wistfully she looked, that he could not refuse and, going to the window, read the letter. It was evidently an answer to a passionate appeal from the young lover, and was written with consummate skill. As he read, Gerald could not help thinking, If this girl writes in this way to a man whom she does *not* love, with what a world of power and passion would she write to one whom she *did* love. And this thought kept returning to him as his eye went over line after line of wise argument, gentle reproof, good counsel, and friendly regard. Here and there a word, a phrase, betrayed what she had already confessed, and Coventry forgot to return the letter, as he stood wondering who was the man whom Jean loved.

The sound of Bella's voice recalled him, for she was saying, half kindly, half petulantly, "Don't look so sad, Jean. Ned will outlive it, I dare say. You remember you said once men never died of love, though women might. In his one note to me, he spoke so beautifully of you, and begged me to be kind to you for his sake, that I try to be with all my heart, though if it was anyone but you, I really think I should hate them for making my dear boy so unhappy."

"You are too kind, Bella, and I often think I'll go away to relieve you of my presence; but unwise and dangerous as it is to stay, I haven't the courage to go. I've been so happy here." And as she spoke, Jean's head dropped lower over the dog as it nestled to her affectionately.

Before Bella could utter half the loving words that sprang to her lips, Coventry came to them with all languor gone from face and mien, and laying Jean's letter before her, he said, with an undertone of deep feeling in his usually emotionless voice, "A right womanly and eloquent letter, but I fear it will only increase the fire it was meant to quench. I pity my brother more than ever now."

"Shall I send it?" asked Jean, looking straight up at him, like one who had entire reliance on his judgment.

"Yes, I have not the heart to rob him of such a sweet sermon upon self-sacrifice. Shall I post it for you?"

"Thank you; in a moment." And with a grateful look, Jean dropped her eyes. Producing her little purse, she selected a penny, folded it in a bit of paper, and then offered both letter and coin to Coventry, with such a pretty air of business, that he could not control a laugh.

"So you won't be indebted to me for a penny? What a proud woman you are, Miss Muir."

"I am; it's a family failing." And she gave him a significant glance, which recalled to him the memory of who she was. He understood her feeling, and liked her the better for it, knowing that he would have done the same had he been in her place. It was a little thing, but if done for effect, it answered admirably, for it showed a quick insight into his character on her part, and betrayed to him the existence of a pride in which he sympathized heartily. He stood by Jean a moment, watching her as she burnt Edward's letter in the blaze of the spirit lamp under the urn.

"Why do you do that?" he asked involuntarily.

"Because it is my duty to forget" was all her answer.

"Can you always forget when it becomes a duty?"

"I wish I could! I wish I could!"

She spoke passionately, as if the words broke from her against her will, and, rising hastily, she went into the garden, as if afraid to stay.

"Poor, dear Jean is very unhappy about something, but I can't discover what it is. Last night I found her crying over a rose, and now she runs away, looking as if her heart was broken. I'm glad I've got no lessons."

"What kind of a rose?" asked Coventry from behind his paper as Bella paused.

"A lovely white one. It must have come from the Hall; we have none like it. I wonder if Jean was ever going to be married, and lost her lover, and felt sad because the flower reminded her of bridal roses."

Coventry made no reply, but felt himself change countenance as he recalled the little scene behind the rose hedge, where he gave Jean the flower which she had refused yet taken. Presently, to Bella's surprise, he flung down the paper, tore Sydney's note to atoms, and rang for his horse with an energy which amazed her.

"Why, Gerald, what has come over you? One would think Ned's restless spirit had suddenly taken possession of you. What are you going to do?"

"I'm going to work" was the unexpected answer, as Coventry turned toward her with an expression so rarely seen on his fine face.

"What has waked you up all at once?" asked Bella, looking more and more amazed.

"You did," he said, drawing her toward him.

"I! When? How?"

"Do you remember saying once that energy was better than beauty in a man, and that no one could respect an idler?"

"I never said anything half so sensible as that. Jean said something like it once, I believe, but I forgot. Are you tired of doing nothing, at last, Gerald?"

"Yes, I neglected my duty to Ned, till he got into trouble, and now I reproach myself for it. It's not too late to do other neglected tasks, so I'm going at them with a will. Don't say anything about it to anyone, and don't laugh at me, for I'm in earnest, Bell."

"I know you are, and I admire and love you for it, my dear old boy," cried Bella enthusiastically, as she threw her arms about his neck and kissed him heartily. "What will you do first?" she asked, as he stood thoughtfully smoothing the bright head that leaned upon his shoulder, with that new expression still clear and steady in his face.

"I'm going to ride over the whole estate, and attend to things as a master should; not leave it all to Bent, of whom I've heard many complaints, but have been too idle to inquire about them. I shall consult Uncle, and endeavor to be all that my father was in his time. Is that a worthy ambition, dear?"

"Oh, Gerald, let me tell Mamma. It will make her so happy. You are her idol, and to hear you say these things, to see you look so like dear Papa, would do more for her spirits than all the doctors in England."

"Wait till I prove what my resolution is worth. When I have really done something, then I'll surprise Mamma with a sample of my work."

"Of course you'll tell Lucia?"

"Not on any account. It is a little secret between us, so keep it till I give you leave to tell it."

"But Jean will see it at once; she knows everything that happens, she is so quick and wise. Do you mind her knowing?"

"I don't see that I can help it if she is so wonderfully gifted. Let her see what she can, I don't mind her. Now I'm off." And with a kiss to his sister, a sudden smile on his face, Coventry sprang upon his horse and rode away at a pace which caused the groom to stare after him in blank amazement.

Nothing more was seen of him till dinnertime, when he came in so exhilarated by his brisk ride and busy morning that he found some difficulty in assuming his customary manner, and more than once astonished the family by talking animatedly on various subjects which till now had always seemed utterly uninteresting to him. Lucia was amazed, his mother delighted, and Bella could hardly control her desire to explain the mystery; but Jean took it very calmly and regarded him with the air of one who said, "I understand, but you will soon tire of it." This nettled him more than he would confess, and he exerted himself to silently contradict that prophecy.

"Have you answered Mr. Sydney's letter?" asked Bella, when they were all scattered about the drawing room after dinner.

"No," answered her brother, who was pacing up and down with restless steps, instead of lounging near his beautiful cousin.

"I ask because I remembered that Ned sent a message for him in my last note, as he thought you would know Sydney's address. Here it is, something about a horse. Please put it in when you write," and Bella laid the note on the writing table nearby.

"I'll send it at once and have done with it," muttered Coventry and, seating himself, he dashed off a few lines, sealed and sent the letter, and then resumed his march, eyeing the three young ladies with three different expressions, as he passed and repassed. Lucia sat apart, feigning to be intent upon a book, and her handsome face looked almost stern in its haughty composure, for though her heart ached, she was too proud to own it. Bella now lay on the sofa, half asleep, a rosy little creature, as unconsciously pretty as a child. Miss Muir sat in the recess of a deep window, in a low lounging chair, working at an embroidery frame with a graceful industry pleasant to see. Of late she had worn colors, for Bella had been generous in gifts, and the pale blue muslin which flowed in soft waves about her was very becoming to her fair skin and golden hair. The close braids were gone, and loose curls dropped here and there from the heavy coil wound around her well-shaped head. The tip of one dainty foot was visible, and a petulant litle gesture which now and then shook back the falling sleeve gave glimpses of a round white arm. Ned's great hound lay nearby, the sunshine flickered on her through the leaves, and as she sat smiling to herself, while the dexterous hands shaped leaf and flower, she made a charming picture of all that is most womanly and winning; a picture which few men's eyes would not have liked to rest upon.

Another chair stood near her, and as Coventry went up and down, a strong desire to take it possessed him. He was tired of his thoughts and wished to be amused by watching the changes of the girl's expressive face, listening to the varying tones of her voice, and trying to discover the spell which so strongly attracted him in spite of himself. More than once he swerved from his course to gratify his whim, but Lucia's presence always restrained him, and with a word to the dog, or a glance from the window, as pretext for a pause, he resumed his walk again. Something in his cousin's face reproached him, but her manner of late was so repellent that he felt no desire to resume their former familiarity, and, wishing to show that he did not consider himself bound, he kept aloof. It was a quiet test of the power of each woman over this man; they instinctively felt it, and both tried to conquer. Lucia spoke several times, and tried to speak frankly and affably; but her manner was constrained, and Coventry, having answered politely, relapsed into silence. Jean said nothing, but silently appealed to eye and ear by the pretty picture she made of herself, the snatches of song she softly sang, as if forgetting that she was not alone, and a shy glance now and then, half wistful, half merry, which was more alluring than graceful figure or sweet voice. When she had tormented Lucia and tempted Coventry long enough, she quietly asserted her supremacy in a way which astonished her rival, who knew nothing of the secret of her birth, which knowledge did much to attract and charm the young man. Letting a ball of silk escape from her lap, she watched it roll toward the promenader, who caught and returned it with an alacrity which added grace to the trifling service. As she took it, she said, in the frank way that never failed to win him, "I think you must be tired; but if exercise is necessary, employ your energies to some purpose and put your mother's basket of silks in order. They are in a tangle, and it will please her to know that you did it, as your brother used to do."

"Hercules at the distaff," said Coventry gaily, and down he sat in the long-desired seat. Jean put the basket on his knee, and as he surveyed it, as if daunted at his task, she leaned back, and indulged in a musical little peal of laughter charming to hear. Lucia sat dumb with surprise, to see her proud, indolent cousin obeying the commands of a governess, and looking as if he heartily enjoyed it. In ten minutes she was as entirely forgotten as if she had been miles away; for Jean seemed in her wittiest, gayest mood, and as she now treated the "young master" like an equal, there was none of the former meek timidity. Yet often her eyes fell, her color changed, and the piquant sallies faltered on her tongue, as Coventry involuntarily looked deep into the fine eyes which had once shone on him so tenderly in that mimic tragedy. He could not forget it, and though neither alluded to it, the memory of the previous evening seemed to haunt both and lend a secret charm to the present moment. Lucia bore this as long as she could, and then left the room with an air of an insulted princess; but Coventry did not, and Jean feigned not to see her go. Bella was fast asleep, and before he knew how it came to pass, the young man was listening to the story of his companion's life. A sad tale, told with wonderful skill, for soon he was absorbed in it. The basket slid unobserved from his knee, the dog was pushed away, and, leaning forward, he listened eagerly as the girl's low voice recounted all the hardships, loneliness, and grief of her short life. In the midst of a touching episode she started, stopped, and looked straight before her, with an intent expression which changed to one of intense contempt, and her eye turned to Coventry's, as she said, pointing to the window behind him, "We are watched."

"By whom?" he demanded, starting up angrily.

"Hush, say nothing, let it pass. I am used to it."

"But *I* am not, and I'll not submit to it. Who was it, Jean?" he answered hotly.

She smiled significantly at a knot of rose-colored ribbon, which a little gust was blowing toward them along the terrace. A black frown darkened the young man's face as he sprang out of the long window and went rapidly out of sight, scrutinizing each green nook as he passed. Jean laughed quietly as she watched him, and said softly to herself, with her eyes on the fluttering ribbon, "That was a fortunate accident, and a happy inspiration. Yes, my dear Mrs. Dean, you will find that playing the spy will only get your mistress as well as yourself into trouble. You would not be warned, and you must take the consequences, reluctant as I am to injure a worthy creature like yourself."

Soon Coventry was heard returning. Jean listened with suspended breath to catch his first words, for he was not alone.

"Since you insist that it was you and not your mistress, I let it pass, although I still have my suspicions. Tell Miss Beaufort I desire to see her for a few moments in the library. Now go, Dean, and be careful for the future, if you wish to stay in my house."

The maid retired, and the young man came in looking both ireful and stern.

"I wish I had said nothing, but I was startled, and spoke involuntarily. Now you are angry, and I have made fresh trouble for poor Miss Lucia. Forgive me as I forgive her, and let it pass. I have learned to bear this surveillance, and pity her causeless jealousy," said Jean, with a self-reproachful air.

"I will forgive the dishonorable act, but I cannot forget it, and I intend to put a stop to it. I am not betrothed to my cousin, as I told you once, but you, like all the rest, seem bent on believing that I am. Hitherto I have cared too little about the matter to settle it, but now I shall prove beyond all doubt that I am free."

As he uttered the last word, Coventry cast on Jean a look that affected her strangely. She grew pale, her work dropped on her lap, and her eyes rose to his, with an eager, questioning expression, which slowly changed to one of mingled pain and pity, as she turned her face away, murmuring in a tone of tender sorrow, "Poor Lucia, who will comfort her?"

For a moment Coventry stood silent, as if weighing some fateful purpose in his mind. As Jean's rapt sigh of compassion reached his ear, he had echoed it within himself, and half repented of his resolution; then his eye rested on the girl before him looking so lonely in her sweet sympathy for another that his heart yearned toward her. Sudden fire shot into his eye, sudden warmth replaced the cold sternness of his face, and his steady voice faltered suddenly, as he said, very low, yet very earnestly, "Jean, I have tried to love her, but I cannot. Ought I to deceive her, and make myself miserable to please my family?"

"She is beautiful and good, and loves you tenderly; is there no hope for her?" asked Jean, still pale, but very quiet, though she held one hand against her heart, as if to still or hide its rapid beating.

"None," answered Coventry.

"But can you not learn to love her? Your will is strong, and most men would not find it a hard task."

"I cannot, for something stronger than my own will controls me."

"What is that?" And Jean's dark eyes were fixed upon him, full of innocent wonder.

His fell, and he said hastily, "I dare not tell you yet."

"Pardon! I should not have asked. Do not consult me in this matter; I am not the person to advise you. I can only say that it seems to me as if any man with an empty heart would be glad to have so beautiful a woman as your cousin."

"My heart is not empty," began Coventry, drawing a step nearer, and speaking in a passionate voice. "Jean, I *must* speak; hear me. I cannot love my cousin, because I love you."

"Stop!" And Jean sprang up with a commanding gesture. "I will not hear you while any promise binds you to another. Remember your mother's wishes, Lucia's hopes, Edward's last words, your own pride, my humble lot. You forget yourself, Mr. Coventry. Think well before you speak, weigh the cost of this act, and recollect who I am before you insult me by any transient passion, any false vows."

"I have thought, I do weigh the cost, and I swear that I desire to woo you as humbly, honestly as I would any lady in the land. You speak of my pride. Do I stoop in loving my equal in rank? You speak of your lowly lot, but poverty is no disgrace, and the courage with which you bear it makes it beautiful. I should have broken with Lucia before I spoke, but I could not control myself. My mother loves you, and will be happy in my happiness. Edward must forgive me, for I have tried to do my best, but love is irresistible. Tell me, Jean, is there any hope for me?"

He had seized her hand and was speaking impetuously, with ardent face and tender tone, but no answer came, for as Jean turned her eloquent countenance toward him, full of maiden shame and timid love, Dean's prim figure appeared at the door, and her harsh voice broke the momentary silence, saying, sternly, "Miss Beaufort is waiting for you, sir."

"Go, go at once, and be kind, for my sake, Gerald," whispered Jean, for he stood as if deaf and blind to everything but her voice, her face.

As she drew his head down to whisper, her cheek touched his, and regardless of Dean, he kissed it, passionately, whispering back, "My little Jean! For your sake I can be anything."

"Miss Beaufort is waiting. Shall I say you will come, sir?" demanded Dean, pale and grim with indignation.

"Yes, yes, I'll come. Wait for me in the garden, Jean." And Coventry hurried away, in no mood for the interview but anxious to have it over.

As the door closed behind him, Dean walked up to Miss Muir, trembling with anger, and laying a heavy hand on her arm, she said below her breath, "I've been expecting this, you artful creature. I saw your game and did my best to spoil it, but you are too quick for me. You think you've got him. There you are mistaken; for as sure as my name is Hester Dean, I'll prevent it, or Sir John shall."

"Take your hand away and treat me with proper respect, or you will be dismissed from this house. Do you know who I am?" And Jean drew herself up with a haughty air, which impressed the woman more deeply than her words. "I am the daughter of Lady Howard and, if I choose it, can be the wife of Mr. Coventry."

Dean drew back amazed, yet not convinced. Being a well-trained servant, as well as a prudent woman, she feared to overstep the bounds of respect, to go too far, and get her mistress as well as herself into trouble.

So, though she still doubted Jean, and hated her more than ever, she controlled herself. Dropping a curtsy, she assumed her usual air of deference, and said, meekly, "I beg pardon, miss. If I'd known, I should have conducted myself differently, of course, but ordinary governesses make so much mischief in a house, one can't help mistrusting them. I don't wish to meddle or be overbold, but being fond of my dear young lady, I naturally take her part, and must say that Mr. Coventry has not acted like a gentleman."

"Think what you please, Dean, but I advise you to say as little as possible if you wish to remain. I have not accepted Mr. Coventry yet, and if he chooses to set aside the engagement his family made for him, I think he has a right to do so. Miss Beaufort would hardly care to marry him against his will, because he pities her for her unhappy love," and with a tranquil smile, Miss Muir walked away.

VII

THE LAST CHANCE

✣✣✣✣✣

"SHE will tell Sir John, will she? Then I must be before her, and hasten events. It will be as well to have all sure before there can be any danger. My poor Dean, you are no match for me, but you may prove annoying, nevertheless."

These thoughts passed through Miss Muir's mind as she went down the hall, pausing an instant at the library door, for the murmur of voices was heard. She caught no word, and had only time for an instant's pause as Dean's heavy step followed her. Turning, Jean drew a chair before the door, and, beckoning to the woman, she said, smiling still, "Sit here and play watchdog. I am going to Miss Bella, so you can nod if you will."

"Thank you, miss. I will wait for my young lady. She may need me when this hard time is over." And Dean seated herself with a resolute face.

Jean laughed and went on; but her eyes gleamed with sudden malice, and she glanced over her shoulder with an expression which boded ill for the faithful old servant.

"I've got a letter from Ned, and here is a tiny note for you," cried Bella as Jean entered the boudoir. "Mine is a very odd, hasty letter, with no news in it, but his meeting with Sydney. I hope yours is better, or it won't be very satisfactory."

As Sydney's name passed Bella's lips, all the color died out of Miss Muir's face, and the note shook with the tremor of her hand. Her very lips were white, but she said calmly, "Thank you. As you are busy, I'll go and read my letter on the lawn." And before Bella could speak, she was gone.

Hurrying to a quiet nook, Jean tore open the note and read the few blotted lines it contained.

I have seen Sydney; he has told me all; and, hard as I found it to believe, it was impossible to doubt, for he has discovered proofs which cannot be denied. I make no reproaches, shall demand no confession or atonement, for I cannot forget that I once loved you. I give you three days to find another home, before I return to tell the family who you are. Go at once, I beseech you, and spare me the pain of seeing your disgrace.

Slowly, steadily she read it twice over, then sat motionless, knitting her brows in deep thought. Presently she drew a long breath, tore up the note, and rising, went slowly toward the Hall, saying to herself, "Three days, only three days! Can it be accomplished in so short a time? It shall be, if wit and will can do it, for it is my last chance. If this fails, I'll not go back to my old life, but end all at once."

Setting her teeth and clenching her hands, as if some memory stung her, she went on through the twilight, to find Sir John waiting to give her a hearty welcome.

"You look tired, my dear. Never mind the reading tonight; rest yourself, and let the book go," he said kindly, observing her worn look.

"Thank you, sir. I am tired, but I'd rather read, else the book will not be finished before I go."

"Go, child! Where are you going?" demanded Sir John, looking anxiously at her as she sat down.

"I will tell you by-and-by, sir." And opening the book, Jean read for a little while.

But the usual charm was gone; there was no spirit in the voice of the reader, no interest in the face of the listener, and soon he said, abruptly, "My dear, pray stop! I cannot listen with a divided mind. What troubles you? Tell your friend, and let him comfort you."

As if the kind words overcame her, Jean dropped the book, covered up her face, and wept so bitterly that Sir John was much alarmed; for such a demonstration was doubly touching in one who usually was all gaiety and smiles. As he tried to soothe her, his words grew tender, his solicitude full of a more than paternal anxiety, and his kind heart overflowed with pity and affection for the weeping girl. As she grew calmer, he urged her to be frank, promising to help and counsel her, whatever the affliction or fault might be.

"Ah, you are too kind, too generous! How can I go away and leave my one friend?" sighed Jean, wiping the tears away and looking up at him with grateful eyes.

"Then you do care a little for the old man?" said Sir John with an eager look, an involuntary pressure of the hand he held.

Jean turned her face away, and answered, very low, "No one ever was so kind to me as you have been. Can I help caring for you more than I can express?"

Sir John was a little deaf at times, but he heard that, and looked well pleased. He had been rather thoughtful of late, had dressed with unusual care, been particularly gallant and gay when the young ladies visited him, and more than once, when Jean paused in the reading to ask a question, he had been forced to confess that he had not been listening; though, as she well knew, his eyes had been fixed upon her. Since the discovery of her birth, his manner had been peculiarly benignant, and many little acts had proved his interest and goodwill. Now, when Jean spoke of going, a panic seized him, and desolation seemed about to fall upon the old Hall. Something in her unusual agitation struck him as peculiar and excited his curiosity. Never had she seemed so interesting as now, when she sat beside him with tearful eyes, and some soft trouble in her heart which she dared not confess.

"Tell me everything, child, and let your friend help you if he can." Formerly he said "father" or "the old man," but lately he always spoke of himself as her "friend."

"I will tell you, for I have no one else to turn to. I must go away because Mr. Coventry has been weak enough to love me."

"What, Gerald?" cried Sir John, amazed.

"Yes; today he told me this, and left me to break with Lucia; so I ran to you to help me prevent him from disappointing his mother's hopes and plans."

Sir John had started up and paced down the room, but as Jean paused he turned toward her, saying, with an altered face. "Then you do not love him? Is it possible?"

"No, I do not love him," she answered promptly.

"Yet he is all that women usually find attractive. How is it that you have escaped, Jean?"

"I love someone else" was the scarcely audible reply.

Sir John resumed his seat with the air of a man bent on getting at a mystery, if possible.

"It will be unjust to let you suffer for the folly of these boys, my little girl. Ned is gone, and I was sure that Gerald was safe; but now that his turn has come, I am perplexed, for he cannot be sent away."

"No, it is I who must go; but it seems so hard to leave this safe and happy home, and wander away into the wide, cold world again. You have all been too kind to me, and now separation breaks my heart."

A sob ended the speech, and Jean's head went down upon her hands again. Sir John looked at her a moment, and his fine old face was full of genuine emotion, as he said slowly, "Jean, will you stay and be a daughter to the solitary old man?"

"No, sir" was the unexpected answer.

"And why not?" asked Sir John, looking surprised, but rather pleased than angry.

"Because I could not be a daughter to you; and even if I could, it would not be wise, for the gossips would say you were not old enough to be the adopted father of a girl like me. Sir John, young as I am, I know much of the world, and am sure that this kind plan is impractical; but I thank you from the bottom of my heart."

"Where will you go, Jean?" asked Sir John, after a pause.

"To London, and try to find another situation where I can do no harm."

"Will it be difficult to find another home?"

"Yes. I cannot ask Mrs. Coventry to recommend me, when I have innocently brought so much trouble into her family; and Lady Sydney is gone, so I have no friend."

"Except John Coventry. I will arrange all that. When will you go, Jean?"

"Tomorrow."

"So soon!" And the old man's voice betrayed the trouble he was trying to conceal.

Jean had grown very calm, but it was the calmness of desperation. She had hoped that the first tears would produce the avowal for which she waited. It had not, and she began to fear that her last chance was slipping from her. Did the old man love her? If so, why did he not speak? Eager to profit by each moment, she was on the alert for any hopeful hint, any propitious word, look, or act, and every nerve was strung to the utmost.

"Jean, may I ask one question?" said Sir John.

"Anything of me, sir."

"This man whom you love—can he not help you?"

"He could if he knew, but he must not."

"If he knew what? Your present trouble?"

"No. My love."

"He does know this, then?"

"No, thank heaven! And he never will."

"Why not?"

"Because I am too proud to own it."

"He loves you, my child?"

"I do not know—I dare not hope it," murmured Jean.

"Can I not help you here? Believe me, I desire to see you safe and happy. Is there nothing I can do?"

"Nothing, nothing."

"May I know the name?"

"No! No! Let me go; I cannot bear this questioning!" And Jean's distressful face warned him to ask no more.

"Forgive me, and let me do what I may. Rest here quietly. I'll write a letter to a good friend of mine, who will find you a home, if you leave us."

As Sir John passed into his inner study, Jean watched him with despairing eyes and wrung her hands, saying to herself, Has all my skill deserted me when I need it most? How can I make him understand, yet not overstep the bounds of maiden modesty? He is so blind, so timid, or so dull he will not see, and time is going fast. What shall I do to open his eyes?

Her own eyes roved about the room, seeking for some aid from inanimate things, and soon she found it. Close behind the couch where she sat hung a fine miniature of Sir John. At first her eye rested on it as she contrasted its placid comeliness with the unusual pallor and disquiet of the living face seen through the open door, as the old man sat at his desk trying to write and casting covert glances at the girlish figure he had left behind him. Affecting unconsciousness of this, Jean gazed on as if forgetful of everything but the picture, and suddenly, as if obeying an irresistible impulse, she took it down, looked long and fondly at it, then, shaking her curls about her face, as if to hide the act, pressed it to her lips and seemed to weep over it in an uncontrollable paroxysm of tender grief. A sound startled her, and like a guilty thing, she turned to replace the picture; but it dropped from her hand as she uttered a faint cry and hid her face, for Sir John stood before her, with an expression which she could not mistake.

"Jean, why did you do that?" he asked, in an eager, agitated voice.

No answer, as the girl sank lower, like one overwhelmed with shame. Laying his hand on the bent head, and bending his own, he whispered, "Tell me, is the name John Coventry?"

Still no answer, but a stifled sound betrayed that his words had gone home.

"Jean, shall I go back and write the letter, or may I stay and tell you that the old man loves you better than a daughter?"

She did not speak, but a little hand stole out from under the falling hair, as if to keep him. With a broken exclamation he seized it, drew her up into his arms, and laid his gray head on her fair one, too happy for words. For a moment Jean Muir enjoyed her success; then, fearing lest some sudden mishap should destroy it, she hastened to make all secure. Looking up with well-feigned timidity and half-confessed affection, she said softly, "Forgive me that I could not hide this better. I meant to go away and never tell it, but you were so kind it made the parting doubly hard. Why did you ask such dangerous questions? Why did you look, when you should have been writing my dismissal?"

"How could I dream that you loved me, Jean, when you refused the only offer I dared make? Could I be presumptuous enough to fancy you would reject young lovers for an old man like me?" asked Sir John caressing her.

"You are not old, to me, but everything I love and honor!" interrupted Jean, with a touch of genuine remorse, as this generous, honorable gentleman gave her both heart and home, unconscious of deceit. "It is I who am presumptuous, to dare to love one so far above me. But I did not know how dear you were to me till I felt that I must go. I ought not to accept this happiness. I am not worthy of it; and you will regret your kindness when the world blames you for giving a home to one so poor, and plain, and humble as I."

"Hush, my darling. I care nothing for the idle gossip of the world. If you are happy here, let tongues wag as they will. I shall be too busy enjoying the sunshine of your presence to heed anything that goes on about me. But, Jean, you are sure you love me? It seems incredible that I should win the heart that has been so cold to younger, better men than I."

"Dear Sir John, be sure of this, I love you truly. I will do my best to be a good wife to you, and prove that, in spite of my many faults, I possess the virtue of gratitude."

If he had known the strait she was in, he would have understood the cause of the sudden fervor of her words, the intense thankfulness that shone in her face, the real humility that made her stoop and kiss the generous hand that gave so much. For a few moments she enjoyed and let him enjoy the happy present, undisturbed. But the anxiety which devoured her, the danger which menaced her, soon recalled her, and forced her to wring yet more from the unsuspicious heart she had conquered.

"No need of letters now," said Sir John, as they sat side by side, with the summer moonlight glorifying all the room. "You have found a home for life; may it prove a happy one."

"It is not mine yet, and I have a strange foreboding that it never will be," she answered sadly.

"Why, my child?"

"Because I have an enemy who will try to destroy my peace, to poison your mind against me, and to drive me out from my paradise, to suffer again all I have suffered this last year."

"You mean that mad Sydney of whom you told me?"

"Yes. As soon as he hears of this good fortune to poor little Jean, he will hasten to mar it. He is my fate; I cannot escape him, and wherever he goes my friends desert me; for he has the power and uses it for my destruction. Let me go away and hide before he comes, for, having shared your confidence, it will break my heart to see you distrust and turn from me, instead of loving and protecting."

"My poor child, you are superstitious. Be easy. No one can harm you now, no one would dare attempt it. And as for my deserting you, that will soon be out of my power, if I have my way."

"How, dear Sir John?" asked Jean, with a flutter of intense relief at her heart, for the way seemed smoothing before her.

"I will make you my wife at once, if I may. This will free you from Gerald's love, protect you from Sydney's persecution, give you a safe home, and me the right to cherish and defend with heart and hand. Shall it be so, my child?"

"Yes; but oh, remember that I have no friend but you! Promise me to be faithful to the last—to believe in me, to trust me, protect and love me, in spite of all misfortunes, faults, and follies. I will be true as steel to you, and make your life as happy as it deserves to be. Let us promise these things now, and keep the promises unbroken to the end."

Her solemn air touched Sir John. Too honorable and upright himself to suspect falsehood in others, he saw only the natural impulse of a lovely girl in Jean's words, and, taking the hand she gave him in both of his, he promised all she asked, and kept that promise to the end. She paused an instant, with a pale, absent expression, as if she searched herself, then looked up clearly in the confiding face above her, and promised what she faithfully performed in afteryears.

"When shall it be, little sweetheart? I leave all to you, only let it be soon, else some gay young lover will appear, and take you from me," said Sir John, playfully, anxious to chase away the dark expression which had stolen over Jean's face.

"Can you keep a secret?" asked the girl, smiling up at him, all her charming self again.

"Try me."

"I will. Edward is coming home in three days. I must be gone before he comes. Tell no one of this; he wishes to surprise them. And if you love me, tell nobody of your approaching marriage. Do not betray that you care for me until I am really yours. There will be such a stir, such remonstrances, explanations, and reproaches that I shall be worn out, and run away from you all to escape the trial. If I could have my wish, I would go to some quiet place tomorrow and wait till you come for me. I know so little of such things, I cannot tell how soon we may be married; not for some weeks, I think."

"Tomorrow, if we like. A special license permits people to marry when and where they please. My plan is better than yours. Listen, and tell me if it can be carried out. I will go to town tomorrow, get the license, invite my friend, the Reverend Paul Fairfax, to return with me, and tomorrow evening you come at your usual time, and, in the presence of my discreet old servants, make me the happiest man in England. How does this suit you, my little Lady Coventry?"

The plan which seemed made to meet her ends, the name which was the height of her ambition, and the blessed sense of safety which came to her filled Jean Muir with such intense satisfaction that tears of real feeling stood in her eyes, and the glad assent she gave was the truest word that had passed her lips for months.

"We will go abroad or to Scotland for our honeymoon, till the storm blows over," said Sir John, well knowing that this hasty marriage would surprise or offend all his relations, and feeling as glad as Jean to escape the first excitement.

"To Scotland, please. I long to see my father's home," said Jean, who dreaded to meet Sydney on the continent.

They talked a little longer, arranging all things, Sir John so intent on hurrying the event that Jean had nothing to do but give a ready assent to all his suggestions. One fear alone disturbed her. If Sir John went to town, he might meet Edward, might hear and believe his statements. Then all would be lost. Yet this risk must be incurred, if the marriage was to be speedily and safely accomplished; and to guard against the meeting was Jean's sole care. As they went through the park—for Sir John insisted upon taking her home—she said, clinging to his arm:

"Dear friend, bear one thing in mind, else we shall be much annoyed, and all our plans disarranged. Avoid your nephews; you are so frank your face will betray you. They both love me, are both hot-tempered, and in the first excitement of the discovery might be violent. You must incur no danger, no disrespect for my sake; so shun them both till we are safe— particularly Edward. He will feel that his brother has wronged him, and that you have succeeded where he failed. This will irritate him, and I fear a stormy scene. Promise to avoid both for a day or two; do not listen to them, do not see them, do not write to or receive letters from them. It is foolish, I know; but you are all I have, and I am haunted by a strange foreboding that I am to lose you."

Touched and flattered by her tender solicitude, Sir John promised everything, even while he laughed at her fears. Love blinded the good gentleman to the peculiarity of the request; the novelty, romance, and secrecy of the affair rather bewildered though it charmed him; and the knowledge that he had outrivaled three young and ardent lovers gratified his vanity more than he would confess. Parting from the girl at the garden gate, he turned homeward, feeling like a boy again, and loitered back, humming a love lay, quite forgetful of evening damps, gout, and the five-and-fifty years which lay so lightly on his shoulders since Jean's arms had rested there. She hurried toward the house, anxious to escape Coventry; but he was waiting for her, and she was forced to meet him.

"How could you linger so long, and keep me in suspense?" he said reproachfully, as he took her hand and tried to catch a glimpse of her face in the shadow of her hat brim. "Come and rest in the grotto. I have so much to say, to hear and enjoy."

"Not now; I am too tired. Let me go in and sleep. Tomorrow we will talk. It is damp and chilly, and my head aches with all this worry." Jean spoke wearily, yet with a touch of petulance, and Coventry, fancying that she was piqued at his not coming for her, hastened to explain with eager tenderness.

"My poor little Jean, you do need rest. We wear you out, among us, and you never complain. I should have come to bring you home, but Lucia detained me, and when I got away I saw my uncle had forestalled me. I shall be jealous of the old gentleman, if he is so devoted. Jean, tell me one thing before we part; I am free as air, now, and have a right to speak. Do you love me? Am I the happy man who has won your heart? I dare to think so, to believe that this telltale face of yours has betrayed you, and to hope that I have gained what poor Ned and wild Sydney have lost."

"Before I answer, tell me of your interview with Lucia. I have a right to know," said Jean.

Coventry hesitated, for pity and remorse were busy at his heart when he recalled poor Lucia's grief. Jean was bent on hearing the humiliation of her rival. As the young man paused, she frowned, then lifted up her face wreathed in softest smiles, and laying her hand on his arm, she said, with most effective emphasis, half shy, half fond, upon his name, "Please tell me, Gerald!"

He could not resist the look, the touch, the tone, and taking the little hand in his, he said rapidly, as if the task was distasteful to him, "I told her that I did not, could not love her; that I had submitted to my mother's wish, and, for a time, had felt tacitly bound to her, though no words had passed between us. But now I demanded my liberty, regretting that the separation was not mutually desired."

"And she—what did she say? How did she bear it?" asked Jean, feeling in her own woman's heart how deeply Lucia's must have been wounded by that avowal.

"Poor girl! It was hard to bear, but her pride sustained her to the end. She owned that no pledge tied me, fully relinquished any claim my past behavior had seemed to have given her, and prayed that I might find another woman to love me as truly, tenderly as she had done. Jean, I felt like a villain; and yet I never plighted my word to her, never really loved her, and had a perfect right to leave her, if I would."

"Did she speak of me?"

"Yes."

"What did she say?"

"Must I tell you?"

"Yes, tell me everything. I know she hates me and I forgive her, knowing that I should hate any woman whom *you* loved."

"Are you jealous, dear?"

"Of you, Gerald?" And the fine eyes glanced up at him, full of a brilliancy that looked like the light of love.

"You make a slave of me already. How do you do it? I never obeyed a woman before. Jean, I think you are a witch. Scotland is the home of weird, uncanny creatures, who take lovely shapes for the bedevilment of poor weak souls. Are you one of those fair deceivers?"

"You are complimentary," laughed the girl. "I *am* a witch, and one day my disguise will drop away and you will see me as I am, old, ugly, bad and lost. Beware of me in time. I've warned you. Now love me at your peril."

Coventry had paused as he spoke, and eyed her with an unquiet look, conscious of some fascination which conquered yet brought no happiness. A feverish yet pleasurable excitement possessed him; a reckless mood, making him eager to obliterate the past by any rash act, any new experience which his passion brought. Jean regarded him with a wistful, almost woeful face, for one short moment; then a strange smile broke over it, as she spoke in a tone of malicious mockery, under which lurked the bitterness of a sad truth. Coventry looked half bewildered, and his eye went from the girl's mysterious face to a dimly lighted window, behind whose curtains poor Lucia hid her aching heart, praying for him the tender prayers that loving women give to those whose sins are all forgiven for love's sake. His heart smote him, and a momentary feeling of repulsion came over him, as he looked at Jean. She saw it, felt angry, yet conscious of a sense of relief; for now that her own safety was so nearly secured, she felt no wish to do mischief, but rather a desire to undo what was already done, and be at peace with all the world. To recall him to his allegiance, she sighed and walked on, saying gently yet coldly, "Will you tell me what I ask before I answer your question, Mr. Coventry?"

"What Lucia said of you? Well, it was this, 'Beward of Miss Muir. We instinctively distrusted her when we had no cause. I believe in instincts, and mine have never changed, for she has not tried to delude me. Her art is wonderful; I feel yet cannot explain or detect it, except in the working of events which her hand seems to guide. She has brought sorrow and dissension into this hitherto happy family. We are all changed, and this girl has done it. Me she can harm no further; you she will ruin, if she can. Beware of her in time, or you will bitterly repent your blind infatuation!"

"And what answer did you make?" asked Jean, as the last words came reluctantly from Coventry's lips.

"I told her that I loved you in spite of myself, and would make you my wife in the face of all opposition. Now, Jean, your answer."

"Give me three days to think of it. Good night." And gliding from him, she vanished into the house, leaving him to roam about half the night, tormented with remorse, suspense, and the old distrust which would return when Jean was not there to banish it by her art.

VIII

SUSPENSE

ALL the next day, Jean was in a state of the most intense anxiety, as every hour brought the crisis nearer, and every hour might bring defeat, for the subtlest human skill is often thwarted by some unforeseen accident. She longed to assure herself that Sir John was gone, but no servants came or went that day, and she could devise no pretext for sending to glean intelligence. She dared not go herself, lest the unusual act should excite suspicion, for she never went till evening. Even had she determined to venture, there was no time, for Mrs. Coventry was in one of her nervous states, and no one but Miss Muir could amuse her; Lucia was ill, and Miss Muir must give orders; Bella had a studious fit, and Jean must help her. Coventry lingered about the house for several hours, but Jean dared not send him, lest some hint of the truth might reach him. He had ridden away to his new duties when Jean did not appear, and the day dragged on wearisomely. Night came at last, and as Jean dressed for the late dinner, she hardly knew herself when she stood before her mirror, excitement lent such color and brilliancy to her countenance. Remembering the wedding which was to take place that evening, she put on a simple white dress and added a cluster of white roses in bosom and hair. She often wore flowers, but in spite of her desire to look and seem as usual, Bella's first words as she entered the drawing room were "Why, Jean, how like a bride you look; a veil and gloves would make you quite complete!"

"You forget one other trifle, Bell," said Gerald, with eyes that brightened as they rested on Miss Muir.

"What is that?" asked his sister.

"A bridegroom."

Bella looked to see how Jean received this, but she seemed quite composed as she smiled one of her sudden smiles, and merely said, "That trifle will doubtless be found when the time comes. Is Miss Beaufort too ill for dinner?"

"She begs to be excused, and said you would be willing to take her place, she thought."

As innocent Bella delivered this message, Jean glanced at Coventry, who evaded her eye and looked ill at ease.

A little remorse will do him good, and prepare him for repentance after the grand coup, *she said to herself, and was particularly gay at dinnertime, though Coventry looked often at Lucia's empty seat, as if he missed her.* As soon as they left the table, Miss Muir sent Bella to her mother; and, knowing that Coventry would not linger long at his wine, she hurried away to the Hall. A servant was lounging at the door, and of him she asked, in a tone which was eager in spite of all efforts to be calm, "Is Sir John at home?"

"No, miss, he's just gone to town."

"Just gone! When do you mean?" cried Jean, forgetting the relief she felt in hearing of his absence in surprise at his late departure.

"He went half an hour ago, in the last train, miss."

"I thought he was going early this morning; he told me he should be back this evening."

"I believe he did mean to go, but was delayed by company. The steward came up on business, and a load of gentlemen called, so Sir John could not get off till night, when he wasn't fit to go, being worn out, and far from well."

"Do you think he will be ill? Did he look so?" And as Jean spoke, a thrill of fear passed over her, lest death should rob her of her prize.

"Well, you know, miss, hurry of any kind is bad for elderly gentlemen inclined to apoplexy. Sir John was in a worry all day, and not like himself. I wanted him to take his man, but he wouldn't; and drove off looking flushed and excited like. I'm anxious about him, for I know something is amiss to hurry him off in this way."

"When will he be back, Ralph?"

"Tomorrow noon, if possible; at night, certainly, he bid me tell anyone that called."

"Did he leave no note or message for Miss Coventry, or someone of the family?"

"No, miss, nothing."

"Thank you." And Jean walked back to spend a restless night and rise to meet renewed suspense.

The morning seemed endless, but noon came at last, and under the pretense of seeking coolness in the grotto, Jean stole away to a slope whence the gate to the Hall park was visible. For two long hours she watched, and no one came. She was just turning away when a horseman dashed through the gate and came galloping toward the Hall. Heedless of everything but the uncontrollable longing to gain some tidings, she ran to meet him, feeling assured that he brought ill news. It was a young man from the station, and as he caught sight of her, he drew bridle, looking agitated and undecided.

"Has anything happened?" she cried breathlessly.

"A dreadful accident on the railroad, just the other side of Croydon. News telegraphed half an hour ago," answered the man, wiping his hot face.

"The noon train? Was Sir John in it? Quick, tell me all!"

"It was that train, miss, but whether Sir John was in it or not, we don't know; for the guard is killed, and everything is in such confusion that nothing can be certain. They are at work getting out the dead and wounded. We heard that Sir John was expected, and I came up to tell Mr. Coventry, thinking he would wish to go down. A train leaves in fifteen minutes; where shall I find him? I was told he was at the Hall."

"Ride on, ride on! And find him if he is there. I'll run home and look for him. Lose no time. Ride! Ride!" And turning, Jean sped back like a deer, while the man tore up the avenue to rouse the Hall.

Coventry was there, and went off at once, leaving both Hall and house in dismay. Fearing to betray the horrible anxiety that possessed her, Jean shut herself up in her room and suffered untold agonies as the day wore on and no news came. At dark a sudden cry rang through the house, and Jean rushed down to learn the cause. Bella was standing in the hall, holding a letter, while a group of excited servants hovered near her.

"What is it?" demanded Miss Muir, pale and steady, though her heart died within her as she recognized Gerald's handwriting. Bella gave her the note, and hushed her sobbing to hear again the heavy tidings that had come.

Dear Bella:

Uncle is safe; he did not go in the noon train. But several persons are sure that Ned was there. No trace of him as yet, but many bodies are in the river, under the ruins of the bridge, and I am doing my best to find the poor lad, if he is there. I have sent to all his haunts in town, and as he has not been seen, I hope it is a false report and he is safe with his regiment. Keep this from my mother till we are sure. I write you, because Lucia is ill. Miss Muir will comfort and sustain you. Hope for the best, dear.

Yours, G. C.

Those who watched Miss Muir as she read these words wondered at the strange expressions which passed over her face, for the joy which appeared there as Sir John's safety was made known did not change to grief or horror at poor Edward's possible fate. The smile died on her lips, but her voice did not falter, and in her downcast eyes shone an inexplicable look of something like triumph. No wonder, for if this was true, the danger which menaced her was averted for a time, and the marriage might be consummated without such desperate haste. This sad and sudden event seemed to her the mysterious fulfilment of a secret wish; and though startled she was not daunted but inspirited, for fate seemed to favor her designs. She did comfort Bella, control the excited household, and keep the rumors from Mrs. Coventry all that dreadful night.

At dawn Gerald came home exhausted, and bringing no tiding of the missing man. He had telegraphed to the headquarters of the regiment and received a reply, stating that Edward had left for London the previous day, meaning to go home before returning. The fact of his having been at the London station was also established, but whether he left by the train or not was still uncertain. The ruins were still being searched, and the body might yet appear.

"Is Sir John coming at noon?" asked Jean, as the three sat together in the rosy hush of dawn, trying to hope against hope.

"No, he had been ill, I learned from young Gower, who is just from town, and so had not completed his business. I sent him word to wait till night, for the bridge won't be passable till then. Now I must try and rest an hour; I've worked all night and have no strength left. Call me the instant any messenger arrives."

With that Coventry went to his room, Bella followed to wait on him, and Jean roamed through house and grounds, unable to rest. The morning was far spent when the messenger arrived. Jean went to receive his tidings, with the wicked hope still lurking at her heart.

"Is he found?" she asked calmly, as the man hesitated to speak.

"Yes, ma'am."

"You are sure?"

"I am certain, ma'am, though some won't say till Mr. Coventry comes to look."

"Is he alive?" And Jean's white lips trembled as she put the question.

"Oh no, ma'am, that warn't possible, under all them stones and water. The poor young gentleman is so wet, and crushed, and torn, no one would know him, except for the uniform, and the white hand with the ring on it."

Jean sat down, very pale, and the man described the finding of the poor shattered body. As he finished, Coventry appeared, and with one look of mingled remorse, shame, and sorrow, the elder brother went away, to find and bring the younger home. Jean crept into the garden like a guilty thing, trying to hide the satisfaction which struggled with a woman's natural pity, for so sad an end for this brave young life.

"Why waste tears or feign sorrow when I must be glad?" she muttered, as she paced to and fro along the terrace. "The poor boy is out of pain, and I am out of danger."

She got no further, for, turning as she spoke, she stood face to face with Edward! Bearing no mark of peril on dress or person, but stalwart and strong as ever, he stood there looking at her, with contempt and compassion struggling in his face. As if turned to stone, she remained motionless, with dilated eyes, arrested breath, and paling cheek. He did not speak but watched her silently till she put out a trembling hand, as if to assure herself by touch that it was really he. Then he drew back, and as if the act convinced as fully as words, she said slowly, "They told me you were dead."

"And you were glad to believe it. No, it was my comrade, young Courtney, who unconsciously deceived you all, and lost his life, as I should have done, if I had not gone to Ascot after seeing him off yesterday."

"To Ascot?" echoed Jean, shrinking back, for Edward's eye was on her, and his voice was stern and cold.

"Yes; you know the place. I went there to make inquiries concerning you and was well satisfied. Why are you still here?"

"The three days are not over yet. I hold you to your promise. Before night I shall be gone; till then you will be silent, if you have honor enough to keep your word."

"I have." Edward took out his watch and, as he put it back, said with cool precision, "It is now two, the train leaves for London at half-past six; a carriage will wait for you at the side door. Allow me to advise you to go then, for the instant dinner is over I shall speak." And with a bow he went into the house, leaving Jean nearly suffocated with a throng of contending emotions.

For a few minutes she seemed paralyzed; but the native energy of the woman forbade utter despair, till the last hope was gone. Frail as that now was, she still clung to it tenaciously, resolving to win the game in defiance of everything. Springing up, she went to her room, packed her few valuables, dressed herself with care, and then sat down to wait. She heard a joyful stir below, saw Coventry come hurrying back, and from a garrulous maid learned that the body was that of young Courtney. The uniform being the same as Edward's and the ring, a gift from him, had caused the men to believe the disfigured corpse to be that of the younger Coventry. No one but the maid came near her; once Bella's voice called her, but some one checked the girl, and the call was not repeated. At five an envelope was brought her, directed in Edward's hand, and containing a check which more than paid a year's salary. No word accompanied the gift, yet the generosity of it touched her, for Jean Muir had the relics of a once honest nature, and despite her falsehood could still admire nobleness and respect virtue. A tear of genuine shame dropped on the paper, and real gratitude filled her heart, as she thought that even if all else failed, she was not thrust out penniless into the world, which had no pity for poverty.

As the clock struck six, she heard a carriage drive around and went down to meet it. A servant put on her trunk, gave the order, "To the station, James," and she drove away without meeting anyone, speaking to anyone, or apparently being seen by anyone. A sense of utter weariness came over her, and she longed to lie down and forget. But the last chance still remained, and till that failed, she would not give up. Dismissing the carriage, she seated herself to watch for the quarter-past-six train from London, for in that Sir John would come if he came at all that night. She was haunted by the fear that Edward had met and told him. The first glimpse of Sir John's frank face would betray the truth. If he knew all, there was no hope, and she would go her way alone. If he knew nothing, there was yet time for the marriage; and once his wife, she knew she was safe, because for the honor of his name he would screen and protect her.

Up rushed the train, out stepped Sir John, and Jean's heart died within her. Grave, and pale, and worn he looked, and leaned heavily on the arm of a portly gentleman in black. The Reverend Mr. Fairfax, why has he come, if the secret is out? thought Jean, slowly advancing to meet them and fearing to read her fate in Sir John's face. He saw her, dropped his friend's arm, and hurried forward with the ardor of a young man, exclaiming, as he seized her hand with a beaming face, a glad voice, "My little girl! Did you think I would never come?"

She could not answer, the reaction was too strong, but she clung to him, regardless of time or place, and felt that her last hope had not failed. Mr. Fairfax proved himself equal to the occasion. Asking no questions, he hurried Sir John and Jean into a carriage and stepped in after them with a bland apology. Jean was soon herself again, and, having told her fears at his delay, listened eagerly while he related the various mishaps which had detained him.

"Have you seen Edward?" was her first question.

"Not yet, but I know he has come, and have heard of his narrow escape. I should have been in that train, if I had not been delayed by the indisposition which I then cursed, but now bless. Are you ready, Jean? Do you repent your choice, my child?"

"No, no! I am ready, I am only too happy to become your wife, dear, generous Sir John," cried Jean, with a glad alacrity, which touched the old man to the heart, and charmed the Reverend Mr. Fairfax, who concealed the romance of a boy under his clerical suit.

They reached the Hall. Sir John gave orders to admit no one and after a hasty dinner sent for his old housekeeper and his steward, told them of his purpose, and desired them to witness his marriage. Obedience had been the law of their lives, and Master could do nothing wrong in their eyes, so they played their parts willingly, for Jean was a favorite at the Hall. Pale as her gown, but calm and steady; she stood beside Sir John, uttering her vows in a clear tone and taking upon herself the vows of a wife with more than a bride's usual docility. When the ring was fairly on, a smile broke over her face. When Sir John kissed and called her his "little wife," she shed a tear or two of sincere happiness; and when Mr. Fairfax addressed her as "my lady," she laughed her musical laugh, and glanced up at a picture of Gerald with eyes full of exultation. As the servants left the room, a message was brought from Mrs. Coventry, begging Sir John to come to her at once.

"You will not go and leave me so soon?" pleaded Jean, well knowing why he was sent for.

"My darling, I must." And in spite of its tenderness, Sir John's manner was too decided to be withstood.

"Then I shall go with you," cried Jean, resolving that no earthly power should part them.

IX

LADY COVENTRY

WHEN the first excitement of Edward's return had subsided, and before they could question him as to the cause of this unexpected visit, he told them that after dinner their curiosity should be gratified, and meantime he begged them to leave Miss Muir alone, for she had received bad news and must not be disturbed. The family with difficulty restrained their tongues and waited impatiently. Gerald confessed his love for Jean and asked his brother's pardon for betraying his trust. He had expected an outbreak, but Edward only looked at him with pitying eyes, and said sadly, "You too! I have no reproaches to make, for I know what you will suffer when the truth is known."

"What do you mean?" demanded Coventry.

"You will soon know, my poor Gerald, and we will comfort one another."

Nothing more could be drawn from Edward till dinner was over, the servants gone, and all the family alone together. Then pale and grave, but very self-possessed, for trouble had made a man of him, he produced a packet of letters, and said, addressing himself to his brother, "Jean Muir has deceived us all. I know her story; let me tell it before I read her letters."

"Stop! I'll not listen to any false tales against her. The poor girl has enemies who belie her!" cried Gerald, starting up.

"For the honor of the family, you must listen, and learn what fools she has made of us. I can prove what I say, and convince you that she has the art of a devil. Sit still ten minutes, then go, if you will."

Edward spoke with authority, and his brother obeyed him with a foreboding heart.

"I met Sydney, and he begged me to beware of her. Nay, listen, Gerald! I know she has told her story, and that you believe it; but her own letters convict her. She tried to charm Sydney as she did us, and nearly succeeded in inducing him to marry her. Rash and wild as he is, he is still a gentleman, and when an incautious word of hers roused his suspicions, he refused to make her his wife. A stormy scene ensued, and, hoping to intimidate him, she feigned to stab herself as if in despair. She did wound herself, but failed to gain her point and insisted upon going to a hospital to die. Lady Sydney, good, simple soul, believed the girl's version of the story, thought her son was in the wrong, and when he was gone, tried to atone for his fault by finding Jean Muir another home. She thought Gerald was soon to marry Lucia, and that I was away, so sent her here as a safe and comfortable retreat."

"But, Ned, are you sure of all this? Is Sydney to be believed?" began Coventry, still incredulous.

"To convince you, I'll read Jean's letter before I say more. They were written to an accomplice and were purchased by Sydney. There was a compact between the two women, that each should keep the other informed of all adventures, plots and plans, and share whatever good fortune fell to the lot of either. Thus Jean wrote freely, as you shall judge. The letters concern us alone. The first was written a few days after she came.

"Dear Hortense:

"Another failure. Sydney was more wily than I thought. All was going well, when one day my old fault beset me, I took too much wine, and I carelessly owned that I had been an actress. He was shocked, and retreated. I got up a scene, and gave myself a safe little wound, to frighten him. The brute was not frightened, but coolly left me to my fate. I'd have died to spite him, if I dared, but as I didn't, I lived to torment him. As yet, I have had no chance, but I will not forget him. His mother is a poor, weak creature, whom I could use as I would, and through her I found an excellent place. A sick mother, silly daughter, and two eligible sons. One is engaged to a handsome iceberg, but that only renders him more interesting in my eyes, rivalry adds so much to the charm of one's conquests. Well, my dear, I went, got up in the meek style, intending to do the pathetic; but before I saw the family, I was so angry I could hardly control myself. Through the indolence of Monsieur the young master, no carriage was sent for me, and I intend he shall atone for that rudeness by-and-by. The younger son, the mother, and the girl received me patronizingly, and I understood the simple souls at once. Monsieur (as I shall call him, as names are unsafe) was unapproachable, and took no pains to conceal his dislike of governesses. The cousin was lovely, but detestable with her pride, her coldness, and her very visible adoration of Monsieur, who let her worship him, like an inanimate idol as he is. I hated them both, of course, and in return for their insolence shall torment her with jealousy, and teach him how to woo a woman by making his heart ache. They are an intensely proud family, but I can humble them all, I think, by captivating the sons, and when they have committed themselves, cast them off, and marry the old uncle, whose title takes my fancy."

"She never wrote that! It is impossible. A woman could not do it," cried Lucia indignantly, while Bella sat bewildered and Mrs. Coventry supported herself with salts and fan. Coventry went to his brother, examined the writing, and returned to his seat, saying, in a tone of suppressed wrath, "She did write it. I posted some of those letters myself. Go on, Ned."

"I made myself useful and agreeable to the amiable ones, and overheard the chat of the lovers. It did not suit me, so I fainted away to stop it, and excite interest in the provoking pair. I thought I had succeeded, but Monsieur suspected me and showed me that he did. I forgot my meek role and gave him a stage look. It had a good effect, and I shall try it again. The man is well worth winning, but I prefer the title, and as the uncle is a hale, handsome gentleman, I can't wait for him to die, though Monsieur is very charming, with his elegant languor, and his heart so fast asleep no woman has had power to wake it yet. I told my story, and they believed it, though I had the audacity to say I was but nineteen, to talk Scotch, and bashfully confess that Sydney wished to marry me. Monsieur knows S. and evidently suspects something. I must watch him and keep the truth from him, if possible.

"I was very miserable that night when I got alone. Something in the atmosphere of this happy home made me wish I was anything but what I am. As I sat there trying to pluck up my spirits, I thought of the days when I was lovely and young, good and gay. My glass showed me an old woman of thirty, for my false locks were off, my paint gone, and my face was without its mask. Bah! how I hate sentiment! I drank your health from your own little flask, and went to bed to dream that I was playing Lady Tartuffe—as I am. Adieu, more soon."

No one spoke as Edward paused, and taking up another letter, he read on:

"My Dear Creature:

"All goes well. Next day I began my task, and having caught a hint of the character of each, tried my power over them. Early in the morning I ran over to see the Hall. Approved of it highly, and took the first step toward becoming its mistress, by piquing the curiosity and flattering the pride of its master. His estate is his idol; I praised it with a few artless compliments to himself, and he was charmed. The cadet of the family adores horses. I risked my neck to pet his beast, and he was charmed. The little girl is romantic about flowers; I made a posy and was sentimental, and she was charmed. The fair icicle loves her departed mamma, I had raptures over an old picture, and she thawed. Monsieur is used to being worshipped. I took no notice of him, and by the natural perversity of human nature, he began to take notice of me. He likes music; I sang, and stopped when he'd listened long enough to want more. He is lazily fond of being amused; I showed him my skill, but refused to exert it in his behalf. In short, I gave him no peace till he began to wake up. In order to get rid of the boy, I fascinated him, and he was sent away. Poor lad, I rather liked him, and if the title had been nearer would have married him.

"Many thanks for the honor." And Edward's lip curled with intense scorn. But Gerald sat like a statue, his teeth set, his eyes fiery, his brows bent, waiting for the end.

"The passionate boy nearly killed his brother, but I turned the affair to good account, and bewitched Monsieur by playing nurse, till Vashti (the icicle) interfered. Then I enacted injured virtue, and kept out of his way, knowing that he would miss me. I mystified him about S. by sending a letter where S. would not get it, and got up all manner of soft scenes to win this proud creature. I get on well and meanwhile privately fascinate Sir J. by being daughterly and devoted. He is a worthy old man, simple as a child, honest as the day, and generous as a prince. I shall be a happy woman if I win him, and you shall share my good fortune; so wish me success.

"This is the third, and contains something which will surprise you," Edward said, as he lifted another paper.

"Hortense:

"I've done what I once planned to do on another occasion. You know my handsome, dissipated father married a lady of rank for his second wife. I never saw Lady H————d but once, for I was kept out of the way. Finding that this good Sir J. knew something of her when a girl, and being sure that he did not know of the death of her little daughter, I boldly said I was the child, and told a pitiful tale of my early life. It worked like a charm; he told Monsieur, and both felt the most chivalrous compassion for Lady Howard's daughter, though before they had secretly looked down on me, and my real poverty and my lowliness. That boy pitied me with an honest warmth and never waited to learn my birth. I don't forget that and shall repay it if I can. Wishing to bring Monsieur's affair to a successful crisis, I got up a theatrical evening and was in my element. One little event I must tell you, because I committed an actionable offense and was nearly discovered. I did not go down to supper, knowing that the moth would return to flutter about the candle, and preferring that the fluttering should be done in private, as Vashti's jealousy is getting uncontrollable. Passing through the gentlemen's dressing room, my

197

quick eye caught sight of a letter lying among the costumes. It was no stage affair, and an odd sensation of fear ran through me as I recognized the hand of S. I had feared this, but I believe in chance; and having found the letter, I examined it. You know I can imitate almost any hand. When I read in this paper the whole story of my affair with S., truly told, and also that he had made inquiries into my past life and discovered the truth, I was in a fury. To be so near success and fail was terrible, and I resolved to risk everything. I opened the letter by means of a heated knife blade under the seal, therefore the envelope was perfect; imitating S.'s hand, I penned a few lines in his hasty style, saying he was at Baden, so that if Monsieur answered, the reply would not reach him, for he is in London, it seems. This letter I put into the pocket whence the other must have fallen, and was just congratulating myself on this narrow escape, when Dean, the maid of Vashti, appeared as if watching me. She had evidently seen the letter in my hand, and suspected something. I took no notice of her, but must be careful, for she is on the watch. After this the evening closed with strictly private theatricals, in which Monsieur and myself were the only actors. To make sure that he received my version of the story first, I told him a romantic story of S.'s persecution, and he believed it. This I followed up by a moonlight episode behind a rose hedge, and sent the young gentleman home in a half-dazed condition. What fools men are!"

"She is right!" muttered Coventry, who had flushed scarlet with shame and anger, as his folly became known and Lucia listened in astonished silence.

"Only one more, and my distasteful task will be nearly over," said Edward, unfolding the last of the papers. "This is not a letter, but a copy of one written three nights ago. Dean boldly ransacked Jean Muir's desk while she was at the Hall, and, fearing to betray the deed by keeping the letter, she made a hasty copy which she gave me today, begging me to save the family from disgrace. This makes the chain complete. Go now, if you will, Gerald. I would gladly spare you the pain of hearing this."

"I will not spare myself; I deserve it. Read on," replied Coventry, guessing what was to follow and nerving himself to hear it. Reluctantly his brother read these lines:

"The enemy has surrendered! Give me joy, Hortense; I can be the wife of this proud monsieur, if I will. Think what an honor for the divorced wife of a disreputable actor. I laugh at the farce and enjoy it, for I only wait till the prize I desire is fairly mine, to turn and reject this lover who has proved himself false to brother, mistress, and his own conscience. I resolved to be revenged on both, and I have kept my word. For my sake he cast off the beautiful woman who truly loved him; he forgot his promise to his brother, and put by his pride to beg of me the worn-out heart that is not worth a good man's love. Ah well, I am satisfied, for Vashti has suffered the sharpest pain a proud woman can endure, and will feel another pang when I tell her that I scorn her recreant lover, and give him back to her, to deal with as she will."

Coventry started from his seat with a fierce exclamation, but Lucia bowed her face upon her hands, weeping, as if the pang had been sharper than even Jean foresaw.

"Send for Sir John! I am mortally afraid of this creature. Take her away; do something to her. My poor Bella, what a companion for you! Send for Sir John at once!" cried Mrs. Coventry incoherently, and clasped her daughter in her arms, as if Jean Muir would burst in to annihilate the whole family. Edward alone was calm.

"I have already sent, and while we wait, let me finish this story. It is true that Jean is the daughter of Lady Howard's husband, the pretended clergyman, but really a worthless man who married her for her money. Her own child died, but this girl, having beauty, wit and a bold spirit, took her fate into her own hands, and became an actress. She married an actor, led a reckless life for some years; quarreled with her husband, was divorced, and went to Paris; left the stage, and tried to support herself as governess and companion. You know how she fared with the Sydneys, how she has duped us, and but for this discovery would have duped Sir John. I was in time to prevent this, thank heaven. She is gone; no one knows the truth but Sydney and ourselves; he will be silent, for his own sake; we will be for ours, and leave this dangerous woman to the fate which will surely overtake her."

"Thank you, it has overtaken her, and a very happy one she finds it."

A soft voice uttered the words, and an apparition appeared at the door, which made all start and recoil with amazement—Jean Muir leaning on the arm of Sir John.

"How dare you return?" began Edward, losing the self-control so long preserved. "How dare you insult us by coming back to enjoy the mischief you have done? Uncle, you do not know that woman!"

"Hush, boy, I will not listen to a word, unless you remember where you are," said Sir John, with a commanding gesture.

"Remember your promise: love me, forgive me, protect me, and do not listen to their accusations," whispered Jean, whose quick eye had discovered the letters.

"I will; have no fears, my child," he answered, drawing her nearer as he took his accustomed place before the fire, always lighted when Mrs. Coventry was down.

Gerald, who had been pacing the room excitedly, paused behind Lucia's chair as if to shield her from insult; Bella clung to her mother; and Edward, calming himself by a strong effort, handed his uncle the letters, saying briefly, "Looking at those, sir, and let them speak."

"I will look at nothing, hear nothing, believe nothing which can in any way lessen my respect and affection for this young lady. She has prepared me for this. I know the enemy who is unmanly enough to belie and threaten her. I know that you both are unsuccessful lovers, and this explains your unjust, uncourteous treatment now. We all have committed faults and follies. I freely forgive Jean hers, and desire to know nothing of them from your lips. If she has innocently offended, pardon it for my sake, and forget the past."

"But, Uncle, we have proofs that this woman is not what she seems. Her own letters convict her. Read them, and do not blindly deceive yourself," cried Edward, indignant at his uncle's words.

A low laugh startled them all, and in an instant they saw the cause of it. While Sir John spoke, Jean had taken the letters from the hand which he had put behind him, a favorite gesture of his, and, unobserved, had dropped them on the fire. The mocking laugh, the sudden blaze, showed what had been done. Both young men sprang forward, but it was too late; the proofs were ashes, and Jean Muir's bold, bright eyes defied them, as she said, with a disdainful little gesture, "Hands off, gentlemen! You may degrade yourselves to the work of detectives, but I am not a prisoner yet. Poor Jean Muir you might harm, but Lady Coventry is beyond your reach."

"Lady Coventry!" echoed the dismayed family, in varying tones of incredulity, indignation, and amazement.

"Aye, my dear and honored wife," said Sir John, with a protecting arm about the slender figure at his side; and in the act, the words, there was a tender dignity that touched the listeners with pity and respect for the deceived man. "Receive her as such, and for my sake, forbear all further accusation," he continued steadily. "I know what I have done. I have no fear that I shall repent it. If I am blind, let me remain so till time opens my eyes. We are going away for a little while, and when we return, let the old life return again, unchanged, except that Jean makes sunshine for me as well as for you."

No one spoke, for no one knew what to say. Jean broke the silence, saying coolly, "May I ask how those letters came into your possession?"

"In tracing out your past life, Sydney found your friend Hortense. She was poor, money bribed her, and your letters were given up to him as soon as received. Traitors are always betrayed in the end," replied Edward sternly.

Jean shrugged her shoulders, and shot a glance at Gerald, saying with her significant smile, "Remember that, monsieur, and allow me to hope that in wedding you will be happier than in wooing. Receive my congratulations, Miss Beaufort, and let me beg of you to follow my example, if you would keep your lovers."

Here all the sarcasm passed from her voice, the defiance from her eye, and the one unspoiled attribute which still lingered in this woman's artful nature shone in her face, as she turned toward Edward and Bella at their mother's side.

"You have been kind to me," she said, with grateful warmth. "I thank you for it, and will repay it if I can. To you I will acknowledge that I am not worthy to be this good man's wife, and to you I will solemnly promise to devote my life to his happiness. For his sake forgive me, and let there be peace between us."

There was no reply, but Edward's indignant eyes fell before hers. Bella half put out her hand, and Mrs. Coventry sobbed as if some regret mingled with her resentment. Jean seemed to expect no friendly demonstration, and to understand that they forbore for Sir John's sake, not for hers, and to accept their contempt as her just punishment.

"Come home, love, and forget all this," said her husband, ringing the bell, and eager to be gone. "Lady Coventry's carriage."

And as he gave the order, a smile broke over her face, for the sound assured her that the game was won. Pausing an instant on the threshold before she vanished from their sight, she looked backward, and fixing on Gerald the strange glance he remembered well, she said in her penetrating voice, "Is not the last scene better than the first?"

HAPPY WOMEN

✼✼✼✼✼✼

ONE of the trials of woman-kind is the fear of being an old maid. To escape this dreadful doom, young girls rush into matrimony with a recklessness which astonishes the beholder; never pausing to remember that the loss of liberty, happiness, and self-respect is poorly repaid by the barren honor of being called "Mrs." instead of "Miss."

Fortunately, this foolish prejudice is fast disappearing, conquered by the success of a certain class belonging to the sisterhood. This class is composed of superior women who, from various causes, remain single, and devote themselves to some earnest work; espousing philanthropy, art, literature, music, medicine, or whatever task taste, necessity, or chance suggests, and remaining as faithful to and as happy in their choice as married women with husbands and homes. It being my good fortune to know several such, I venture to offer a little sketch of them to those of my young countrywomen who, from choice or necessity, stand along, seeking to find the happiness which is the right of all.

Here is L., a rich man's daughter; pretty, accomplished, sensible, and good. She tried fashionable life and found that it did not satisfy her. No lover was happy enough to make a response in her heart, and at twenty-three she looked about her for something to occupy and interest her. She was attracted towards the study of medicine; became absorbed in it; went alone to Paris and London; studied faithfully; received her diploma, and, having practised successfully for a time, was appointed the resident physician of a city hospital. Here, doing a truly womanly work, she finds no time for ennui, unhappiness, or the vague longing for something to fill heart and life, which leads so many women to take refuge in frivolous or dangerous amusements and pursuits. She never talks of her mission or her rights, but beautifully fulfils the one and quietly assumes the others. Few criticise or condemn her course, and none question her success. Respected and beloved by all who know her, she finds genuine satisfaction in her work, and is the busiest, happiest, most useful woman whom I know.

Next comes M., a brilliant, talented girl, full of energy, ambition, and noble aspirations. Poor, yet attractive, through natural gifts and graces, to her came the great temptation of such a girl's life—a rich lover; an excellent young man, but her inferior in all respects. She felt this, and so did he, but hoping that love would make them equals, he urged his suit.

"If I loved him," she said, "my way would be plain, and I should not hesitate a minute. But I do not; I've tried, and I am sure I *never* can feel toward him as I should. It is a great temptation, for I long to cultivate my talent to help my family, to see the world, and enjoy life, and all this may be done if I said 'Yes.' People tell me that I am foolish to reject this good fortune; that it is my duty to accept it; that I shall get on very well without love, and talk as if it were a business transaction. It is hard to say 'No'; but I *must,* for in marriage I want to look up, not down. I cannot make it seem right to take this offer, and I must let it go, for I dare not sell my liberty."

She made her choice, turned away from the pleasant future laid before her, and took up her load again. With her one talent in her hand she faced poverty, cheerfully teaching music, year after year; hoping always, complaining never, and finding herself a stronger, happier woman for that act: A richer woman also; for, though the husband was lost a true friend was gained—since the lover, with respect added to his love, said manfully, "She is right; God bless her!"

S. is poor, plain, ungifted, and ordinary in all things but one—a cheerful, helpful spirit, that loves its neighbor better than itself, and cannot rest till it has proved its sincerity. Few, so placed, would have lived forty hard, dull years without becoming either sharp and sour, or bitter and blue. But S. is as sweet and sunny as a child; and, to those who know her, the personification of content. The only talent she possesses is that of loving every helpless, suffering, forlorn and outcast creature whom she meets. Finding her round of home duties too small for her benevolence, she became one of the home missionaries, whose reports are never read, whose salaries are never paid of earth. Poverty-stricken homes, sick-beds, sinful souls, and sorrowing hearts attract her as irrestibly as pleasure attracts other women, and she faithfully ministers to such, unknown and unrewarded.

"I never had a lover, and I never can have you know. I'm *so* plain," she says, with a smile that is pathetic in its humility, its unconscious wistfulness.

She is mistaken here; for there are many to whom that plain face is beautiful, that helpful hand very dear. Her lovers are not of the romantic sort; but old women, little children, erring men, and forlorn girls give her an affections as endearing and sincere as any husband could have done. Few will know her worth here, but, in the long hereafter, I am sure S. will be blest with eternal beauty, happiness, and love.

A. is a woman of a strongly individual type, who in the course of an unusually varied experience has seen so much of what a wise man has called "the tragedy of modern married life," that she is afraid to try it. Knowing that for one of a peculiar nature like herself such an experiment would be doubly hazardous, she has obeyed instinct and become a chronic old maid. Filial and fraternal love must satisfy her, and grateful that such ties are possible, she lives for them and is content. Literature is a fond and faithful spouse, and the little family that has sprung up around her, though perhaps unlovely and uninteresting to others, is a profitable source of satisfaction to her maternal heart. After a somewhat tempestuous voyage, she is glad to find herself in a quiet haven whence she can look back upon her vanished youth and feel that though the blossom time of life is past, a little fruit remains to ripen in the early autumn coming on. Not lonely, for parents, brothers and sisters, friends and babies keep her heart full and warm; not idle, for necessity, stern, yet kindly teacher, has taught her the worth of work; not unhappy, for love and labor, like good angels, walk at either hand, and the divine Friend fills the world with strength and beauty for the soul and eyes that have learned to see it thankfully.

My sisters, don't be afraid of the words, "old maid," for it is in your power to make this a term of honor, not reproach. It is not necessary to be a sour, spiteful spinster, with nothing to do but brew tea, talk scandal and tend a pocket-handkerchief. No, the world is full of work, needing all the heads, hearts, and hands we can bring to do it. Never was there so splendid an opportunity for women to enjoy their liberty and prove that they deserve it be using it wisely. If love comes as it should come, accept it in God's name and be worth of His best blessing. If it never comes, then in God's name reject the shadow of it, for that can never satisfy a hungry heart. Do not be ashamed to own the truth—do not be daunted by the fear of ridicule and loneliness, nor saddened by the loss of a woman's tenderest ties. Be true to yourselves; cherish whatever talent you possess, and in using it faithfully for the good of others you will most assuredly find happiness for yourself, and make of life no failure, but a beautiful success.

PSYCHE'S ART

※※※※※※

"Handsome is that handsome does."

I

ONCE upon a time there raged in a certain city one of those fashionable epidemics which occasionally attack our youthful population. It wasn't the music mania, nor gymnastic convulsions, nor that wide-spread malady, croquet. Neither was it one of the new dances which, like a tarantula-bite, set every one a-twirling, nor stage madness, nor yet that American lecturing influenza which yearly sweeps over the land. No, it was a new disease called the Art fever, and it attacked the young women of the community with great violence.

Nothing but time could cure it, and it ran its course to the dismay, amusement, or edification of the beholders, for its victims did all manner of queer things in their delirium. They besieged potteries for clay, drove Italian plaster-workers out of their wits with unexecutable orders, got neuralgia and rheumatism sketching perched on fences and trees like artistic hens, and caused a rise in the price of bread, paper, and charcoal, by their order in crayoning. They covered canvas with the expedition of scene-painters, had classes, lectures, receptions, and exhibitions, made models of each other, and rendered their walls hideous with bad likenesses of all their friends. Their conversation ceased to be intelligible to the uninitiated, and they prattled prettily of "chiaro-oscuro, French sauce, refraction of the angle of the eye, seventh spinus process, depth and juiciness of color, tender touch, and a good tone." Even in dress the artistic disorder was visible; some cast aside crinoline altogether, and stalked about with a severe simplicity of outline worthy of Flaxman.[1] Others flushed themselves with scarlet, that no landscape which they adorned should be without some touch of Turner's favorite tint. Some were *blue* in every sense of the word, and the heads of all were adorned with classic braids, curls tied Hebe-wise, or hair dressed à la hurricane.

It was found impossible to keep them safe at home, and, as the fever grew, these harmless maniacs invaded the sacred retreats where artists of the other sex did congregate, startling those anchorites with visions of large-eyed damsels bearing portfolios in hands delicately begrimed with crayon, chalk, and clay, gliding through the corridors hitherto haunted only by shabby paletots, shadowy hats, and cigar smoke. This irruption was borne with manly fortitude, not to say cheerfulness, for studio doors stood hospitably open as the fair invaders passed, and studies from life were generously offered them in glimpses of picturesque gentlemen posed before easels, brooding over master-pieces in "a divine despair," or attitudinizing upon couches as if exhausted by the soarings of genius.

An atmosphere of romance began to pervade the old buildings when the girls came, and nature and art took turns. There were peepings and whisperings, much stifled laughter and whisking in and out; not to mention the accidental rencontres, small services, and eye telegrams, which somewhat lightened the severe studies of all parties.

Half-a-dozen young victims of this malady met daily in one of the cells of a great art bee-hive called "Raphael's Rooms," and devoted their shining hours to modelling fancy heads, gossiping the while; for the poor things found the road to fame rather dull and dusty without such verbal sprinklings.

"Psyche Dean, you've had an adventure! I see it in your face; so tell it at once, for we are as stupid as owls here to-day," cried one of the sisterhood, as a bright-eyed girl entered with some precipitation.

"I dropped my portfolio, and a man picked it up, that's all," replied Psyche, hurrying on her gray linen pinafore.

"That won't do; I know something interesting happened, for you've been blushing, and you look brisker than usual this morning," said the first speaker, polishing off the massive nose of her Homer.

"It wasn't anything," began Psyche, a little reluctantly. "I was coming up in a hurry when I ran against a man coming down in a hurry. My portfolio slipped, and my papers went flying all about the landing. Of course we both laughed and begged pardon, and I began to pick them up, but he wouldn't let me; so I held the book while he collected the sketches. I saw him glance at them as he did so, and that made me blush, for they are wretched things, you know."

"Not a bit of it; they are capital, and you are a regular genius, as we all agree," cut in the Homeric Miss Cutter.

"Never tell people they are geniuses unless you wish to spoil them," returned Psyche, severely. "Well, when the portfolio was put to rights I was going on, but he fell to picking up a little bunch of violets I had dropped; you know I always wear a posy into town to give me inspiration. I didn't care for the dusty flowers, and told him so, and scrambled away before any one came. At the top of the stairs I peeped over the railing, and there he was, gathering up every one of those half-dead violets as carefully as if they had been tea-roses."

"Psyche Dean, you have met your fate this day!" exclaimed a third damsel, with straw-colored tresses, and a good deal of weedy shrubbery in her hat, which gave an Ophelia-like expression to her sentimental countenance.

Psyche frowned and shook her head as if half sorry she had told her little story.

"Was he handsome?" asked Miss Larkins, the believer in fate.

"I didn't particularly observe."

"It was the red-headed man, whom we call Titian; he's always on the stairs."

"No, it wasn't; his hair was brown and curly," cried Psyche, innocently falling into the trap.

"Like Peerybingle's baby [2] when its cap was taken off," quoted Miss Dickenson, who pined to drop the last two letters of her name.

"Was it Murillo, the black-eyed one?" asked the fair Cutter, for the girls had a name for all the attitudinizers and promenaders whom they oftenest met.

"No, he had gray eyes, and very fine ones they were too," answered Psyche, adding, as if to herself, "he looked as I imagine Michael Angelo might have looked when young."

"Had he a broken nose like the great Mike?" asked an irreverent damsel.

"If he had, no one would mind it, for his head is splendid; he took his hat off, so I had a fine view. He isn't handsome, but he'll *do* something," said Psyche, prophetically, as she recalled the strong, ambitious face which she had often observed, but never mentioned before.

"Well, dear, considering that you didn't 'particularly look' at the man, you've given us a very good idea of his appearance. We'll call him Michael Angelo, and he shall be your idol. I prefer stout old Rembrandt myself, and Larkie adores that dandefied Raphael," said the lively Cutter, slapping away at Homer's bald pate energetically, as she spoke.

"Raphael is a dear, but Rubens is more to my taste now," returned Miss Larkins. "He was in the hall yesterday talking with Sir Joshua, who had his inevitable umbrella, like a true Englishman. Just as I came up, the umbrella fell right before me. I started back; Sir Joshua laughed but Rubens said, 'Deuce take it!' and caught up the umbrella, giving me a never-to-be-forgotten look. It was perfectly thrilling."

"Which,—the umbrella, the speech, or the look?" asked Psyche, who was not sentimental.

"Ah, you have no soul for art in nature, and nature in art," sighed the amber-tressed Larkins. "I have, for I feed upon a glance, a tint, a curve, with exquisite delight. Rubens is adorable (*as a study*); that lustrous eye, that night of hair, that sumptuous cheek, are perfect. He only needs a cloak, lace collar, and slouching hat to be the genuine thing."

"This isn't the genuine thing by any means. What *does* it need?" said Psyche, looking with a despondent air at the head on her stand.

Many would have pronounced it a clever thing; the nose was strictly Greek, the chin curved upward gracefully, the mouth was sweetly haughty, the brow classically smooth and low, and the breezy hair well done. But something was wanting; Psyche felt that, and could have taken her Venus by the dimpled shoulders, and given her a hearty shake, if that would have put strength and spirit into the lifeless face.

"Now *I* am perfectly satisfied with my Apollo, though you all insist that it is the image of Theodore Smythe. He says so himself, and assures me it will make a sensation when we exhibit," remarked Miss Larkins, complacently caressing the ambrosial locks of her Symthified Phebus.

"What shall you do if it don't?" asked Miss Cutter, with elegance.

"I shall feel that I have mistaken my sphere, shall drop my tools, veil my bust, and cast myself into the arms of Nature, since Art rejects me," replied Miss Larkins, with a tragic gesture and an expression which strongly suggested that in her eyes Nature meant Theodore.

"She must have capacious arms if she is to receive all Art's rejected admirers. Shall I be one of them?"

Psyche put the question to herself as she turned to work, but somehow ambitious aspirations were not in a flourishing condition that morning; her heart was not in tune, and head and hands sympathized. Nothing went well, for certain neglected home-duties had dogged her into town, and now worried her more than dust, or heat, or the ceaseless clatter of tongues. Tom, Dick, and Harry's unmended hose persisted in dancing a spectral jig before her mental eye, mother's querulous complaints spoilt the song she hummed to cheer herself, and little May's wistful face put the goddess of beauty entirely out of countenance.

"It's no use; I can't work till the clay is wet again. Where is Giovanni?" she asked, throwing down her tools with a petulant gesture and a dejected air.

"He is probably playing truant in the empty upper rooms as usual. I can't wait for him any longer, so I'm doing his work myself," answered Miss Dickenson, who was tenderly winding a wet bandage round her Juno's face, one side of which was so much plumper than the other that it looked as if the Queen of Olympus was being hydropathically treated for a severe fit of ague.

"I'll go and find the little scamp; a run will do me good; so will a breath of air and a view of the park from the upper windows."

Doffing her apron, Psyche strolled away up an unfrequented staircase to the empty apartments, which seemed to be too high even for the lovers of High Art. On the western side they were shady and cool, and, leaning from one of the windows, Psyche watched the feathery treetops ruffled by the balmy wind, that brought spring odors from the hills, lying green and sunny far away. Silence and solitude were such pleasant companions that the girl forgot herself, till a shrill whistle disturbed her day-dreams, and reminded her what she came for. Following the sound she found the little Italian errandboy busily uncovering a clay model which stood in the middle of a scantily furnished room near by.

"He is not here; come and look; it is greatly beautiful," cried Giovanni, beckoning with an air of importance.

Psyche did look and speedily forgot both her errand and herself. It was the figure of a man, standing erect, and looking straight before him with a wonderfully life-like expression. It was neither a mythological nor a historical character, Psyche thought, and was glad of it, being tired to death of gods and heroes. She soon ceased to wonder what it was, feeling only the indescribable charm of something higher than beauty. Small as her knowledge was, she could see and enjoy the power visible in every part of it; the accurate anatomy of the vigorous limbs, the grace of the pose, the strength and spirit in the countenance, clay though it was. A majestic figure, but the spell lay in the face, which, while it suggested the divine, was full of human truth and tenderness, for pain and passion seemed to have passed over it and a humility half-pathetic, a courage half-heroic, seemed to have been born from some great loss or woe.

How long she stood there Psyche did not know. Giovanni went away unseen, to fill his water-pail, and in the silence, she just stood and looked. Her eyes kindled, her color rose, despondency and discontent vanished, and her soul was in her face, for she loved beauty passionately, and all that was best and truest in her did honor to the genius of the unknown worker.

"If I could do a thing like that I'd die happy!" she exclaimed, impetuously, as a feeling of despair came over her at the thought of her own poor attempts.

"Who did it, Giovanni?" she asked, still looking up at the grand face with unsatisfied eyes.

"Paul Gage."

It was not the boy's voice, and, with a start, Psyche turned to see her Michael Angelo, standing in the door-way attentively observing her. Being too full of artless admiration to think of herself just yet, she neither blushed nor apologized, but looked straight at him, saying heartily:—

"You have done a wonderful piece of work, and I envy you more than I can tell."

The enthusiasm in her face, the frankness of her manner, seemed to please him, for there was no affectation about either. He gave her a keen, kind glance out of the "fine gray eyes," a little bow, and a grateful smile, saying quietly:—

"Then my Adam is not a failure in spite of his fall?"

Psyche turned from the sculptor to his model with increased admiration in her face, and earnestness in her voice, as she exclaimed, delighted:—

"Adam! I might have known it was he. O sir, you have indeed succeeded, for you have given that figure the power and pathos of the first man who sinned and suffered, and began again."

"Then I am satisfied." That was all he said, but the look he gave his work was a very eloquent one, for it betrayed that he had paid the price of success in patience and privation, labor and hope.

"What can one do to learn your secret?" asked the girl wistfully, for there was nothing in the man's manner to disturb her self-forgetful mood, but much to foster it, because to the solitary worker this confiding guest was as welcome as the doves who often hopped in at his window.

"Work and wait, and meantime feed heart, soul, and imagination with the best food one can get," he answered slowly, finding it impossible to give a receipt for genius.

"I can work and wait a long time to gain my end; but I don't know where to find the food you speak of," she answered, looking at him like a hungry child.

"I wish I could tell you, but each needs different fare, and each must look for it in different places."

The kindly tone and the sympathizing look, as well as the lines in his forehead, and a few gray hairs among the brown, gave Psyche courage to say more.

"I love beauty so much that I not only want to possess it myself, but to gain the power of seeing it in all things, and the art of reproducing it with truth. I have tried very hard to do it, but something is wanting; and in spite of my intense desire I never get on."

As she spoke the girl's eyes filled and fell in spite of herself, and turning a little with sudden shamefacedness she saw, lying on the table beside her among other scraps in manuscript and print, the well-known lines:—

> "I slept, and dreamed that life was beauty;
> I woke, and found that life was duty.
> Was thy dream then a shadowy lie?
> Toil on, sad heart, courageously,
> And thou shalt find thy dream to be
> A noonday light and truth to thee.: [3]

She knew them at a glance, had read them many times, but now they came home to her with sudden force, and, seeing that his eye had followed hers, she said in her impulsive fashion:—

"Is doing one's duty a good way to feed heart, soul, and imagination?"

As if he had caught a glimpse of what was going on in her mind, Paul answered emphatically:—

"Excellent; for if one is good, one is happy, and if happy, one can work well. Moulding character is the highest sort of sculpture, and all of us should learn that art before we touch clay or marble."

He spoke with the energy of a man who believed what he said, and did his best to be worthy of the rich gift bestowed upon him. The sight of her violets in a glass of water, and Giovanni staring at her with round eyes, suddenly recalled Psyche to a sense of the proprieties which she had been innocently outraging for the last ten minutes. A sort of panic seized her; she blushed deeply, retreated precipitately to the door, and vanished murmuring thanks and apologies as she went.

"Did you find him? I thought you had forgotten," said Miss Dickenson, now hard at work.

"Yes, I found him. No, I shall not forget," returned Psyche, thinking of Gage, not Giovanni.

She stood before her work eying it intently for several minutes; then, with an expression of great contempt for the whole thing, she suddenly tilted her cherished Venus on to the floor, gave the classical face a finishing crunch, and put on her hat in a decisive manner, saying briefly to the dismayed damsels:—

Psyche's Art

"Good-by, girls; I shan't come any more, for I'm going to work at home hereafter."

II

THE prospect of pursuing artistic studies at home was not brilliant, as one may imagine when I mention that Psyche's father was a painfully prosaic man, wrapt in flannel, so to speak; for his woollen mills left him no time for anything but sleep, food, and newspapers. Mrs. Dean was one of those exasperating women who pervade their mansions like a domestic steam-engine one week and take to their sofas the next, absorbed by fidgets and foot-stoves, shawls, and lamentations. There were three riotous and robust young brothers, whom it is unnecessary to describe except by stating that they were *boys* in the broadest sense of that delightful word. There was a feeble little sister, whose patient, suffering face demanded constant love and care to mitigate the weariness of a life of pain. And last, but not least by any means, there were two Irish ladies, who, with the best intentions imaginable, produced a universal state of topsy-turvyness when left to themselves for a moment.

But being very much in earnest about doing her duty, not because it *was* her duty, but as a means toward an end, Psyche fell to work with a will, hoping to serve both masters at once. So she might have done, perhaps, if flesh and blood had been as plastic as clay, but the live models were so exacting in their demands upon her time and strength, that the poor statues went to the wall. Sculpture and sewing, calls and crayons, Ruskin [4] and receipt-books, didn't work well together, and poor Psyche found duties and desires desperately antagonistic. Take a day as a sample.

"The washing and ironing is well over, thank goodness, ma used up and quiet, the boys out of the way, and May comfortable, so I'll indulge myself in a blissful day after my own heart," Psyche said, as she shut herself into her little studio, and prepared to enjoy a few hours of hard study and happy day-dreams.

With a book on her lap, and her own round, white arm going through all manner of queer evolutions, she was placidly repeating,

"Deltoids, Biceps, Triceps, Pronator, Supinator, Palmanis, Flexor carpi ulnaris—"

"Here's Flexis what-you-call-ums for you," interrupted a voice, which began in a shrill falsetto and ended in a gruff bass, as a flushed, dusty, long-legged boy burst in, with a bleeding hand obligingly extended for inspection.

"Mercy on us, Harry, what have you done to yourself now? Split your fingers with a cricket-ball again?" cried Psyche, as her arms went up and her book went down.

"No, sir. I just pitched into one of the fellows because he got mad and said pa was going to fail."

"O Harry, is he?"

"Course he isn't! It's hard times for every one, but pa will pull through like a brick. No use to try and explain it all; girls can't understand business; so you just tie me up, and don't bother," was the characteristic reply of the young man, who, being three years her junior, of course treated the weaker vessel with lordly condescension.

"What a dreadful wound! I hope nothing is broken, for I haven't studied the hand much yet, and may do mischief doing it up," said Psyche, examining the great grimy paw with tender solicitude.

"Much good your biceps, and deltoids, and things do you, if you can't right up a little cut like that," squeaked the ungrateful hero.

"I'm not going to be a surgeon, thank Heaven; I intend to make perfect hands and arms, not mend damaged ones," retorted Psyche, in a dignified tone, somewhat marred by a great piece of court-plaster on her tongue.

"I should say a surgeon could improve *that* perfect thing, if he didn't die a-laughing before he began," growled Harry, pointing with a scornful grin at a clay arm humpy with muscles all carefully developed in the wrong places.

"Don't hoot, Hal, for you don't know anything about it. Wait a few years and see if you're not proud of me."

"Sculp away then, do your prettiest, and I'll hurrah for your mud-pies like a good one;" with which cheering promise the youth departed, having effectually disturbed his sister's peaceful mood.

Anxious thoughts of her father rendered "biceps, deltoids, and things" uninteresting, and, hoping to compose her mind, she took up The Old Painters and went on with the story of Claude Lorraine.[5] She had just reached the tender scene where:—

"Calista gazed with enthusiasm, while she looked like a being of heaven rather than earth. 'My friend,' she cried, 'I read in thy picture thy immortality!' As she spoke, her head sunk upon his bosom, and it was several moments before Claude perceived that he supported a lifeless form."

"How sweet!" said Psyche, with a romantic sigh.

"Faith, and swate it is thin!" echoed Katy, whose red head had just appeared round the half-opened door. "It's gingybread I'm making the day, miss, and will I be puttin' purlash or sallyrathis into it, if ye plase?"

"Purlash by all means," returned the girl, keeping her countenance, fearing to enrage Katy by a laugh; for the angry passions of the red-haired one rose more quickly than her bread. As she departed with alacrity to add a spoonful of starch and a pinch of whiting to her cake, Psyche, feeling better for her story and her smile, put on her bib and paper cap and fell to work on the deformed arm. An hour of bliss, then came a ring at the door-bell, followed by Biddy to announce callers, and add that as "the mistress was in her bed, miss must go and take care of 'em." Whereat "miss" cast down her tools in despair, threw her cap one way, her bib another, and went in to her guests with anything but a rapturous welcome.

Dinner being accomplished after much rushing up and down stairs with trays and messages for Mrs. Dean, Psyche fled again to her studio, ordering no one to approach under pain of a scolding. All went well till, going in search of something, she found her little sister sitting on the floor with her cheek against the studio door.

"I didn't mean to be naughty, Sy, but ma's asleep, and the boys all gone, so I just came to be near you; it's so lonely everywhere," she said, apologetically, as she lifted up the heavy head that always ached.

"The boys are very thoughtless. Come in and stay with me; you are such a mouse you won't disturb me. Wouldn't you like to play be a model, and let me draw your arm, and tell you all about the nice little bones and muscles?" asked Psyche, who had the fever very strong upon her just then.

May didn't look as if the proposed amusement overwhelmed her with delight, but meekly consented to be perched upon a high stool with one arm propped up by a dropsical plaster cherub, while Psyche drew busily, feeling that duty and pleasure were being delightfully combined.

"Can't you hold your arm still, child? It shakes so I can't get it right," she said, rather impatiently.

"No, it will tremble, 'cause it's weak. I try hard, Sy, but there don't seem to be any strongness in me lately."

"That's better; keep it so a few minutes and I'll be done," cried the artist, forgetting that a few minutes may seem ages.

"My arm is so thin you can see the bunches nicely,—can't you?"

"Yes, dear."

Psyche glanced up at the wasted limb and when she drew again there was a blur before her eyes for a minute.

"I wish I was as fat as this white boy; but I get thinner every day somehow, and pretty soon there won't be any of me left but my little bones," said the child, looking at the winged cherub with sorrowful envy.

"Don't, my darling; don't say that," cried Psyche, dropping her work with a sudden pang at her heart. "I'm a sinful, selfish girl to keep you here; you're weak for want of air; come out and see the chickens, and pick dandelions, and have a good romp with the boys."

The weak arms were strong enough to clasp Psyche's neck, and the tired face brightened beautifully as the child exclaimed, with grateful delight:—

"Oh, I'd like it very much! I wanted to go dreadfully; but everybody is so busy all the time. I don't want to play, Sy; but just to lie on the grass with my head in your lap while you tell stories and draw me pretty things as you used to."

The studio was deserted all that afternoon, for Psyche sat in the orchard drawing squirrels on the wall, pert robbins hopping by, buttercups and mosses, elves and angels; while May lay contentedly enjoying sun and air, sisterly care, and the "pretty things" she loved so well. Psyche did not find the task a hard one; for this time her heart was in it, and if she needed any reward she surely found it; for the little face on her knee lost its weary look, and the peace and beauty of nature soothed her own troubled spirit, cheered her heart, and did her more good than hours of solitary study.

Finding, much to her own surprise, that her fancy was teeming with lovely conceits, she did hope for a quiet evening. But ma wanted a dish of gossip, pa must have his papers read to him, the boys had lessons and rips and grievances to be attended to, May's lullaby could not be forgotten, and the maids had to be looked after, lest burly "cousins" should be hidden in the boiler, or lucifer matches among the shavings. So Psyche's day ended, leaving her very tired, rather discouraged, and almost heart-sick with the shadow of a coming sorrow.

All summer she did her best, but accomplished very little as she thought; yet this was the teaching she most needed, and in time she came to see it. In the autumn May died, whispering with her arms about her sister's neck:—

"You make me so happy, Sy, I wouldn't mind the pain if I could stay a little longer. But if I can't, good-by, dear, good-by."

Her last look and word and kiss were all for Psyche, who felt then with grateful tears that her summer had not been wasted; for the smile upon the little dead face was more to her than any marble perfection her hands could have carved.

In the solemn pause which death makes in every family, Psyche said, with the sweet self-forgetfulness of a strong yet tender nature:—

"I must not think of myself, but try to comfort them;' and with this resolution she gave herself heart and soul to duty, never thinking of reward.

A busy, anxious, humdrum winter, for, as Harry said, "it was hard times for every one." Mr. Dean grew gray with the weight of business cares about which he never spoke; Mrs. Dean, laboring under the delusion that an invalid was a necessary appendage to the family, installed herself in the place the child's death left vacant, and the boys needed much comforting, for the poor lads never knew how much they loved "the baby" till the little chair stood empty. All turned to Sy for help and consolation, and her strength seemed to increase with the demand upon it. Patience and cheerfulness, courage and skill, came at her call like good fairies who had bided their time. House-keeping ceased to be hateful, and peace reigned in parlor and kitchen, while Mrs. Dean, shrouded in shawls, read Hahnemann's Lesser Writings on her sofa. Mr. Dean sometimes forgot his mills when a bright face came to meet him, a gentle hand smoothed the wrinkles out of his anxious forehead, and a daughterly heart sympathized with all his cares. The boys found home very pleasant with Sy always there ready to "lend a hand," whether it was to make fancy ties, help conjugate "a confounded verb," pull candy, or sing sweetly in the twilight when all thought of little May and grew quiet.

The studio door remained locked till her brothers begged Psyche to open it and make a bust of the child. A flush of joy swept over her face at the request, and her patient eyes grew bright and eager, as a thirsty traveller's might at the sight or sound of water. Then it faded as she shook her head, saying, with a regretful sigh, "I'm afraid I've lost the little skill I ever had."

But she tried, and with great wonder and delight discovered that she could work as she had never done before. She thought the newly found power lay in her longing to see the little face again; for it grew like magic under her loving hands, while every tender memory, sweet thought, and devout hope she had ever cherished, seemed to lend their aid. But when it was done and welcomed with tears and smiles, and praise more precious than any the world could give, then Psyche said within herself like one who saw light at last:—

"He was right; doing one's duty *is* the way to feed heart, soul, and imagination; for if one is good, one is happy, and if happy, one can work well."

III

"SHE broke her head, and went home to come no more," was Giovanni's somewhat startling answer when Paul asked about Psyche, finding that he no longer met her on the stairs or in the halls. He understood what the boy meant, and with an approving nod turned to his work again, saying, "I like that! If there is any power in her, she has taken the right way to find it out, I suspect."

How she prospered he never asked; for, though he met her more than once that year, the interviews were brief ones in street, concert-room, or picture-gallery, and she carefully avoided speaking of herself. But, possessing the gifted eyes which can look below the surface of things, he detected in the girl's face something better than beauty, though each time he saw it, it looked older and more thoughtful, often anxious and sad.

"She is getting on," he said to himself with a cordial satisfaction which gave his manner a friendliness as grateful to Psyche as his wise reticence.

Adam was finished at last, proved a genuine success, and Paul heartily enjoyed the well-earned reward for years of honest work. One blithe May morning, he slipped early into the art-gallery, where the statue now stood, to look at his creation with paternal pride. He was quite alone with the stately figure that shone white against the purple draperies and seemed to offer him a voiceless welcome from its marble lips. He gave it one loving look, and then forgot it, for at the feet of his Adam lay a handful of wild violets, with the dew still on them. A sudden smile broke over his face as he took them up, with the thought, "She has been here and found my work good."

For several moments he stood thoughtfully turning the flowers to and fro in his hands; then, as if deciding some question within himself, he said, still smiling:—

"It is just a year since she went home; she must have accomplished something in that time; I'll take the violets as a sign that I may go and ask her what."

He knew she lived just out of the city, between the river and the mills, and as he left the streets behind him, he found more violets blooming all along the way like flowery guides to lead him right. Greener grew the road, balmier blew the wind, and blither sang the birds, as he went on enjoying his holiday with the zest of a boy, until he reached a most attractive little path winding away across the fields. The gate swung invitingly open, and all the ground before it was blue with violets. Still following their guidance he took the narrow path, till, coming to a mossy stone beside a brook, he sat down to listen to the blackbirds singing deliciously in the willows overhead. Close by the stone, half hidden in the grass lay a little book, and, taking it up, he found it was a pocket-diary. No name appeared on the fly-leaf, and, turning the pages to find some clue to its owner, he read here and there enough to give him glimpses into an innocent and earnest heart which seemed to be learning some hard lesson patiently. Only near the end did he find the clue in words of his own, spoken long ago, and a name. Then, though longing intensely to know more, he shut the little book and went on, showing by his altered face that the simple record of a girl's life had touched him deeply.

Soon an old house appeared nestling to the hillside with the river shining in the low green meadows just before it.

"She lives there," he said, with as much certainty as if the pansies by the door-stone spelt her name, and, knocking, he asked for Psyche.

"She's gone to town, but I expect her home every minute." "Ask the gentleman to walk in and wait, Katy," cried a voice from above, where the whisk of skirts was followed by the appearance of an inquiring eye over the banisters.

The gentleman did walk in, and while he waited looked about him. The room, though very simply furnished, had a good deal of beauty in it, for the pictures were few and well chosen, the books such as never grow old, the music lying on the well-worn piano of the sort which is never out of fashion, and standing somewhat apart was one small statue in a recess full of flowers. Lovely in its simple grace and truth was the figure of a child looking upward as if watching the airy flight of some butterfly which had evidently escaped from the chrysalis still lying in the little hand.

Paul was looking at it with approving eyes when Mrs. Dean appeared with his card in her hand, three shawls on her shoulders, and in her face a somewhat startled expression, as if she expected some novel demonstration from the man whose genius her daughter so much admired.

"I hope Miss Psyche is well," began Paul, with great discrimination if not originality.

The delightfully commonplace remark tranquillized Mrs. Dean at once, and, taking off the upper shawl with a fussy gesture, she settled herself for a chat.

"Yes, thank Heaven, Sy is well. I don't know what would become of us if she wasn't. It has been a hard and sorrowful year for us with Mr. Dean's business embarrassments, my feeble health, and May's death. I don't know that you were aware of our loss, sir;" and unaffected maternal grief gave sudden dignity to the faded, fretful face of the speaker.

Paul murmured his regrets, understanding better now the pathetic words on a certain tear-stained page of the little book still in his pocket.

"Poor dear, she suffered everything, and it came very hard upon Sy, for the child wasn't happy with any one else, and almost lived in her arms," continued Mrs. Dean, dropping the second shawl to get her handkerchief.

"Miss Psyche has not had much time for art-studies this year, I suppose?" said Paul, hoping to arrest the shower natural as it was.

"How could she, with two invalids, the housekeeping, pa and the boys to attend to? No, she gave that up last spring, and though it was a great disappointment to her at the time, she has got over it now, and is happier than she ever was before, I think," added her mother, remembering as she spoke that Psyche even now went about the house sometimes pale and silent, with a hungry look in her eyes.

"I am glad to hear it," though a little shadow passed over his face as Paul spoke, for he was too true an artist to believe that any work could be as happy as that which he loved and lived for. "I thought there was much promise in Miss Psyche, and I sincerely believe that time will prove me a true prophet," he said with mingled regret and hope in his voice as he glanced about the room, which betrayed the tastes still cherished by the girl.

"I'm afraid ambition isn't good for women; I mean the sort that makes 'em known by coming before the public in any way. But Sy deserves some reward, I'm sure, and I know she'll have it, for a better daughter never lived."

Here the third shawl was cast off, as if the thought of Psyche, or the presence of a genial guest, had touched Mrs. Dean's chilly nature with a comfortable warmth.

Further conversation was interrupted by the avalanche of boys, which came tumbling down the front stairs as Tom, Dick, and Harry shouted in a sort of chorus:—

"Sy, my balloon has got away; lend us a hand at catching him!"

"Sy, I want a lot of paste made, right off."

"Sy, I've split my jacket down the back; come sew me up, there's a dear!"

On beholding a stranger the young gentlemen suddenly lost their voices, found their manners, and with nods and grins took themselves away as quietly as could be expected of six clumping boots and an unlimited quantity of animal spirits in a high state of effervescence. As they trooped off an unmistakable odor of burnt milk pervaded the air, and the crash of china, followed by an Irish wail, caused Mrs. Dean to clap on her three shawls again and excuse herself in visible trepidation.

Paul laughed quietly to himself, then turned sober and said, "Poor Psyche!" with a sympathetic sigh. He roamed about the room impatiently till the sound of voices drew him to the window to behold the girl coming up the walk with her clumsy old father leaning on one arm, the other loaded with baskets and bundles, and her hands occupied by a remarkably ugly turtle.

"Here we are!" cried a cheery voice, as they entered without observing the new-comer. "I've done all my errands and had a lovely time. There is Tom's gunpowder, Dick's fishhooks, and one of Professor Gazzy's famous turtles for Harry. Here are your bundles, mother dear, and, best of all, here's pa, home in time for a good rest before dinner. I went to the mill and got him."

Psyche spoke as if she had brought a treasure; and so she had, for though Mr. Dean's face usually was about as expressive as the turtle's, it woke and warmed with the affection which his daughter had fostered till no amount of flannel could extinguish it. His big hand patted her cheek very gently as he said, in a tone of fatherly love and pride:—

"My little Sy never forgets old pa, does she?"

"Good gracious me, my dear, there's *such* a mess in the kitchen! Katy's burnt up the pudding, put castor-oil instead of olive in the salad, smashed the best meat-dish, and here's Mr. Gage come to dinner," cried Mrs. Dean in accents of despair as she tied up her head in a fourth shawl.

"Oh, I'm so glad; I'll go in and see him a few minutes, and then I'll come and attend to everything; so don't worry, mother."

"How did you find me out?" asked Psyche as she shook hands with her guest and stood looking up at him with all the old confiding frankness in her face and manner.

"The violets showed me the way."

She glanced at the posy in his button-hole and smiled.

"Yes, I gave them to Adam, but I didn't think you would guess. I enjoyed your work for an hour to-day, and I have no words strong enough to express my admiration."

"There is no need of any. Tell me about yourself; what have you been doing all this year?" he asked, watching with genuine satisfaction the serene and sunny face before him, for discontent, anxiety, and sadness were no longer visible there.

"I've been working and waiting," she began.

"And succeeding, if I may believe what I see and hear and read," he said with an expressive little wave of the book as he laid it down before her.

"My diary! I didn't know I had lost it. Where did you find it?"

"By the brook where I stopped to rest. The moment I saw your name I shut it up. Forgive me, but I can't ask pardon for reading a few pages of that little gospel of patience, love, and self-denial."

She gave him a reproachful look and hurried the telltale book out of sight as she said, with a momentary shadow on her face:—

"It has been a hard task; but I think I have learned it, and am just beginning to find that my dream *is* 'a noonday light and truth,' to me."

"Then you do not relinquish your hopes and lay down your tools?" he asked with some eagerness.

"Never! I thought at first that I could not serve two masters; but in trying to be faithful to one I find I am nearer and dearer to the other. My cares and duties are growing lighter every day (or I have learned to bear them better), and when my leisure does come I shall know how to use it, for my head is full of ambitious plans, and I feel that I can do something *now*."

All the old enthusiasm shone in her eyes, and a sense of power betrayed itself in voice and gesture as she spoke.

"I believe it," he said heartily. "You have learned the secret, as that proves."

Psyche looked at the childish image as he pointed to it, and into her face there came a motherly expression that made it very sweet.

"That little sister was so dear to me I could not fail to make her lovely, for I put my heart into my work. The year has gone, but I don't regret it, though this is all I have done."

"You forgot your three wishes; I think the year has granted them."

"What were they?"

"To possess beauty in yourself, the power of seeing it in all things, and the art of reproducing it with truth."

She colored deeply under the glance which accompanied the three-fold compliment, and answered with grateful humility,—

"You are very kind to say so; I wish I could believe it." Then, as if anxious to forget herself, she added rather abruptly,—

"I hear you think of giving your Adam a mate,—have you begun yet?"

"Yes, my design is finished, all but the face."

"I should think you could image Eve's beauty since you have succeeded so well with Adam's."

"The features perhaps, but not the expression. That is the charm of feminine faces, a charm so subtile that few can catch and keep it. I want a truly womanly face, one that shall be sweet and strong without being either weak or hard. A hopeful, loving, earnest face, with a tender touch of motherliness in it, and perhaps the shadow of a grief that has softened but not saddened it."

"It will be hard to find a face like that."

"I don't expect to find it in perfection; but one sometimes sees faces which suggest all this, and in rare moments give glimpses of a lovely possibility."

"I sincerely hope you will find one then," said Psyche, thinking of the dinner.

"Thank you; *I* think I have."

Now, in order that every one may be suited, we will stop here, and leave our readers to finish the story as they like. Those who prefer the good old fashion may believe that the hero and heroine fell in love, were married and lived happily ever afterward. But those who can conceive of a world outside of a wedding-ring may believe that the friends remained faithful friends all their lives, while Paul won fame and fortune, and Psyche grew beautiful with the beauty of a serene and sunny nature, happy in duties which became pleasures, rich in the art which made life lovely to herself and others.

THE SUNNY SIDE

"*SUPPOSE* you come and see some of my friends instead! They are not fine or ceremonious, but lively, odd, and pleasant. Come, it will amuse you."

"I will," cried Fanny, whose spirits seemed improved by the shower.

"Nice little old lady, isn't she?" added Fan, as she caught sight of Miss Mills, on their way out, sitting at a table piled with work, and sewing away with an energy that made the gray curls vibrate.

"Saint Mehitable, I call her. Now, there is a rich woman who knew how to get happiness out of her money," said Polly, as they walked away. "She was poor till she was nearly fifty; then a comfortable fortune was left her, and she knew just how to use it. That house was given her, but instead of living in it all alone, she filled it with poor gentlefolks who needed neat, respectable homes, but couldn't get anything comfortable for their little money. I'm one of them, and I know the worth of what she does for me. Two old widow ladies live below me, several students overhead, poor Mrs. Kean and her lame boy have the back parlor, and Jenny the little bedroom next Miss Mills. Each pays what they can; that's independent, and makes us feel better: but that dear woman does a thousand things that money can't pay for, and we feel her influence all through the house. I'd *rather* be married, and have a home of my own; but next to that, I should like to be an old maid like Miss Mills."

Polly's sober face and emphatic tone made Fanny laugh, and at the cheery sound a young girl pushing a baby-carriage looked round and smiled.

"What lovely eyes!" whispered Fanny.

"Yes, that's little Jane," returned Polly, adding, when she had passed, with a nod and a friendly "Don't get tired, Jenny," "we help one another at our house, and every fine morning Jenny takes Johnny Kean out when she goes for her own walk. That gives his mother time to rest, does both the children good, and keeps things neighborly. Miss Mills suggested it, and Jenny is so glad to do anything for anybody, it's a pleasure to let her."

"I've heard of Miss Mills before. But I should think she would get tired to death, sitting there making hoods and petticoats day after day," said Fanny, after thinking over Jenny's story for a few minutes, for seeing the girl seemed to bring it nearer, and make it more real to her.

"But she don't sit there all the time. People come to her with their troubles, and she goes to them with all sorts of help, from soap and soup, to shrouds for the dead and comfort for the living. I go with her sometimes, and it is more exciting than any play, to see and hear the lives and stories of the poor."

"How can you bear the dreadful sights and sounds, the bad air, and the poverty that can't be cured?"

"But it isn't all dreadful. There are good and lovely things among them, if one only has eyes to see them. It makes me grateful and contented, shows me how rich I am, and keeps me ready to do all I can for these poor souls."

"My good Polly!" and Fanny gave her friend's arm an affectionate squeeze, wondering if it was this alone that had worked the change in Polly.

"You have seen two of my new friends, Miss Mills and Jenny, now I'll show you two more," said Polly, presently, as they reached a door, and she led the way up several flights of public stairs. "Rebecca Jeffrey is a regularly splendid girl, full of talent; she won't let us call it genius; she will be famous some day, I know, she is so modest, and yet so intent on her work. Lizzie Small is an engraver and designs the most delightful little pictures. Becky and she live together, and take care of one another in true Damon and Pythias style. This studio is their home,—they work, eat, sleep, and live here, going halves in everything. They are all alone in the world, but as happy and independent as birds; real friends, whom nothing will part."

"Let a lover come between them, and their friendship won't last long," said Fanny.

"I think it will. Take a look at them, and you'll change your mind," answered Polly, tapping at a door, on which two modest cards were tacked.

"Come in!" said a voice, and obeying, Fanny found herself in a large, queerly furnished room, lighted from above, and occupied by two girls. One stood before a great clay figure, in a corner. This one was tall, with a strong face, keen eyes, short, curly hair, and a fine head. Fanny was struck at once by this face and figure, though the one was not handsome, and the other half hidden by a great pinafore covered with clay. At a table where the light was clearest, sat a frail-looking girl, with a thin face, big eyes, and pale hair,—a dreamy, absorbed little person, who bent over a block, skilfully wielding her tools.

"Becky and Bess, how do you do? This is my friend, Fanny Shaw. We are out on a rampage; so go on with your work, and let us lazy ones look on and admire."

As Polly spoke, both girls looked up and nodded, smilingly; Bess gave Fan the one easy-chair; Becky took an artistic survey of the new-comer, with eyes that seemed to see everything; then each went on with her work, and all began to talk.

"You are just what I want, Polly. Pull up your sleeve, and give me an arm while you sit; the muscles here aren't right, and you've got just what I want," said Becky, slapping the round arm of the statue, at which Fan was gazing with awe.

"How do you get on?" asked Polly, throwing off her cloak, and rolling up her sleeves, as if going to wash.

"Slowly. The idea is working itself clear, and I follow as fast as my hands can. Is the face better, do you think?" said Becky, taking off a wet cloth, and showing the head of the statue.

"How beautiful it is!" cried Fanny, staring at it with increased respect.

"What does it mean to you?" asked Rebecca, turning to her with a sudden shine in her keen eyes.

"I don't know whether it is meant for a saint or a muse, a goddess or a fate; but to me it is only a beautiful woman, bigger, lovelier, and more imposing than any woman I ever saw," answered Fanny, slowly, trying to express the impression the statue made upon her.

Rebecca smiled brightly, and Bess looked round to nod approvingly, but Polly clapped her hands, and said,—

"Well done, Fan! I didn't think you'd get the idea so well, but you have, and I'm proud of your insight. Now I'll tell you, for Becky will let me, since you have paid her the compliment of understanding her work. Some time ago we got into a famous talk about what women should be, and Becky said she'd show us her idea of the coming woman. There she is, as you say, bigger, lovelier, and more imposing than any we see nowadays; and at the same time, she is a true woman. See what a fine forehead, yet the mouth is both firm and tender, as if it could say strong, wise things, as well as teach children and kiss babies. We couldn't decide what to put in the hands as the most appropriate symbol. What do you say?"

"Give her a sceptre; she would make a fine queen," answered Fanny.

"No, we have had enough of that; women have been called queens a long time, but the kingdom given them isn't worth ruling," answered Rebecca.

"I don't think it is nowadays," said Fanny, with a tired sort of sigh.

"Put a man's hand in hers to help her along, then," said Polly, whose happy fortune it had been to find friends and helpers in father and brothers.

"No; my woman is to stand alone, and help herself," said Rebecca, decidedly.

"She's to be strong-minded, is she?" and Fanny's lip curled a little as she uttered the misused words.

"Yes, strong-minded, strong-hearted, strong-souled, and strong-bodied; that is why I made her larger than the miserable, pinched-up woman of our day. Strength and beauty must go together. Don't you think these broad shoulders can bear burdens without breaking down, these hands work well, these eyes see clearly, and these lips do something besides simper and gossip?"

Fanny was silent; but a voice from Bess's corner said,—

"Put a child in her arms, Becky."

"Not that even, for she is to be something more than a nurse."

"Give her a ballot-box," cried a new voice, and turning round, they saw an odd-looking woman perched on a sofa behind them.

"Thank you for the suggestion, Kate. I'll put that with the other symbols at her feet; for I'm going to have needle, pen, palette, and broom somewhere, to suggest the various talents she owns, and the ballot-box will show that she has earned the right to use them. How goes it?" and Rebecca offered a clay-daubed hand, which the new-comer cordially shook.

"Great news, girls! Anna is going to Italy!" cried Kate, tossing up her bonnet like a school-boy.

"Oh, how splendid! Who takes her! Has she had a fortune left her? Tell all about it," exclaimed the girls, gathering round the speaker.

"Yes, it *is* splendid; just one of the beautiful things that does everybody heaps of good, it is so generous and so deserved. You know Anna has been longing to go; working and hoping for a chance, and never getting it, till all of a sudden Miss Burton is inspired to invite the girl to go with her for several years to Italy. Think of the luck of that dear soul, the advantages she'll have, the good it will do her, and, best of all, the lovely way in which it comes to her. Miss Burton wants her as a friend, asks nothing of her but her company, and Anna will go through fire and water for her, of course. Now, isn't that fine?"

It was good to see how heartily these girls sympathized in their comrade's good fortune. Polly danced all over the room, Bess and Becky hugged one another, Kate laughed with her eyes full, while even Fanny felt a glow of pride and pleasure at the kind act.

"Who is that?" she whispered to Polly, who had subsided into a corner.

"Why, it's Kate King, the authoress. Bless me, how rude not to introduce you! Here, my King, is an admirer of yours, Fanny Shaw, and my well-beloved friend," cried Polly, presenting Fan, who regarded the shabby young woman with as much respect, as if she had been arrayed in velvet and ermine; for Kate had written a successful book by accident, and happened to be the fashion, just then.

"It's time for lunch, girls, and I brought mine along with me, it's so much jollier to eat in sisterhood. Let's club together, and have a revel," said Kate, producing a bag of oranges, and several big, plummy buns.

"We've got sardines, crackers, and cheese," said Bess, clearing off a table with all speed.

"Wait a bit, and I'll add my share," cried Polly, and catching up her cloak, she ran off to the grocery store near by.

"You'll be shocked at our performances, Miss Shaw, but you can call it a picnic, and never tell what dreadful things you saw us do," said Rebecca, polishing a paint knife by rubbing it up and down in a pot of ivy, while Kate spread forth the feast in several odd plates, and a flat shell or two.

"Let us have coffee to finish off with; put on the pot, Bess, and skim the milk," added Becky, as she produced cups, mugs, and a queer little vase, to supply drinking vessels for the party.

"Here's nuts, a pot of jam, and some cake. Fan likes sweet things, and we want to be elegant when we have company," said Polly, flying in again, and depositing her share on the table.

"Now, then, fall to, ladies, and help yourselves. Never mind if the china don't hold out; take the sardines by their little tails, and wipe your fingers on my brown-paper napkins," said Kate, setting the example with such a relish, that the others followed it in a gale of merriment.

Fanny had been to many elegant lunches, but never enjoyed one more than that droll picnic in the studio; for there was a freedom about it that was charming, an artistic flavor to everything, and such a spirit of good-will and gayety, that she felt at home at once. As they ate, the others talked and she listened, finding it as interesting as any romance to hear these young women discuss their plans, ambitions, successes, and defeats. It was a new world to her, and they seemed a different race of creatures from the girls whose lives were spent in dress, gossip, pleasure, or ennui. They were girls still, full of spirits, fun, and youth; but below the light-heartedness each cherished a purpose, which seemed to ennoble her womanhood, to give her a certain power, a sustaining satisfaction, a daily stimulus, that led her on to daily effort, and in time to some success in circumstance or character, which was worth all the patience, hope, and labor of her life.

Fanny was just then in the mood to feel the beauty of this, for the sincerest emotion she had even known was beginning to make her dissatisfied with herself, and the aimless life she led. "Men must respect such girls as these," she thought; "yes, and love them too, for in spite of their independence, they are womanly. I wish I had a talent to live for, if it would do as much for me as it does for them. It is this sort of thing that is improving Polly, that makes her society interesting to Sydney, and herself so dear to every one. Money can't buy these things for me, and I want them very much."

As these thoughts were passing through her mind, Fanny was hearing all sorts of topics discussed with feminine enthusiasm and frankness. Art, morals, politics, society, books, religion, housekeeping, dress, and economy, for the minds and tongues roved from subject to subject with youthful rapidity, and seemed to get something from the dryest and the dullest.

"How does the new book come on?" asked Polly, sucking her orange in public with a composure which would have scandalized the good ladies of "Cranford." [1]

"Better than it deserves. My children, beware of popularity; it is a delusion and a snare; it puffeth up the heart of man, and especially of woman; it blindeth the eyes to faults; it exalteth unduly the humble powers of the victim; it is apt to be capricious, and just as one gets to liking the taste of this intoxicating draught, it suddenly faileth, and one is left gasping, like a fish out of water," and Kate emphasized her speech by spearing a sardine with a penknife, and eating it with a groan.

"It won't hurt you much, I guess; you have worked and waited so long, a large dose will do you good," said Rebecca, giving her a generous spoonful of jam, as if eager to add as much sweetness as possible to a life that had not been an easy one.

"When are you and Becky going to dissolve partnership?" asked Polly, eager for news of all.

"Never! George knows he can't have one without the other, and has not suggested such a thing as parting us. There is always room in my house for Becky, and she lets me do as she would if she was in my place," answered Bess, with a look which her friend answered by a smile.

"The lover won't separate this pair of friends, you see," whispered Polly to Fan. "Bess is to be married in the spring, and Becky is to live with her."

"By the way, Polly, I've got some tickets for you. People are always sending me such things, and as I don't care for them, I'm glad to make them over to you young and giddy infants. There are passes for the statuary exhibition, Becky shall have those; here are the concert tickets for you, my musical girl; and that is for a course of lectures on literature, which I'll keep for myself."

As Kate dealt out the colored cards to the grateful girls, Fanny took a good look at her, wondering if the time would ever come when women could earn a little money and success, without paying such a heavy price for them; for Kate looked sick, tired, and too early old. Then her eye went to the unfinished statue, and she said, impulsively,—

"I hope you'll put that in marble, and show us what we ought to be."

"I wish I could!" And an intense desire shone in Rebecca's face, as she saw her faulty work, and felt how fair her model was.

For a minute, the five young women sat silent, looking up at the beautiful, strong figure before them, each longing to see it done, and each unconscious that she was helping, by her individual effort and experience, to bring the day when their noblest ideal of womanhood should be embodied in flesh and blood, not clay.

The city bells rung one, and Polly started up.

"I must go, for I promised a neighbor of mine a lesson at two."

"I thought this was a holiday," said Fanny.

"So it is, but this is a little labor of love, and doesn't spoil the day at all. The child has talent, loves music, and needs help. I can't give her money, but I *can* teach her; so I do, and she is the most promising pupil I have. Help one another, is part of the religion of our sisterhood, Fan."

"I must put you in a story, Polly. I want a heroine, and you will do," said Kate.

"Me! why, there never was such a humdrum, unromantic thing as I am," cried Polly, amazed.

"I've booked you, nevertheless, so in you go; but you may add as much romance as you like, it's time you did."

"I'm ready for it when it comes, but it can't be forced, you know," and Polly blushed and smiled as if some little spice of that delightful thing *had* stolen into her life, for all its prosaic seeming.

Fanny was amused to see that the girls did not kiss at parting, but shook hands in a quiet, friendly fashion, looking at one another with eyes that said more than the most "gushing" words.

"I like your friends very much, Polly. I was afraid I should find them mannish and rough, or sentimental and conceited. But they are simple, sensible creatures, full of talent, and all sorts of fine things. I admire and respect them, and want to go again, if I may."

"Oh, Fan, I *am* so glad! I hoped you'd like them, I knew they'd do you good, and I'll take you any time, for you stood the test better than I expected. Becky asked me to bring you again, and she seldom does that for fashionable young ladies, let me tell you."

"I want to be ever so much better, and I think you and they might show me how," said Fanny, with a traitorous tremble in her voice.

"We'll show you the sunny side of poverty and work, and that is a useful lesson for any one, Miss Mills says," answered Polly, hoping that Fan *would* learn how much the poor can teach the rich, and what helpful friends girls may be to one another.

WORK: A STORY OF EXPERIENCE

I

CHRISTIE

"*AUNT BETSEY*, there's going to be a new Declaration of Independence."

"Bless and save us, what do you mean, child?" And the startled old lady precipitated a pie into the oven with destructive haste.

"I mean that, being of age, I'm going to take care of myself, and not be a burden any longer. Uncle wishes me out of the way; thinks I ought to go, and, sooner or later, will tell me so. I don't intend to wait for that, but, like the people in fairy tales, travel away into the world and seek my fortune. I know I can find it."

Christie emphasized her speech by energetic demonstrations in the bread-trough, kneading the dough as if it was her destiny, and she was shaping it to suit herself; while Aunt Betsey stood listening, with uplifted pie-fork, and as much astonishment as her placid face was capable of expressing. As the girl paused, with a decided thump, the old lady exclaimed:

"What crazy idee you got into your head now?"

"A very sane and sensible one that's got to be worked out, so please listen to it, ma'am. I've had it a good while, I've thought it over thoroughly, and I'm sure it's the right thing for me to do. I'm old enough to take care of myself; and if I'd been a boy, I should have been told to do it long ago. I hate to be dependent; and now there's no need of it, I can't bear it any longer. If you were poor, I wouldn't leave you; for I never forget how kind *you* have been to me. But Uncle doesn't love or understand me; I *am* a burden to

239

him, and I must go where I can take care of myself. I can't be happy till I do, for there's nothing here for me. I'm sick of this dull town, where the one idea is eat, drink, and get rich; I don't find any friends to help me as I want to be helped, or any work that I can do well; so let me go, Aunty, and find my place, wherever it is."

"But I do need you, deary; and you mustn't think Uncle don't like you. He does, only he don't show it; and when your odd ways fret him, he ain't pleasant, I know. I don't see why you can't be contented; I've lived here all my days, and never found the place lonesome, or the folks unneighborly." And Aunt Betsey looked perplexed by the new idea.

"You and I are very different, ma'am. There was more yeast put into my composition, I guess; and, after standing quiet in a warm corner so long, I begin to ferment, and ought to be kneaded up in time, so that I may turn out a wholesome loaf. You can't do this; so let me go where it can be done, else I shall turn sour and good for nothing. Does that make the matter any clearer?" And Christie's serious face relaxed into a smile as her aunt's eye went down from her to the nicely moulded loaf offered as an illustration.

"I see what you mean, Kitty; but I never thought on't before. You be better riz than me; though, let me tell you, too much emptins makes bread poor stuff, like baker's trash; and too much workin' up makes it hard and dry. Now fly 'round, for the big oven is most het, and this cake takes a sight of time in the mixin'."

"You haven't said I might go, Aunty," began the girl, after a long pause devoted by the old lady to the preparation of some compound which seemed to require great nicety of measurement in its ingredients; for when she replied, Aunt Betsey curiously interlarded her speech with inaudible directions to herself from the receipt-book before her.

"I ain't no right to keep you, dear, ef you choose to take (a pinch of salt). I'm sorry you ain't happy, and think you might be ef you'd only (beat six eggs, yolks and whites together). But ef you can't, and feel that you need (two cups of sugar), only speak to Uncle, and ef he says (a squeeze of fresh lemon), go, my dear, and take my blessin' with you (not forgettin' to cover with a piece of paper)."

Christie's laugh echoed through the kitchen; and the old lady smiled benignly, quite unconscious of the cause of the girl's merriment.

"I shall ask Uncle to-night, and I know he won't object. Then I shall write to see if Mrs. Flint has a room for me, where I can stay till I get something to do. There is plenty of work in the world, and I'm not afraid of it; so you'll soon hear good news of me. Don't look sad, for you know I never could forget *you,* even if I should become the greatest lady in the land." And Christie left the prints of two floury but affectionate hands on the old lady's shoulders, as she kissed the wrinkled face that had never worn a frown to her.

Full of hopeful fancies, Christie salted the pans and buttered the dough in pleasant forgetfulness of all mundane affairs, and the ludicrous dismay of Aunt Betsey, who followed her about rectifying her mistakes, and watching over her as if this sudden absence of mind had roused suspicions of her sanity.

"Uncle, I want to go away, and get my own living, if you please," was Christie's abrupt beginning, as they sat round the evening fire.

"Hey! what's that?" said Uncle Enos, rousing from the doze he was enjoying, with a candle in perilous proximity to his newspaper and his nose.

Christie repeated her request, and was much relieved, when, after a meditative stare, the old man briefly answered:

"Wal, go ahead."

"I was afraid you might think it rash or silly, sir."

"I think it's the best thing you could do; and I like your good sense in pupposin' on't."

"Then I may really go?"

"Soon's ever you like. Don't pester me about it till you're ready; then I'll give you a little suthing to start off with." And Uncle Enos returned to "The Farmer's Friend," as if cattle were more interesting than kindred.

Christie was accustomed to his curt speech and careless manner; had expected nothing more cordial; and, turning to her aunt, said, rather bitterly:

"Didn't I tell you he'd be glad to have me go? No matter! When I've done something to be proud of, he will be as glad to see me back again." Then her voice changed, her eyes kindled, and the firm lips softened with a smile. "Yes, I'll try my experiment; then I'll get rich; found a home for girls like myself; or, better, still, be a Mrs. Fry,[1] a Florence Nightingale, or"—

"How are you on't for stockin's, dear?"

Christie's castles in the air vanished at the prosaic question; but, after a blank look, she answered pleasantly:

"Thank you for bringing me down to my feet again, when I was soaring away too far and too fast. I'm poorly off, ma'am; but if you are knitting these for me, I shall certainly start on a firm foundation." And, leaning on Aunt Betsey's knee, she patiently discussed the wardrobe question from hose to head-gear.

"Don't you think you could be contented any way, Christie, ef I make the work lighter, and leave you more time for your books and things?" asked the old lady, loth to lose the one youthful element in her quiet life.

"No, ma'am, for I can't find what I want here," was the decided answer.

"What *do* you want, child?"

"Look in the fire, and I'll try to show you."

The old lady obediently turned her spectacles that way; and Christie said in a tone half serious, half playful:

"Do you see those two logs? Well that one smouldering dismally away in the corner is what my life is now; the other blazing and singing is what I want my life to be."

"Bless me, what an idee! They are both a-burnin' where they are put, and both will be ashes to-morrow; so what difference *doos* it make?"

Christie smiled at the literal old lady; but, following the fancy that pleased her, she added earnestly:

"I know the end is the same; but it *does* make a difference *how* they turn to ashes, and *how* I spend my life. That log, with its one dull spot of fire, gives neither light nor warmth, but lies sizzling despondently among the cinders. But the other glows from end to end with cheerful little flames that go singing up the chimney with a pleasant sound. Its light fills the room and shines out into the dark; its warmth draws us nearer, making the hearth the cosiest place in the house, and we shall all miss the friendly blaze when it dies. Yes," she added, as if to herself, "I hope my life may be like that, so that, whether it be long or short, it will be useful and cheerful while it lasts, will be missed when it ends, and leave something behind besides ashes."

Though she only half understood them, the girl's words touched the kind old lady, and made her look anxiously at the eager young face gazing so wistfully into the fire.

"A good smart blowin' up with the belluses would make the green stick burn most as well as the dry one after a spell. I guess contentedness is the best bellus for young folks, ef they would only think so."

"I dare say you are right, Aunty; but I want to try for myself; and if I fail, I'll come back and follow your advice. Young folks always have discontented fits, you know. Didn't you when you were a girl?"

"Shouldn't wonder ef I did; but Enos came along, and I forgot 'em."

"My Enos has not come along yet, and never may; so I'm not going to sit and wait for any man to give me independence, if I can earn it for myself." And a quick glance at the gruff, gray old man in the corner plainly betrayed that, in Christie's opinion, Aunt Betsey made a bad bargain when she exchanged her girlish aspirations for a man whose soul was in his pocket.

"Jest like her mother, full of hifalutin notions, discontented, and sot in her own idees. Poor capital to start a fortin' on."

Christie's eye met that of her uncle peering over the top of his paper with an expression that always tried her patience. Now it was like a dash of cold water on her enthusiasm, and her face fell as she asked quickly:

"How do you mean, sir?"

"I mean that you are startin' all wrong; your redic'lus notions about independence and self-cultur won't come to nothin' in the long run, and you'll make as bad a failure of your life as your mother did of her'n."

"Please, don't say that to me; I can't bear it, for *I* shall never think her life a failure, because she tried to help herself, and married a good man in spite of poverty, when she loved him! You call that folly; but I'll do the same if I can; and I'd rather have what my father and mother left me, than all the money you are piling up, just for the pleasure of being richer than your neighbors."

"Never mind, dear, he don't mean no harm!" whispered Aunt Betsey, fearing a storm.

But though Christie's eyes had kindled and her color deepened, her voice was low and steady, and her indignation was of the inward sort.

"Uncle likes to try me by saying such things, and this is one reason why I want to go away before I get sharp and bitter and distrustful as he is. I don't suppose I can make you understand my feeling, but I'd like to try, and then I'll never speak of it again;" and, carefully controlling voice and face, Christie slowly added, with a look that would have been pathetically eloquent to one who could have understood the instincts of a strong nature for light and freedom: "You say I am discontented, proud and ambitious; that's true, and I'm glad of it. I am discontented, because I can't help feeling that there is a better sort of life than this dull one made up of everlasting work, with no object but money. I can't starve my soul for the sake of my body, and I mean to get out of the treadmill if I can. I'm proud, as you call it, because I hate dependence where there isn't any love to make it bearable. You don't say so in words, but I know you begrudge me a home, though you will call me ungrateful when I'm gone. I'm willing to work, but I want work that I can put my heart into, and feel that it does me good, no matter how hard it is. I only ask for a chance to be a useful, happy woman, and I don't think that is a bad ambition. Even if I only do what my dear mother did, earn my living honestly and happily, and leave a beautiful example behind me, to help one other woman as hers helps me, I shall be satisfied."

Christie's voice faltered over the last words, for the thoughts and feelings which had been working within her during the last few days had stirred her deeply, and the resolution to cut loose from the old life had not been lightly made. Mr. Devon had listened behind his paper to this unusual outpouring with a sense of discomfort which was new to him. But though the words reproached and annoyed, they did not soften him, and when Christie paused with tearful eyes, her uncle rose, saying, slowly, as he lighted his candle:

"Ef I'd refused to let you go before, I'd agree to it now; for you need breakin' in, my girl, and you are goin' where you'll get it, so the sooner you're off the better for all on us. Come, Betsey, we may as wal leave, for we can't understand the wants of her higher nater, as Christie calls it, and we've had lecterin' enough for one night." And with a grim laugh the old man quitted the field, worsted but in good order.

"There, there, dear, hev a good cry, and forgit all about it!" purred Aunt Betsey, as the heavy footsteps creaked away, for the good soul had a most old-fashioned and dutiful awe of her lord and master.

Work: A Story of Experience

"I shan't cry but act; for it is high time I *was* off. I've stayed for your sake; now I'm more trouble than comfort, and away I go. Good-night, my dear old Aunty, and don't look troubled, for I'll be a lamb while I stay."

Having kissed the old lady, Christie swept her work away, and sat down to write the letter which was the first step toward freedom. When it was done, she drew nearer to her friendly *confidante* the fire, and till late into the night sat thinking tenderly of the past, bravely of the present, hopefully of the future. Twenty-one to-morrow, and her inheritance a head, a heart, a pair of hands; also the dower of most New England girls, intelligence, courage, and common sense, many practical gifts, and, hidden under the reserve that soon melts in a genial atmosphere, much romance and enthusiasm, and the spirit which can rise to heroism when the great moment comes.

Christie was one of that large class of women who, moderately endowed with talents, earnest and true-hearted, are driven by necessity, temperament, or principle out into the world to find support, happiness, and homes for themselves. Many turn back discouraged; more accept shadow for substance, and discover their mistake too late; the weakest lose their purpose and themselves; but the strongest struggle on, and, after danger and defeat, earn at last the best success this world can give us, the possession of a brave and cheerful spirit, rich in self-knowledge, self-control, self-help. This was the real desire of Christie's heart; this was to be her lesson and reward, and to this happy end she was slowly yet surely brought by the long discipline of life and labor.

Sitting alone there in the night, she tried to strengthen herself with all the good and helpful memories she could recall, before she went away to find her place in the great unknown world. She thought of her mother, so like herself, who had borne the commonplace life of home till she could bear it no longer. Then had gone away to teach, as most country girls are forced to do. Had met, loved, and married a poor gentleman, and, after a few years of genuine happiness, untroubled even by much care and poverty, had followed him out of the world, leaving her little child to the protection of her brother.

Christie looked back over the long, lonely years she had spent in the old farm-house, plodding to school and church, and doing her tasks with kind Aunt Betsey while a child; and slowly growing into girlhood, with a world of romance locked up in a heart hungry for love and a larger, nobler life.

She had tried to appease this hunger in many ways, but found little help. Her father's old books were all she could command, and these she wore out with much reading. Inheriting his refined tastes, she found nothing to attract her in the society of the commonplace and often coarse people about her. She tried to like the buxom girls whose one ambition was to "get married," and whose only subjects of conversation were "smart bonnets" and "nice dresses." She tried to believe that the admiration and regard of the bluff young farmers was worth striving for; but when one well-to-do neighbor laid his acres at her feet, she found it impossible to accept for her life's companion a man whose soul was wrapped up in prize cattle and big turnips.

Uncle Enos never could forgive her for this piece of folly, and Christie plainly saw that one of three things would surely happen, if she lived on there with no vent for her full heart and busy mind. She would either marry Joe Butterfield in sheer desperation, and become a farmer's household drudge; settle down into a sour spinster, content to make butter, gossip, and lay up money all her days; or do what poor Mary Stone had done, try to crush and curb her needs and aspirations till the struggle grew too hard, and then in a fit of despair end her life, and leave a tragic story to haunt their quiet river.

To escape these fates but one way appeared; to break loose from this narrow life, go out into the world and see what she could do for herself. This idea was full of enchantment to the eager girl, and, after much earnest thought, she had resolved to try it.

"If I fail, I can come back," she said to herself, even while she scorned the idea of failure, for with all her shy pride she was both brave and ardent, and her dreams were of the rosiest sort.

"I won't marry Joe; I won't wear myself out in a district-school for the mean sum they give a woman; I won't delve away here where I'm not wanted; and I won't end my life like a coward, because it is dull and hard. I'll try my fate as mother did, and perhaps I may succeed as well." And Christie's thoughts went wandering away into the dim, sweet past when she, a happy child, lived with loving parents in a different world from that.

Lost in these tender memories, she sat till the old moon-faced clock behind the door struck twelve, then the visions vanished, leaving their benison behind them.

As she glanced backward at the smouldering fire, a slender spire of flame shot up from the log that had blazed so cheerily, and shone upon her as she went. A good omen, gratefully accepted then, and remembered often in the years to come.

SERVANT

A FORTNIGHT later, and Christie was off. Mrs. Flint had briefly answered that she had a room, and that work was always to be found in the city. So the girl packed her one trunk, folding away splendid hopes among her plain gowns, and filling every corner with happy fancies, utterly impossible plans, and tender little dreams, so lovely at the time, so pathetic to remember, when contact with the hard realities of life has collapsed our bright bubbles, and the frost of disappointment nipped all our morning glories in their prime.

The old red stage stopped at Enos Devon's door, and his niece crossed the threshold after a cool handshake with the master of the house, and a close embrace with the mistress, who stood pouring out last words with spectacles too dim for seeing. Fat Ben swung up the trunk, slammed the door, mounted his perch, and the ancient vehicle swayed with pre-monitory symptoms of departure.

Then something smote Christie's heart. "Stop!" she cried, and springing out ran back into the dismal room where the old man sat. Straight up to him she went with outstretched hand, saying steadily, though her face was full of feeling:

"Uncle, I'm not satisfied with that good-bye. I don't mean to be sentimental, but I do want to say, 'Forgive me!' I see now that I might have made you sorry to part with me, if I had tried to make you love me more. It's too late now, but I'm not too proud to confess when I'm wrong. I want to part kindly; I ask your pardon; I thank you for all you've done for me, and I say good-bye affectionately now."

Mr. Devon had a heart somewhere, though it seldom troubled him; but it did make itself felt when the girl looked at him with his dead sister's eyes, and spoke in a tone whose unaccustomed tenderness was a reproach.

Conscience had pricked him more than once that week, and he was glad to own it now; his rough sense of honor was touched by her frank expression, and, as he answered, his hand was offered readily.

"I like that, Kitty, and think the better of you for't. Let bygones be bygones. I gen'lly got as good as I give, and I guess I deserved some on't. I wish you wal, my girl, I heartily wish you wal, and hope you won't forgit that the old house ain't never shet aginst you."

Christie astonished him with a cordial kiss; then bestowing another warm hug on Aunt Niobe, as she called the old lady in a tearful joke, she ran into the carriage, taking with her all the sunshine of the place.

Christie found Mrs. Flint a dreary woman, with "boarders" written all over her sour face and faded figure. Butcher's bills and house rent seemed to fill her eyes with sleepless anxiety; thriftless cooks and saucy housemaids to sharpen the tones of her shrill voice; and an incapable husband to burden her shoulders like a modern "Old man of the sea.

A little room far up in the tall house was at the girl's disposal for a reasonable sum, and she took possession, feeling very rich with the hundred dollars Uncle Enos gave her, and delightfully independent, with no milk-pans to scald; no heavy lover to elude; no humdrum district school to imprison her day after day.

For a week she enjoyed her liberty heartily, then set about finding something to do. Her wish was to be a governess, that being the usual refuge for respectable girls who have a living to get. But Christie soon found her want of accomplishments a barrier to success in that line, for the mammas thought less of the solid than of the ornamental branches, and wished their little darlings to learn French before English, music before grammar, and drawing before writing.

So, after several disappointments, Christie decided that her education was too old-fashioned for the city, and gave up the idea of teaching. Sewing she resolved not to try till every thing else failed; and, after a few more attempts to get writing to do, she said to herself, in a fit of humility and good sense: "I'll begin at the beginning, and work my way up. I'll put my pride in my pocket, and go out to service. Housework I like, and can do well, thanks to Aunt Betsey. I never thought it degradation to do it for her, so why should I mind doing it for others if they pay for it? It isn't what I want, but it's better than idleness, so I'll try it!"

Full of this wise resolution, she took to haunting that purgatory of the poor, an intelligence office. Mrs. Flint gave her a recommendation, and she hopefully took her place among the ranks of buxom German, incapable Irish, and "smart" American women; for in those days foreign help had not driven farmers' daughters out of the field, and made domestic comfort a lost art.

At first Christie enjoyed the novelty of the thing, and watched with interest the anxious housewives who flocked in demanding that *rara avis,* an angel at nine shillings a week; and not finding it, bewailed the degeneracy of the times. Being too honest to profess herself absolutely perfect in every known branch of house-work, it was some time before she suited herself. Meanwhile, she was questioned and lectured, half engaged and kept waiting, dismissed for a whim, and so worried that she began to regard herself as the incarnation of all human vanities and shortcomings.

"A desirable place in a small, genteel family," was at last offered her, and she posted away to secure it, having reached a state of desperation and resolved to go as a first-class cook rather than sit with her hands before her any longer.

A well-appointed house, good wages, and light duties seemed things to be grateful for, and Christie decided that going out to service was not the hardest fate in life, as she stood at the door of a handsome house in a sunny square waiting to be inspected.

Mrs. Stuart, having just returned from Italy, affected the artistic, and the new applicant found her with a Roman scarf about her head, a rosary like a string of small cannon balls at her side, and azure draperies which became her as well as they did the sea-green furniture of her marine boudoir, where unwary walkers tripped over coral and shells, grew sea-sick looking at pictures of tempestuous billows engulfing every sort of craft, from a man-of-war to a hencoop with a ghostly young lady clinging to it with one hand, and had their appetites effectually taken away by a choice collection of water-bugs and snakes in a glass globe, that looked like a jar of mixed pickles in a state of agitation.

Madame was intent on a water-color copy of Turner's "Rain, Wind, and Hail," that pleasing work which was sold upsidedown and no one found it out. Motioning Christie to a seat she finished some delicate sloppy process before speaking. In that little pause Christie examined her, and the impression then received was afterward confirmed.

Mrs. Stuart possessed some beauty and chose to think herself a queen of society. She assumed majestic manners in public and could not entirely divest herself of them in private, which often produced comic effects. Zenobia troubled about fish-sauce, or Aspasia indignant at the price of eggs will give some idea of this lady when she condescended to the cares of housekeeping.[2]

Presently she looked up and inspected the girl as if a new servant were no more than a new bonnet, a necessary article to be ordered home for examination. Christie presented her recommendation, made her modest little speech, and awaited her doom.

Mrs. Stuart read, listened, and then demanded with queenly brevity:

"Your name?"

"Christie Devon."

"Too long; I should prefer to call you Jane as I am accustomed to the name."

"As you please, ma'am."

"Your age?"

"Twenty-one."

"You are an American?"

"Yes, ma'am."

Mrs. Stuart gazed into space a moment, then delivered the following address with impressive solemnity.

"I wish a capable, intelligent, honest, neat, well-conducted person who knows her place and keeps it. The work is light, as there are but two in the family. I am very particular and so is Mr. Stuart. I pay two dollars and a half, allow one afternoon out, one service on Sunday, and no followers. My table-girl must understand her duties thoroughly, be extremely neat, and always wear white aprons."

"I think I can suit you, ma'am, when I have learned the ways of the house," meekly replied Christie.

Mrs. Stuart looked graciously satisfied and returned the paper with a gesture that Victoria might have used in restoring a granted petition, though her next words rather marred the effect of the regal act, "My cook is black."

"I have no objection to color, ma'am."

An expression of relief dawned upon Mrs. Stuart's countenance, for the black cook had been an insurmountable obstacle to all the Irish ladies who had applied. Thoughtfully tapping her Roman nose with the handle of her brush Madame took another survey of the new applicant, and seeing that she looked neat, intelligent, and respectful, gave a sigh of thankfulness and engaged her on the spot.

Much elated Christie rushed home, selected a bag of necessary articles, bundled the rest of her possessions into an empty closet (lent her rent-free owing to a profusion of cockroaches), paid up her board, and at two o'clock introduced herself to Hepsey Johnson, her fellow servant.

Hepsey was a tall, gaunt woman, bearing the tragedy of her race written in her face, with its melancholy eyes, subdued expression, and the pathetic patience of a wronged dumb animal. She received Christie with an air of resignation, and speedily bewildered her with an account of the duties she would be expected to perform.

A long and careful drill enabled Christie to set the table with but few mistakes, and to retain a tolerably clear recollection of the order of performances. She had just assumed her badge of servitude, as she called the white apron, when the bell rang violently and Hepsey, who was hurrying away to "dish up," said:

"It's de marster. You has to answer de bell, honey, and he likes it done bery spry."

Christie ran and admitted an impetuous, stout gentleman, who appeared to be incensed against the elements, for he burst in as if blown, shook himself like a Newfoundland dog, and said all in one breath:

"You're the new girl, are you? Well, take my umbrella and pull off my rubbers."

"Sir?"

Mr. Stuart was struggling with his gloves, and, quite unconscious of the astonishment of his new maid, impatiently repeated his request.

"Take this wet thing away, and pull off my overshoes. Don't you see it's raining like the very deuce!"

Christie folded her lips together in a peculiar manner as she knelt down and removed a pair of muddy overshoes, took the dripping umbrella, and was walking away with her agreeable burden when Mr. Stuart gave her another shock by calling over the banister:

"I'm going out again; so clean those rubbers, and see that the boots I sent down this morning are in order."

"Yes, sir," answered Christie meekly, and immediately afterward startled Hepsey by casting overshoes and umbrella upon the kitchen floor, and indignantly demanding:

"Am I expected to be a boot-jack to that man?"

"I 'spects you is, honey."

"Am I also expected to clean his boots?"

"Yes, chile. Katy did, and de work ain't hard when you gits used to it."

"It isn't the work; it's the degradation; and I won't submit to it."

Christie looked fiercely determined; but Hepsey shook her head, saying quietly as she went on garnishing a dish:

"Dere's more 'gradin' works dan dat, chile, and dem dat's bin 'bliged to do um finds dis sort bery easy. You's paid for it, honey; and if you does it willin, it won't hurt you more dan washin' de marster's dishes, or sweepin' his rooms."

"There ought to be a boy to do this sort of thing. Do you think it's right to ask it of me?" cried Christie, feeling that being servant was not as pleasant a task as she had thought it.

"Dunno, chile. I'se shore I'd never ask it of any woman if I was a man, 'less I was sick or ole. But folks don't seem to 'member dat we've got feelin's, and de best way is not to mind dese ere little trubbles. You jes leave de boots to me; blackin' can't do dese ole hands no hurt, and dis ain't no deggydation to me now; I's a free woman."

"Why, Hepsey, were you ever a slave?" asked the girl, forgetting her own small injury at this suggestion of the greatest of all wrongs.

"All my life, till I run away five year ago. My ole folks, and eight brudders and sisters, is down dere in de pit now, waitin' for the Lord to set 'em free. And He's gwine to do it soon, *soon!*" As she uttered the last words, a sudden light chased the tragic shadow from Hepsey's face, and the solemn fervor of her voice thrilled Christie's heart. All her anger died out in a great pity, and she put her hand on the woman's shoulder, saying earnestly:

"I hope so; and I wish I could help to bring that happy day at once!"

For the first time Hepsey smiled, as she said gratefully, "De Lord bress you for dat wish, chile." then, dropping suddenly into her old, quiet way, she added, turning to her work:

"Now you tote up de dinner, and I'll be handy by to 'fresh your mind 'bout how de dishes goes, for missis is bery 'ticular, and don't like no 'stakes in tendin'."

Thanks to her own neat-handed ways and Hepsey's prompting through the slide, Christie got on very well; managed her salver dexterously, only upset one glass, clashed one dish-cover, and forgot to sugar the pie before putting it on the table; an omission which was majestically pointed out, and graciously pardoned as a first offence.

By seven o'clock the ceremonial was fairly over, and Christie dropped into a chair quite tired out with frequent pacings to and fro. In the kitchen she found the table spread for one, and Hepsey busy with the boots.

"Aren't you coming to your dinner, Mrs. Johnson?" she asked, not pleased at the arrangement.

"When you's done, honey; dere's no hurry 'bout me. Katy liked dat way best, and I'se used ter waitin'."

"But *I* don't like that way, and I won't have it. I suppose Katy thought her white skin gave her a right to be disrespectful to a woman old enough to be her mother just because she was black. I don't; and while I'm here, there must be no difference made. If we can work together, we can eat together; and because you have been a slave is all the more reason I should be good to you now."

If Hepsey had been surprised by the new girl's protest against being made a boot-jack of, she was still more surprised at this sudden kindness, for she had set Christie down in her own mind as "one ob dem toppin' smart ones dat don't stay long nowheres." She changed her opinion now, and sat watching the girl with a new expression on her face, as Christie took boot and brush from her, and fell to work energetically, saying as she scrubbed:

"I'm ashamed of complaining about such a little thing as this, and don't mean to feel degraded by it, though I should by letting you do it for me. I never lived out before: that's the reason I made a fuss. There's a polish, for you, and I'm in a good humor again; so Mr. Stuart may call for his boots whenever he likes, and we'll go to dinner like fashionable people, as we are."

There was something so irresistible in the girl's hearty manner, that Hepsey submitted at once with a visible satisfaction, which gave a relish to Christie's dinner, though it was eaten at a kitchen table, with a bare-armed cook sitting opposite, and three rows of burnished dish-covers reflecting the dreadful spectacle.

After this, Christie got on excellently, for she did her best, and found both pleasure and profit in her new employment. It gave her real satisfaction to keep the handsome rooms in order, to polish plate, and spread bountiful meals. There was an atmosphere of ease and comfort about her which contrasted agreeably with the shabbiness of Mrs. Flint's boarding-house, and the bare simplicity of the old home. Like most young people, Christie loved luxury, and was sensible enough to see and value the comforts of her situation, and to wonder why more girls placed as she was did not choose a life like this rather than the confinements of a sewing-room, or the fatigue and publicity of a shop.

She did not learn to love her mistress, because Mrs. Stuart evidently considered herself as one belonging to a superior race of beings, and had no desire to establish any of the friendly relations that may become so helpful and pleasant to both mistress and maid. She made a royal progress through her dominions every morning, issued orders, found fault liberally, bestowed praise sparingly, and took no more personal interest in her servants than if they were clocks, to be wound up once a day, and sent away the moment they got out of repair.

Mr. Stuart was absent from morning till night, and all Christie ever knew about him was that he was a kind-hearted, hot-tempered, and very conceited man; fond of his wife, proud of the society they managed to draw about them, and bent on making his way in the world at any cost.

If masters and mistresses knew how skillfully they are studied, criticised, and imitated by their servants, they would take more heed to their ways, and set better examples, perhaps. Mrs. Stuart never dreamed that her quiet, respectful Jane kept a sharp eye on all her movements, smiled covertly at her affectations, envied her accomplishments, and practised certain little elegancies that struck her fancy.

Mr. Stuart would have become apoplectic with indignation if he had known that this too intelligent table-girl often contrasted her master with his guests, and dared to think him wanting in good breeding when he boasted of his money, flattered a great man, or laid plans to lure some lion into his house. When he lost his temper, she always wanted to laugh, he bounced and bumbled about so like an angry blue-bottle fly; and when he got himself up elaborately for a party, this disrespectful hussy confided to Hepsey her opinion that "master was a fat dandy, with nothing to be vain of but his clothes,"—a sacrilegious remark which would have caused her to be summarily ejected from the house if it had reached the august ears of master or mistress.

"My father was a gentleman; and I shall never forget it, though I do go out to service. I've got no rich friends to help me up, but, sooner or later, I mean to find a place among cultivated people; and while I'm working and waiting, I can be fitting myself to fill that place like a gentlewoman, as I am."

With this ambition in her mind, Christie took notes of all that went on in the polite world, of which she got frequent glimpses while "living out." Mrs. Stuart received one evening of each week, and on these occasions Christie, with an extra frill on her white apron, served the company, and enjoyed herself more than they did, if the truth had been known.

While helping the ladies with their wraps, she observed what they wore, how they carried themselves, and what a vast amount of prinking they did, not to mention the flood of gossip they talked while shaking out their flounces and settling their topknots.

Later in the evening, when she passed cups and glasses, this demure-looking damsel heard much fine discourse, saw many famous beings, and improved her mind with surreptitious studies of the rich and great when on parade. But her best time was after supper, when, through the crack of the door of the little room where she was supposed to be clearing away the relics of the feast, she looked and listened at her ease; laughed at the wits, stared at the lions, heard the music, was impressed by the wisdom, and much edified by the gentility of the whole affair.

After a time, however, Christie got rather tired of it, for there was an elegant sameness about these evenings that became intensely wearisome to the uninitiated, but she fancied that as each had his part to play he managed to do it with spirit. Night after night the wag told his stories, the poet read his poems, the singers warbled, the pretty women simpered and dressed, the heavy scientific was duly discussed by the elect precious, and Mrs. Stuart, in amazing costumes, sailed to and fro in her most swan-like manner; while my lord stirred up the lions he had captured, till they roared their best, great and small.

"Good heavens! why don't they do or say something new and interesting, and not keep twaddling on about art, and music, and poetry, and cosmos? The papers are full of appeals for help for the poor, reforms of all sorts, and splendid work that others are doing; but these people seem to think it isn't genteel enough to be spoken of here. I suppose it is all very elegant to go on like a set of trained canaries, but it's very dull fun to watch them, and Hepsey's stories are a deal more interesting to me."

Having come to this conclusion, after studying dilettanteism through the crack of the door for some months, Christie left the "trained canaries" to twitter and hop about their gilded cage, and devoted herself to Hepsey, who gave her glimpses into another sort of life so bitterly real that she never could forget it.

Friendship had prospered in the lower regions, for Hepsey had a motherly heart, and Christie soon won her confidence by bestowing her own. Her story was like many another; yet, being the first Christie had ever heard, and told with the unconscious eloquence of one who had suffered and escaped, it made a deep impression on her, bringing home to her a sense of obligation so forcibly that she began at once to pay a little part of the great debt which the white race owes the black.

Christie loved books; and the attic next her own was full of them. To this store she found her way by a sort of instinct as sure as that which leads a fly to a honey-pot, and, finding many novels, she read her fill. This amusement lightened many heavy hours, peopled the silent house with troops of friends, and, for a time, was the joy of her life.

Hepsey used to watch her as she sat buried in her book when the day's work was done, and once a heavy sigh roused Christie from the most exciting crisis of "The Abbot."[3]

"What's the matter? Are you very tired, Aunty?" she asked, using the name that came most readily to her lips.

"No, honey; I was only wishin' I could read fast like you does. I's berry slow 'bout readin' and I want to learn a heap," answered Hepsey, with such a wistful look in her soft eyes that Christie shut her book, saying briskly:

"Then I'll teach you. Bring out your primer and let's begin at once."

"Dear chile, it's orful hard work to put learnin' in my ole head, and I wouldn't 'cept such a ting from you only I needs dis sort of help so bad, and I can trust you to gib it to me as I wants it."

Then in a whisper that went straight to Christie's heart, Hepsey told her plan and showed what help she craved.

For five years she had worked hard, and saved her earnings for the purpose of her life. When a considerable sum had been hoarded up, she confided it to one whom she believed to be a friend, and sent him to buy her old mother. But he proved false, and she never saw either mother or money. It was a hard blow, but she took heart and went to work again, resolving this time to trust no one with the dangerous part of the affair, but when she had scraped together enough to pay her way she meant to go South and steal her mother at the risk of her life.

"I don't want much money, but I must know little 'bout readin' and countin' up, else I'll get lost and cheated. You'll help me do dis, honey, and I'll bless you all my days, and so will my old mammy, if I ever gets her safe away."

With tears of sympathy shining on her cheeks, and both hands stretched out to the poor soul who implored this small boon of her, Christie promised all the help that in her lay, and kept her word religiously.

From that time, Hepsey's cause was hers; she laid by a part of her wages for "ole mammy," she comforted Hepsey with happy prophecies of success, and taught with an energy and skill she had never known before.

Novels lost their charms now, for Hepsey could give her a comedy and tragedy surpassing any thing she found in them, because truth stamped her tales with a power and pathos the most gifted fancy could but poorly imitate.

The select receptions upstairs seemed duller than ever to her now, and her happiest evenings were spent in the tidy kitchen, watching Hepsey laboriously shaping A's and B's, or counting up on her worn fingers the wages they had earned by months of weary work, that she might purchase one treasure,—a feeble, old woman, worn out with seventy years of slavery far away there in Virginia.

For a year Christie was a faithful servant to her mistress, who appreciated her virtues, but did not encourage them; a true friend to poor Hepsey, who loved her dearly, and found in her sympathy and affection a solace for many griefs and wrongs. But Providence had other lessons for Christie, and when this one was well learned she was sent away to learn another phase of woman's life and labor.

While their domestics amused themselves with privy conspiracy and rebellion at home, Mr. and Mrs. Stuart spent their evenings in chasing that bright bubble called social success, and usually came home rather cross because they could not catch it.

On one of these occasions they received a warm welcome, for, as they approached the house, smoke was seen issuing from an attic window, and flames flickering behind the half-drawn curtain. Bursting out of the carriage with his usual impetuosity, Mr. Stuart let himself in and tore upstairs shouting "Fire!" like an engine company.

In the attic Christie was discovered lying dressed upon her bed, asleep or suffocated by the smoke that filled the room. A book had slipped from her hand, and in falling had upset the candle on a chair beside her; the long wick leaned against a cotton gown hanging on the wall, and a greater part of Christie's wardrobe was burning brilliantly.

"I forbade her to keep the gas lighted so late, and see what the deceitful creature has done with her private candle!" cried Mrs. Stuart with a shrillness that roused the girl from her heavy sleep more effectually than the anathemas Mr. Stuart was fulminating against the fire.

Sitting up she looked dizzily about her. The smoke was clearing fast, a window having been opened; and the tableau was a striking one. Mr. Stuart with an excited countenance was dancing frantically on a heap of half-consumed clothes pulled from the wall. He had not only drenched them with water from bowl and pitcher, but had also cast those articles upon the pile like extinguishers, and was skipping among the fragments with an agility which contrasted with his stout figure in full evening costume, and his besmirched face, made the sight irresistibly ludicrous.

Mrs. Stuart, though in her most regal array, seemed to have left her dignity downstairs with her opera cloak, for with skirts gathered closely about her, tiara all askew, and face full of fear and anger, she stood upon a chair and scolded like any shrew.

The comic overpowered the tragic, and being a little hysterical with the sudden alarm, Christie broke into a peal of laughter that sealed her fate.

"Look at her! look at her!" cried Mrs. Stuart gesticulating on her perch as if about to fly. "She has been at the wine, or lost her wits. She must go, Horatio, she must go! I cannot have my nerves shattered by such dreadful scenes. She is too fond of books, and it has turned her brain. Hepsey can watch her to-night, and at dawn she shall leave the house for ever."

"Not till after breakfast, my dear. Let us have that in comfort I beg, for upon my soul we shall need it," panted Mr. Stuart, sinking into a chair exhausted with the vigorous measures which had quenched the conflagration.

Christie checked her untimely mirth, explained the probable cause of the mischief, and penitently promised to be more careful for the future.

Mr. Stuart would have pardoned her on the spot, but Madame was inexorable, for she had so completely forgotten her dignity that she felt it would be impossible ever to recover it in the eyes of this disrespectful menial. Therefore she dismissed her with a lecture that made both mistress and maid glad to part.

She did not appear at breakfast, and after that meal Mr. Stuart paid Christie her wages with a solemnity which proved that he had taken a curtain lecture to heart. There was a twinkle in his eye, however, as he kindly added a recommendation, and after the door closed behind him Christie was sure that he exploded into a laugh at the recollection of his last night's performance.

This lightened her sense of disgrace very much, so, leaving a part of her money to repair damages, she packed up her dilapidated wardrobe, and, making Hepsey promise to report progress from time to time, Christie went back to Mrs. Flint's to compose her mind and be ready *à la* Micawber "for something to turn up."[4]

III

ACTRESS

FEELING that she had all the world before her where to choose, and that her next step ought to take her up at least one round higher on the ladder she was climbing, Christie decided not to try going out to service again. She knew very well that she would never live with Irish mates, and could not expect to find another Hepsey. So she tried to get a place as companion to an invalid, but failed to secure the only situation of the sort that was offered her, because she mildly objected to waiting on a nervous cripple all day, and reading aloud half the night. The old lady called her an "impertinent baggage," and Christie retired in great disgust, resolving not to be a slave to anybody.

Things seldom turn out as we plan them, and after much waiting and hoping for other work Christie at last accepted about the only employment which had not entered her mind.

Among the boarders at Mrs. Flint's were an old lady and her pretty daughter, both actresses at a respectable theatre. Not stars by any means, but good second-rate players, doing their work creditably and earning an honest living. The mother had been kind to Christie in offering advice, and sympathizing with her disappointments. The daughter, a gay little lass, had taken Christie to the theatre several times, there to behold her in all the gauzy glories that surround the nymphs of spectacular romance.

To Christie this was a great delight, for, though she had pored over

262

her father's Shakespeare till she knew many scenes by heart, she had never seen a play till Lucy led her into what seemed an enchanted world. Her interest and admiration pleased the little actress, and sundry lifts when she was hurried with her dresses made her grateful to Christie.

The girl's despondent face, as she came in day after day from her unsuccessful quest, told its own story, though she uttered no complaint, and these friendly souls laid their heads together, eager to help her in their own dramatic fashion.

"I've got it! I've got it! All hail to the queen!" was the cry that one day startled Christie as she sat thinking anxiously, while sewing mock-pearls on a crown for Mrs. Black.

Looking up she saw Lucy just home from rehearsal, going through a series of pantomimic evolutions suggestive of a warrior doing battle with incredible valor, and a very limited knowledge of the noble art of self-defence.

"What have you got? Who is the queen?" she asked, laughing, as the breathless hero lowered her umbrella, and laid her bonnet at Christie's feet.

"*You* are to be the Queen of the Amazons in our new spectacle, at half a dollar a night for six or eight weeks, if the piece goes well."

"No!" cried Christie, with a gasp.

"Yes!" cried Lucy, clapping her hands; and then she proceeded to tell her news with theatrical volubility. "Mr. Sharp, the manager, wants a lot of tallish girls, and I told him I knew of a perfect dear. He said: 'Bring her on, then,' and I flew home to tell you. Now, don't look wild, and say no. You've only got to sing in one chorus, march in the grand procession, and lead your band in the terrific battle-scene. The dress is splendid! Red tunic, tiger-skin over shoulder, helmet, shield, lance, fleshings, sandals, hair down, and as much cork to your eyebrows as you like."

Christie certainly did look wild, for Lucy had burst into the room like a small hurricane, and her rapid words rattled about the listeners' ears as if a hail-storm had followed the gust. While Christie still sat with her mouth open, too bewildered to reply, Mrs. Black said in her cosey voice:

"Try it, me dear, it's just what you'll enjoy, and a capital beginning I assure ye; for if you do well old Sharp will want you again, and then, when some one slips out of the company, you can slip in, and there you are quite comfortable. Try it, me dear, and if you don't like it drop it when the piece is over, and there's no harm done."

"It's much easier and jollier than any of the things you are after. We'll stand by you like bricks, and in a week you'll say it's the best lark you ever had in your life. Don't be prim, now, but say yes, like a trump, as you are," added Lucy, waving a pink satin train temptingly before her friend.

"I will try it!" said Christie, with sudden decision, feeling that something entirely new and absorbing was what she needed to expend the vigor, romance, and enthusiasm of her youth upon.

With a shriek of delight Lucy swept her off her chair, and twirled her about the room as excitable young ladies are fond of doing when their joyful emotions need a vent. When both were giddy they subsided into a corner and a breathless discussion of the important step.

Though she had consented, Christie had endless doubts and fears, but Lucy removed many of the former, and her own desire for pleasant employment conquered many of the latter. In her most despairing moods she had never thought of trying this. Uncle Enos considered "play-actin'" as the sum of all iniquity. What would he say if she went calmly to destruction by that road? Sad to relate, this recollection rather strengthened her purpose, for a delicious sense of freedom pervaded her soul, and the old defiant spirit seemed to rise up within her at the memory of her Uncle's grim prophecies and narrow views.

"Lucy is happy, virtuous, and independent, why can't I be so too if I have any talent? It isn't exactly what I should choose, but any thing honest is better than idleness. I'll try it any way, and get a little fun, even if I don't make much money or glory out of it."

So Christie held to her resolution in spite of many secret misgivings, and followed Mrs. Black's advice on all points with a docility which caused that sanguine lady to predict that she would be a star before she knew where she was.

"Is this the stage? How dusty and dull it is by daylight!" said Christie next day, as she stood by Lucy on the very spot where she had seen Hamlet die in great anguish two nights before.

"Bless you, child, it's in curl-papers now, as I am of a morning. Mr. Sharp, here's an Amazon for you."

As she spoke, Lucy hurried across the stage, followed by Christie, wearing any thing but an Amazonian expression just then.

"Ever on before?" abruptly asked a keen-faced, little man, glancing with an experienced eye at the young person who stood before him bathed in blushes.

"No, sir."

"Do you sing?"

"A little, sir."

"Dance, of course?"

"Yes, sir."

"Just take a turn across the stage, will you? Must walk well to lead a march."

As she went, Christie heard Mr. Sharp taking notes audibly:

"Good tread; capital figure; fine eye. She'll make up well, and behave herself, I fancy."

A strong desire to make off seized the girl; but, remembering that she had presented herself for inspection, she controlled the impulse, and returned to him with no demonstration of displeasure, but a little more fire in "the fine eye," and a more erect carriage of the "capital figure."

"All right, my dear. Give your name to Mr. Tripp, and your mind to the business, and consider yourself engaged,"—with which satisfactory remark the little man vanished like a ghost.

"Lucy, did you hear that impertinent 'my dear'?" asked Christie, whose sense of propriety had received its first shock.

"Lord, child, all managers do it. They don't mean any thing; so be resigned, and thank your stars he didn't say 'love' and 'darling,' and kiss you, as old Vining used to," was all the sympathy she got.

Having obeyed orders, Lucy initiated her into the mysteries of the place, and then put her in a corner to look over the scenes in which she was to appear. Christie soon caught the idea of her part,—not a difficult matter, as there were but few ideas in the whole piece, after which she sat watching the arrival of the troop she was to lead. A most forlorn band of warriors they seemed, huddled together, and looking as if afraid to speak, lest they should infringe some rule; or to move, lest they be swallowed up by some unsuspected trapdoor.

Presently the ballet-master appeared, the orchestra struck up, and

Christie found herself marching and counter-marching at word of command. At first, a most uncomfortable sense of the absurdity of her position oppressed and confused her; then the ludicrous contrast between the solemn anxiety of the troop and the fantastic evolutions they were performing amused her till the novelty wore off; the martial music excited her; the desire to please sharpened her wits; and natural grace made it easy for her to catch and copy the steps and poses given her to imitate. Soon she forgot herself, entered into the spirit of the thing, and exerted every sense to please, so successfully that Mr. Tripp praised her quickness at comprehension, Lucy applauded heartily from a fairy car, and Mr. Sharp popped his head out of a palace window to watch the Amazon's descent from the Mountains of the Moon.

When the regular company arrived, the troop was dismissed till the progress of the play demanded their reappearance. Much interested in the piece, Christie stood aside under a palm-tree, the foliage of which was strongly suggestive of a dilapidated green umbrella, enjoying the novel sights and sounds about her.

Yellow-faced gentlemen and sleepy-eyed ladies roamed languidly about with much incoherent jabbering of parts, and frequent explosions of laughter. Princes, with varnished boots and suppressed cigars, fought, bled, and died, without a change of countenance. Damsels of unparalleled beauty, according to the text, gaped in the faces of adoring lovers, and crocheted serenely on the brink of annihilation. Fairies, in rubber-boots and woollen head-gear, disported themselves on flowery barks of canvas, or were suspended aloft with hooks in their backs like young Hindoo devotees. Demons, guiltless of hoof or horn, clutched their victims with the inevitable "Ha! ha!" and vanished darkly, eating pea-nuts. The ubiquitous Mr. Sharp seemed to pervade the whole theatre; for his voice came shrilly from above or spectrally from below, and his active little figure darted to and fro like a critical will-o-the-wisp.

The grand march and chorus in the closing scene were easily accomplished; for, as Lucy bade her, Christie "sung with all her might," and kept step as she led her band with the dignity of a Boadicea.[5] No one spoke to her; few observed her; all were intent on their own affairs; and when the final shriek and bang died away without lifting the roof by its din, she could hardly believe that the dreaded first rehearsal was safely over.

A visit to the wardrobe-room to see her dress came next; and here Christie had a slight skirmish with the mistress of that department relative to the length of her classical garments. As studies from the nude had not yet become one of the amusements of the *élite* of Little Babel, Christie was not required to appear in the severe simplicity of a costume consisting of a necklace, sandals, and a bit of gold fringe about the waist, but was allowed an extra inch or two on her tunic, and departed, much comforted by the assurance that her dress would not be "a shock to modesty," as Lucy expressed it.

"Now, look at yourself, and, for my sake, prove an honor to your country and a terror to the foe," said Lucy, as she led her *protégée* before the green-room mirror on the first night of "The Demon's Daughter, or The Castle of the Sun!! The most Magnificent Spectacle ever produced upon the American Stage!!!"

Christie looked, and saw a warlike figure with glittering helmet, shield and lance, streaming hair and savage cloak. She liked the picture, for there was much of the heroic spirit in the girl, and even this poor counterfeit pleased her eye and filled her fancy with martial memories of Joan of Arc, Zenobia, and Britomarte.[6]

"Go to!" cried Lucy, who affected theatrical modes of speech. "Don't admire yourself any longer, but tie up your sandals and come on. Be sure you rush down the instant I cry, 'Demon, I defy thee!' Don't break your neck, or pick your way like a cat in wet weather, but come *with effect,* for I want that scene to make a hit."

Princess Caremfil swept away, and the Amazonian queen climbed to her perch among the painted mountains where her troop already sat like a flock of pigeons shining in the sun. The gilded breast-plate rose and fell with the quick beating of her heart, the spear shook with the trembling of her hand, her lips were dry, her head dizzy, and more than once, as she waited for her cue, she was sorely tempted to run away and take the consequences.

But the thought of Lucy's good-will and confidence kept her, and when the cry came she answered with a ringing shout, rushed down the ten-foot precipice, and charged upon the foe with an energy that inspired her followers, and quite satisfied the princess struggling in the demon's grasp.

With clashing of arms and shrill war-cries the rescuers of innocence assailed the sooty fiends who fell before their unscientific blows with a rapidity which inspired in the minds of beholders a suspicion that the goblins' own voluminous tails tripped them up and gallantry kept them prostrate. As the last groan expired, the last agonized squirm subsided, the conquerors performed the intricate dance with which it appears the Amazons were wont to celebrate their victories. Then the scene closed with a glare of red light and a "grand tableau" of the martial queen standing in a bower of lances, the rescued princess gracefully fainting in her arms, and the vanquished demon scowling fiercely under her foot, while four-and-twenty dishevelled damsels sang a song of exultation, to the barbaric music of a tattoo on their shields.

All went well that night, and when at last the girls doffed crown and helmet, they confided to one another the firm opinion that the success of the piece was in a great measure owing to their talent, their exertions, and went gaily home predicting for themselves careers as brilliant as those of Siddons and Rachel.[7]

It would be a pleasant task to paint the vicissitudes and victories of a successful actress; but Christie was no dramatic genius born to shine before the world and leave a name behind her. She had no talent except that which may be developed in any girl possessing the lively fancy, sympathetic nature, and ambitious spirit which make such girls naturally dramatic. This was to be only one of many experiences which were to show her her own weakness and strength, and through effort, pain, and disappointment fit her to play a nobler part on a wider stage.

For a few weeks Christie's illusions lasted; then she discovered that the new life was nearly as humdrum as the old, that her companions were ordinary men and women, and her bright hopes were growing as dim as her tarnished shield. She grew unutterably weary of "The Castle of the Sun," and found the "Demon's Daughter" an unmitigated bore. She was not tired of the profession, only dissatisfied with the place she held in it, and eager to attempt a part that gave some scope for power and passion.

Mrs. Black wisely reminded her that she must learn to use her wings before she tried to fly, and comforted her with stories of celebrities who had begun as she was beginning, yet who had suddenly burst from their grub-like obscurity to adorn the world as splendid butterflies.

"We'll stand by you, Kit; so keep up your courage, and do your best. Be clever to every one in general, old Sharp in particular, and when a chance comes, have your wits about you and grab it. That's the way to get on," said Lucy, as sagely as if she had been a star for years.

"If I had beauty I should stand a better chance," sighed Christie, surveying herself with great disfavor, quite unconscious that to a cultivated eye the soul of beauty was often visible in that face of hers, with its intelligent eyes, sensitive mouth, and fine lines about the forehead, making it a far more significant and attractive countenance than that of her friend, possessing only piquant prettiness.

"Never mind, child; you've got a lovely figure, and an actress's best feature,—fine eyes and eyebrows. I heard old Kent say so, and he's a judge. So make the best of what you've got, as I do," answered Lucy, glancing at her own comely little person with an air of perfect resignation.

Christie laughed at the adviser, but wisely took the advice, and, though she fretted in private, was cheerful and alert in public. Always modest, attentive, and obliging, she soon became a favorite with her mates, and, thanks to Lucy's good offices with Mr. Sharp, whose favorite she was, Christie got promoted sooner than she otherwise would have been.

A great Christmas spectacle was brought out the next season, and Christie had a good part in it. When that was over she thought there was no hope for her, as the regular company was full and a different sort of performance was to begin. But just then her chance came, and she "grabbed it." The first soubrette died suddenly, and in the emergency Mr. Sharp offered the place to Christie till he could fill it to his mind. Lucy was second soubrette, and had hoped for this promotion; but Lucy did not sing well. Christie had a good voice, had taken lessons and much improved of late, so she had the preference and resolved to stand the test so well that this temporary elevation should become permanent.

She did her best, and though many of the parts were distasteful to her she got through them successfully, while now and then she had one which she thoroughly enjoyed. Her Tilly Slowboy[8] was a hit, and a proud girl was Christie when Kent, the comedian, congratulated her on it, and told her he had seldom seen it better done.

To find favor in Kent's eyes was an honor indeed, for he belonged to the old school, and rarely condescended to praise modern actors. His own style was so admirable that he was justly considered the first comedian in the country, and was the pride and mainstay of the old theatre where he had played for years. Of course he possessed much influence in that little world, and being a kindly man used it generously to help up any young aspirant who seemed to him deserving.

He had observed Christie, attracted by her intelligent face and modest manners, for in spite of her youth there was a native refinement about her that made it impossible for her to romp and flirt as some of her mates did. But till she played Tilly he had not thought she possessed any talent. That pleased him, and seeing how much she valued his praise, and was flattered by his notice, he gave her the wise but unpalatable advice always offered young actors. Finding that she accepted it, was willing to study hard, work faithfully, and wait patiently, he predicted that in time she would make a clever actress, never a great one.

Of course Christie thought he was mistaken, and secretly resolved to prove him a false prophet by the triumphs of her career. But she meekly bowed to his opinion; this docility pleased him, and he took a paternal sort of interest in her, which, coming from the powerful favorite, did her good service with the higher powers, and helped her on more rapidly than years of meritorious effort.

Toward the end of that second season several of Dickens's dramatized novels were played, and Christie earned fresh laurels. She loved those books, and seemed by instinct to understand and personate the humor and pathos of many of those grotesque creations. Believing she had little beauty to sacrifice, she dressed such parts to the life, and played them with a spirit and ease that surprised those who had considered her a dignified and rather dull young person.

"I'll tell you what it is, Sharp, that girl is going to make a capital character actress. When her parts suit, she forgets herself entirely and does admirably well. Her Miggs was nearly the death of me to-night.⁹ She's got that one gift, and it's a good one. You'd better give her a chance, for I think she'll be a credit to the old concern."

Kent said that,—Christie heard it, and flew to Lucy, waving Miggs's cap for joy as she told the news.

"What did Mr. Sharp say," asked Lucy, turning round with her face half "made up."

"He merely said 'Hum,' and smiled. Wasn't that a good sign?" said Christie, anxiously.

"Can't say," and Lucy touched up her eyebrows as if she took no interest in the affair.

Christie's face fell, and her heart sunk at the thought of failure; but she kept up her spirits by working harder than ever, and soon had her reward. Mr. Sharp's "Hum" did mean yes, and the next season she was regularly engaged, with a salary of thirty dollars a week.

It was a grand step, and knowing that she owed it to Kent, Christie did her utmost to show that she deserved his good opinion. New trials and temptations beset her now, but hard work and an innocent nature kept her safe and busy. Obstacles only spurred her on to redoubled exertion, and whether she did well or ill, was praised or blamed, she found a never-failing excitement in her attempts to reach the standard of perfection she had set up for herself. Kent did not regret his patronage. Mr. Sharp was satisfied with the success of the experiment, and Christie soon became a favorite in a small way, because behind the actress the public always saw a woman who never "forgot the modesty of nature."

But as she grew prosperous in outward things, Christie found herself burdened with a private cross that tried her very much. Lucy was no longer her friend; something had come between them, and a steadily increasing coldness took the place of the confidence and affection which had once existed. Lucy was jealous for Christie had passed her in the race. She knew she could not fill the place Christie had gained by favor, and now held by her own exertions, still she was bitterly envious, though ashamed to own it.

Christie tried to be just and gentle, to prove her gratitude to her first friend, and to show that her heart was unchanged. But she failed to win Lucy back and felt herself injured by such unjust resentment. Mrs. Black took her daughter's part, and though they preserved the peace outwardly the old friendliness was quite gone.

Hoping to forget this trouble in excitement Christie gave herself entirely to her profession, finding in it a satisfaction which for a time consoled her.

But gradually she underwent the sorrowful change which comes to strong natures when they wrong themselves through ignorance or wilfulness.

Pride and native integrity kept her from the worst temptations of such a life, but to the lesser ones she yielded, growing selfish, frivolous, and vain,—intent on her own advancement, and careless by what means she reached it. She had no thought now beyond her art, no desire beyond the commendation of those whose opinion was serviceable, no care for any one but herself.

Her love of admiration grew by what it fed on, till the sound of applause became the sweetest music to her ear. She rose with this hope, lay down with this satisfaction, and month after month passed in this feverish life, with no wish to change it, but a growing appetite for its unsatisfactory delights, an ever-increasing forgetfulness of any higher aspiration than dramatic fame.

"Give me joy, Lucy, I'm to have a benefit next week! Everybody else has had one, and I've played for them all, so no one seemed to begrudge me my turn when dear old Kent proposed it," said Christie, coming in one night still flushed and excited with the good news.

"What shall you have?" asked Lucy, trying to look pleased, and failing decidedly.

"'Masks and Faces.'¹⁰ I've always wanted to play Peg and it has good parts for you and Kent, and St. George. I chose it for that reason, for I shall need all the help I can get to pull me through, I dare say."

The smile vanished entirely at this speech, and Christie was suddenly seized with a suspicion that Lucy was not only jealous of her as an actress, but as a woman. St. George was a comely young actor who usually played lovers' parts with Christie, and played them very well, too, being possessed of much talent, and a gentleman. They had never thought of falling in love with each other, though St. George wooed and won Christie night after night in vaudeville and farce. But it was very easy to imagine that so much mock passion had a basis of truth, and Lucy evidently tormented herself with this belief.

"Why didn't you choose Juliet: St. George would do Romeo so well?" said Lucy, with a sneer.

"No, that is beyond me. Kent says Shakespeare will never be my line, and I believe him. I should think you'd be satisfied with 'Masks and Faces,' for you know Mabel gets her husband safely back in the end," answered Christie, watching the effect of her words.

"As if I wanted the man! No, thank you, other people's leavings won't suit me," cried Lucy, tossing her head, though her face belied her words.

"Not even though he has 'heavenly eyes,' 'distracting legs,' and 'a melting voice?'" asked Christie maliciously, quoting Lucy's own rapturous speeches when the new actor came.

"Come, come, girls, don't quarrel. I won't 'ave it in me room. Lucy's tired to death, and it's not nice of you, Kitty, to come and crow over her this way," said Mamma Black, coming to the rescue, for Lucy was in tears, and Christie looking dangerous.

"It's impossible to please you, so I'll say good-night," and Christie went to her room with resentment burning hotly in her heart.

As she crossed the chamber her eye fell on her own figure reflected in the long glass, and with a sudden impulse she turned up the gas, wiped the rouge from her cheeks, pushed back her hair, and studied her own face intently for several moments. It was pale and jaded now, and all its freshness seemed gone; hard lines had come about the mouth, a feverish disquiet filled the eyes, and on the forehead seemed to lie the shadow of a discontent that saddened the whole face. If one could believe the testimony of that countenance things were not going well with Christie, and she owned it with a regretful sigh, as she asked herself, "Am I what I hoped I should be? No, and it is my fault. If three years of this life have made me this, what shall I be in ten? A fine actress perhaps, but how good a woman?"

With gloomy eyes fixed on her altered face she stood a moment struggling with herself. Then the hard look returned, and she spoke out defiantly, as if in answer to some warning voice within herself. "No one cares what I am, so why care myself? Why not go on and get as much fame as I can? Success gives me power if it cannot give me happiness, and I must have some reward for my hard work. Yes! a gay life and a short one, then out with the lights and down with the curtain!"

But in spite of her reckless words Christie sobbed herself to sleep that night like a child who knows it is astray, yet cannot see the right path or hear its mother's voice calling it home.

On the night of the benefit, Lucy was in a most exasperating mood,

Christie in a very indignant one, and as they entered their dressing-room they looked as if they might have played the Rival Queens with great effect.[11] Lucy offered no help and Christie asked none, but putting her vexation resolutely out of sight fixed her mind on the task before her. As the pleasant stir began all about her, actress-like, she felt her spirits rise, her courage increase with every curl she fastened up, every gay garment she put on, and soon smiled approvingly at herself, for excitement lent her cheeks a better color than rouge, her eyes shone with satisfaction, and her heart beat high with the resolve to make a hit or die.

Christie needed encouragement that night, and found it in the hearty welcome that greeted her, and the full house, which proved how kind a regard was entertained for her by many who knew her only by a fictitious name. She felt this deeply, and it helped her much, for she was vexed with many trials those before the footlights knew nothing of.

The other players were full of kindly interest in her success, but Lucy took a naughty satisfaction in harassing her by all the small slights and unanswerable provocations which one actress has it in her power to inflict upon another.

Christie was fretted almost beyond endurance, and retaliated by an ominous frown when her position allowed, threatening asides when a moment's by-play favored their delivery, and angry protests whenever she met Lucy off the stage.

But in spite of all annoyances she had never played better in her life. She liked the part, and acted the warm-hearted, quick-witted, sharp-tongued Peg with a spirit and grace that surprised even those who knew her best. Especially good was she in the scenes with Triplet, for Kent played the part admirably, and cheered her on with many an encouraging look and word. Anxious to do honor to her patron and friend she threw her whole heart into the work; in the scene where she comes like a good angel to the home of the poor play-wright, she brought tears to the eyes of her audience; and when at her command Triplet strikes up a jig to amuse the children she "covered the buckle" in gallant style, dancing with all the frolicsome *abandon* of the Irish orange-girl who for a moment forgot her grandeur and her grief.

That scene was her best, for it is full of those touches of nature that need very little art to make them effective; and when a great bouquet fell with a thump at Christie's feet, as she paused to bow her thanks for an encore, she felt that she had reached the height of earthly bliss.

In the studio scene Lucy seemed suddenly gifted with unsuspected skill; for when Mabel kneels to the picture, praying her rival to give her back her husband's heart, Christie was amazed to see real tears roll down Lucy's cheeks, and to hear real love and longing thrill her trembling words with sudden power and passion.

"That is not acting. She does love St. George, and thinks I mean to keep him from her. Poor dear! I'll tell her all about it to-night, and set her heart at rest," thought Christie; and when Peg left the frame, her face expressed the genuine pity that she felt, and her voice was beautifully tender as the promised to restore the stolen treasure.

Lucy felt comforted without knowing why, and the piece went smoothly on to its last scene. Peg was just relinquishing the repentant husband to his forgiving wife with those brave words of hers, when a rending sound above their heads made all look up and start back; all but Lucy, who stood bewildered. Christie's quick eye saw the impending danger, and with a sudden spring she caught her friend from it. It was only a second's work, but it cost her much; for in the act, down crashed one of the mechanical contrivances used in a late spectacle, and in its fall stretched Christie stunned and senseless on the stage.

A swift uprising filled the house with tumult; a crowd of actors hurried forward, and the panic-stricken audience caught glimpses of poor Peg lying mute and pallid in Mabel's arms, while Vane wrung his hands, and Triplet audibly demanded, "Why the devil somebody didn't go for a doctor?"

Then a brilliant view of Mount Parnassus, with Apollo and the Nine Muses in full blast, shut the scene from sight, and soon Mr. Sharp appeared to ask their patience till the after-piece was ready, for Miss Douglas was too much injured to appear again. And with an unwonted expression of feeling, the little man alluded to "the generous act which perhaps had changed the comedy to a tragedy and robbed the beneficiary of her well-earned reward at their hands."

All had seen the impulsive spring toward, not from, the danger, and this unpremeditated action won heartier applause than Christie ever had received for her best rendering of more heroic deeds.

But she did not hear the cordial round they gave her. She had said she would "make a hit or die;" and just then it seemed as if she had done both, for she was deaf and blind to the admiration and the sympathy bestowed upon her as the curtain fell on the first, last benefit she ever was to have.

IV

GOVERNESS

꠹꠹꠹꠹꠹꠹

DURING the next few weeks Christie learned the worth of many things which she had valued very lightly until then. Health became a boon too precious to be trifled with; life assumed a deeper significance when death's shadow fell upon its light, and she discovered that dependence might be made endurable by the sympathy of unsuspected friends.

Lucy waited upon her with a remorseful devotion which touched her very much, and won entire forgiveness for the past, long before it was repentantly implored. All her comrades came with offers of help and affectionate regrets. Several whom she had most disliked now earned her gratitude by the kindly thoughtfulness which filled her sick-room with fruit and flowers, supplied carriages for the convalescent, and paid her doctor's bill without her knowledge.

Thus Christie learned, like many another needy member of the gay profession, that though often extravagant and jovial in their way of life, these men and women give as freely as they spend, wear warm, true hearts under their motley, and make misfortune only another link in the bond of good-fellowship which binds them loyally together.

Slowly Christie gathered her energies after weeks of suffering, and took up her life again, grateful for the gift, and anxious to be more worthy of it. Looking back upon the past she felt that she had made a mistake and lost more than she had gained in those three years. Others might lead that life of alternate excitement and hard work unharmed, but she could not.

The very ardor and insight which gave power to the actress made that mimic life unsatisfactory to the woman, for hers was an earnest nature that took fast hold of whatever task she gave herself to do, and lived in it heartily while duty made it right, or novelty lent it charms. But when she saw the error of a step, the emptiness of a belief, with a like earnestness she tried to retrieve the one and to replace the other with a better substitute.

In the silence of wakeful nights and the solitude of quiet days, she took counsel with her better self, condemned the reckless spirit which had possessed her, and came at last to the decision which conscience prompted and much thought confirmed.

"The stage is not the place for me," she said. "I have no genius to glorify the drudgery, keep me from temptation, and repay me for any sacrifice I make. Other women can lead this life safely and happily: I cannot, and I must not go back to it, because, with all my past experience, and in spite of all my present good resolutions, I should do no better, and I might do worse. I'm not wise enough to keep steady there; I must return to the old ways, dull but safe, and plod along till I find my real place and work."

Great was the surprise of Lucy and her mother when Christie told her resolution, adding, in a whisper, to the girl, "I leave the field clear for you, dear, and will dance at your wedding with all my heart when St. George asks you to play the 'Honeymoon' with him, as I'm sure he will before long."

Many entreaties from friends, as well as secret longings, tried and tempted Christie sorely, but she withstood them all, carried her point, and renounced the profession she could not follow without self-injury and self-reproach. The season was nearly over when she was well enough to take her place again, but she refused to return, relinquished her salary, sold her wardrobe, and never crossed the threshold of the theatre after she had said good-bye.

Then she asked, "What next?" and was speedily answered. An advertisement for a governess met her eye, which seemed to combine the two things she most needed just then,—employment and change of air.

"Mind you don't mention that you've been an actress or it will be all up with you, me dear," said Mrs. Black, as Christie prepared to investigate the matter, for since her last effort in that line she had increased her knowledge of music, and learned French enough to venture teaching it to very young pupils.

"I'd rather tell in the beginning, for if you keep any thing back it's sure to pop out when you least expect or want it. I don't believe these people will care so long as I'm respectable and teach well," returned Christie, wishing she looked stronger and rosier.

"You'll be sorry if you do tell," warned Mrs. Black, who knew the ways of the world.

"I shall be sorry if I don't," laughed Christie, and so she was, in the end.

"L. N. Saltonstall" was the name on the door, and L. N. Saltonstall's servant was so leisurely about answering Christie's meek solo on the bell, that she had time to pull out her bonnet-strings half-a-dozen times before a very black man in a very white jacket condescended to conduct her to his mistress.

A frail, tea-colored lady appeared, displaying such a small proportion of woman to such a large proportion of purple and fine linen, that she looked as if she was literally as well as figuratively "dressed to death."

Christie went to the point in a business-like manner that seemed to suit Mrs. Saltonstall, because it saved so much trouble, and she replied, with a languid affability:

"I wish some one to teach the children a little, for they are getting too old to be left entirely to nurse. I am anxious to get to the sea-shore as soon as possible, for they have been poorly all winter, and my own health has suffered. Do you feel inclined to try the place? And what compensation do you require?"

Christie had but a vague idea of what wages were usually paid to nursery governesses, and hesitatingly named a sum which seemed reasonable to her, but was so much less than any other applicant had asked, that Mrs. Saltonstall began to think she could not do better than secure this cheap young person, who looked firm enough to manage her rebellious son and heir, and well-bred enough to begin the education of a fine little lady. Her winter had been an extravagant one, and she could economize in the governess better perhaps than elsewhere; so she decided to try Christie, and get out of town at once.

"Your terms are quite satisfactory, Miss Devon, and if my brother approves, I think we will consider the matter settled. Perhaps you would like to see the children? They are little darlings, and you will soon be fond of them, I am sure."

A bell was rung, an order given, and presently appeared an eight-year-old boy, so excessively Scotch in his costume that he looked like an animated checkerboard; and a little girl, who presented the appearance of a miniature opera-dancer staggering under the weight of an immense sash.

"Go and speak prettily to Miss Devon, my pets, for she is coming to play with you, and you must mind what she says," commanded mamma.

The pale, fretful-looking little pair went solemnly to Christie's knee, and stood there staring at her with a dull composure that quite daunted her, it was so sadly unchildlike.

"What is your name, dear?" she asked, laying her hand on the young lady's head.

"Villamena Temmatina Taltentall. You mustn't touch my hair; it's just turled," was the somewhat embarrassing reply.

"Mine's Louy 'Poleon Thaltensthall, like papa's," volunteered the other young person, and Christie privately wondered if the possession of names nearly as long as themselves was not a burden to the poor dears.

Feeling that she must say something, she asked, in her most persuasive tone:

"Would you like to have me come and teach you some nice lessons out of your little books?"

If she had proposed corporal punishment on the spot it could not have caused greater dismay. Wilhelmina cast herself upon the floor passionately, declaring that she "touldn't tuddy," and Saltonstall, Jr., retreated precipitately to the door, and from that refuge defied the whole race of governesses and "nasty lessons" jointly.

"There, run away to Justine. They are sadly out of sorts, and quite pining for sea-air," said mamma, with both hands at her ears, for the war-cries of her darlings were piercing as they departed, proclaiming their wrongs while swarming up stairs, with a skirmish on each landing.

With a few more words Christie took leave and scandalized the sable retainer by smiling all through the hall, and laughing audibly as the door closed. The contrast of the plaid boy and beruffled girl's irritability with their mother's languid affectation, and her own unfortunate efforts, was too much for her. In the middle of her merriment she paused suddenly, saying to herself:

"I never told about my acting. I must go back and have it settled." She retraced a few steps, then turned and went on again, thinking, "No; for once I'll be guided by other people's advice, and let well alone."

A note arrived soon after, bidding Miss Devon consider herself engaged, and desiring her to join the family at the boat on Monday next.

At the appointed time Christie was on board, and looked about for her party. Mrs. Saltonstall appeared in the distance with her family about her, and Christie took a survey before reporting herself. Madame looked more like a fashion-plate than ever, in a mass of green flounces, and an impressive bonnet flushed with poppies and bristling with wheat-ears. Beside her sat a gentleman, rapt in a newspaper, of course, for to an American man life is a burden till the daily news have been absorbed. Mrs. Saltonstall's brother was the possessor of a handsome eye without softness, thin lips without benevolence, but plenty of will; a face and figure which some thirty-five years of ease and pleasure had done their best to polish and spoil, and a costume without flaw, from his aristocratic boots to the summer hat on his head.

The little boy more checkered and the little girl more operatic than before, sat on stools eating *bonbons,* while a French maid and the African footman hovered in the background.

Feeling very much like a meek gray moth among a flock of butterflies, Christie modestly presented herself.

"Good morning," said Madame with a nod, which, slight as it was, caused a great commotion among the poppies and the wheat; "I began to be anxious about you. Miss Devon, my brother, Mr. Fletcher."

The gentleman bowed, and as Christie sat down he got up, saying, as he sauntered away with a bored expression:

"Will you have the paper, Charlotte? There's nothing in it."

As Mrs. Saltonstall seemed going to sleep and she felt delicate about addressing the irritable infants in public, Christie amused herself by watching Mr. Fletcher as he roamed listlessly about, and deciding, in her usual rash way, that she did not like him because he looked both lazy and cross, and *ennui* was evidently his bosom friend. Soon, however, she forgot every thing but the shimmer of the sunshine on the sea, the fresh wind that brought color to her pale cheeks, and the happy thoughts that left a smile upon her lips. Then Mr. Fletcher put up his glass and stared at her, shook his head, and said, as he lit a cigar:

"Poor little wretch, what a time she will have of it between Charlotte and the brats!"

But Christie needed no pity, and thought herself a fortunate young woman when fairly established in her corner of the luxurious apartments occupied by the family. Her duties seemed light compared to those she had left, her dreams were almost as bright as of old, and the new life looked pleasant to her, for she was one of those who could find little bits of happiness for herself and enjoy them heartily in spite of loneliness or neglect.

One of her amusements was studying her companions, and for a time this occupied her, for Christie possessed penetration and a feminine fancy for finding out people.

Mrs. Saltonstall's mission appeared to be the illustration of each new fashion as it came, and she performed it with a devotion worthy of a better cause. If a color reigned supreme she flushed herself with scarlet or faded into primrose, made herself pretty in the bluest of blue gowns, or turned livid under a gooseberry colored bonnet. Her hat-brims went up or down, were preposterously wide or dwindled to an inch, as the mode demanded. Her skirts were rampant with sixteen frills, or picturesque with landscapes down each side, and a Greek border or a plain hem. Her waists were as pointed as those of Queen Bess or as short as Diana's; and it was the opinion of those who knew her that if the autocrat who ruled her life decreed the wearing of black cats as well as of vegetables, bugs, and birds, the blackest, glossiest Puss procurable for money would have adorned her head in some way.

Her time was spent in dressing, driving, dining and dancing; in skimming novels, and embroidering muslin; going to church with a velvet prayer-book and a new bonnet; and writing to her husband when she wanted money, for she had a husband somewhere abroad, who so happily combined business with pleasure that he never found time to come home. Her children were inconvenient blessings, but she loved them with the love of a shallow heart, and took such good care of their little bodies that there was none left for their little souls. A few days' trial satisfied her as to Christie's capabilities, and, relieved of that anxiety, she gave herself up to her social duties, leaving the ocean and the governess to make the summer wholesome and agreeable to "the darlings."

Mr. Fletcher, having tried all sorts of pleasure and found that, like his newspaper, there was "nothing in it," was now paying the penalty for that unsatisfactory knowledge. Ill health soured his temper and made his life a burden to him. Having few resources within himself to fall back upon, he was very dependent upon other people, and other people were so busy amusing themselves, they seemed to find little time or inclination to amuse a man who had never troubled himself about them. He was rich, but while his money could hire a servant to supply each want, gratify each caprice, it could not buy a tender, faithful friend to serve for love, and ask no wages but his comfort.

He knew this, and felt the vain regret that inevitably comes to those who waste life and learn the value of good gifts by their loss. But he was not wise or brave enough to bear his punishment manfully, and lay the lesson honestly to heart. Fretful and imperious when in pain, listless and selfish when at ease, his one aim in life now was to kill time, and any thing that aided him in this was most gratefully welcomed.

For a long while he took no more notice of Christie than if she had been a shadow, seldom speaking beyond the necessary salutations, and merely carrying his finger to his hat-brim when he passed her on the beach with the children. Her first dislike was softened by pity when she found he was an invalid, but she troubled herself very little about him, and made no romances with him, for all her dreams were of younger, nobler lovers.

Busied with her own affairs, the days though monotonous were not unhappy. She prospered in her work and the children soon believed in her as devoutly as young Turks in their Prophet. She devised amusements for herself as well as for them; walked, bathed, drove, and romped with the little people till her own eyes shone like theirs, her cheek grew rosy, and her thin figure rounded with the promise of vigorous health again.

Christie was at her best that summer, physically speaking, for sickness had refined her face, giving it that indescribable expression which pain often leaves upon a countenance as if in compensation for the bloom it takes away. The frank eyes had a softer shadow in their depths, the firm lips smiled less often, but when it came the smile was the sweeter for the gravity that went before, and in her voice there was a new undertone of that subtle music, called sympathy, which steals into the heart and nestles there.

She was unconscious of this gracious change, but others saw and felt it, and to some a face bright with health, intelligence, and modesty was more attractive than mere beauty. Thanks to this and her quiet, cordial manners, she found friends here and there to add charms to that summer by the sea.

The dashing young men took no more notice of her than if she had been a little gray peep on the sands; not so much, for they shot peeps now and then, but a governess was not worth bringing down. The fashionable belles and beauties were not even aware of her existence, being too entirely absorbed in their yearly husband-hunt to think of any one but themselves and their prey. The dowagers had more interesting topics to discuss, and found nothing in Christie's humble fortunes worthy of a thought, for they liked their gossip strong and highly flavored, like their tea.

But a kind-hearted girl or two found her out, several lively old maids, as full of the romance of the past as ancient novels, a bashful boy, three or four invalids, and *all* the children, for Christie had a motherly heart and could find charms in the plainest, crossest baby that ever squalled.

Of her old friends she saw nothing, as her theatrical ones were off on their vacations, Hepsey had left her place for one in another city, and Aunt Betsey seldom wrote.

But one day a letter came, telling her that the dear old lady would never write again, and Christie felt as if her nearest and dearest friend was lost. She had gone away to a quiet spot among the rocks to get over her first grief alone, but found it very hard to check her tears, as memory brought back the past, tenderly recalling every kind act, every loving word, and familiar scene. She seldom wept, but when any thing did unseal the fountains that lay so deep, she cried with all her heart, and felt the better for it.

With the letter crumpled in her hand, her head on her knees, and her hat at her feet, she was sobbing like a child, when steps startled her, and, looking up, she saw Mr. Fletcher regarding her with an astonished countenance from under his big sun umbrella.

Something in the flushed, wet face, with its tremulous lips and great tears rolling down, seemed to touch even lazy Mr. Fletcher, for he furled his umbrella with unusual rapidity, and came up, saying, anxiously:

"My dear Miss Devon, what's the matter? Are you hurt? Has Mrs. S. been scolding? Or have the children been too much for you?"

"No; oh, no! it's bad news from home," and Christie's head went down again, for a kind word was more than she could bear just then.

"Some one ill, I fancy? I'm sorry to hear it, but you must hope for the best, you know," replied Mr. Fletcher, really quite exerting himself to remember and present this well-worn consolation.

"There is no hope; Aunt Betsey's dead!"

"Dear me! that's very sad."

Mr. Fletcher tried not to smile as Christie sobbed out the old-fashioned name, but a minute afterward there were actually tears in his eyes, for, as if won by his sympathy, she poured out the homely little story of Aunt Betsey's life and love, unconsciously pronouncing the kind old lady's best epitaph in the unaffected grief that made her broken words so eloquent.

For a minute Mr. Fletcher forgot himself, and felt as he remembered feeling long ago, when, a warm-hearted boy, he had comforted his little sister for a lost kitten or a broken doll. It was a new sensation, therefore interesting and agreeable while it lasted, and when it vanished, which it speedily did, he sighed, then shrugged his shoulders and wished "the girl would stop crying like a water-spout."

"It's hard, but we all have to bear it, you know; and sometimes I fancy if half the pity we give the dead, who don't need it, was given to the living, who do, they'd bear their troubles more comfortably. I know *I* should," added Mr. Fletcher, returning to his own afflictions, and vaguely wondering if any one would cry like that when he departed this life.

Christie minded little what he said, for his voice was pitiful and it comforted her. She dried her tears, put back her hair, and thanked him with a grateful smile, which gave him another pleasant sensation; for, though young ladies showered smiles upon him with midsummer radiance, they seemed cool and pale beside the sweet sincerity of this one given by a girl whose eyes were red with tender tears.

"That's right, cheer up, take a little run on the beach, and forget all about it," he said, with a heartiness that surprised himself as much as it did Christie.

"I will, thank you. Please don't speak of this; I'm used to bearing my troubles alone, and time will help me to do it cheerfully."

"That's brave! If I can do any thing, let me know; I shall be most happy." And Mr. Fletcher evidently meant what he said.

Christie gave him another grateful "Thank you," then picked up her hat and went away along the sands to try his prescription; while Mr. Fletcher walked the other way, so rapt in thought that he forgot to put up his umbrella till the end of his aristocratic nose was burnt a deep red.

That was the beginning of it; for when Mr. Fletcher found a new amusement, he usually pursued it regardless of consequences. Christie took his pity for what it was worth, and thought no more of that little interview, for her heart was very heavy. But he remembered it, and, when they met on the beach next day, wondered how the governess would behave. She was reading as she walked, and, with a mute acknowledgment of his nod, tranquilly turned a page and read on without a pause, a smile, or change of color.

Mr. Fletcher laughed as he strolled away; but Christie was all the more amusing for her want of coquetry, and soon after he tried her again. The great hotel was all astir one evening with bustle, light, and music; for the young people had a hop, as an appropriate entertainment for a melting July night. With no taste for such folly, even if health had not forbidden it, Mr. Fletcher lounged about the piazzas, tantalizing the fair fowlers who spread their nets for him, and goading sundry desperate spinsters to despair by his erratic movements. Coming to a quiet nook, where a long window gave a fine view of the brilliant scene, he found Christie leaning in, with a bright, wistful face, while her hand kept time to the enchanting music of a waltz.

"Wisely watching the lunatics, instead of joining in their antics," he said, sitting down with a sigh.

Christie looked around and answered, with the wistful look still in her eyes:

"I'm very fond of that sort of insanity; but there is no place for me in Bedlam at present."

"I daresay I can find you one, if you care to try it. I don't indulge myself." And Mr. Fletcher's eye went from the rose in Christie's brown hair to the silvery folds of her best gown, put on merely for the pleasure of wearing it because every one else was in festival array.

She shook her head. "No, thank you. Governesses are very kindly treated in America; but ball-rooms like that are not for them. I enjoy looking on, fortunately; so I have my share of fun after all."

"I shan't get any complaints out of her. Plucky little soul! I rather like that," said Mr. Fletcher to himself; and, finding his seat comfortable, the corner cool, and his companion pleasant to look at, with the moonlight doing its best for her, he went on talking for his own satisfaction.

Christie would rather have been left in peace; but fancying that he did it out of kindness to her, and that she had done him injustice before, she was grateful now, and exerted herself to seem so; in which endeavor she succeeded so well that Mr. Fletcher proved he could be a very agreeable companion when he chose. He talked well; and Christie was a good listener. Soon interest conquered her reserve, and she ventured to ask a question, make a criticism, or express an opinion in her own simple way. Unconsciously she piqued the curiosity of the man; for, though he knew many lovely, wise, and witty women, he had never chanced to meet with one like this before; and novelty was the desire of his life. Of course he did not find moonlight, music, and agreeable chat as delightful as she did; but there *was* something animating in the fresh face opposite, something flattering in the eager interest she showed, and something most attractive in the glimpses unconsciously given him of a nature genuine in its womanly sincerity and strength. Something about this girl seemed to appeal to the old self, so long neglected that he thought it dead. He could not analyze the feeling, but was conscious of a desire to seem better than he was as he looked into those honest eyes; to talk well, that he might bring that frank smile to the lips that grew either sad or scornful when he tried worldly gossip or bitter satire; and to prove himself a man under all the elegance and polish of the gentleman.

He was discovering then, what Christie learned when her turn came, that fine natures seldom fail to draw out the finer traits of those who approach them, as the little witch-hazel wand, even in the hand of a child, detects and points to hidden springs in unsuspected spots. Women often possess this gift, and when used worthily find it as powerful as beauty; for, if less alluring, it is more lasting and more helpful, since it appeals, not to the senses, but the souls of men.

Christie was one of these; and in proportion as her own nature was sound and sweet so was its power as a touchstone for the genuineness of others. It was this unconscious gift that made her wonder at the unexpected kindness she found in Mr. Fletcher, and this which made him, for an hour or two at least, heartily wish he could live his life over again and do it better.

After that evening Mr. Fletcher spoke to Christie when he met her, turned and joined her sometimes as she walked with the children, and fell into the way of lounging near when she sat reading aloud to an invalid friend on piazza or sea-shore. Christie much preferred to have no auditor but kind Miss Tudor; but finding the old lady enjoying his chat she resigned herself, and when he brought them new books as well as himself, she became quite cordial.

Everybody sauntered and lounged, so no one minded the little group that met day after day among the rocks. Christie read aloud, while the children revelled in sand, shells, and puddles; Miss Tudor spun endless webs of gay silk and wool; and Mr. Fletcher, with his hat over his eyes, lay sunning himself like a luxurious lizard, as he watched the face that grew daily fairer in his sight, and listened to the pleasant voice that went reading on till all his ills and *ennui* seemed lulled to sleep as by a spell.

A week or two of this new caprice set Christie to thinking. She knew that Uncle Philip was not fond of "the darlings;" it was evident that good Miss Tudor, with her mild twaddle and eternal knitting, was not the attraction, so she was forced to believe that he came for her sake alone. She laughed at herself for this fancy at first; but not possessing the sweet unconsciousness of those heroines who can live through three volumes with a burning passion before their eyes, and never see it till the proper moment comes, and Eugene goes down upon his knees, she soon felt sure that Mr. Fletcher found her society agreeable, and wished her to know it.

Being a mortal woman, her vanity was flattered, and she found herself showing that she liked it by those small signs and symbols which lovers' eyes are so quick to see and understand,—an artful bow on her hat, a flower in her belt, fresh muslin gowns, and the most becoming arrangement of her hair.

"Poor man, he has so few pleasures I'm sure I needn't grudge him such a small one as looking at and listening to me if he likes it," she said to herself one day, as she was preparing for her daily stroll with unusual care. "But how will it end? If he only wants a mild flirtation he is welcome to it; but if he really cares for me, I must make up my mind about it, and not deceive him. I don't believe he loves me; how can he? such an insignificant creature as I am."

Here she looked in the glass, and as she looked the color deepened in her cheek, her eyes shone, and a smile would sit upon her lips, for the reflection showed her a very winning face under the coquettish hat put on to captivate.

"Don't be foolish, Christie! Mind what you do, and be sure vanity doesn't delude you, for you are only a woman, and in things of this sort we are so blind and silly. I'll think of this possibility soberly, but I won't flirt, and then which ever way I decide I shall have nothing to reproach myself with."

Armed with this virtuous resolution, Christie sternly replaced the pretty hat with her old brown one, fastened up a becoming curl, which of late she had worn behind her ear, and put on a pair of stout, rusty boots, much fitter for rocks and sand than the smart slippers she was preparing to sacrifice. Then she trudged away to Miss Tudor, bent on being very quiet and reserved, as became a meek and lowly governess.

But, dear heart, how feeble are the resolutions of womankind! When she found herself sitting in her favorite nook, with the wide, blue sea glittering below, the fresh wind making her blood dance in her veins, and all the earth and sky so full of summer life and loveliness, her heart *would* sing for joy, her face *would* shine with the mere bliss of living, and underneath all this natural content the new thought, half confessed, yet very sweet, *would* whisper, "Somebody cares for me."

If she had doubted it, the expression of Mr. Fletcher's face that morning would have dispelled the doubt, for, as she read, he was saying to himself: "Yes, this healthful, cheery, helpful creature is what I want to make life pleasant. Every thing else is used up; why not try this, and make the most of my last chance? She does me good, and I don't seem to get tired of her. I can't have a long life, they tell me, nor an easy one, with the devil to pay with my vitals generally; so it would be a wise thing to provide myself with a good-tempered, faithful soul to take care of me. My fortune would pay for loss of time, and my death leave her a bonny widow. I won't be rash, but I think I'll try it."

With this mixture of tender, selfish, and regretful thoughts in his mind, it is no wonder Mr. Fletcher's eyes betrayed him, as he lay looking at Christie. Never had she read so badly, for she could not keep her mind on her book. It *would* wander to that new and troublesome fancy of hers; she could not help thinking that Mr. Fletcher must have been a handsome man before he was so ill; wondering if his temper was *very* bad, and fancying that he might prove both generous and kind and true to one who loved and served him well. At this point she was suddenly checked by a slip of the tongue that covered her with confusion.

She was reading "John Halifax," and instead of saying "Phineas Fletcher" she said Philip, and then colored to her forehead, and lost her place.[12] Miss Tudor did not mind it, but Mr. Fletcher laughed, and Christie thanked Heaven that her face was half hidden by the old brown hat.

Nothing was said, but she was much relieved to find that Mr. Fletcher had joined a yachting party next day and he would be away for a week. During that week Christie thought over the matter, and fancied she had made up her mind. She recalled certain speeches she had heard, and which had more weight with her than she suspected. One dowager had said to another: "P. F. intends to marry, I assure you, for his sister told me so, with tears in her eyes. Men who have been gay in their youth make very good husbands when their wild oats are sowed. Clara could not do better, and I should be quite content to give her to him."

"Well, dear, I should be sorry to see my Augusta his wife, for whoever he marries will be a perfect slave to him. His fortune would be a nice thing if he did not live long; but even for that my Augusta shall not be sacrificed," returned the other matron whose Augusta had vainly tried to captivate "P. F.," and revenged herself by calling him "a wreck, my dear, a perfect wreck."

At another time Christie heard some girls discussing the eligibility of several gentlemen, and Mr. Fletcher was considered the best match among them.

"You can do any thing you like with a husband a good deal older than yourself. He's happy with his business, his club, and his dinner, and leaves you to do what you please; just keep him comfortable and he'll pay your bills without much fuss," said one young thing who had seen life at twenty.

"I'd take him if I had the chance, just because everybody wants him. Don't admire him a particle, but it will make a jolly stir whenever he does marry, and I wouldn't mind having a hand in it," said the second budding belle.

"I'd take him for the diamonds alone. Mamma says they are splendid, and have been in the family for ages. He won't let Mrs. S. wear them, for they always go to the eldest son's wife. Hope he'll choose a handsome woman who will show them off well," said a third sweet girl, glancing at her own fine neck.

"He won't; he'll take some poky old maid who will cuddle him when he is sick, and keep out of his way when he is well. See if he don't."

"I saw him dawdling round with old Tudor, perhaps he means to take her: she's a capital nurse, got ill herself taking care of her father, you know."

"Perhaps he's after the governess; she's rather nice looking, though she hasn't a bit of style."

"Gracious, no! she's a dowdy thing, always trailing round with a book and those horrid children. No danger of his marrying *her*." And a derisive laugh seemed to settle that question beyond a doubt.

"Oh, indeed!" said Christie, as the girls went trooping out of the bath-house, where this pleasing chatter had been carried on regardless of listeners. She called them "mercenary, worldly, unwomanly flirts," and felt herself much their superior. Yet the memory of their gossip haunted her, and had its influence upon her decision, though she thought she came to it through her own good judgment and discretion.

"If he really cares for me I will listen, and not refuse till I know him well enough to decide. I'm tired of being alone, and should enjoy ease and pleasure so much. He's going abroad for the winter, and that would be charming. I'll try not to be worldly-minded and marry without love, but it does look tempting to a poor soul like me."

So Christie made up her mind to accept, if this promotion was offered her; and while she waited, went through so many alternations of feeling, and was so harassed by doubts and fears that she sometimes found herself wishing it had never occurred to her.

Mr. Fletcher, meantime, with the help of many meditative cigars, was making up *his* mind. Absence only proved to him how much he needed a better time-killer than billiards, horses, or newspapers, for the long, listless days seemed endless without the cheerful governess to tone him up, like a new and agreeable sort of bitters. A gradually increasing desire to secure this satisfaction had taken possession of him, and the thought of always having a pleasant companion, with no nerves, nonsense, or affectation about her, was an inviting idea to a man tired of fashionable follies and tormented with the *ennui* of his own society.

The gossip, wonder, and chagrin such a step would cause rather pleased his fancy; the excitement of trying almost the only thing as yet untried allured him; and deeper than all the desire to forget the past in a better future led him to Christie by the nobler instincts that never wholly die in any soul. He wanted her as he had wanted many other things in his life, and had little doubt that he could have her for the asking. Even if love was not abounding, surely his fortune, which hitherto had procured him all he wished (except health and happiness) could buy him a wife, when his friends made better bargains every day. So, having settled the question, he came home again, and every one said the trip had done him a world of good.

Christie sat in her favorite nook one bright September morning, with the inevitable children hunting hapless crabs in a pool near by. A book lay on her knee, but she was not reading; her eyes were looking far across the blue waste before her with an eager gaze, and her face was bright with some happy thought. The sound of approaching steps disturbed her reverie, and, recognizing them, she plunged into the heart of the story, reading as if utterly absorbed, till a shadow fell athwart the page, and the voice she had expected to hear asked blandly:

"What book now, Miss Devon?"

"'Jane Eyre,' sir."

Mr. Fletcher sat down just where her hat-brim was no screen, pulled off his gloves, and leisurely composed himself for a comfortable lounge.

"What is your opinion of Rochester?" he asked, presently.

"Not a very high one."

"Then you think Jane was a fool to love and try to make a saint of him, I suppose?"

"I like Jane, but never can forgive her marrying that man, as I haven't much faith in the saints such sinners make."

"But don't you think a man who had only follies to regret might expect a good woman to lend him a hand and make him happy?"

"If he has wasted his life he must take the consequences, and be content with pity and indifference, instead of respect and love. Many good women do 'lend a hand,' as you say, and it is quite Christian and amiable, I've no doubt; but I cannot think it a fair bargain."

Mr. Fletcher liked to make Christie talk, for in the interest of the subject she forget herself and her chief charm for him was her earnestness. But just then the earnestness did not seem to suit him, and he said, rather sharply:

"What hard-hearted creatures you women are sometimes! Now, I fancied you were one of those who wouldn't leave a poor fellow to his fate, if his salvation lay in your hands."

"I can't say what I should do in such a case; but it always seemed to me that a man should have energy enough to save himself, and not expect the 'weaker vessel,' as he calls her, to do it for him," answered Christie, with a conscious look, for Mr. Fletcher's face made her feel as if something was going to happen.

Evidently anxious to know what she *would* do in aforesaid case, Mr. Fletcher decided to put one before her as speedily as possible, so he said, in a pensive tone, and with a wistful glance:

"You looked very happy just now when I came up. I wish I could believe that my return had any thing to do with it."

Christie wished she could control her tell-tale color, but finding she could not, looked hard at the sea, and, ignoring his tender insinuation, said, with suspicious enthusiasm:

"I was thinking of what Mrs. Saltonstall said this morning. She asked me if I would like to go to Paris with her for the winter. It has always been one of my dreams to go abroad, and I do hope I shall not be disappointed."

Christie's blush seemed to be a truer answer than her words, and, leaning a little nearer, Mr. Fletcher said, in his most persuasive tone:

"Will you go to Paris as *my* governess, instead of Charlotte's?"

Christie thought her reply was all ready; but when the moment came, she found it was not, and sat silent, feeling as if that "Yes" would promise far more than she could give. Mr. Fletcher had no doubt what the answer would be, and was in no haste to get it, for that was one of the moments that are so pleasant and so short-lived they should be enjoyed to the uttermost. He liked to watch her color come and go, to see the asters on her bosom tremble with the quickened beating of her heart, and tasted, in anticipation, the satisfaction of the moment when that pleasant voice of hers would falter out its grateful assent. Drawing yet nearer, he went on, still in the persuasive tone that would have been more lover-like if it had been less assured.

"I think I am not mistaken in believing that you care for me a little. You must know how fond I am of you, how much I need you, and how glad I should be to give all I have if I might keep you always to make my hard life happy. May I, Christie?"

"You would soon tire of me. I have no beauty, no accomplishments, no fortune,—nothing but my heart and my hand to give the man I marry. Is that enough?" asked Christie, looking at him with eyes that betrayed the hunger of an empty heart longing to be fed with genuine food.

But Mr. Fletcher did not understand its meaning; he saw the humility in her face, thought she was overcome by the weight of the honor he did her, and tried to reassure her with the gracious air of one who wishes to lighten the favor he confers.

"It might not be for some men, but it is for me, because I want you very much. Let people say what they will, if you say yes I am satisfied. You shall not regret it Christie; I'll do my best to make you happy; you shall travel wherever I can go with you, have what you like, if possible, and when we come back by and by, you shall take your place in the world as my wife. You will fill it well, I fancy, and I shall be a happy man. I've had my own way all my life, and I mean to have it now, so smile, and say, 'Yes, Philip,' like a sweet soul, as you are."

But Christie did not smile, and felt no inclination to say "Yes, Philip," for that last speech of his jarred on her ear. The tone of unconscious condescension in it wounded the woman's sensitive pride; self was too apparent, and the most generous words seemed to her like bribes. This was not the lover she had dreamed of, the brave, true man who gave her all, and felt it could not half repay the treasure of her innocent, first love. This was not the happiness she had hoped for, the perfect faith, the glad surrender, the sweet content that made all things possible, and changed this work-a-day world into a heaven while the joy lasted.

She had decided to say "yes," but her heart said "no" decidedly, and with instinctive loyalty she obeyed it, even while she seemed to yield to the temptation which appeals to three of the strongest foibles in most women's nature,—vanity, ambition, and the love of pleasure.

"You are very kind, but you may repent it, you know so little of me," she began, trying to soften her refusal, but sadly hindered by a feeling of contempt.

"I know more about you than you think; but it makes no difference," interrupted Mr. Fletcher, with a smile that irritated Christie, even before she understood its significance. "I thought it would at first, but I found I couldn't get on without you, so I made up my mind to forgive and forget that my wife had ever been an actress."

Christie had forgotten it, and it would have been well for him if he had held his tongue. Now she understood the tone that had chilled her, the smile that angered her, and Mr. Fletcher's fate was settled in the drawing of a breath.

"Who told you that?" she asked, quickly, while every nerve tingled with the mortification of being found out then and there in the one secret of her life.

"I saw you dancing on the beach with the children one day, and it reminded me of an actress I had once seen. I should not have remembered it but for the accident which impressed it on my mind. Powder, paint, and costume made 'Miss Douglas' a very different woman from Miss Devon, but a few cautious inquiries settled the matter, and I then understood where you got that slight *soupçon* of dash and daring which makes our demure governess so charming when with me."

As he spoke, Mr. Fletcher smiled again, and kissed his hand to her with a dramatic little gesture that exasperated Christie beyond measure.

She would not make light of it, as he did, and submit to be forgiven for a past she was not ashamed of. Heartily wishing she had been frank at first, she resolved to have it out now, and accept nothing Mr. Fletcher offered her, not even silence.

"Yes," she said, as steadily as she could, "I *was* an actress for three years, and though it was a hard life it was an honest one, and I'm not ashamed of it. I ought to have told Mrs. Saltonstall, but I was warned that if I did it would be difficult to find a place, people are so prejudiced. I sincerely regret it now, and shall tell her at once, so you may save yourself the trouble."

"My dear girl, I never dreamed of telling any one!" cried Mr. Fletcher in an injured tone. "I beg you won't speak, but trust me, and let it be a little secret between us two. I assure you it makes no difference to me, for I should marry an opera dancer if I chose, so forget it, as I do, and set my mind at rest upon the other point. I'm still waiting for my answer, you know."

"It is ready."

"A kind one, I'm sure. What is it, Christie?"

"No, I thank you."

"But you are not in earnest?"

"Perfectly so."

Mr. Fletcher got up suddenly and set his back against the rock, saying in a tone of such unaffected surprise and disappointment that her heart reproached her:

"Am I to understand that as your final answer, Miss Devon?"

"Distinctly and decidedly my final answer, Mr. Fletcher."

Christie tried to speak kindly, but she was angry with herself and him, and unconsciously showed it both in face and voice, for she was no actress off the stage, and wanted to be very true just then as a late atonement for that earlier want of candor.

A quick change passed over Mr. Fletcher's face; his cold eyes kindled with an angry spark, his lips were pale with anger, and his voice was very bitter, as he slowly said:

"I've made many blunders in my life, and this is one of the greatest; for I believed in a woman, was fool enough to care for her with the sincerest love I ever knew, and fancied that she would be grateful for the sacrifice I made."

He got no further, for Christie rose straight up and answered him with all the indignation she felt burning in her face and stirring the voice she tried in vain to keep as steady as his own.

"The sacrifice would not have been *all* yours, for it is what we *are,* not what we *have,* that makes one human being superior to another. I am as well-born as you in spite of my poverty; my life, I think, has been a better one than yours; my heart, I know, is fresher, and my memory has fewer faults and follies to reproach me with. What can you give me but money and position in return for the youth and freedom I should sacrifice in marrying you? Not love, for you count the cost of your bargain, as no true lover could, and you reproach me for deceit when in your heart you know you only cared for me because I can amuse and serve you. I too deceived myself, I too see my mistake, and I decline the honor you would do me, since it is so great in your eyes that you must remind me of it as you offer it."

In the excitement of the moment Christie unconsciously spoke with something of her old dramatic fervor in voice and gesture; Mr. Fletcher saw it, and, while he never had admired her so much, could not resist avenging himself for the words that angered him, the more deeply for their truth. Wounded vanity and baffled will can make an ungenerous man as spiteful as a woman; and Mr. Fletcher proved it then, for he saw where Christie's pride was sorest, and touched the wound with the skill of a resentful nature.

As she paused, he softly clapped his hands, saying, with a smile that made her eyes flash:

"Very well done! infinitely superior to your 'Woffington,' Miss Devon.[13] I am disappointed in the woman, but I make my compliment to the actress, and leave the stage free for another and a more successful Romeo."

Still smiling, he bowed and went away apparently quite calm and much amused, but a more wrathful, disappointed man never crossed those sands than the one who kicked his dog and swore at himself for a fool that day when no one saw him.

For a minute Christie stood and watched him, then, feeling that she must either laugh or cry, wisely chose the former vent for her emotions, and sat down feeling inclined to look at the whole scene from a ludicrous point of view.

"My second love affair is a worse failure than my first, for I did pity poor Joe, but this man is detestable, and I never will forgive him that last insult. I dare say I *was* absurdly tragical, I'm apt to be when very angry, but what a temper he has got! The white, cold kind, that smoulders and stabs, instead of blazing up and being over in a minute. Thank Heaven, I'm not his wife! Well, I've made an enemy and lost my place, for of course Mrs. Saltonstall won't keep me after this awful discovery. I'll tell her at once, for I will have no 'little secrets' with him. No Paris either, and that's the worst of it all! Never mind, I haven't sold my liberty for the Fletcher diamonds, and that's a comfort. Now a short scene with my lady and then exit governess."

But though she laughed, Christie felt troubled at the part she had played in this affair; repented of her worldly aspirations; confessed her vanity; accepted her mortification and disappointment as a just punishment for her sins; and yet at the bottom of her heart she did enjoy it mightily.

She tried to spare Mr. Fletcher in her interview with his sister, and only betrayed her own iniquities. But, to her surprise, Mrs. Saltonstall, though much disturbed at the discovery, valued Christie as a governess, and respected her as a woman, so she was willing to bury the past, she said, and still hoped Miss Devon would remain.

Then Christie was forced to tell her why it was impossible for her to do so; and, in her secret soul, she took a naughty satisfaction in demurely mentioning that she had refused my lord.

Mrs. Saltonstall's consternation was comical, for she had been so absorbed in her own affairs she had suspected nothing; and horror fell upon her when she learned how near dear Philip had been to the fate from which she jealously guarded him, that his property might one day benefit the darlings.

In a moment every thing was changed; and it was evident to Christie that the sooner she left the better it would suit madame. The proprieties were preserved to the end, and Mrs. Saltonstall treated her with unusual respect, for she had come to honor, and also conducted herself in a most praiseworthy manner. How she could refuse a Fletcher visibly amazed the lady; but she forgave the slight, and gently insinuated that "my brother" was, perhaps, only amusing himself.

Christie was but too glad to be off; and when Mrs. Saltonstall asked when she would prefer to leave, promptly replied, "To-morrow," received her salary, which was forthcoming with unusual punctuality, and packed her trunks with delightful rapidity.

As the family was to leave in a week, her sudden departure caused no surprise to the few who knew her, and with kind farewells to such of her summer friends as still remained, she went to bed that night all ready for an early start. She saw nothing more of Mr. Fletcher that day, but the sound of excited voices in the drawing-room assured her that madame was having it out with her brother; and with truly feminine inconsistency Christie hoped that she would not be too hard upon the poor man, for, after all, it was kind of him to overlook the actress, and ask the governess to share his good things with him.

She did not repent, but she got herself to sleep, imagining a bridal trip to Paris, and dreamed so delightfully of lost splendors that the awakening was rather blank, the future rather cold and hard.

She was early astir, meaning to take the first boat and so escape all disagreeable *recontres,* and having kissed the children in their little beds, with tender promises not to forget them, she took a hasty breakfast and stepped into the carriage waiting at the door. The sleepy waiters stared, a friendly housemaid nodded, and Miss Walker, the hearty English lady who did her ten miles a day, cried out, as she tramped by, blooming and bedraggled:

"Bless me, are you off?"

"Yes, thank Heaven!" answered Christie; but as she spoke Mr. Fletcher came down the steps looking as wan and heavy-eyed as if a sleepless night had been added to his day's defeat. Leaning in at the window, he asked abruptly, but with a look she never could forget:

"Will nothing change your answer, Christie?"

"Nothing."

His eyes said, "Forgive me," but his lips only said, "Good-by," and the carriage rolled away.

Then, being a woman, two great tears fell on the hand still red with the lingering grasp he had given it, and Christie said, as pitifully as if she loved him:

"He *has* got a heart, after all, and perhaps I might have been glad to fill it if he had only shown it to me sooner. Now it is too late."

V

COMPANION

BEFORE she had time to find a new situation, Christie received a note from Miss Tudor, saying that hearing she had left Mrs. Saltonstall she wanted to offer her the place of companion to an invalid girl, where the duties were light and the compensation large.

"How kind of her to think of me," said Christie, gratefully. "I'll go at once and do my best to secure it, for it must be a good thing or she wouldn't recommend it."

Away went Christie to the address sent by Miss Tudor, and as she waited at the door she thought:

"What a happy family in the Carrols must be!" for the house was one of an imposing block in a West End square, which had its own little park where a fountain sparkled in the autumn sunshine, and pretty children played among the fallen leaves.

Mrs. Carrol was a stately woman, still beautiful in spite of her fifty years. But though there were few lines on her forehead, few silver threads in the dark hair that lay smoothly over it, and a gracious smile showed the fine teeth, an indescribable expression of unsubmissive sorrow touched the whole face, betraying that life had brought some heavy cross, from which her wealth could purchase no release, for which her pride could find no effectual screen.

She looked at Christie with a searching eye, listened attentively when she spoke, and seemed testing her with covert care as if the place she was to fill demanded some unusual gift or skill.

"Miss Tudor tells me that you read aloud well, sing sweetly, possess a cheerful temper, and the quiet, patient ways which are peculiarly grateful to an invalid," began Mrs. Carrol, with that keen yet wistful gaze, and an anxious accent in her voice that went to Christie's heart.

"Miss Tudor is very kind to think so well of me and my few accomplishments. I have never been with an invalid, but I think I can promise to be patient, willing, and cheerful. My own experience of illness has taught me how to sympathize with others and love to lighten pain. I shall be very glad to try if you think I have any fitness for the place."

"I do," and Mrs. Carrol's face softened as she spoke, for something in Christie's words or manner seemed to please her. Then slowly, as if the task was a hard one, she added:

"My daughter has been very ill and is still weak and nervous. I must hint to you that the loss of one very dear to her was the cause of the illness and the melancholy which now oppresses her. Therefore we must avoid any thing that can suggest or recall this trouble. She cares for nothing as yet, will see no one, and prefers to live alone. She is still so feeble this is but natural; yet solitude is bad for her, and her physician thinks that a new face might rouse her, and the society of one in no way connected with the painful past might interest and do her good. You see it is a little difficult to find just what we want, for a young companion is best, yet must be discreet and firm, as few young people are."

Fancying from Mrs. Carrol's manner that Miss Tudor had said more in her favor than had been repeated to her, Christie in a few plain words told her little story, resolving to have no concealments here, and feeling that perhaps her experiences might have given her more firmness and discretion than many women of her age possessed. Mrs. Carrol seemed to find it so; the anxious look lifted a little as she listened, and when Christie ended she said, with a sigh of relief:

"Yes, I think Miss Tudor is right, and you *are* the one we want. Come and try it for a week and then we can decide. Can you begin to-day?" she added, as Christie rose. "Every hour is precious, for my poor girl's sad solitude weighs on my heart, and this is my one hope."

"I will stay with pleasure," answered Christie, thinking Mrs. Carrol's anxiety excessive, yet pitying the mother's pain, for something in her face suggested the idea that she reproached herself in some way for her daughter's state.

With secret gratitude that she had dressed with care, Christie took off her things and followed Mrs. Carrol upstairs. Entering a room in what seemed to be a wing of the great house, they found an old woman sewing.

"How is Helen to-day, Nurse?" asked Mrs. Carrol, pausing.

"Poorly, ma'am. I've been in every hour, but she only says: 'Let me be quiet,' and lies looking up at the picture till it's fit to break your heart to see her," answered the woman, with a shake of the head.

"I have brought Miss Devon to sit with her a little while. Doctor advises it, and I fancy the experiment may succeed if we can only amuse the dear child, and make her forget herself and her troubles."

"As you please, ma'am," said the old woman, looking with little favor at the new-comer, for the good soul was jealous of any interference between herself and the child she had tended for years.

"I won't disturb her, but you shall take Miss Devon in and tell Helen mamma sends her love, and hopes she will make an effort for all our sakes."

"Yes, ma'am."

"Go, my dear, and do your best." With these words Mrs. Carrol hastily left the room, and Christie followed Nurse.

A quick glance showed her that she was in the daintily furnished boudoir of a rich man's daughter, but before she could take a second look her eyes were arrested by the occupant of this pretty place, and she forgot all else. On a low luxurious couch lay a girl, so beautiful and pale and still, that for an instant Christie thought her dead or sleeping. She was neither, for at the sound of a voice the great eyes opened wide, darkening and dilating with a strange expression as they fell on the unfamiliar face.

"Nurse, who is that? I told you I would see no one. I'm too ill to be so worried," she said, in an imperious tone.

"Yes, dear, I know, but your mamma wished you to make an effort. Miss Devon is to sit with you and try to cheer you up a bit," said the old woman in a dissatisfied tone, that contrasted strangely with the tender way in which she stroked the beautiful disordered hair that hung about the girl's shoulders.

Helen knit her brows and looked most ungracious, but evidently tried to be civil, for with a courteous wave of her hand toward an easy chair in the sunny window she said, quietly:

"Please sit down, Miss Devon, and excuse me for a little while. I've had a bad night, and am too tired to talk just yet. There are books of all sorts, or the conservatory if you like it better."

"Thank you. I'll read quietly till you want me. Then I shall be very glad to do any thing I can for you."

With that Christie retired to the big chair, and fell to reading the first book she took up, a good deal embarrassed by her reception, and very curious to know what would come next.

The old woman went away after folding the down coverlet carefully over her darling's feet, and Helen seemed to go to sleep.

For a time the room was very still; the fire burned softly on the marble hearth, the sun shone warmly on velvet carpet and rich hangings, the delicate breath of flowers blew in through the half-open door that led to a gay little conservatory, and nothing but the roll of a distant carriage broke the silence now and then.

Christie's eyes soon wandered from her book to the lovely face and motionless figure on the couch. Just opposite, in a recess, hung the portrait of a young and handsome man, and below it stood a vase of flowers, a graceful Roman lamp, and several little relics, as if it were the shrine where some dead love was mourned and worshipped still.

As she looked from the living face, so pale and so pathetic in its quietude, to the painted one so full of color, strength, and happiness, her heart ached for poor Helen, and her eyes were wet with tears of pity. A sudden movement on the couch gave her no time to hide them, and as she hastily looked down upon her book a treacherous drop fell glittering on the page.

"What have you there so interesting?" asked Helen, in that softly imperious tone of hers.

"Don Quixote," answered Christie, too much abashed to have her wits about her.

Helen smiled a melancholy smile as she rose, saying wearily:

"They gave me that to make me laugh, but I did not find it funny; neither was it sad enough to make me cry as you do."

"I was not reading, I was"—there Christie broke down, and could have cried with vexation at the bad beginning she had made. But that involuntary tear was better balm to Helen than the most perfect tact, the most brilliant conversation. It touched and won her without words, for sympathy works miracles. Her whole face changed, and her mournful eyes grew soft as with the gentle freedom of a child she lifted Christie's downcast face and said, with a falter in her voice:

"I know you were pitying me. Well, I need pity, and from you I'll take it, because you don't force it on me. Have *you* been ill and wretched too? I think so, else you would never care to come and shut yourself up here with me!"

"I have been ill, and I know how hard it is to get one's spirits back again. I've had my troubles, too, but not heavier than I could bear, thank God!"

"What made you ill? Would you mind telling me about it? I seem to fancy hearing other people's woes, though it can't make mine seem lighter."

"A piece of the Castle of the Sun fell on my head and nearly killed me," and Christie laughed in spite of herself at the astonishment in Helen's face. "I was an actress once; your mother knows and didn't mind," she added, quickly.

"I'm glad of that. I used to wish I could be one, I was so fond of the theatre. They should have consented, it would have given me something to do, and, however hard it is, it couldn't be worse than this." Helen spoke vehemently and an excited flush rose to her white cheeks; then she checked herself and dropped into a chair, saying, hurriedly:

"Tell me about it: don't let me think; it's bad for me."

Glad to be set to work, and bent on retrieving her first mistake, Christie plunged into her theatrical experiences and talked away in her most lively style. People usually get eloquent when telling their own stories, and true tales are always the most interesting. Helen listened at first with a half-absent air, but presently grew more attentive, and when the catastrophe came sat erect, quite absorbed in the interest of this glimpse behind the curtain.

Charmed with her success, Christie branched off right and left, stimulated by questions, led on by suggestive incidents, and generously supplied by memory. Before she knew it, she was telling her whole history in the most expansive manner, for women soon get sociable together, and

Helen's interest flattered her immensely. Once she made her laugh at some droll trifle, and as if the unaccustomed sound had startled her, old nurse popped in her head; but seeing nothing amiss retired, wondering what on earth that girl could be doing to cheer up Miss Helen so.

"Tell about your lovers: you must have had some; actresses always do. Happy women, they can love as they like!" said Helen, with the inquisitive frankness of an invalid for whom etiquette has ceased to exist.

Remembering in time that this was a forbidden subject, Christie smiled and shook her head.

"I had a few, but one does not tell those secrets, you know."

Evidently disappointed, and a little displeased at being reminded of her want of good-breeding, Helen got up and began to wander restlessly about the room. Presently, as if wishing to atone for her impatience, she bade Christie come and see her flowers. Following her, the new companion found herself in a little world where perpetual summer reigned. Vines curtained the roof, slender shrubs and trees made leafy walls on either side, flowers bloomed above and below, birds carolled in half-hidden prisons, aquariums and ferneries stood all about, and the soft plash of a little fountain made pleasant music as it rose and fell.

Helen threw herself wearily down on a pile of cushions that lay beside the basin, and beckoning Christie to sit near, said, as she pressed her hands to her hot forehead and looked up with a distressful brightness in the haggard eyes that seemed to have no rest in them:

"Please sing to me; any humdrum air will do. I am so tired, and yet I cannot sleep. If my head would only stop this dreadful thinking and let me forget one hour it would do me so much good."

"I know the feeling, and I'll try what Lucy used to do to quiet me. Put your poor head in my lap, dear, and lie quite still while I cool and comfort it."

Obeying like a worn-out child, Helen lay motionless while Christie, dipping her fingers in the basin, passed the wet tips softly to and fro across the hot forehead, and the thin temples where the pulses throbbed so fast. And while she soothed she sang the "Land o' the Leal," and sang it well; for the tender words, the plaintive air were dear to her, because her mother loved and sang it to her years ago. Slowly the heavy eyelids drooped, slowly the lines of pain were smoothed away from the broad brow, slowly the restless hands grew still, and Helen lay asleep.

So intent upon her task was Christie, that she forgot herself till the discomfort of her position reminded her that she had a body. Fearing to wake the poor girl in her arms, she tried to lean against the basin, but could not reach a cushion to lay upon the cold stone ledge. An unseen hand supplied the want, and, looking round, she saw two young men standing behind her.

Helen's brothers, without doubt; for, though utterly unlike in expression, some of the family traits were strongly marked in both. The elder wore the dress of a priest, had a pale, ascetic face, with melancholy eyes, stern mouth, and the absent air of one who leads an inward life. The younger had a more attractive face, for, though bearing marks of dissipation, it betrayed a generous, ardent nature, proud and wilful, yet lovable in spite of all defects. He was very boyish still, and plainly showed how much he felt, as, with a hasty nod to Christie, he knelt down beside his sister, saying, in a whisper:

"Look at her, Augustine! so beautiful, so quiet! What a comfort it is to see her like herself again."

"Ah, yes; and but for the sin of it, I could find it in my heart to wish she might never wake!" returned the other, gloomily.

"Don't say that! How could we live without her?" Then, turning to Christie, the younger said, in a friendly tone:

"You must be very tired; let us lay her on the sofa. It is very damp here, and if she sleeps long you will faint from weariness."

Carefully lifting her, the brothers carried the sleeping girl into her room, and laid her down. She sighed as her head touched the pillow, and her arm clung to Harry's neck, as if she felt his nearness even in sleep. He put his cheek to hers, and lingered over her with an affectionate solicitude beautiful to see. Augustine stood silent, grave and cold as if he had done with human ties, yet found it hard to sever this one, for he stretched his hand above his sister as if he blessed her, then, with another grave bow to Christie, went away as noiselessly as he had come. But Harry kissed the sleeper tenderly, whispered, "Be kind to her," with an imploring voice, and hurried from the room as if to hide the feeling that he must not show.

A few minutes later the nurse brought in a note from Mrs. Carrol.

"My son tells me that Helen is asleep, and you look very tired. Leave her to Hester, now; you have done enough to-day, so let me thank you heartily, and send you home for a quiet night before you continue your good work to-morrow."

Christie went, found a carriage waiting for her, and drove home very happy at the success of her first attempt at companionship.

The next day she entered upon the new duties with interest and good-will, for this was work in which heart took part, as well as head and hand. Many things surprised, and some things perplexed her, as she came to know the family better. But she discreetly held her tongue, used her eyes, and did her best to please.

Mrs. Carrol seemed satisfied, often thanked her for her faithfulness to Helen, but seldom visited her daughter, never seemed surprised or grieved that the girl expressed no wish to see her; and, though her handsome face always wore its gracious smile, Christie soon felt very sure that it was a mask put on to hide some heavy sorrow from a curious world.

Augustine never came except when Helen was asleep: then, like a shadow, he passed in and out, always silent, cold, and grave, but in his eyes the gloom of some remorseful pain that prayers and penances seemed powerless to heal.

Harry came every day, and no matter how melancholy, listless, or irritable his sister might be, for him she always had a smile, an affectionate greeting, a word of praise, or a tender warning against the reckless spirit that seemed to possess him. The love between them was very strong, and Christie found a never-failing pleasure in watching them together, for then Helen showed what she once had been, and Harry was his best self. A boy still, in spite of his one-and-twenty years, he seemed to feel that Helen's room was a safe refuge from the temptations that beset one of his thoughtless and impetuous nature. Here he came to confess his faults and follies with the frankness which is half sad, half comical, and wholly charming in a good-hearted young scatter-brain. Here he brought gay gossip, lively descriptions, and masculine criticisms of the world he moved in. All his hopes and plans, joys and sorrows, successes and defeats, he told to Helen. And she, poor soul, in this one happy love of her sad life, forgot a little the burden of despair that darkened all the world to her. For his sake she smiled, to him she talked when others got no word from her, and Harry's salvation was the only duty that she owned or tried to fulfill.

A younger sister was away at school, but the others seldom spoke of her, and Christie tired herself with wondering why Bella never wrote to Helen, and why Harry seemed to have nothing but a gloomy sort of pity to bestow upon the blooming girl whose picture hung in the great drawing-room below.

It was a very quiet winter, yet a very pleasant one to Christie, for she felt herself loved and trusted, saw that she suited, and believed that she was doing good, as women best love to do it, by bestowing sympathy and care with generous devotion.

Helen and Harry loved her like an elder sister; Augustine showed that he was grateful, and Mrs. Carrol sometimes forgot to put on her mask before one who seemed fast becoming *confidante* as well as companion.

In the spring the family went to the fine old country-house just out of town, and here Christie and her charge led a freer, happier life. Walking and driving, boating and gardening, with pleasant days on the wide terrace, where Helen swung idly in her hammock, while Christie read or talked to her; and summer twilights beguiled with music, or the silent reveries more eloquent than speech, which real friends may enjoy together, and find the sweeter for the mute companionship.

Harry was with them, and devoted to his sister, who seemed slowly to be coming out of her sad gloom, won by patient tenderness and the cheerful influences all about her.

Christie's heart was full of pride and satisfaction, as she saw the altered face, heard the tone of interest in that once hopeless voice, and felt each day more sure that Helen had outlived the loss that seemed to have broken her heart.

Alas, for Christie's pride, for Harry's hope, and for poor Helen's bitter fate! When all was brightest, the black shadow came; when all looked safest, danger was at hand; and when the past seemed buried, the ghost which haunted it returned, for the punishment of a broken law is as inevitable as death.

When settled in town again Bella came home, a gay, young girl, who should have brought sunshine and happiness into her home. But from the hour she returned a strange anxiety seemed to possess the others. Mrs. Carrol watched over her with sleepless care, was evidently full of maternal pride in the lovely creature, and began to dream dreams about her future. She seemed to wish to keep the sisters apart, and said to Christie, as if to explain this wish:

"Bella was away when Helen's trouble and illness came, she knows very little of it, and I do not want her to be saddened by the knowledge. Helen cares only for Hal, and Bella is too young to be of any use to my poor girl; therefore the less they see of each other the better for both. I am sure you agree with me?" she added, with that covert scrutiny which Christie had often felt before.

She could but acquiesce in the mother's decision, and devote herself more faithfully than ever to Helen, who soon needed all her care and patience, for a terrible unrest grew upon her, bringing sleepless nights again, moody days, and all the old afflictions with redoubled force.

Bella "came out" and began her career as a beauty and a belle most brilliantly. Harry was proud of her, but seemed jealous of other men's admiration for his charming sister, and would excite both Helen and himself over the flirtations into which "that child" as they called her, plunged with all the zest of a light-hearted girl whose head was a little turned with sudden and excessive adoration.

In vain Christie begged Harry not to report these things, in vain she hinted that Bella had better not come to show herself to Helen night after night in all the dainty splendor of her youth and beauty; in vain she asked Mrs. Carrol to let her go away to some quieter place with Helen, since she never could be persuaded to join in any gayety at home or abroad. All seemed wilful, blind, or governed by the fear of the gossiping world. So the days rolled on till an event occurred which enlightened Christie, with startling abruptness, and showed her the skeleton that haunted this unhappy family.

Going in one morning to Helen she found her walking to and fro as she often walked of late, with hurried steps and excited face as if driven by some power beyond her control.

"Good morning, dear. I'm so sorry you had a restless night, and wish you had sent for me. Will you come out now for an early drive? It's a lovely day, and your mother thinks it would do you good," began Christie, troubled by the state in which she found the girl.

But as she spoke Helen turned on her, crying passionately:

"My mother! don't speak of her to me, I hate her!"

"Oh, Helen, don't say that. Forgive and forget if she has displeased you, and don't exhaust yourself by brooding over it. Come, dear, and let us soothe ourselves with a little music. I want to hear that new song again, though I can never hope to sing it as you do."

"Sing!" echoed Helen, with a shrill laugh, "you don't know what you ask. Could *you* sing when your heart was heavy with the knowledge of a sin about to be committed by those nearest to you? Don't try to quiet me, I *must* talk whether you listen or not; I shall go frantic if I don't tell some one; all the world will know it soon. Sit down, I'll not hurt you, but don't thwart me or you'll be sorry for it."

Speaking with a vehemence that left her breathless, Helen thrust Christie down upon a seat, and went on with an expression in her face that bereft the listener of power to move or speak.

"Harry has just told me of it; he was very angry, and I saw it, and made him tell me. Poor boy, he can keep nothing from *me*. I've been dreading it, and now it's coming. You don't know it, then? Young Butler is in love with Bella, and no one has prevented it. Think how wicked when such a curse is on us all."

The question, "What curse?" rose involuntarily to Christie's lips, but did not pass them, for, as if she read the thought, Helen answered it in a whisper that made the blood tingle in the other's veins, so full of ominous suggestion was it.

"The curse of insanity I mean. We are all mad, or shall be; we come of a mad race, and for years we have gone recklessly on bequeathing this awful inheritance to our descendants. It should end with us, we are the last; none of us should marry; none dare think of it but Bella, and she knows nothing. She must be told, she must be kept from the sin of deceiving her lover, the agony of seeing her children become what I am, and what we all may be."

Here Helen wrung her hands and paced the room in such a paroxysm of impotent despair that Christie sat bewildered and aghast, wondering if this were true, or but the fancy of a troubled brain. Mrs. Carrol's face and manner returned to her with sudden vividness, so did Augustine's gloomy expression, and the strange wish uttered over his sleeping sister long ago.

Harry's reckless, aimless life might be explained in this way; and all that had perplexed her through that year. Every thing confirmed the belief that this tragical assertion was true, and Christie covered up her face, murmuring, with an involuntary shiver:

"My God, how terrible!"

Helen came and stood before her with such grief and penitence in her countenance that for a moment it conquered the despair that had broken bonds.

"We should have told you this at first; I longed to do it, but I was afraid you'd go and leave me. I was so lonely, so miserable, Christie. I could not give you up when I had learned to love you; and I did learn very soon, for no wretched creature ever needed help and comfort more than I. For your sake I tried to be quiet, to control my shattered nerves, and hide my desperate thoughts. You helped me very much, and your unconsciousness made me doubly watchful. Forgive me; don't desert me now, for the old horror may be coming back, and I want you more than ever."

Too much moved to speak, Christie held out her hands, with a face full of pity, love, and grief. Poor Helen clung to them as if her only help lay there, and for a moment was quite still. But not long; the old anguish was too sharp to be borne in silence; the relief of confidence once tasted was too great to be denied; and, breaking loose, she went to and fro again, pouring out the bitter secret which had been weighing upon heart and conscience for a year.

"You wonder that I hate my mother; let me tell you why. When she was beautiful and young she married, knowing the sad history of my father's family. He was rich, she poor and proud; ambition made her wicked, and she did it after being warned that, though he might escape, his children were sure to inherit the curse, for when one generation goes free it falls more heavily upon the rest. She knew it all, and yet she married him. I have her to thank for all I suffer, and I cannot love her though she is my mother. It may be wrong to say these things, but they are true; they burn in my heart, and I must speak out; for I tell you there comes a time when children judge their parents as men and women, in spite of filial duty, and woe to those whose actions change affection and respect to hatred or contempt."

The bitter grief, the solemn fervor of her words, both touched and awed Christie too much for speech. Helen had passed beyond the bounds of ceremony, fear, or shame: her hard lot, her dark experience, set her apart, and gave her the right to utter the bare truth. To her heart's core Christie felt that warning; and for the first time saw what many never see or wilfully deny,—the awful responsibility that lies on every man and woman's soul forbidding them to entail upon the innocent the burden of their own infirmities, the curse that surely follows their own sins.

Sad and stern, as an accusing angel, that most unhappy daughter spoke:

"If ever a woman had cause to repent, it is my mother; but she will not, and till she does, God has forsaken us. Nothing can subdue her pride, not even an affliction like mine. She hides the truth; she hides me, and lets the world believe I am dying of consumption; not a word about insanity, and no one knows the secret beyond ourselves, but doctor, nurse, and you. This is why I was not sent away, but for a year was shut up in that room yonder where the door is always locked. If you look in, you'll see barred windows, guarded fire, muffled walls, and other sights to chill your blood, when you remember all those dreadful things were meant for me."

"Don't speak, don't think of them! Don't talk any more; let me do something to comfort you, for my heart is broken with all this," cried Christie, panic-stricken at the picture Helen's words had conjured up.

"I *must* go on! There is no rest for me till I have tried to lighten this burden by sharing it with you. Let me talk, let me wear myself out, then you shall help and comfort me, if there is any help and comfort for such as I. Now I can tell you all about my Edward, and you'll listen, though mamma forbade it. Three years ago my father died, and we came here. I was well then, and oh, how happy!"

Clasping her hands above her head, she stood like a beautiful, pale image of despair; tearless and mute, but with such a world of anguish in the eyes lifted to the smiling picture opposite that it needed no words to tell the story of a broken heart.

"How I loved him!" she said, softly, while her whole face glowed for an instant with the light and warmth of a deathless passion. "How I loved him, and how he loved me! Too well to let me darken both our lives with a remorse which would come too late for a just atonement. I thought him cruel then,—I bless him for it now. I had far rather be the innocent sufferer I am, than a wretched woman like my mother. I shall never see him any more, but I know he thinks of me far away in India, and when I die one faithful heart will remember me."

There her voice faltered and failed, and for a moment the fire of her eyes was quenched in tears. Christie thought the reaction had come, and rose to go and comfort her. But instantly Helen's hand was on her shoulder, and pressing her back into her seat, she said, almost fiercely:

"I'm not done yet; you must hear the whole, and help me to save Bella. We knew nothing of the blight that hung over us till father told Augustine upon his death-bed. August, urged by mother, kept it to himself, and went away to bear it as he could. He should have spoken out and saved me in time. But not till he came home and found me engaged did he have courage to warn me of the fate in store for us. So Edward tore himself away, although it broke his heart, and I—do you see that?"

With a quick gesture she rent open her dress, and on her bosom Christie saw a scar that made her turn yet paler than before.

"Yes, I tried to kill myself; but they would not let me die, so the old tragedy of our house begins again. August became a priest, hoping to hide his calamity and expiate his father's sin by endless penances and prayers. Harry turned reckless; for what had he to look forward to? A short life, and a gay one, he says, and when his turn comes he will spare himself long suffering, as I tried to do it. Bella was never told; she was so young they kept her ignorant of all they could, even the knowledge of my state. She was long away at school, but now she has come home, now she has learned to love, and is going blindly as I went, because no one tells her what she *must* know soon or late. Mamma will not. August hesitates, remembering me. Harry swears he will speak out, but I implore him not to do it, for he will be too violent; and I am powerless. I never knew about this man till Hal told me to-day. Bella only comes in for a moment, and I have no chance to tell her she must *not* love him."

Pressing her hands to her temples, Helen resumed her restless march again, but suddenly broke out more violently than before:

"Now do you wonder why I am half frantic? Now will you ask me to sing and smile, and sit calmly by while this wrong goes on? You have done much for me, and God will bless you for it, but you cannot keep me sane. Death is the only cure for a mad Carrol, and I'm so young, so strong, it will be long in coming unless I hurry it."

She clenched her hands, set her teeth, and looked about her as if ready for any desperate act that should set her free from the dark and dreadful future that lay before her.

For a moment Christie feared and trembled; then pity conquered fear. She forgot herself, and only remembered this poor girl, so hopeless, helpless, and afflicted. Led by a sudden impulse, she put both arms about her, and held her close with a strong but silent tenderness better than any bonds. At first, Helen seemed unconscious of it, as she stood rigid and motionless, with her wild eyes dumbly imploring help of earth and heaven. Suddenly both strength and excitement seemed to leave her, and she would have fallen but for the living, loving prop that sustained her.

Still silent, Christie laid her down, kissed her white lips, and busied herself about her till she looked up quite herself again, but so wan and weak, it was pitiful to see her.

"It's over now," she whispered, with a desolate sigh. "Sing to me, and keep the evil spirit quiet for a little while. To-morrow, if I'm strong enough, we'll talk about poor little Bella."

And Christie sang, with tears dropping fast upon the keys, that made a soft accompaniment to the sweet old hymns which soothed this troubled soul as David's music brought repose to Saul.

When Helen slept at last from sheer exhaustion, Christie executed the resolution she had made as soon as the excitement of that stormy scene was over. She went straight to Mrs. Carrol's room, and, undeterred by the presence of her sons, told all that had passed. They were evidently not unprepared for it, thanks to old Hester, who had overheard enough of Helen's wild words to know that something was amiss, and had reported accordingly; but none of them had ventured to interrupt the interview, lest Helen should be driven to desperation as before.

"Mother, Helen is right; we should speak out, and not hide this bitter fact any longer. The world will pity us, and we must bear the pity, but it would condemn us for deceit, and we should deserve the condemnation if we let this misery go on. Living a lie will ruin us all. Bella will be destroyed as Helen was; I am only the shadow of a man now, and Hal is killing himself as fast as he can, to avoid the fate we all dread."

Augustine spoke first, for Mrs. Carrol sat speechless with her trouble as Christie paused.

"Keep to your prayers, and let me go my own way, it's the shortest," muttered Harry, with his face hidden, and his head down on his folded arms.

"Boys, boys, you'll kill me if you say such things! I have more now than I can bear. Don't drive me wild with your reproaches to each other!" cried their mother, her heart rent with the remorse that came too late.

"No fear of that; *you* are not a Carrol," answered Harry, with the pitiless bluntness of a resentful and rebellious boy.

Augustine turned on him with a wrathful flash of the eye, and a warning ring in his stern voice, as he pointed to the door.

"You shall not insult your mother! Ask her pardon, or go!"

"She should ask mine! I'll go. When you want me, you'll know where to find me." And, with a reckless laugh, Harry stormed out of the room.

Augustine's indignant face grew full of a new trouble as the door banged below, and he pressed his thin hands tightly together, saying, as if to himself:

"Heaven help me! Yes, I do know; for, night after night, I find and bring the poor lad home from gambling-tables and the hells where souls like his are lost."

Here Christie thought to slip away, feeling that it was no place for her now that her errand was done. But Mrs. Carrol called her back.

"Miss Devon—Christie—forgive me that I did not trust you sooner. It was so hard to tell; I hoped so much from time; I never could believe that my poor children would be made the victims of my mistake. Do not forsake us: Helen loves you so. Stay with her, I implore you, and let a most unhappy mother plead for a most unhappy child." Then Christie went to the poor woman, and earnestly assured her of her love and loyalty; for now she felt doubly bound to them because they trusted her.

"What shall we do?" they said to her, with pathetic submission, turning like sick people to a healthful soul for help and comfort.

"Tell Bella all the truth, and help her to refuse her lover. Do this just thing, and God will strengthen you to bear the consequences," was her answer, though she trembled at the responsibility they put upon her.

"Not yet," cried Mrs. Carrol. "Let the poor child enjoy the holidays with a light heart,—then we will tell her; and then Heaven help us all!"

So it was decided; for only a week or two of the old year remained, and no one had the heart to rob poor Bella of the little span of blissful ignorance that now remained to her.

A terrible time was that to Christie; for, while one sister, blessed with beauty, youth, love, and pleasure, tasted life at its sweetest, the other sat in the black shadow of a growing dread, and wearied Heaven with piteous prayers for her relief.

"The old horror is coming back; I feel it creeping over me. Don't let it come, Christie! Stay by me! Help me! Keep me sane! And if you cannot, ask God to take me quickly!"

With words, like these, poor Helen clung to Christie; and, soul and body, Christie devoted herself to the afflicted girl. She would not see her mother; and the unhappy woman haunted that closed door, hungering for the look, the word, that never came to her. Augustine was her consolation, and, during those troublous days, the priest was forgotten in the son. But Harry was all in all to Helen then; and it was touching to see how these unfortunate young creatures clung to one another, she tenderly trying to keep him from the wild life that was surely hastening the fate he might otherwise escape for years, and he patiently bearing all her moods, eager to cheer and soothe the sad captivity from which he could not save her.

These tender ministrations seemed to be blessed at last; and Christie began to hope the haunting terror would pass by, as quiet gloom succeeded to wild excitement. The cheerful spirit of the season seemed to reach even that sad room; and, in preparing gifts for others, Helen seemed to find a little of that best of all gifts,—peace for herself.

On New Year's morning, Christie found her garlanding her lover's picture with white roses and the myrtle sprays brides wear.

"These were his favorite flowers, and I meant to make my wedding wreath of this sweet-scented myrtle, because he gave it to me," she said, with a look that made Christie's eyes grow dim. "Don't grieve for me, dear; we shall surely meet hereafter, though so far asunder here. Nothing can part us there, I devoutly believe; for we leave our burdens all behind us when we go." Then, in a lighter tone, she said, with her arm on Christie's neck:

"This day is to be a happy one, no matter what comes after it. I'm going to be my old self for a little while, and forget there's such a word as sorrow. Help me to dress, so that when the boys come up they may find the sister Nell they have not seen for two long years."

"Will you wear this, my darling? Your mother sends it, and she tried to have it dainty and beautiful enough to please you. See, your own colors, though the bows are only laid on that they might be changed for others if you like."

As she spoke Christie lifted the cover of the box old Hester had just brought in, and displayed a cashmere wrapper, creamy-white, silk-lined, down-trimmed, and delicately relieved by rosy knots, like holly berries lying upon snow. Helen looked at it without a word for several minutes, then gathering up the ribbons, with a strange smile, she said:

"I like it better so; but I'll not wear it yet."

"Bless and save us, deary; it *must* have a bit of color somewhere, else it looks just like a shroud," cried Hester, and then wrung her hands in dismay as Helen answered, quietly:

"Ah, well, keep it for me, then. I shall be happier when I wear it so than in the gayest gown I own, for when you put it on, this poor head and heart of mine will be quiet at last."

Motioning Hester to remove the box, Christie tried to banish the cloud her unlucky words had brought to Helen's face, by chatting cheerfully as she helped her make herself "pretty for the boys."

All that day she was unusually calm and sweet, and seemed to yield herself wholly to the happy influences of the hour, gave and received her gifts so cheerfully that her brothers watched her with delight; and unconscious Bella said, as she hung about her sister, with loving admiration in her eyes:

"I always thought you would get well, and now I'm sure of it, for you look as you used before I went away to school, and seem just like our own dear Nell."

"I'm glad of that; I wanted you to feel so, my Bella. I'll accept your happy prophecy, and hope I may get well soon, very soon."

So cheerfully she spoke, so tranquilly she smiled, that all rejoiced over her believing, with love's blindness, that she might yet conquer her malady in spite of their forebodings.

It was a very happy day to Christie, not only that she was generously remembered and made one of them by all the family, but because this change for the better in Helen made her heart sing for joy. She had given time, health, and much love to the task, and ventured now to hope they had not been given in vain. One thing only marred her happiness, the sad estrangement of the daughter from her mother, and that evening she resolved to take advantage of Helen's tender mood, and plead for the poor soul who dared not plead for herself.

As the brothers and sisters said good-night, Helen clung to them as if loth to part, saying, with each embrace:

"Keep hoping for me, Bella; kiss me, Harry; bless me, Augustine, and all wish for me a happier New Year than the last."

When they were gone she wandered slowly round the room, stood long before the picture with its fading garland, sung a little softly to herself, and came at last to Christie, saying, like a tired child:

"I have been good all day; now let me rest."

"One thing has been forgotten, dear," began Christie, fearing to disturb the quietude that seemed to have been so dearly bought.

Helen understood her, and looked up with a sane sweet face, out of which all resentful bitterness had passed.

"No, Christie, not forgotten, only kept until the last. To-day is a good day to forgive, as we would be forgiven, and I mean to do it before I sleep." Then holding Christie close, she added, with a quiver of emotion in her voice: "I have no words warm enough to thank you, my good angel, for all you have been to me, but I know it will give you a great pleasure to do one thing more. Give dear mamma my love, and tell her that when I am quiet for the night I want her to come and get me to sleep with the old lullaby she used to sing when I was a little child."

No gift bestowed that day was so precious to Christie as the joy of carrying this loving message from daughter to mother. How Mrs. Carrol received it need not be told. She would have gone at once, but Christie begged her to wait till rest and quiet, after the efforts of the day, had prepared Helen for an interview which might undo all that had been done if too hastily attempted.

Hester always waited upon her child at night; so, feeling that she might be wanted later, Christie went to her own room to rest. Quite sure that Mrs. Carrol would come to tell her what had passed, she waited for an hour or two, then went to ask of Hester how the visit had sped.

"Her mamma came up long ago, but the dear thing was fast asleep, so I wouldn't let her be disturbed, and Mrs. Carrol went away again," said the old woman, rousing from a nap.

Grieved at the mother's disappointment, Christie stole in, hoping that Helen might rouse. She did not, and Christie was about to leave her, when, as she bent to smooth the tumbled coverlet, something dropped at her feet. Only a little pearl-handled penknife of Harry's; but her heart stood still with fear, for it was open, and, as she took it up, a red stain came off upon her hand.

Helen's face was turned away, and, bending nearer, Christie saw how deathly pale it looked in the shadow of the darkened room. She listened at her lips; only a faint flutter of breath parted them; she lifted up the averted head, and on the white throat saw a little wound, from which the blood still flowed. Then, like a flash of light, the meaning of the sudden change which came over her grew clear,—her brave efforts to make the last day happy, her tender good-night partings, her wish to be at peace with every one, the tragic death she had chosen rather than live out the tragic life that lay before her.

Christie's nerves had been tried to the uttermost; the shock of this discovery was too much for her, and, in the act of calling for help, she fainted, for the first time in her life.

When she was herself again, the room was full of people; terror-stricken faces passed before her; broken voices whispered, "It is too late," and, as she saw the group about the bed, she wished for unconsciousness again.

Helen lay in her mother's arms at last, quietly breathing her life away, for though every thing that love and skill could devise had been tried to save her, the little knife in that desperate hand had done its work, and this world held no more suffering for her. Harry was down upon his knees beside her, trying to stifle his passionate grief. Augustine prayed audibly above her, and the fervor of his broken words comforted all hearts but one. Bella was clinging, panic-stricken, to the kind old doctor, who was sobbing like a boy, for he had loved and served poor Helen as faithfully as if she had been his own.

"Can nothing save her?" Christie whispered, as the prayer ended, and a sound of bitter weeping filled the room.

"Nothing; she is sane and safe at last, thank God!"

Christie could not but echo his thanksgiving, for the blessed tranquillity of the girl's countenance was such as none but death, the great healer, can bring; and, as they looked, her eyes opened, beautifully clear and calm before they closed for ever. From face to face they passed, as if they looked for some one, and her lips moved in vain efforts to speak.

Christie went to her, but still the wide, wistful eyes searched the room as if unsatisfied; and, with a longing that conquered the mortal weakness of the body, the heart sent forth one tender cry:

"My mother—I want my mother!"

There was no need to repeat the piteous call, for, as it left her lips, she saw her mother's face bending over her, and felt her mother's arms gathering her in an embrace which held her close even after death had set its seal upon the voiceless prayers for pardon which passed between those reunited hearts.

When she was asleep at last, Christie and her mother made her ready for her grave; weeping tender tears as they folded her in the soft, white garment she had put by for that sad hour; and on her breast they laid the flowers she had hung about her lover as a farewell gift. So beautiful she looked when all was done, that in the early dawn they called her brothers, that they might not lose the memory of the blessed peace that shone upon her face, a mute assurance that for her the new year had happily begun.

"Now my work here is done, and I must go," thought Christie, when the waves of life closed over the spot where another tired swimmer had gone down. But she found that one more task remained for her before she left the family which, on her coming, she had thought so happy.

Mrs. Carrol, worn out with the long effort to conceal her secret cross, broke down entirely under this last blow, and besought Christie to tell Bella all that she must know. It was a hard task, but Christie accepted it, and, when the time came, found that there was very little to be told, for at the death-bed of the eldest sister, the younger had learned much of the sad truth. Thus prepared, she listened to all that was most carefully and tenderly confided to her, and, when the heavy tale was done, she surprised Christie by the unsuspected strength she showed. No tears, no lamentations, for she was her mother's daughter, and inherited the pride that can bear heavy burdens, if they are borne unseen.

"Tell me what I must do, and I will do it," she said, with the quiet despair of one who submits to the inevitable, but will not complain.

When Christie with difficulty told her that she should give up her lover, Bella bowed her head, and for a moment could not speak, then lifted it as if defying her own weakness, and spoke out bravely:

"It shall be done, for it is right. It is very hard for *me,* because I love him; he will not suffer much, for he can love again. I should be glad of that, and I'll try to wish it for his sake. He is young, and if, as Harry says, he cares more for my fortune than myself, so much the better. What next, Christie?"

Amazed and touched at the courage of the creature she had fancied a sort of lovely butterfly to be crushed by a single blow, Christie took heart, and, instead of soothing sympathy, gave her the solace best fitted for strong natures, something to do for others. What inspired her, Christie never knew; perhaps it was the year of self-denying service she had rendered for pity's sake; such devotion is its own reward, and now, in herself, she discovered unsuspected powers.

"Live for your mother and your brothers, Bella; they need you sorely, and in time I know you will find true consolation in it, although you must relinquish much. Sustain your mother, cheer Augustine, watch over Harry, and be to them what Helen longed to be."

"And fail to do it, as she failed!" cried Bella, with a shudder.

"Listen, and let me give you this hope, for I sincerely do believe it. Since I came here, I have read many books, thought much, and talked often with Dr. Shirley about this sad affliction. He thinks you and Harry may escape it, if you will. You are like your mother in temperament and temper; you have self-control, strong wills, good nerves, and cheerful spirits. Poor Harry is wilfully spoiling all his chances now; but you may save him, and, in the endeavor, save yourself."

"Oh, Christie, may I hope it? Give me one chance of escape, and I will suffer any hardship to keep it. Let me see any thing before me but a life and death like Helen's, and I'll bless you for ever!" cried Bella, welcoming this ray of light as a prisoner welcomes sunshine in his cell.

Christie trembled at the power of her words, yet, honestly believing them, she let them uplift this disconsolate soul, trusting that they might be in time fulfilled through God's mercy and the saving grace of sincere endeavor.

Holding fast to this frail spar, Bella bravely took up arms against her sea of troubles, and rode out the storm. When her lover came to know his fate, she hid her heart, and answered "no," finding a bitter satisfaction in the end, for Harry was right, and, when the fortune was denied him, young Butler did not mourn the woman long. Pride helped Bella to bear it; but it needed all her courage to look down the coming years so bare of all that makes life sweet to youthful souls, so desolate and dark, with duty alone to cheer the thorny way, and the haunting shadow of her race lurking in the background.

Submission and self-sacrifice are stern, sad angels, but in time one learns to know and love them, for when they have chastened, they uplift and bless. Dimly discerning this, poor Bella put her hands in theirs, saying, "Lead me, teach me; I will follow and obey you."

All soon felt that they could not stay in a house so full of heavy memories, and decided to return to their old home. They begged Christie to go with them, using every argument and entreaty their affection could suggest. But Christie needed rest, longed for freedom, and felt that in spite of their regard it would be very hard for her to live among them any longer. Her healthy nature needed brighter influences, stronger comrades, and the memory of Helen weighed so heavily upon her heart that she was eager to forget it for a time in other scenes and other work.

So they parted, very sadly, very tenderly, and laden with good gifts Christie went on her way weary, but well satisfied, for she had earned her rest.

VI

SEAMSTRESS

FOR some weeks Christie rested and refreshed herself by making her room gay and comfortable with the gifts lavished on her by the Carrols, and by sharing with others the money which Harry had smuggled into her possession after she had steadily refused to take one penny more than the sum agreed upon when she first went to them.

She took infinite satisfaction in sending one hundred dollars to Uncle Enos, for she had accepted what he gave her as a loan, and set her heart on repaying every fraction of it. Another hundred she gave to Hepsey, who found her out and came to report her trials and tribulations. The good soul had ventured South and tried to buy her mother. But "ole missis" would not let her go at any price, and the faithful chattel would not run away. Sorely disappointed, Hepsey had been obliged to submit; but her trip was not a failure, for she liberated several brothers and sent them triumphantly to Canada.

"You *must* take it, Hepsey, for I could not rest happy if I put it away to lie idle while you can save men and women from torment with it. I'd give it if it was my last penny, for I can help in no other way; and if I need money, I can always earn it, thank God!" said Christie, as Hepsey hesitated to take so much from a fellow-worker.

The thought of that investment lay warm at Christie's heart, and never woke a regret, for well she knew that every dollar of it would be blessed, since shares in the Underground Railroad pay splendid dividends that never fail.

Another portion of her fortune, as she called Harry's gift, was bestowed in wedding presents upon Lucy, who at length succeeded in winning the heart of the owner of the "heavenly eyes" and "distracting legs;" and, having gained her point, married him with dramatic celerity, and went West to follow the fortunes of her lord.

The old theatre was to be demolished and the company scattered, so a farewell festival was held, and Christie went to it, feeling more solitary than ever as she bade her old friends a long good-bye.

The rest of the money burned in her pocket, but she prudently put it by for a rainy day, and fell to work again when her brief vacation was over.

Hearing of a chance for a good needle-woman in a large and well-conducted mantua-making establishment, she secured it as a temporary thing, for she wanted to divert her mind from that last sad experience by entirely different employment and surroundings. She liked to return at night to her own little home, solitary and simple as it was, and felt a great repugnance to accept any place where she would be mixed up with family affairs again.

So day after day she went to her seat in the workroom where a dozen other young women sat sewing busily on gay garments, with as much lively gossip to beguile the time as Miss Cotton, the forewoman, would allow.

For a while it diverted Christie, as she had a feminine love for pretty things, and enjoyed seeing delicate silks, costly lace, and all the indescribable fantasies of fashion. But as spring came on, the old desire for something fresh and free began to haunt her, and she had both waking and sleeping dreams of a home in the country somewhere, with cows and flowers, clothes bleaching on green grass, bob-o'-links making rapturous music by the river, and the smell of new-mown hay, all lending their charms to the picture she painted for herself.

Most assuredly she would have gone to find these things, led by the instincts of a healthful nature, had not one slender tie held her till it grew into a bond so strong she could not break it.

Among her companions was one, and one only, who attracted her. The others were well-meaning girls, but full of the frivolous purposes and pleasures which their tastes prompted and their dull life fostered. Dress, gossip, and wages were the three topics which absorbed them. Christie soon tired of the innumerable changes rung upon these themes, and took refuge in her own thoughts, soon learning to enjoy them undisturbed by the clack of many tongues about her. Her evenings at home were devoted to books, for she had the true New England woman's desire for education, and read or studied for the love of it. Thus she had much to think of as her needle flew, and was rapidly becoming a sort of sewing-machine when life was brightened for her by the finding of a friend.

Among the girls was one quiet, skilful creature whose black dress, peculiar face, and silent ways attracted Christie. Her evident desire to be let alone amused the new comer at first, and she made no effort to know her. But presently she became aware that Rachel watched her with covert interest, stealing quick, shy glances at her as she sat musing over her work. Christie smiled at her when she caught these glances, as if to reassure the looker of her good-will. But Rachel only colored, kept her eyes fixed on her work, and was more reserved than ever.

This interested Christie, and she fell to studying this young woman with some curiosity, for she was different from the others. Though evidently younger than she looked, Rachel's face was that of one who had known some great sorrow, some deep experience; for there were lines on the forehead that contrasted strongly with the bright, abundant hair above it; in repose, the youthfully red, soft lips had a mournful droop, and the eyes were old with that indescribable expression which comes to those who count their lives by emotions, not by years.

Strangely haunting eyes to Christie, for they seemed to appeal to her with a mute eloquence she could not resist. In vain did Rachel answer her with quiet coldness, nod silently when she wished her a cheery "good morning," keep resolutely in her own somewhat isolated corner, though invited to share the sunny window where the other sat. Her eyes belied her words, and those fugitive glances betrayed the longing of a lonely heart that dared not yield itself to the genial companionship so freely offered it.

Christie was sure of this, and would not be repulsed; for her own heart was very solitary. She missed Helen, and longed to fill the empty place. She wooed this shy, cold girl as patiently and as gently as a lover might, determined to win her confidence, because all the others had failed to do it. Sometimes she left a flower in Rachel's basket, always smiled and nodded as she entered, and often stopped to admire the work of her tasteful fingers. It was impossible to resist such friendly overtures, and slowly Rachel's coldness melted; into the beseeching eyes came a look of gratitude, the more touching for its wordlessness, and an irrepressible smile broke over her face in answer to the cordial ones that made the sunshine of her day.

Emboldened by these demonstrations, Christie changed her seat, and quietly established between them a daily interchange of something beside needles, pins, and spools. Then, as Rachel did not draw back offended, she went a step farther, and, one day when they chanced to be left alone to finish off a delicate bit of work, she spoke out frankly:

"Why can't we be friends? I want one sadly, and so do you, unless your looks deceive me. We both seem to be alone in the world, to have had trouble, and to like one another. I won't annoy you by any impertinent curiosity, nor burden you with uninteresting confidences; I only want to feel that you like me a little and don't mind my liking you a great deal. Will you be my friend, and let me be yours?"

A great tear rolled down upon the shining silk in Rachel's hands as she looked into Christie's earnest face, and answered with an almost passionate gratitude in her own:

"You can never need a friend as much as I do, or know what a blessed thing it is to find such an one as you are."

"Then I may love you, and not be afraid of offending?" cried Christie, much touched.

"Yes. But remember *I* didn't ask it first," said Rachel, half dropping the hand she had held in both her own.

"You proud creature! I'll remember; and when we quarrel, I'll take all the blame upon myself."

Then Christie kissed her warmly, whisked away the tear, and began to paint the delights in store for them in her most enthusiastic way, being much elated with her victory; while Rachel listened with a newly kindled light in her lovely eyes, and a smile that showed how winsome her face had been before many tears washed its bloom away, and much trouble made it old too soon.

Christie kept her word,—asked no questions, volunteered no confidences, but heartily enjoyed the new friendship, and found that it gave to life the zest which it had lacked before. Now some one cared for her, and, better still, she could make some one happy, and in the act of lavishing the affection of her generous nature on a creature sadder and more solitary than herself, she found a satisfaction that never lost its charm. There was nothing in her possession that she did not offer Rachel, from the whole of her heart to the larger half of her little room.

"I'm tired of thinking only of myself. It makes me selfish and low-spirited; for I'm not a bit interesting. I must love somebody, and 'love them hard,' as children say; so why can't you come and stay with me? There's room enough, and we could be so cosy evenings with our books and work. I know you need some one to look after you, and I love dearly to take care of people. Do come," she would say, with most persuasive hospitality.

But Rachel always answered steadily: "Not yet, Christie, not yet. I've got something to do before I can think of doing any thing so beautiful as that. Only love me, dear, and some day I'll show you all my heart, and thank you as I ought."

So Christie was content to wait, and, meantime, enjoyed much; for, with Rachel as a friend, she ceased to care for country pleasures, found happiness in the work that gave her better food than mere daily bread, and never thought of change; for love can make a home for itself anywhere.

A very bright and happy time was this in Christie's life; but, like most happy times, it was very brief. Only one summer allowed for the blossoming of the friendship that budded so slowly in the spring; then the frost came and killed the flowers; but the root lived long underneath the snows of suffering, doubt, and absence.

Coming to her work late one morning, she found the usually orderly room in confusion. Some of the girls were crying; some whispering to-gether,—all looking excited and dismayed. Mrs. King sat majestically at her table, with an ominous frown upon her face. Miss Cotton stood beside her, looking unusually sour and stern, for the ancient virgin's temper was not of the best. Alone, before them all, with her face hidden in her hands, and despair in every line of her drooping figure, stood Rachel,—a meek culprit at the stern bar of justice, where women try a sister woman.

"What's the matter?" cried Christie, pausing on the threshold.

Rachel shivered, as if the sound of that familiar voice was a fresh wound, but she did not lift her head; and Mrs. King answered, with a nervous emphasis that made the bugles of her head-dress rattle dismally:

"A very sad thing, Miss Devon,—*very* sad, indeed; a thing which *never* occurred in my establishment before, and *never* shall again. It appears that Rachel, whom we all considered a most respectable and worthy girl, has been quite the reverse. I shudder to think what the consequences of my taking her without a character (a thing I never do, and was only tempted by her superior taste as a trimmer) might have been if Miss Cotton, having suspicions, had not made strict inquiry and confirmed them."

"That was a kind and generous act, and Miss Cotton must feel proud of it," said Christie, with an indignant recollection of Mr. Fletcher's "cautious inquiries" about herself.

"It was perfectly right and proper, Miss Devon; and I thank her for her care of my interests." And Mrs. King bowed her acknowledgment of the service with a perfect castanet accompaniment, whereat Miss Cotton bridled with malicious complacency.

"Mrs. King, are you sure of this?" said Christie. "Miss Cotton does not like Rachel because her work is so much praised. May not her jealousy make her unjust, or her zeal for you mislead her?"

"I thank you for your polite insinuations, miss," returned the irate forewoman. "*I* never make mistakes; but you will find that *you* have made a very great one in choosing Rachel for your bosom friend instead of some one who would be a credit to you. Ask the creature herself if all I've said of her isn't true. She can't deny it."

With the same indefinable misgiving which had held her aloof, Christie turned to Rachel, lifted up the hidden face with gentle force, and looked into it imploringly, as she whispered, "Is it true?"

The woful countenance she saw made any other answer needless. Involuntarily her hands fell away, and she hid her own face, uttering the one reproach, which, tender and tearful though it was, seemed harder to be borne than the stern condemnation gone before.

"Oh, Rachel, I so loved and trusted you!"

The grief, affection, and regret that trembled in her voice roused Rachel from her state of passive endurance and gave her courage to plead for herself. But it was Christie whom she addressed, Christie whose pardon she implored, Christie's sorrowful reproach that she most keenly felt.

"Yes, it *is* true," she said, looking only at the woman who had been the first to befriend and now was the last to desert her. "It is true that I once went astray, but God knows I have repented; that for years I've tried to be an honest girl again, and that but for His help I should be a far sadder creature than I am this day. Christie, you can never know how bitter hard it is to outlive a sin like mine, and struggle up again from such a fall. It clings to me; it won't be shaken off or buried out of sight. No sooner do I find a safe place like this, and try to forget the past, than some one reads my secret in my face and hunts me down. It seems very cruel, very hard, yet it is my punishment, so I try to bear it, and begin again. What hurts me now more than all the rest, what breaks my heart, is that I deceived *you*. I never meant to do it. I did not seek you, did I? I tried to be cold and stiff; never asked for love, though starving for it, till you came to me, so kind, so generous, so dear,—how could I help it? Oh, how could I help it then?"

Christie had watched Rachel while she spoke, and spoke to her alone; her heart yearned toward this one friend, for she still loved her, and, loving, she believed in her.

"I don't reproach you, dear: I don't despise or desert you, and though I'm grieved and disappointed, I'll stand by you still, because you need me more than ever now, and I want to prove that I am a true friend. Mrs. King, please forgive and let poor Rachel stay here, safe among us."

"Miss Devon, I'm surprised at you! By no means; it would be the ruin of my establishment; not a girl would remain, and the character of my rooms would be lost for ever," replied Mrs. King, goaded on by the relentless Cotton.

"But where will she go if you send her away? Who will employ her if you inform against her? What stranger will believe in her if we, who have known her so long, fail to befriend her now? Mrs. King, think of your own daughters, and be a mother to this poor girl for their sake."

That last stroke touched the woman's heart; her cold eye softened, her hard mouth relaxed, and pity was about to win the day, when prudence, in the shape of Miss Cotton, turned the scale, for that spiteful spinster suddenly cried out, in a burst of righteous wrath:

"If that hussy stays, *I* leave this establishment for ever!" and followed up the blow by putting on her bonnet with a flourish.

At this spectacle, self-interest got the better of sympathy in Mrs.

King's worldly mind. To lose Cotton was to lose her right hand, and charity at that price was too expensive a luxury to be indulged in; so she hardened her heart, composed her features, and said, impressively:

"Take off your bonnet, Cotton; I have no intention of offending you, or any one else, by such a step. I forgive you, Rachel, and I pity you; but I can't think of allowing you to stay. There are proper institutions for such as you, and I advise you to go to one and repent. You were paid Saturday night, so nothing prevents your leaving at once. Time is money here, and we are wasting it. Young ladies, take your seats."

All but Christie obeyed, yet no one touched a needle, and Mrs. King sat, hurriedly stabbing pins into the fat cushion on her breast, as if testing the hardness of her heart.

Rachel's eyes went round the room; saw pity, aversion, or contempt, on every face, but met no answering glance, for even Christie's eyes were bent thoughtfully on the ground, and Christie's heart seemed closed against her. As she looked her whole manner changed; her tears ceased to fall, her face grew hard, and a reckless mood seemed to take possession of her, as if finding herself deserted by womankind, she would desert her own womanhood.

"I might have known it would be so," she said abruptly, with a bitter smile, sadder to see than her most hopeless tears. "It's no use for such as me to try; better go back to the old life, for there are kinder hearts among the sinners than among the saints, and no one can live without a bit of love. Your Magdalen Asylums are penitentiaries, not homes; I won't go to any of them. Your piety isn't worth much, for though you read in your Bible how the Lord treated a poor soul like me, yet when I stretch out my hand to you for help, not one of all you virtuous, Christian women dare take it and keep me from a life that's worse than hell."

As she spoke Rachel flung out her hand with a half-defiant gesture, and Christie took it. That touch, full of womanly compassion, seemed to exorcise the desperate spirit that possessed the poor girl in her despair, for, with a stifled exclamation, she sunk down at Christie's feet, and lay there weeping in all the passionate abandonment of love and gratitude, remorse and shame. Never had human voice sounded so heavenly sweet to her as that which broke the silence of the room, as this one friend said, with the earnestness of a true and tender heart:

"Mrs. King, if you send her away, I must take her in; for if she does go back to the old life, the sin of it will lie at our door, and God will remember it against us in the end. Some one must trust her, help her, love her, and so save her, as nothing else will. Perhaps I can do this better than you,—at least, I'll try; for even if I risk the loss of my good name, I could bear that better than the thoughts that Rachel had lost the work of these hard years for want of upholding now. She shall come home with me; no one there need know of this discovery, and I will take any work to her that you will give me, to keep her from want and its temptations. Will you do this, and let me sew for less, if I can pay you for the kindness in no other way?"

Poor Mrs. King was "much tumbled up and down in her own mind;" she longed to consent, but Cotton's eye was upon her, and Cotton's departure would be an irreparable loss, so she decided to end the matter in the most summary manner. Plunging a particularly large pin into her cushioned breast, as if it was a relief to inflict that mock torture upon herself, she said sharply:

"It is impossible. You can do as you please, Miss Devon, but I prefer to wash my hands of the affair at once and entirely."

Christie's eye went from the figure at her feet to the hard-featured woman who had been a kind and just mistress until now, and she asked, anxiously:

"Do you mean that you wash your hands of me also, if I stand by Rachel?"

"I do. I'm very sorry, but my young ladies *must* keep respectable company, or leave my service," was the brief reply, for Mrs. King grew grimmer externally as the mental rebellion increased internally.

"Then I *will* leave it!" cried Christie, with an indignant voice and eye. "Come, dear, we'll go together." And without a look or word for any in the room, she raised the prostrate girl, and led her out into the little hall.

There she essayed to comfort her, but before many words had passed her lips Rachel looked up, and she was silent with surprise, for the face she saw was neither despairing nor defiant, but beautifully sweet and clear, as the unfallen spirit of the woman shone through the grateful eyes, and blessed her for her loyalty.

"Christie, you have done enough for me," she said. "Go back, and keep the good place you need, for such are hard to find. I can get on alone; I'm used to this, and the pain will soon be over."

"I'll not go back!" cried Christie, hotly. "I'll do slop-work and starve, before I'll stay with such a narrow-minded, cold-hearted woman. Come home with me at once, and let us lay our plans together."

"No, dear; if I wouldn't go when you first asked me, much less will I go now, for I've done you harm enough already. I never can thank you for your great goodness to me, never tell you what it has been to me. We must part now; but some day I'll come back and show you that I've not forgotten how you loved and helped and trusted me, when all the others cast me off."

Vain were Christie's arguments and appeals. Rachel was immovable, and all her friend could win from her was a promise to send word, now and then, how things prospered with her.

"And, Rachel, I charge you to come to me in any strait, no matter what it is, no matter where I am; for if any thing could break my heart, it would be to know that you had gone back to the old life, because there was no one to help and hold you up."

"I *never* can go back; you have saved me, Christie, for you love me, you have faith in me, and that will keep me strong and safe when you are gone. Oh, my dear, my dear, God bless you for ever and for ever!"

Then Christie, remembering only that they were two loving women, alone in a world of sin and sorrow, took Rachel in her arms, kissed and cried over her with sisterly affection, and watched her prayerfully, as she went away to begin her hard task anew, with nothing but the touch of innocent lips upon her cheek, the baptism of tender tears upon her forehead to keep her from despair.

Still cherishing the hope that Rachel would come back to her, Christie neither returned to Mrs. King nor sought another place of any sort, but took home work from a larger establishment, and sat sewing diligently in her little room, waiting, hoping, longing for her friend. But month after month went by, and no word, no sign came to comfort her. She would not doubt, yet she could not help fearing, and in her nightly prayer no petition was more fervently made than that which asked the Father of both saint and sinner to keep poor Rachel safe, and bring her back in his good time.

Never had she been so lonely as now, for Christie had a social heart, and, having known the joy of a cordial friendship even for a little while, life seemed very barren to her when she lost it. No new friend took Rachel's place, for none came to her, and a feeling of loyalty kept her from seeking one. But she suffered for the want of genial society, for all the tenderness of her nature seemed to have been roused by that brief but most sincere affection. Her hungry heart clamored for the happiness that was its right, and grew very heavy as she watched friends or lovers walking in the summer twilight when she took her evening stroll. Often her eyes followed some humble pair, longing to bless and to be blessed by the divine passion whose magic beautifies the little milliner and her lad with the same tender grace as the poet and the mistress whom he makes immortal in a song. But neither friend nor lover came to Christie, and she said to herself, with a sad sort of courage:

"I shall be solitary all my life, perhaps; so the sooner I make up my mind to it, the easier it will be to bear."

At Christmas-tide she made a little festival for herself, by giving to each of the household drudges the most generous gift she could afford, for no one else thought of them, and having known some of the hardships of servitude herself, she had much sympathy with those in like case.

Then, with the pleasant recollection of two plain faces, brightened by gratitude, surprise, and joy, she went out into the busy streets to forget the solitude she left behind her.

Very gay they were with snow and sleigh-bells, holly-boughs, and garlands, below, and Christmas sunshine in the winter sky above. All faces shone, all voices had a cheery ring, and everybody stepped briskly on errands of good-will. Up and down went Christie, making herself happy in the happiness of others. Looking in at the shop-windows, she watched, with interest, the purchases of busy parents, calculating how best to fill the little socks hung up at home, with a childish faith that never must be disappointed, no matter how hard the times might be. She was glad to see so many turkeys on their way to garnish hospitable tables, and hoped that all the dear home circles might be found unbroken, though she had place in none. No Christmas-tree went by leaving a whiff of piny sweetness behind, that she did not wish it all success, and picture to herself the merry little people dancing in its light. And whenever she saw a ragged child eying a window full of goodies, smiling even while it shivered, she could not resist playing Santa Claus till her purse was empty, sending the poor little souls enraptured home with oranges and apples in either hand, and splendid sweeties in their pockets, for the babies.

No envy mingled with the melancholy that would not be dispelled even by these gentle acts, for her heart was very tender that night, and if any one had asked what gifts she desired most, she would have answered with a look more pathetic than any shivering child had given her:

"I want the sound of a loving voice; the touch of a friendly hand."

Going home, at last, to the lonely little room where no Christmas fire burned, no tree shone, no household group awaited her, she climbed the long, dark stairs, with drops on her cheeks, warmer than any melted snowflake could have left, and opening her door paused on the threshold, smiling with wonder and delight, for in her absence some gentle spirit *had* remembered her. A fire burned cheerily upon the hearth, her lamp was lighted, a lovely rose-tree, in full bloom, filled the air with its delicate breath, and in its shadow lay a note from Rachel.

"A merry Christmas and a happy New Year, Christie! Long ago you gave me your little rose; I have watched and tended it for your sake, dear, and now when I want to show my love and thankfulness, I give it back again as my one treasure. I crept in while you were gone, because I feared I might harm you in some way if you saw me. I longed to stay and tell you that I am safe and well, and busy, with your good face looking into mine, but I don't deserve that yet. Only love me, trust me, pray for me, and some day you shall know what you have done for me. Till then, God bless and keep you, dearest friend, your   RACHEL."

Never had sweeter tears fallen than those that dropped upon the little tree as Christie took it in her arms, and all the rosy clusters leaned toward her as if eager to deliver tender messages. Surely her wish was granted now, for friendly hands had been at work for her. Warm against her heart lay words as precious as if uttered by a loving voice, and nowhere, on that happy night, stood a fairer Christmas tree than that which bloomed so beautifully from the heart of a Magdalen who loved much and was forgiven. . . .

XX

AT FORTY

"*NEARLY* twenty years since I set out to seek my fortune. It has been a long search, but I think I have found it at last. I only asked to be a useful, happy woman, and my wish is granted: for, I believe I *am* useful; I *know* I am happy."

Christie looked so as she sat alone in the flowery parlor one September afternoon, thinking over her life with a grateful cheerful spirit. Forty to-day, and pausing at that half-way house between youth and age, she looked back into the past without bitter regret or unsubmissive grief, and forward into the future with courageous patience; for three good angels attended her, and with faith, hope, and charity to brighten life, no woman need lament lost youth or fear approaching age. Christie did not, and though her eyes filled with quiet tears as they were raised to the faded cap and sheathed sword hanging on the wall, none fell; and in a moment tender sorrow changed to still tenderer joy as her glance wandered to rosy little Ruth playing hospital with her dollies in the porch. Then they shone with genuine satisfaction as they went from the letters and papers on her table to the garden, where several young women were at work with a healthful color in the cheeks that had been very pale and thin in the spring.

"I think David is satisfied with me; for I have given all my heart and strength to his work, and it prospers well," she said to herself, and then her face grew thoughtful, as she recalled a late event which seemed to have opened a new field of labor for her if she chose to enter it.

Work: A Story of Experience

A few evenings before she had gone to one of the many meetings of working-women, which had made some stir of late. Not a first visit, for she was much interested in the subject and full of sympathy for this class of workers.

There were speeches of course, and of the most unparliamentary sort, for the meeting was composed almost entirely of women, each eager to tell her special grievance or theory. Any one who chose got up and spoke; and whether wisely or foolishly each proved how great was the ferment now going on, and how difficult it was for the two classes to meet and help one another in spite of the utmost need on one side and the sincerest good-will on the other. The workers poured out their wrongs and hardships passionately or plaintively, demanding or imploring justice, sympathy, and help; displaying the ignorance, incapacity, and prejudice, which make their need all the more pitiful, their relief all the more imperative.

The ladies did their part with kindliness, patience, and often uncon-scious condescension, showing in their turn how little they knew of the real trials of the women whom they longed to serve, how very narrow a sphere of usefulness they were fitted for in spite of culture and intelligence, and how rich they were in generous theories, how poor in practical methods of relief.

One accomplished creature with learning radiating from every pore, delivered a charming little essay on the strong-minded women of antiq-uity; then, taking labor into the region of art, painted delightful pictures of the time when all would work harmoniously together in an Ideal Republic, where each did the task she liked, and was paid for it in liberty, equality, and fraternity.

Unfortunately she talked over the heads of her audience, and it was like telling fairy tales to hungry children to describe Aspasia discussing Greek politics with Pericles and Plato reposing upon ivory couches, or Hypatia modestly delivering philosophical lectures to young men behind a Tyrian purple curtain;[14] and the Ideal Republic met with little favor from anxious seamstresses, type-setters, and shop-girls, who said ungratefully among themselves, "That's all very pretty, but I don't see how it's going to better wages among us *now*."

Another eloquent sister gave them a political oration which fired the

337

revolutionary blood in their veins, and made them eager to rush to the State-house *en masse,* and demand the ballot before one-half of them were quite clear what it meant, and the other half were as unfit for it as any ignorant Patrick bribed with a dollar and a sup of whiskey.

A third well-wisher quenched their ardor like a wet blanket, by reading reports of sundry labor reforms in foreign parts; most interesting, but made entirely futile by differences of climate, needs, and customs. She closed with a cheerful budget of statistics, giving the exact number of needle-women who had starved, gone mad, or committed suicide during the past year; the enormous profits wrung by capitalists from the blood and muscles of their employés; and the alarming increase in the cost of living, which was about to plunge the nation into debt and famine, if not destruction generally.

When she sat down despair was visible on many countenances, and immediate starvation seemed to be waiting at the door to clutch them as they went out; for the impressible creatures believed every word and saw no salvation anywhere.

Christie had listened intently to all this; had admired, regretted, or condemned as each spoke; and felt a steadily increasing sympathy for all, and a strong desire to bring the helpers and the helped into truer relations with each other.

The dear ladies were so earnest, so hopeful, and so unpractically benevolent, that it grieved her to see so much breath wasted, so much good-will astray; while the expectant, despondent, or excited faces of the work-women touched her heart; for well she knew how much they needed help, how eager they were for light, how ready to be led if some one would only show a possible way.

As the statistical extinguisher retired, beaming with satisfaction at having added her mite to the good cause, a sudden and uncontrollable impulse moved Christie to rise in her place and ask leave to speak. It was readily granted, and a little stir of interest greeted her; for she was known to many as Mr. Power's friend, David Sterling's wife, or an army nurse who had done well. Whispers circulated quickly, and faces brightened as they turned toward her; for she had a helpful look, and her first words pleased them. When the president invited her to the platform she paused on the lowest step, saying with an expressive look and gesture:

"I am better here, thank you; for I have been and mean to be a working-woman all my life."

"Hear! hear!" cried a stout matron in a gay bonnet, and the rest indorsed the sentiment with a hearty round. Then they were very still, and then in a clear, steady voice, with the sympathetic undertone to it that is so magical in its effect, Christie made her first speech in public since she left the stage.

That early training stood her in good stead now, giving her self-possession, power of voice, and ease of gesture; while the purpose at her heart lent her the sort of simple eloquence that touches, persuades, and convinces better than logic, flattery, or oratory.

What she said she hardly knew: words came faster than she could utter them, thoughts pressed upon her, and all the lessons of her life rose vividly before her to give weight to her arguments, value to her counsel, and the force of truth to every sentence she uttered. She had known so many of the same trials, troubles, and temptations that she could speak understandingly of them; and, better still, she had conquered or outlived so many of them, that she could not only pity but help others to do as she had done. Having found in labor her best teacher, comforter, and friend, she could tell those who listened that, no matter how hard or humble the task at the beginning, if faithfully and bravely performed, it would surely prove a stepping-stone to something better, and with each honest effort they were fitting themselves for the nobler labor, and larger liberty God meant them to enjoy.

The women felt that this speaker was one of them; for the same lines were on her face that they saw on their own, her hands were no fine lady's hands, her dress plainer than some of theirs, her speech simple enough for all to understand; cheerful, comforting, and full of practical suggestion, illustrations out of their own experience, and a spirit of companionship that uplifted their despondent hearts.

Yet more impressive than any thing she said was the subtle magnetism of character, for that has a universal language which all can understand. They saw and felt that a genuine woman stood down there among them like a sister, ready with head, heart, and hand to help them help themselves; not offering pity as an alms, but justice as a right. Hardship and sorrow, long effort and late-won reward had been hers they knew;

wifehood, motherhood, and widowhood brought her very near to them; and behind her was the background of an earnest life, against which this figure with health on the cheeks, hope in the eyes, courage on the lips, and the ardor of a wide benevolence warming the whole countenance stood out full of unconscious dignity and beauty; an example to comfort, touch, and inspire them.

It was not a long speech, and in it there was no learning, no statistics, and no politics; yet it was the speech of the evening, and when it was over no one else seemed to have any thing to say. As the meeting broke up Christie's hand was shaken by many roughened by the needle, stained with printer's ink, or hard with humbler toil; many faces smiled gratefully at her, and many voices thanked her heartily. But sweeter than any applause were the words of one woman who grasped her hand, and whispered with wet eyes:

"I knew your blessed husband; he was very good to me, and I've been thanking the Lord he had such a wife for his reward!"

Christie was thinking of all this as she sat alone that day, and asking herself if she should go on; for the ladies had been as grateful as the women; had begged her to come and speak again, saying they needed just such a mediator to bridge across the space that now divided them from those they wished to serve. She certainly seemed fitted to act as interpreter between the two classes; for, from the gentleman her father she had inherited the fine instincts, gracious manners, and unblemished name of an old and honorable race; from the farmer's daughter, her mother, came the equally valuable dower of practical virtues, a sturdy love of independence, and great respect for the skill and courage that can win it.

Such women were much needed and are not always easy to find; for even in democratic America the hand that earns its daily bread must wear some talent, name, or honor as an ornament, before it is very cordially shaken by those that wear white gloves.

"Perhaps this is the task my life has been fitting me for," she said. "A great and noble one which I should be proud to accept and help accomplish if I can. Others have finished the emancipation work and done it splendidly, even at the cost of all this blood and sorrow. I came too late to do any thing but give my husband and behold the glorious end. This new task seems to offer me the chance of being among the pioneers, to do the hard work, share the persecution, and help lay the foundation of a new emancipation whose happy success I may never see. Yet I had rather be remembered as those brave beginners are, though many of them missed the triumph, than as the late comers will be, who only beat the drums and wave the banners when the victory is won."

Just then the gate creaked on its hinges, a step sounded in the porch, and little Ruth ran in to say in an audible whisper:

"It's a lady, mamma, a very pretty lady; can you see her?"

"Yes, dear, ask her in."

There was a rustle of sweeping silks through the narrow hall, a vision of a very lovely woman in the door-way, and two daintily gloved hands were extended as an eager voice asked: "Dearest Christie, don't you remember Bella Carrol?"

Christie did remember, and had her in her arms directly, utterly regardless of the imminent destruction of a marvellous hat, or the bad effect of tears on violet ribbons. Presently they were sitting close together, talking with April faces, and telling their stories as women must when they meet after the lapse of years. A few letters had passed between them, but Bella had been abroad, and Christie too busy living her life to have much time to write about it.

"Your mother, Bella? how is she, and where?"

"Still with Augustine, and he you know is melancholy mad; very quiet, very patient, and very kind to every one but himself. His penances for the sins of his race would soon kill him if mother was not there to watch over him. And her penance is never to leave him."

"Dear child, don't tell me any more; it is too sad. Talk of yourself and Harry. Now you smile, so I'm sure all is well with him."

"Yes, thank heaven! Christie, I do believe fate means to spare us as dear old Dr. Shirley said. I never can be gay again, but I keep as cheerful and busy as I can, for Harry's sake, and he does the same for mine. We shall always be together, and all in all to one another, for we can never marry and have homes apart you know. We have wandered over the face of the earth for several years, and now we mean to settle down and be as happy and as useful as we can."

"That's brave! I am so glad to hear it, and so truly thankful it is possible. But tell me, Bella, what Harry means to do? You spoke in one of your first letters of his being hard at work studying medicine. Is that to be his profession?"

"Yes; I don't know what made him choose it, unless it was the hope that he might spare other families from a curse like ours, or lighten it if it came. After Helen's death he was a changed creature; no longer a wild boy, but a man. I told him what you said to me, and it gave him hope. Dr. Shirley confirmed it as far as he dared; and Hal resolved to make the most of his one chance by interesting himself in some absorbing study, and leaving no room for fear, no time for dangerous recollections. I was so glad, and mother so comforted, for we both feared that sad trouble would destroy him. He studied hard, got on splendidly, and then went abroad to finish off. I went with him; for poor August was past hope, and mamma would not let me help her. The doctor said it was best for me to be away, and excellent for Hal to have me with him, to cheer him up, and keep him steady with a little responsibility. We have been happy together in spite of our trouble, he in his profession, and I in him; now he is ready, so we have come home, and now the hardest part begins for me."

"How, Bella?"

"He has his work and loves it: I have nothing after my duty to him is done. I find I've lost my taste for the old pleasures and pursuits, and though I have tried more sober, solid ones, there still remains much time to hang heavy on my hands, and such an empty place in my heart, that even Harry's love cannot fill it. I'm afraid I shall get melancholy,—that is the beginning of the end for us, you know."

As Bella spoke the light died out of her eyes, and they grew despairing with the gloom of a tragic memory. Christie drew the beautiful, pathetic face down upon her bosom, longing to comfort, yet feeling very powerless to lighten Bella's burden.

But Christie's little daughter did it for her. Ruth had been standing near regarding the "pretty lady," with as much wonder and admiration as if she thought her a fairy princess, who might vanish before she got a good look at her. Divining with a child's quick instinct that the princess was in trouble, Ruth flew into the porch, caught up her latest and dearest treasure, and presented it as a sure consolation, with such sweet good-will, that Bella could not refuse, although it was only a fuzzy caterpillar in a little box.

"I give it to you because it is my nicest one and just ready to spin up. Do you like pussy-pillars, and know how they do it?" asked Ruth, emboldened by the kiss she got in return for her offering.

"Tell me all about it, darling," and Bella could not help smiling, as the child fixed her great eyes upon her, and told her little story with such earnestness, that she was breathless by the time she ended.

"At first they are only grubs you know, and stay down in the earth; then they are like this, nice and downy and humpy, when they walk; and when it's time they spin up and go to sleep. It's all dark in their little beds, and they don't know what may happen to 'em; but they are not afraid 'cause God takes care of 'em. So they wait and don't fret, and when it's right for 'em they come out splendid butterflies, all beautiful and shining like your gown. They are happy then, and fly away to eat honey, and live in the air, and never be creeping worms any more."

"That's a pretty lesson for me," said Bella softly, "I accept and thank you for it, little teacher; I'll try to be a patient 'pussy-pillar' though it *is* dark, and I don't know what may happen to me; and I'll wait hopefully till it's time to float away a happy butterfly."

"Go and get the friend some flowers, the gayest and sweetest you can find, Pansy," said Christie, and, as the child ran off, she added to her friend:

"Now we must think of something pleasant for you to do. It may take a little time, but I know we shall find your niche if we give our minds to it."

"That's one reason why I came. I heard some friends of mine talking about you yesterday, and they seemed to think you were equal to any thing in the way of good works. Charity is the usual refuge for people like me, so I wish to try it. I don't mind doing or seeing sad or disagreeable things, if it only fills up my life and helps me to forget."

"You will help more by giving of your abundance to those who know how to dispense it wisely, than by trying to do it yourself, my dear. I never advise pretty creatures like you to tuck up their silk gowns and go down into the sloughs with alms for the poor, who don't like it any better than you do, and so much pity and money are wasted in sentimental charity."

"Then what shall I do?"

"If you choose you can find plenty of work in your own class; for, if you will allow me to say it, they need help quite as much as the paupers, though in a very different way."

"Oh, you mean I'm to be strong-minded, to cry aloud and spare not, to denounce their iniquities, and demand their money or their lives?"

"Now, Bella, that's personal; for I made my first speech a night or two ago."

"I know you did, and I wish I'd heard it. I'd make mine to-night if I could do it half as well as I'm told you did," interrupted Bella, clapping her hands with a face full of approval.

But Christie was in earnest, and produced her new project with all speed.

"I want you to try a little experiment for me, and if it succeeds you shall have all the glory; I've been waiting for some one to undertake it, and I fancy you are the woman. Not every one could attempt it; for it needs wealth and position, beauty and accomplishments, much tact, and more than all a heart that has not been spoilt by the world, but taught through sorrow how to value and use life well."

"Christie, what is it? this experiment that needs so much, and yet which you think me capable of trying?" asked Bella, interested and flattered by this opening.

"I want you to set a new fashion: you know you can set almost any you choose in your own circle; for people are very like sheep, and will follow their leader if it happens to be one they fancy. I don't ask you to be a De Staël, and have a brilliant *salon*.[15] I only want you to provide employment and pleasure for others like yourself, who are now dying of frivolity or *ennui*."

"I should love to do that if I could. Tell me how."

"Well, dear, I want you to make Harry's home as beautiful and attractive as you can; to keep all the elegance and refinement of former times, and to add to it a new charm by setting the fashion of common sense. Invite all the old friends, and as many new ones as you choose; but have it understood that they are to come as intelligent men and women, not as pleasure-hunting beaux and belles; give them conversation instead of gossip; less food for the body and more for the mind; the healthy stimulus of the nobler pleasures they can command, instead of the harmful excitements of present dissipation. In short, show them the sort of society we need more of, and might so easily have if those who possess the means of culture cared for the best sort, and took pride in acquiring it. Do you understand, Bella?"

"Yes, but it's a great undertaking, and you could do it better than I."

"Bless you, no! I haven't a single qualification for it but the will to have it done. I'm 'strong-minded,' a radical, and a reformer. I've done all sorts of dreadful things to get my living, and I have neither youth, beauty, talent, or position to back me up; so I should only be politely ignored if I tried the experiment myself. I don't want you to break out and announce your purpose with a flourish; or try to reform society at large, but I *do* want you to devote yourself and your advantages to quietly insinuating a better state of things into one little circle. The very fact of your own want, your own weariness, proves how much such a reform is needed. There are so many fine young women longing for something to fill up the empty places that come when the first flush of youth is over, and the serious side of life appears; so many promising young men learning to conceal or condemn the high ideals and the noble purposes they started with, because they find no welcome for them. You might help both by simply creating a purer atmosphere for them to breathe, sunshine to foster instead of frost to nip their good aspirations, and so, even if you planted no seed, you might encourage a timid sprout or two that would one day be a lovely flower or a grand tree all would admire and enjoy."

As Christie ended with the figure suggested by her favorite work, Bella said after a thoughtful pause:

"But few of the women I know can talk about any thing but servants, dress, and gossip. Here and there one knows something of music, art, or literature; but the superior ones are not favorites with the larger class of gentlemen."

"Then let the superior women cultivate the smaller class of men who do admire intelligence as well as beauty. There are plenty of them, and you had better introduce a few as samples, though their coats may not be of the finest broadcloth, nor their fathers 'solid men.' Women lead in society, and when men find that they can not only dress with taste, but talk with sense, the lords of creation will be glad to drop mere twaddle and converse as with their equals. Bless my heart!" cried Christie, walking about the room as if she had mounted her hobby, and was off for a canter, "how people can go on in such an idiotic fashion passes my understanding. Why keep up an endless clatter about gowns and dinners, your neighbors' affairs, and your own aches, when there is a world full of grand questions to settle, lovely things to see, wise things to study, and noble things to imitate. Bella, you *must* try the experiment, and be the queen of a better society than any you can reign over now."

"It looks inviting, and I *will* try it with you to help me. I know Harry would like it, and I'll get him to recommend it to his patients. If he is as successful here as elsewhere they will swallow any dose he orders; for he knows how to manage people wonderfully well. He prescribed a silk dress to a despondent, dowdy patient once, telling her the electricity of silk was good for her nerves: she obeyed, and when well dressed felt so much better that she bestirred herself generally and recovered; but to this day she sings the praises of Dr. Carrol's electric cure."

Bella was laughing gaily as she spoke, and so was Christie as she replied:

"That's just what I want you to do with *your* patients. Dress up their minds in their best; get them out into the air; and cure their ills by the magnetism of more active, earnest lives."

They talked over the new plan with increasing interest; for Christie did not mean that Bella should be one of the brilliant women who shine for a little while, and then go out like a firework. And Bella felt as if she had found something to do in her own sphere, a sort of charity she was fitted for, and with it a pleasant sense of power to give it zest.

When Letty and her mother came in, they found a much happier looking guest than the one Christie had welcomed an hour before. Scarcely had she introduced them when voices in the lane made all look up to see old Hepsey and Mrs. Wilkins approaching.

"Two more of my dear friends, Bella: a fugitive slave and a laundress. One has saved scores of her own people, and is my pet heroine. The other has the bravest, cheeriest soul I know, and is my private oracle."

The words were hardly out of Christie's mouth when in they came;

Hepsey's black face shining with affection, and Mrs. Wilkins as usual running over with kind words.

"My dear creeter, the best of wishes and no end of happy birthdays. There's a triflin' keepsake; tuck it away, and look at it byme by. Mis' Sterlin', I'm proper glad to see you lookin' so well. Aunt Letty, how's that darlin' child? I ain't the pleasure of your acquaintance, Miss, but I'm pleased to see you. The children all sent love, likewise Lisha, whose bones is better sense I tried the camfire and red flannel."

Then they settled down like a flock of birds of various plumage and power of song, but all amicably disposed, and ready to peck socially at any topic which might turn up.

Mrs. Wilkins started one by exclaiming as she "laid off" her bonnet: "Sakes alive, there's a new picter! Ain't it beautiful?"

"Colonel Fletcher brought it this morning. A great artist painted it for him, and he gave it to me in a way that added much to its value," answered Christie, with both gratitude and affection in her face; for she was a woman who could change a lover to a friend, and keep him all her life.

It was a quaint and lovely picture of Mr. Greatheart, leading the fugitives from the City of Destruction. A dark wood lay behind; a wide river rolled before; Mercy and Christiana pressed close to their faithful guide, who went down the rough and narrow path bearing a cross-hilted sword in his right hand, and holding a sleeping baby with the left. The sun was just rising, and a long ray made a bright path athwart the river, turned Greatheart's dinted armor to gold, and shone into the brave and tender face that seemed to look beyond the sunrise.[16]

"There's just a hint of Davy in it that is very comforting to me," said Mrs. Sterling, as she laid her old hands softly together, and looked up with her devout eyes full of love.

"Dem women oughter bin black," murmured Hepsey, tearfully; for she considered David worthy of a place with old John Brown and Colonel Shaw.[17]

"The child looks like Pansy, we all think," added Letty, as the little girl brought her nosegay for Aunty to tie up prettily.

Christie said nothing, because she felt too much; and Bella was also silent because she knew too little. But Mrs. Wilkins with her kindly tact changed the subject before it grew painful, and asked with sudden interest:

"When be you a goin' to hold forth agin, Christie? Jest let me know before hand, and I'll wear my old gloves: I tore my best ones all to rags clappin' of you; it was so extra good."

"I don't deserve any credit for the speech, because it spoke itself, and I couldn't help it. I had no thought of such a thing till it came over me all at once, and I was up before I knew it. I'm truly glad you liked it, but I shall never make another, unless you think I'd better. You know I always ask your advice, and what is more remarkable usually take it," said Christie, glad to consult her oracle.

"Hadn't you better rest a little before you begin any new task, my daughter? You have done so much these last years you must be tired," interrupted Mrs. Sterling, with a look of tender anxiety.

"You know I work for two, mother," answered Christie, with the clear, sweet expression her face always wore when she spoke of David. "I am not tired yet: I hope I never shall be, for without my work I should fall into despair or *ennui*. There is so much to be done, and it is so delightful to help do it, that I never mean to fold my hands till they are useless. I owe all I can do, for in labor, and the efforts and experiences that grew out of it, I have found independence, education, happiness, and religion."

"Then, my dear, you are ready to help other folks into the same blessed state, and it's your duty to do it!" cried Mrs. Wilkins, her keen eyes full of sympathy and commendation as they rested on Christie's cheerful, earnest face. "Ef the sperrit moves you to speak, up and do it without no misgivin's. *I* think it was a special leadin' that night, and I hope you'll foller, for it ain't every one that can make folks laugh and cry with a few plain words that go right to a body's heart and stop there real comfortable and fillin'. I guess this is your next job, my dear, and you'd better ketch hold and give it the right turn; for it's goin' to take time, and women ain't stood alone for so long they'll need a sight of boostin'."

There was a general laugh at the close of Mrs. Wilkins's remarks; but Christie answered seriously: "I accept the task, and will do my share faithfully with words or work, as shall seem best. We all need much preparation for the good time that is coming to us, and can get it best by trying to know and help, love and educate one another,—as we do here."

With an impulsive gesture Christie stretched her hands to the friends about her, and with one accord they laid theirs on hers, a loving league of sisters, old and young, black and white, rich and poor, each ready to do her part to hasten the coming of the happy end.

"Me too!" cried little Ruth, and spread her chubby hand above the rest: a hopeful omen, seeming to promise that the coming generation of women will not only receive but deserve their liberty, by learning that the greatest of God's gifts to us is the privilege of sharing His great work.

HOW I WENT OUT TO SERVICE

WHEN I was eighteen I wanted something to do. I had tried teaching for two years, and hated it; I had tried sewing, and could not earn my bread in that way, at the cost of health; I tried story-writing and got five dollars for stories which now bring a hundred; I had thought seriously of going upon the stage, but certain highly respectable relatives were so shocked at the mere idea that I relinquished my dramatic aspirations.

"What *shall* I do?" was still the question that perplexed me. I was ready to work, eager to be independent, and too proud to endure patronage. But the right task seemed hard to find, and my bottled energies were fermenting in a way that threatened an explosion before long.

My honored mother was a city missionary that winter, and not only served the clamorous poor, but often found it in her power to help decayed gentlefolk by quietly placing them where they could earn their bread without the entire sacrifice of taste and talent which makes poverty so hard for such to bear. Knowing her tact and skill, people often came to her for companions, housekeepers, and that class of the needy who do not make their wants known through an intelligence office.

One day, as I sat dreaming splendid dreams, while I made a series of little petticoats out of the odds and ends sent in for the poor, a tall, ministerial gentleman appeared, in search of a companion for his sister. He possessed an impressive nose, a fine flow of language, and a pair of large hands, encased in black kid gloves. With much waving of these somber members, Mr. R. set forth the delights awaiting the happy soul who should secure this home. He described it as a sort of heaven on earth. "There are books, pictures, flowers, a piano, and the best of society," he said. "This person will be one of the family in all respects, and only required to help about the lighter work, which my sister has done herself hitherto, but is now a martyr to neuralgia and needs a gentle friend to assist her."

My mother, who never lost her faith in human nature, in spite of many impostures, believed every word, and quite beamed with benevolent interest as she listened and tried to recall some needy young woman to whom this charming home would be a blessing. I also innocently thought:

"That sounds inviting. I like housework and can do it well. I should have time to enjoy the books and things I love, and D——is not far away from home. Suppose I try it."

So, when my mother turned to me, asking if I could suggest any one, I became as red as a poppy and said abruptly:

"Only myself."

"Do you really mean it?" cried my astonished parent.

"I really do if Mr. R. thinks I should suit," was my steady reply, as I partially obscured my crimson countenance behind a little flannel skirt, still redder.

The Reverend Josephus gazed upon me with the benign regard which a bachelor of five and thirty may accord a bashful damsel of eighteen. A smile dawned upon his countenance, "sicklied o'er with the pale cast of thought," or dyspepsia; and he softly folded the black gloves, as if about to bestow a blessing as he replied, with emphasis:

"I am sure you would, and we should think ourselves most fortunate if we could secure your society, and——ahem——services for my poor sister."

"Then I'll try it," responded the impetuous maid.

"We will talk it over a little first, and let you know to-morrow, sir," put in my prudent parent, adding, as Mr. R. arose: "What wages do you pay?"

"My dear madam, in a case like this let me not use such words as those. Anything you may think proper we shall gladly give. The labor is very light, for there are but three of us and our habits are of the simplest sort. I am a frail reed and may break at any moment; so is my sister, and my aged father cannot long remain; therefore, money is little to us, and any one who comes to lend her youth and strength to our feeble household will not be forgotten in the end, I assure you." And, with another pensive smile, a farewell wave of the impressive gloves, the Reverend Josephus bowed like a well-sweep and departed.

"My dear, are you in earnest?" asked my mother.

"Of course, I am. Why not try this experiment? It can but fail, like all the others."

"I have no objection; only I fancied you were rather too proud for this sort of thing."

"I am too proud to be idle and dependent, ma'am. I'll scrub floors and take in washing first. I do housework at home for love; why not do it abroad for money? I like it better than teaching. It is healthier than sewing and surer than writing. So why not try it?"

"It is going out to service, you know, though you are called a companion. How does that suit?"

"I don't care. Every sort of work that is paid for is service; and I don't mind being a companion, if I can do it well. I may find it is my mission to take care of neuralgic old ladies and lackadaisical clergymen. It does not sound exciting, but it's better than nothing," I answered, with a sigh; for it *was* rather a sudden downfall to give up being a Siddons and become a Betcinder.[1]

How my sisters laughed when they heard the new plan! But they soon resigned themselves, sure of fun, for Lu's adventures were the standing joke of the family. Of course, the highly respectable relatives held up their hands in holy horror at the idea of one of the clan degrading herself by going out to service. Teaching a private school was the proper thing for an indigent gentlewoman. Sewing even, if done in the seclusion of home and not mentioned in public, could be tolerated. Story-writing was a genteel accomplishment and reflected credit upon the name. But leaving the paternal roof to wash other people's teacups, nurse other people's ails, and obey other people's orders for hire—this, this was degradation; and headstrong Louisa would disgrace her name forever if she did it.

Opposition only fired the revolutionary blood in my veins, and I crowned my iniquity by the rebellious declaration:

"If doing this work hurts my respectability, I wouldn't give much for it. My aristocratic ancestors don't feed or clothe me and my democratic ideas of honesty and honor won't let me be idle or dependent. You need not know me if you are ashamed of me, and I won't ask you for a penny; so, if I never do succeed in anything, I shall have the immense satisfaction of knowing I am under no obligation to any one."

In spite of the laughter and the lamentation, I got ready my small wardrobe, consisting of two calico dresses and one delaine, made by myself, also several large and uncompromising blue aprons and three tidy little sweeping-caps; for I had some English notions about housework and felt that my muslin hair-protectors would be useful in some of the "light labors" I was to undertake. It is needless to say they were very becoming. Then, firmly embracing my family, I set forth, one cold January day, with my little trunk, a stout heart, and a five-dollar bill for my fortune.

"She will be back in a week," was my sister's prophecy, as she wiped her weeping eye.

"No, she won't, for she has promised to stay the month out and she will keep her word," answered my mother, who always defended the black sheep of her flock.

I heard both speeches, and registered a tremendous vow to keep that promise, if I died in the attempt—little dreaming, poor innocent, what lay before me.

Josephus meantime had written me several remarkable letters, describing the different members of the family I was about to enter. His account was peculiar, but I believed every word of it and my romantic fancy was much excited by the details he gave. The principal ones are as follows, condensed from the voluminous epistles which he evidently enjoyed writing:

"You will find a stately mansion, fast falling to decay, for my father will have nothing repaired, preferring that the old house and its master should crumble away together. I have, however, been permitted to rescue a few rooms from ruin; and here I pass my recluse life, surrounded by the things I love. This will naturally be more attractive to you than the gloomy apartments my father inhabits, and I hope you will here allow me to minister to your young and cheerful nature when your daily cares are over. I need such companionship and shall always welcome you to my abode.

"Eliza, my sister, is a child at forty, for she has lived alone with my father and an old servant all her life. She is a good creature, but not lively, and needs stirring up, as you will soon see. Also I hope by your means to rescue her from the evil influence of Puah, who, in my estimation, is a *wretch*. She has gained entire control over Eliza, and warps her mind with great skill, prejudicing her against *me* and thereby desolating my home. Puah hates *me* and always has. Why I know not, except that I will not yield to her control. She ruled here for years while I was away, and my return upset all her nefarious plans. It will always be my firm opinion that she has tried to *poison me,* and may again. But even this dark suspicion will not deter me from my duty. I cannot send her away, for both my deluded father and my sister have entire faith in her, and I cannot shake it. She is faithful and kind to them, so I submit and remain to guard them, even at the risk of my life.

"I tell you these things because I wish you to know all and be warned, for this old hag has a specious tongue, and I should grieve to see you deceived by her lies. Say nothing, but watch her silently, and help me to thwart her evil plots; but do not trust her, or beware."

Now this was altogether romantic and sensational, and I felt as if about to enter one of those delightfully dangerous houses we read of in novels, where perils, mysteries, and sins freely disport themselves, till the newcomer sets all to rights, after unheard of trials and escapes.

I arrived at twilight, just the proper time for the heroine to appear; and, as no one answered my modest solo on the rusty knocker, I walked in and looked about me. Yes, here was the long, shadowy hall, where the ghosts doubtless walked at midnight. Peering in at an open door on the right, I saw a parlor full of ancient furniture, faded, dusty, and dilapidated. Old portraits stared at me from the walls and a damp child froze the marrow of my bones in the most approved style.

"The romance opens well," I thought, and, peeping in at an opposite door, beheld a luxurious apartment, full of the warm glow of firelight, the balmy breath of hyacinths and roses, the white glimmer of piano keys, and tempting rows of books along the walls.

The contrast between the two rooms was striking, and, after an admiring survey, I continued my explorations, thinking that I should not mind being "ministered to" in that inviting place when my work was done.

A third door showed me a plain, dull sitting room, with an old man napping in his easy-chair. I heard voices in the kitchen beyond, and, entering there, beheld Puah the fiend. Unfortunately, for the dramatic effect of the tableaux, all I saw was a mild-faced old woman, buttering toast, while she conversed with her familiar, a comfortable gray cat.

The old lady greeted me kindly, but I fancied her faded blue eye had a weird expression and her amiable words were all a snare, though I own I was rather disappointed at the commonplace appearance of this humble Borgia.

She showed me to a tiny room, where I felt more like a young giantess than ever, and was obliged to stow away my possessions as snugly as in a ship's cabin. When I presently descended, armed with a blue apron and "a heart for any fate," I found the old man awake and received from him a welcome full of ancient courtesy and kindliness. Miss Eliza crept in like a timid mouse, looking so afraid of her buxom companion that I forgot my own shyness in trying to relieve hers. She was so enveloped in shawls that all I could discover was that my mistress was a very nervous little woman, with a small button of pale hair on the outside of her head and the vaguest notions of work inside. A few spasmodic remarks and many awkward pauses brought me to teatime, when Josephus appeared, as tall, thin, and cadaverous as ever. After his arrival there was no more silence, for he preached all suppertime something in this agreeable style.

"My young friend, our habits, as you see, are of the simplest. We eat in the kitchen, and all together, in the primitive fashion; for it suits my father and saves labor. I could wish more order and elegance; but *my* wishes are not consulted and I submit. I live above these petty crosses, and, though my health suffers from bad cookery, I do not murmur. Only, I must say, in passing, that if you *will* make your battercakes green with saleratus, Puah, I shall feel it my duty to throw them out of the window. *I* am used to poison; but I cannot see the coals of this blooming girl's stomach destroyed, as mine have been. And, speaking of duties, I may as well mention to you, Louisa (I call you so in a truly fraternal spirit), that I like to find my study in order when I come down in the morning; for I often need a few moments of solitude before I face the daily annoyances of my life. I shall permit *you* to perform this light task, for *you* have some idea of order (I see it in the formation of your brow), and feel sure that *you* will respect the sanctuary of thought. Eliza is so blind she does not see dust, and Puah enjoys devastating the one poor refuge I can call my own this side the grave. We are all waiting for you, sir. My father keeps up the old formalities, you observe; and I endure them, though *my* views are more advanced."

The old gentleman hastily finished his tea and returned thanks, when his son stalked gloomily away, evidently oppressed with the burden of his wrongs, also, as I irreverently fancied, with the seven "green" flapjacks he had devoured during the sermon.

I helped wash up the cups, and during that domestic rite Puah chatted in what I should have considered a cheery, social way had I not been darkly warned against her wiles.

"You needn't mind half Josephus says, my dear. He likes to hear himself talk and always goes on so before folks. I sometimes thinks his books and new ideas have sort of muddled his wits, for he is as full of notions as a paper is of pins; and he gets dreadfully put out if we don't give in to 'em. But, gracious me! they are so redicklus sometimes and so selfish I can't allow him to make a fool of himself or plague Lizy. She don't dare to say her soul is her own; so I have to stand up for her. His pa don't know half his odd doings; for I try to keep the old gentleman comfortable and have to manage 'em all, which is not an easy job I do assure you."

I had a secret conviction that she was right, but did not commit myself in any way, and we joined the social circle in the sitting room. The prospect was not a lively one, for the old gentleman nodded behind his newspaper; Eliza, with her head pinned up in a little blanket, slumbered on the sofa, Puah fell to knitting silently; and the plump cat dozed under the stove. Josephus was visible, artistically posed in the luxurious recesses of his cell, with the light beaming on his thoughtful brow, as he pored over a large volume or mused with upturned eye.

Having nothing else to do, I sat and stared at him, till, emerging from a deep reverie, with an effective start, he became conscious of my existence and beckoned me to approach the "sanctuary of thought" with a dramatic waft of his large hand.

I went, took possession of an easy chair, and prepared myself for elegant conversation. I was disappointed, however; for Josephus showed me a list of his favorite dishes, sole fruit of all that absorbing thought, and, with an earnestness that flushed his saffron countenance, gave me hints as to the proper preparation of these delicacies.

I mildly mentioned that I was not a cook; but was effectually silenced by being reminded that I came to be generally useful, to take his sister's place, and see that the flame of life which burned so feebly in this earthly tabernacle was fed with proper fuel. Mince pies, Welsh rarebits, sausages, and strong coffee did not strike me as strictly spiritual fare; but I listened meekly and privately resolved to shift this awful responsibility to Puah's shoulders.

Detecting me in gape, after an hour of this high converse, he presented me with an overblown rose, which fell to pieces before I got out of the room, pressed my hand, and dismissed me with a fervent "God bless you, child. Don't forget the dropped eggs for breakfast."

I was up betimes next morning and had the study in perfect order before the recluse appeared, enjoying a good prowl among the books as I worked and becoming so absorbed that I forgot the eggs, till a gusty sigh startled me, and I beheld Josephus, in dressing gown and slippers, languidly surveying the scene.

"Nay, do not fly," he said, as I grasped my duster in guilty haste. "It pleases me to see you here and lends a sweet, domestic charm to my solitary room. I like that graceful cap, that housewifely apron, and I beg you to wear them often; for it refreshes my eye to see something tasteful, young, and womanly about me. Eliza makes a bundle of herself and Puah is simply detestable."

He sank languidly into a chair and closed his eyes, as if the mere thought of his enemy was too much for him. I took advantage of this momentary prostration to slip away, convulsed with laughter at the looks and words of this bald-headed sentimentalist.

After breakfast I fell to work with a will, eager to show my powers and glad to put things to rights, for many hard jobs had evidently been waiting for a stronger arm than Puah's and a more methodical head than Eliza's.

Everything was dusty, moldy, shiftless, and neglected, except the domain of Josephus. Up-stairs the paper was dropping from the walls, the ancient furniture was all more or less dilapidated, and every hold and corner was full of relics tucked away by Puah, who was a regular old magpie. Rats and mice reveled in the empty rooms and spiders wove their tapestry undisturbed, for the old man would have nothing altered or repaired and his part of the house was fast going to ruin.

I longed to have a grand "clearing up"; but was forbidden to do more than to keep things in livable order. On the whole, it was fortunate, for I soon found that my hands would be kept busy with the realms of Josephus, whose ethereal being shrank from dust, shivered at a cold breath, and needed much cosseting with dainty food, hot fires, soft beds, and endless service, else, as he expressed it, the frail reed would break.

I regret to say that a time soon came when I felt supremely indifferent as to the breakage, and very skeptical as to the fragility of a reed that ate, slept, dawdled, and scolded so energetically. The rose that fell to pieces so suddenly was a good symbol of the rapid disappearance of all the romantic delusions I had indulged in for a time. A week's acquaintance with the inmates of this old house quite settled my opinion, and further developments only confirmed it.

Miss Eliza was a nonentity and made no more impression on me than a fly. The old gentleman passed his days in a placid sort of doze and took no notice of what went on about him. Puah had been a faithful drudge for years, and, instead of being a "wretch," was, as I soon satisfied myself, a motherly old soul, with no malice in her. The secret of Josephus's dislike was that the reverend tyrant ruled the house, and all obeyed him but Puah, who had nursed him as a baby, boxed his ears as a boy, and was not afraid of him even when he became a man and a minister. I soon repented of my first suspicions, and grew fond of her, for without my old gossip I should have fared ill when my day of tribulation came.

At first I innocently accepted the fraternal invitations to visit the study, feeling that when my day's work was done I earned a right to rest and read. But I soon found that this was not the idea. I was not to read; but to be read to. I was not to enjoy the flowers, pictures, fire, and books; but to keep them in order for my lord to enjoy. I was also to be a passive bucket, into which he was to pour all manner of philosophic, metaphysical, and sentimental rubbish. I was to serve his needs, soothe his sufferings, and sympathize with all his sorrows—be a galley slave, in fact.

As soon as I clearly understood this, I tried to put an end to it by shunning the study and never lingering there an instant after my work was done. But it availed little, for Josephus demanded much sympathy and was bound to have it. So he came and read poems while I washed dishes, discussed his pet problems all meal-times, and put reproachful notes under my door, in which were comically mingled complaints of neglect and orders for dinner.

I bore it as long as I could, and then freed my mind in a declaration of independence, delivered in the kitchen, where he found me scrubbing the hearth. It was not an impressive attitude for an orator, nor was the occupation one a girl would choose when receiving calls; but I have always felt grateful for the intense discomfort of that moment, since it gave me the courage to rebel outright. Stranded on a small island of mat, in a sea of soapsuds, I brandished a scrubbing brush, as I indignantly informed him that I came to be a companion to his sister, not to him, and I should keep that post or none. This I followed up by reproaching him with the delusive reports he had given me of the place and its duties, and assuring him that I should not stay long unless matters mended.

"But I offer you lighter tasks, and you refuse them," he began, still hovering in the doorway, whither he had hastily retired when I opened my batteries.

"But I don't like the tasks, and consider them much worse than hard work," was my ungrateful answer, as I sat upon my island, with the softsoap conveniently near.

"Do you mean to say you prefer to scrub the hearth to sitting in my charming room while I read Hegel to you?" he demanded, glaring down upon me.

"Infinitely," I responded promptly, and emphasized my words by beginning to scrub with a zeal that made the bricks white with foam.

"Is it possible!" and, with a groan at my depravity, Josephus retired, full of ungodly wrath.

I remember that I immediately burst into jocund song, so that no doubt might remain in his mind, and continued to warble cheerfully till my task was done. I also remember that I cried heartily [?] when I got to my room, I was so vexed, disappointed, and tired. But my bower was so small I should soon have swamped the furniture if I had indulged copiously in tears; therefore I speedily dried them up, wrote a comic letter home, and waited with interest to see what would happen next.

Far be it from me to accuse one of the nobler sex of spite or the small revenge of underhand annoyances and slights to one who could not escape and would not retaliate; but after that day a curious change came over the spirit of that very unpleasant dream. Gradually all the work of the house had been slipping into my hands; for Eliza was too poorly to help and direct, and Puah too old to do much besides the cooking. About this time I found that even the roughest work was added to my share, for Josephus was unusually feeble and no one was hired to do his chores. Having made up my mind to go when the month was out, I said nothing, but dug paths, brought water from the well, split kindlings, made fires, and sifted ashes, like a true Cinderella.

There never had been any pretense of companionship with Eliza, who spent her days mulling over the fire, and seldom exerted herself except to find odd jobs for me to do—rusty knives to clean, sheets to turn, old stockings to mend, and, when all else failed, some paradise of moths and mice to be cleared up; for the house was full of such "glory holds."

If I remonstrated, Eliza at once dissolved into tears and said she must do as she was told; Puah begged me to hold on till spring, when things would be much better; and pity pleaded for the two poor souls. But I don't think I could have stood it if my promise had not bound me, for when the fiend said "Budge" honor said "Budge not" and I stayed.

But, being a mortal worm, I turned now and then when ireful Josephus trod upon me too hard, especially in the matter of boot-blacking. I really don't know why that is considered such humiliating work for a woman; but so it is, and there I drew the line. I would have cleaned the old man's shoes without a murmur; but he preferred to keep their native rustiness intact. Eliza never went out, and Puah affected carpet-slippers of the Chinese-junk pattern. Josephus, however, plumed himself upon his feet, which, like his nose, were large, and never took his walks abroad without having his boots in a high state of polish. He had brushed them himself at first; but soon after the explosion I discovered a pair of muddy boots in the shed, set suggestively near the blacking-box. I did not take the hint; feeling instinctively that this amiable being was trying how much I would bear for the sake of peace.

The boots remained untouched; and another pair soon came to keep them company, whereat I smiled wickedly as I chopped just kindlings enough for my own use. Day after day the collection grew, and neither party gave in. Boots were succeeded by shoes, then rubbers gave a pleasing variety to the long line, and then I knew the end was near.

"Why are not my boots attended to?" demanded Josephus, one evening, when obliged to go out.

"I'm sure I don't know," was Eliza's helpless answer.

"I told Louizy I guessed you'd want some of 'em before long," observed Puah with an exasperating twinkle in her old eye.

"And what did she say?" asked my lord with an ireful whack of his velvet slippers as he cast them down.

"Oh! she said she was so busy doing your other work you'd have to do that yourself; and I thought she was about right."

"Louizy" heard it all through the slide, and could have embraced the old woman for her words, but kept still till Josephus had resumed his slippers with a growl and retired to the shed, leaving Eliza in tears, Puah chuckling, and the rebellious handmaid exulting in the china-closet.

Alas! for romance and the Christian virtues, several pairs of boots were cleaned that night, and my sinful soul enjoyed the spectacle of the reverend bootblack at his task. I even found my "fancy work," as I called the evening job of pairing a bucketful of hard russets with a dull knife, much cheered by the shoe-brush accompaniment played in the shed.

Thunder-clouds rested upon the martyr's brow at breakfast, and I was as much ignored as the cat. And what a relief that was! The piano was locked up, so were the bookcases, the newspapers mysteriously disappeared, and a solemn silence reigned at table, for no one dared to talk when that gifted tongue was mute. Eliza fled from the gathering storm and had a comfortable fit of neuralgia in her own room, where Puah nursed her, leaving me to skirmish with the enemy.

It was not a fair fight, and that experience lessened my respect for mankind immensely. I did my best, however—grubbed about all day and amused my dreary evenings as well as I could; too proud even to borrow a book, lest it should seem like a surrender. What a long month it was, and how eagerly I counted the hours of that last week, for my time was up Saturday and I hoped to be off at once. But when I announced my intention such dismay fell upon Eliza that my heart was touched, and Puah so urgently begged me to stay till they could get some one that I consented to remain a few days longer, and wrote posthaste to my mother, telling her to send a substitute quickly or I should do something desperate.

That blessed woman, little dreaming of all the woes I had endured, advised me to be patient, to do the generous thing, and be sure I should not regret it in the end. I groaned, submitted, and did regret it all the days of my life.

Three mortal weeks I waited; for, though two other victims came, I was implored to set them going, and tried to do it. But both fled after a day or two, condemning the place as a very hard one and calling me a fool to stand it another hour. I entirely agreed with them on both points, and, when I had cleared up after the second incapable lady, I tarried not for the coming of a third, but clutched my property and announced my departure by the next train.

Of course, Eliza wept, Puah moaned, the old man politely regretted, and the younger one washed his hands of the whole affair by shutting himself up in his room and forbidding me to say farewell because "he could not bear it." I laughed, and fancied it done for effect then; but I soon understood it better and did not laugh.

At the last moment, Eliza nervously tucked a sixpenny pocketbook into my hand and shrouded herself in the little blanket with a sob. But Puah kissed me kindly and whispered, with an odd look: "Don't blame us for anything. Some folks is liberal and some ain't." I thanked the poor old soul for her kindness to me and trudged gayly away to the station, whither my property had preceded me on a wheelbarrow, hired at my own expense.

I never shall forget that day. A bleak March afternoon, a sloppy, lonely road, and one hoarse crow stalking about a field, so like Josephus that I could not resist throwing a snowball at him. Behind me stood the dull old house, no longer either mysterious or romantic in my disenchanted eyes; before me rumbled the barrow, bearing my dilapidated wardrobe; and in my pocket reposed what I fondly hoped was, if not a liberal, at least an honest return for seven weeks of the hardest work I ever did.

Unable to resist the desire to see what my earnings were, I opened the purse and beheld *four dollars*.

I have had a good many bitter minutes in my life; but one of the bitterest came to me as I stood there in the windy road, with the sixpenny pocket-book open before me, and looked from my poor chapped, grimy, chill-blained hands to the paltry sum that was considered reward enough for all the hard and humble labor they had done.

A girl's heart is a sensitive thing. And mine had been very full lately; for it had suffered many of the trials that wound deeply yet cannot be told; so I think it as but natural that my first impulse was to go straight back to that sacred study and fling this insulting money at the feet of him who sent it. But I was so boiling over with indignation that I could not trust myself in his presence, lest I should be unable to resist the temptation to shake him, in spite of his cloth.

No, I would go home, show my honorable wounds, tell my pathetic tale, and leave my parents to avenge my wrongs. I did so; but over that harrowing scene I drop a veil, for my feeble pen refuses to depict the emotions of my outraged family. I will merely mention that the four dollars went back and the reverend Josephus never heard the last of it in that neighborhood.

My experiment seemed a dire failure and I mourned it as such for years; but more than once in my life I have been grateful for that serio-comico experience, since it has taught me many lessons. One of the most useful of these has been the power of successfully making a companion, not a servant, of those whose aid I need, and helping to gild their honest wages with the sympathy and justice which can sweeten the humblest and lighten the hardest task.

TRANSCENDENTAL WILD OATS

ON THE FIRST day of June, 184-, a large wagon, drawn by a small horse and containing a motley load, went lumbering over certain New England hills, with the pleasing accompaniments of wind, rain, and hail. A serene man with a serene child upon his knee was driving, or rather being driven, for the small horse had it all his own way. A brown boy with a William Penn style of countenance sat beside him, firmly embracing a bust of Socrates. Behind them was an energetic-looking woman, with a benevolent brow, satirical mouth, and eyes brimful of hope and courage. A baby reposed upon her lap, a mirror leaned against her knee, and a basket of provisions danced about at her feet, as she struggled with a large, unruly umbrella. Two blue-eyed little girls, with hands full of childish treasures, sat under one old shawl, chatting happily together.

In front of this lively party stalked a tall, sharp-featured man, in a long blue cloak; and a fourth small girl trudged along beside him through the mud as if she rather enjoyed it.

The wind whistled over the bleak hills; the rain fell in a despondent drizzle, and twilight began to fall. But the calm man gazed as tranquilly into the fog as if he beheld a radiant bow of promise spanning the gray sky. The cheery woman tried to cover every one but herself with the big umbrella. The brown boy pillowed his head on the bald pate of Socrates and slumbered peacefully. The little girls sang lullabies to their dolls in soft, maternal murmurs. The sharp-nosed pedestrian marched steadily on, with the blue cloak streaming out behind him like a banner; the the lively infant splashed through the puddles with a duck-like satisfaction pleasant to behold.

Thus these modern pilgrims journeyed hopefully out of the old world, to found a new one in the wilderness.

The editors of *The Transcendental Tripod* had received from Messrs. Lion & Lamb (two of the aforesaid pilgrims) a communication from which the following statement is an extract:

"We have made arrangements with the proprietor of an estate of about a hundred acres which liberates this tract from human ownership. Here we shall prosecute our effort to initiate a Family in harmony with the primitive instincts of man.

"Ordinary secular farming is not our object. Fruit, grain, pulse, herbs, flax, and other vegetable products, receiving assiduous attention, will afford ample manual occupation, and chaste supplies for the bodily needs. It is intended to adorn the pastures with orchards, and to supersede the labor of cattle by the spade and the pruning-knife.

"Consecrated to human freedom, the land awaits the sober culture of devoted men. Beginning with small pecuniary means, this enterprise must be rooted in a reliance on the succors of an ever-bounteous Providence, whose vital affinities being secured by this union with uncorrupted field and unworldly persons, the cares and injuries of a life of gain are avoided.

"The inner nature of each member of the Family is at no time neglected. Our plan contemplates all such disciplines, cultures, and habits as evidently conduce to the purifying of the inmates.

"Pledged to the spirit alone, the founders anticipate no hasty or numerous addition to their numbers. The kingdom of peace is entered only through the gates of self-denial; and felicity is the test and the reward of loyalty to the unswerving law of Love."

This prospective Eden at present consisted of an old red farm-house, a dilapidated barn, many acres of meadow-land, and a grove. Ten ancient apple trees were all the "chaste supply" which the place offered as yet; but, in the firm belief that plenteous orchards were soon to be evoked from their inner consciousness, these sanguine founders had christened their domain Fruitlands.

Here Timon Lion intended to found a colony of Latter Day Saints, who, under his patriarchal sway, should regenerate the world and glorify his name for ever. Here Abel Lamb, with the devoutest faith in the high ideal which was to him a living truth, desired to plant a Paradise, where Beauty, Virtue, Justice, and Love might live happily together, without the possibility of a serpent entering in. And here his wife, unconverted but faithful to the end, hoped, after many wanderings over the face of the earth, to find rest for herself and a home for her children.

"There is our new abode, announced the enthusiast, smiling with a satisfaction quite undamped by the drops dripping from his hatbrim, as they turned at length into a cart-path that wound along a steep hillside into a barren-looking valley.

"A little difficult of access," observed his practical wife, as she endeavored to keep her various household gods from going overboard with every lurch of the laden ark.

"Like all good things. But those who earnestly desire and patiently seek will soon find us," placidly responded the philosopher from the mud, through which he was now endeavoring to pilot the much-enduring horse.

"Truth lies at the bottom of a well, Sister Hope," said Brother Timon, pausing to detach his small comrade from a gate, whereon she was perched for a clearer gaze into futurity.

"That's the reason we so seldom get at it, I suppose," replied Mrs. Hope, making a vain clutch at the mirror, which a sudden jolt sent flying out of her hands.

"We want no false reflections here," said Timon, with a grim smile, as he crunched the fragments under foot in his onward march.

Sister Hope held her peace, and looked wistfully through the mist at her promised home. The old red house with a hospitable glimmer at its windows cheered her eyes; and considering the weather, was a fitter refuge than the sylvan bowers some of the more ardent souls might have preferred.

The newcomers were welcomed by one of the elect precious—a regenerate farmer, whose idea of reform consisted chiefly in wearing white cotton raiment and shoes of untanned leather. This costume, with a snowy beard, gave him a venerable, and at the same time a somewhat bridal appearance.

The goods and chattels of the Society not having arrived, the weary family reposed before the fire on blocks of wood, while Brother Moses White regaled them with roasted potatoes, brown bread and water, in two plates, a tin pan, and one mug—his table service being limited. But, having cast the forms and vanities of a depraved world behind them, the elders welcomed hardship with the enthusiasm of new pioneers, and the children heartily enjoyed this foretaste of what they believed was to be a sort of perpetual picnic.

During the progress of this frugal meal, two more brothers appeared. One a dark, melancholy man, clad in homespun, whose particular mission was to turn his name hind part before and use as few words as possible. The other was a bland, bearded Englishman, who expected to be saved by eating uncooked food and going without clothes. He had not yet adopted the primitive costume, however; but contented himself with meditatively chewing dry beans out of a basket.

"Every meal should be a sacrament, and the vessels used beautiful and symbolical," observed Brother Lamb, mildly, righting the tin pan slipping about on his knees. "I priced a silver service when in town, but it was too costly; so I got some graceful cups and vases of Britannia ware."

"Hardest things in the world to keep bright. Will whiting be allowed in the community?" inquired Sister Hope, with a housewife's interest in labor-saving institutions.

"Such trivial questions will be discussed at a more fitting time," answered Brother Timon, sharply, as he burnt his fingers with a very hot potato. "Neither sugar, molasses, milk, butter, cheese, nor flesh are to be used among us, for nothing is to be admitted which has caused wrong or death to man or beast."

"Our garments are to be linen till we learn to raise our own cotton or some substitute for woollen fabrics," added Brother Abel, blissfully basking in an imaginary future as warm and brilliant as the generous fire before him.

"Haou abaout shoes?" asked Brother Moses, surveying his own with interest.

"We must yield that point till we can manufacture an innocent substitute for leather. Bark, wood, or some durable fabric will be invented in time. Meanwhile, those who desire to carry out our idea to the fullest extent can go barefooted," said Lion, who liked extreme measures.

"I never will, nor let my girls," murmured rebellious Sister Hope, under her breath.

"Haou do you cattle'ate to treat the ten-acre lot? Ef things ain't 'tended to right smart, we shan't hev no crops," observed the practical patriarch in cotton.

"We shall spade it," replied Abel, in such perfect good faith that Moses said no more, though he indulged in a shake of the head as he glanced at hands that had held nothing heavier than a pen for years. He was a paternal old soul and regarded the younger men as promising boys on a new sort of lark.

"What shall we do for lamps, if we cannot use any animal substance? I do hope light of some sort is to be thrown upon the enterprise," said Mrs. Lamb, with anxiety, for in those days kerosene and camphene were not, and gas unknown in the wilderness.

"We shall go without till we have discovered some vegetable oil or wax to serve us," replied Brother Timon, in a decided tone, which caused Sister Hope to resolve that her private lamp should always be trimmed, if not burning.

"Each member is to perform the work for which experience, strength, and taste best fit him," continued Dictator Lion. "Thus drudgery and disorder will be avoided and harmony prevail. We shall arise at dawn, begin the day by bathing, followed by music, and then a chaste repast of fruit and bread. Each one finds congenial occupation till the meridian meal; when some deep-searching conversation gives rest to the body and development to the mind. Healthful labor again engages us till the last meal, when we assemble in social communion, prolonged till sunset, when we retire to sweet repose, ready for the next day's activity."

"What part of the work do you incline to yourself?" asked Sister Hope, with a humorous glimmer in her keen eyes.

"I shall wait till it is made clear to me. Being in preference to doing is the great aim, and this comes to us rather by a resigned willingness than a willful activity, which is a check to all divine growth," responded Brother Timon.

"I thought so." And Mrs. Lamb sighed audibly, for during the year he had spent in her family Brother Timon had so faithfully carried out his idea of "being, not doing," that she had found his "divine growth" both an expensive and unsatisfactory process.

Here her husband struck into the conversation, his face shining with the light and joy of the splendid dreams and high ideals hovering before him.

"In these steps of reform, we do not rely so much on scientific reasoning or physiological skill as on the spirit's dictates. The greater part of man's duty consists in leaving alone much that he now does. Shall I stimulate with tea, coffee, or wine? No. Shall I consume flesh? Not if I value health. Shall I subjugate cattle? Shall I claim property in any created thing? Shall I trade? Shall I adopt a form of religion? Shall I interest myself in politics? To how many of these questions—could we ask them deeply enough and could they be heard as having relation to our eternal welfare—would the response be 'Abstain'?"

A mild snore seemed to echo the last word of Abel's rhapsody, for brother Moses had succumbed to mundane slumber and sat nodding like a massive ghost. Forest Absalom, the silent man, and John Pease, the English member, now departed to the barn; and Mrs. Lamb led her flock to a temporary fold, leaving the founders of the "Consociate Family" to build castles in the air till the fire went out and the symposium ended in smoke.

The furniture arrived next day, and was soon bestowed; for the principal property of the community consisted in books. To this rare library was devoted the best room in the house, and the few busts and pictures that still survived many flittings were added to beautify the sanctuary, for here the family was to meet for amusement, instruction, and worship.

Any housewife can imagine the emotions of Sister Hope, when she took possession of a large, dilapidated kitchen, containing an old stove and the peculiar stores out of which food was to be evolved for her little family of eleven. Cakes of maple sugar, dried peas and beans, barley and hominy, meal of all sorts, potatoes, and dried fruit. No milk, butter, cheese, tea, or meat, appeared. Even salt was considered a useless luxury and spice entirely forbidden by these lovers of Spartan simplicity. A ten years' experience of vegetarian vagaries had been good for training for this new freak, and her sense of the ludicrous supported her through many trying scenes.

Unleavened bread, porridge, and water for breakfast; bread, vegetables, and water for dinner; bread, fruit, and water for supper was the bill of fare ordained by the elders. No teapot profaned that sacred stove, no gory steak cried aloud for vengeance from her chaste gridiron; and only a brave woman's taste, time, and temper were sacrificed on that domestic altar.

The vexed question of light was settled by buying a quantity of bayberry wax for candles; and, on discovering that no one knew how to make them, pine knots were introduced, to be used when absolutely necessary. Being summer, the evenings were not long, and the weary fraternity found it no great hardship to retire with the birds. The inner light was sufficient for most of them. But Mrs. Lamb rebelled. Evening was the only time she had to herself, and while the tired feet rested the skilful hands mended torn frocks and little stockings, or anxious heart forgot its burden in a book.

So "mother's lamp" burned steadily, while the philosophers built a new heaven and earth by moonlight; and through all the metaphysical mists and philanthropic pyrotechnics of that period Sister Hope played her own little game of "throwing light," and none but the moths were the worse for it.

Such farming probably was never seen before since Adam delved. The band of brothers began by spading garden and field; but a few days of it lessened their ardor amazingly. Blistered hands and aching backs suggested the expediency of permitting the use of cattle till the workers were better fitted for noble toil by a summer of the new life.

Brother Moses brought a yoke of oxen from his farm—at least, the philosophers thought so till it was discovered that one of the animals was a cow; and Moses confessed that he "must be let down easy, for he couldn't live on garden sarse entirely."

Great was Dictator Lion's indignation at this lapse from virtue. But time pressed, the work must be done; so the meek cow was permitted to wear the yoke and the recreant brother continued to enjoy forbidden draughts in the barn, which dark proceeding caused the children to regard him as one set apart for destruction.

The sowing was equally peculiar, for, owing to some mistake, the three brethren, who devoted themselves to this graceful task, found when about half through the job that each had been sowing a different sort of grain in the same field; a mistake which caused much perplexity, as it could not be remedied; but, after a long consultation and a good deal of laughter, it was decided to say nothing and see what would come of it.

The garden was planted with a generous supply of useful roots and herbs; but, as manure was not allowed to profane the virgin soil, few of these vegetable treasures ever came up. Purslane reigned supreme, and the disappointed planters ate it philosophically, deciding that Nature knew what was best for them, and would generously supply their needs, if they could only learn to digest her "sallets" and wild roots.

The orchard was laid out, a little grafting done, new trees and vines set, regardless of the unfit season and entire ignorance of the husbandmen, who honestly believed that in the autumn they would reap a bounteous harvest.

Slowly things got into order, and rapidly rumors of the new experiment went abroad, causing many strange spirits to flock thither, for in those days communities were the fashion and transcendentalism raged wildly. Some came to look on and laugh, some to be supported in poetic idleness, a few to believe sincerely and work heartily. Each member was allowed to mount his favorite hobby and ride it to his heart's content. Very queer were some of these riders, and very rampant some of the hobbies.

One youth, believing that language was of little consequence if the spirit was only right, startled newcomers by blandly greeting them with "good morning, damn you," and other remarks of an equally mixed order. A second irrepressible being held that all the emotions of the soul should be freely expressed, and illustrated his theory by antics that would have sent him to a lunatic asylum, if, as an unregenerate wag said, he had not already been in one. When his spirit soared, he climbed trees and shouted; when doubt assailed him, he lay upon the floor and groaned lamentably. At joyful periods, he raced, leaped, and sang; when sad, he wept aloud; and when a great thought burst upon him in the watches of the night, he crowed like a jocund cockerel, to the great delight of the children and the great annoyance of the elders. One musical brother fiddled whenever so moved, sang sentimentally to the four little girls, and put a music-box on the wall when he hoed corn.

Brother Pease ground away at his uncooked food, or browsed over the farm on sorrel, mint, green fruit, and new vegetables. Occasionally he took his walks abroad, airily attired in an unbleached cotton *poncho,* which was the nearest approach to the primeval costume he was allowed to indulge in. At midsummer he retired to the wilderness, to try his plan where the woodchucks were without prejudices and huckleberry bushes were hospitably full. A sunstroke unfortunately spoilt his plan, and he returned to semi-civilization a sadder and wiser man.

Forest Absalom preserved his Pythagorean silence, cultivated his fine dark locks, and worked like a beaver, setting an excellent example of brotherly love, justice, and fidelity by his upright life. He it was who helped overworked Sister Hope with her heavy washes, kneaded the endless succession of batches of bread, watched over the children, and did the many tasks left undone by the brethren, who were so busy discussing and defining great duties that they forgot to perform the small ones.

Moses White placidly plodded about, "chorin' raound," as he called it, looking like an old-time patriarch, with his silver hair and flowing beard, and saving the community from many a mishap by his thrift and Yankee shrewdness.

Brother Lion domineered over the whole concern; for, having put the most money into the speculation, he was resolved to make it pay—as if anything founded on an ideal basis could be expected to do so by any but enthusiasts.

Abel Lamb simply revelled in the Newness, firmly believing that his dream was to be beautifully realized, and in time not only little Fruitlands, but the whole earth, be turned into a Happy Valley. He worked with every muscle of his body, for *he* was in deadly earnest. He taught with his whole head and heart; planned and sacrificed, preached and prophesied, with a soul full of the purest aspirations, most unselfish purposes, and desires for a life devoted to God and man, too high and tender to bear the rough usage of this world.

It was a little remarkable that only one woman ever joined this community. Mrs. Lamb merely followed wheresoever her husband led—"as ballast for his balloon," as she said, in her bright way.

Miss Jane Gage was a stout lady of mature years, sentimental, amiable, and lazy. She wrote verses copiously, and had vague yearnings and graspings after the unknown, which led her to believe herself fitted for a higher sphere than any she had yet adorned.

Having been a teacher, she was set to instructing the children in the common branches. Each adult member took a turn at the infants; and, as each taught in his own way, the result was a chronic state of chaos in the minds of these much-afflicted innocents.

Sleep, food, and poetic musings were the desires of dear Jane's life, and she shirked all duties as clogs upon her spirit's wings. Any thought of lending a hand with the domestic drudgery never occurred to her; and when to the question, "Are there any beasts of burden on the place?" Mrs. Lamb answered, with a face that told its own tale, "Only one woman!" the buxom Jane took no shame to herself, but laughed at the joke, and let the stout-hearted sister tug on alone.

Unfortunately, the poor lady hankered after the fleshpots, and endeavored to stay herself with private sips of milk, crackers, and cheese, and on one dire occasion she partook of fish at a neighbor's table.

One of the children reported this sad lapse from virtue, and poor Jane was publicly reprimanded by Timon.

"I only took a little bit of the tail," sobbed the penitent poetess.

"Yes, but the whole fish had to be tortured and slain that you might tempt your carnal appetite with that one taste of the tail. Know ye not, consumers of flesh meat, that ye are nourishing the wolf and tiger in your bosoms?"

At this awful question and the peal of laughter which arose from some of the younger brethren, tickled by the ludicrous contrast between the stout sinner, the stern judge, and the naughty satisfaction of the young detective, poor Jane fled from the room to pack her trunk, and return to a world were fishes' tails were not forbidden fruit.

Transcendental wild oats were sown broadcast that year, and the fame thereof has not yet ceased in the land; for, futile as this crop seemed to outsiders, it bore an invisible harvest, worth much to those who planted in earnest. As none of the members of this particular community have ever recounted their experiences before, a few of them may not be amiss, since the interest in these attempts has never died out and Fruitlands was the most ideal of all these castles in Spain.

A new dress was invented, since cotton, silk, and wool were forbidden as the product of slave-labor, worm-slaughter, and sheep-robbery. Tunics and trowsers of brown linen were the only wear. The women's skirts were longer, and their straw hat-brims wider than the men's and this was the only difference. Some persecution lent a charm to the costume, and the long-haired, linen-clad reformers quite enjoyed the mild martyrdom they endured when they left home.

Money was abjured, as the root of all evil. The produce of the land was to supply most of their wants, or be exchanged for the few things they could not grow. This idea had its inconveniences; but self-denial was the fashion, and it was surprising how many things one can do without. When they desired to travel, they walked, if possible, begged the loan of a vehicle, or boldly entered car or coach, and, stating their principles to the officials, took the consequences. Usually their dress, their earnest frankness, and gentle resolution won them a passage; but now and then they met with hard usage, and had the satisfaction of suffering for their principles.

On one of these penniless pilgrimages they took passage on a boat, and, when fare was demanded, artlessly offered to talk, instead of pay. As the boat was well under way and they actually had not a cent, there was no help for it. So Brothers Lion and Lamb held forth to the assembled passengers in their most eloquent style. There must have been something effective in this conversation, for the listeners were moved to take up a contribution for these inspired lunatics, who preached peace on earth and goodwill to man so earnestly, with empty pockets. A goodly sum was collected; but when the captain presented it the reformers proved that they were consistent even in their madness, for not a penny would they accept, saying, with a look at the group about them, whose indifference or contempt had changed to interest and respect, "You see how well we get on without money;" and so went serenely on their way, with their linen blouses flapping airily in the cold October wind.

They preached vegetarianism everywhere and resisted all temptations of the flesh, contentedly eating apples and bread at well-spread tables, and much afflicting hospitable hostesses by denouncing their food and taking away their appetites, discussing the "horrors of shambles," the "incorporation of the brute in man," and "on elegant abstinence the sign of a pure soul." But, when the perplexed or offended ladies asked what they should eat, they got in reply a bill of fare consisting of "bowls of sunrise for breakfast," "solar seeds of the sphere," "dishes from Plutarch's chaste table," and other viands equally hard to find in any modern market.

Reform conventions of all sorts were haunted by these brethren, who said many wise things and did many foolish ones. Unfortunately, these wanderings interfered with their harvest at home; but the rule was to do what the spirit moved, so they left their crops to Providence and went a-reaping in wider and, let us hope, more fruitful fields than their own.

Luckily, the earthly providence who watched over Abel Lamb was at hand to glean the scanty crop yielded by the "uncorrupted land," which, "consecrated to human freedom," had received "the sober culture of devout men."

About the same time the grain was ready to house, some call of the Oversoul wafted all the men away. An easterly storm was coming up and the yellow stacks were sure to be ruined. Then Sister Hope gathered her forces. Three little girls, one boy (Timon's son), and herself, harnessed to clothes-baskets and Russia-linen sheets, were the only teams she could command; but with these poor appliances the indomitable woman got in the grain and saved food for her young, with the instinct and energy of a mother-bird with a brood of hungry nestlings to feed.

This attempt at regeneration had its tragic as well as comic side, though the world only saw the former.

With the first frosts, the butterflies, who had sunned themselves in the new light through the summer, took flight, leaving the few bees to see what honey they had stored for winter use. Precious little appeared beyond the satisfaction of a few months of holy living.

At first it seemed as if a chance to try holy dying was also to be offered them. Timon, much disgusted with the failure of the scheme, decided to retire to the Shakers, who seemed to be the only successful community going.

"What is to become of us?" asked Mrs. Hope, for Abel was heart-broken at the bursting of his lovely bubble.

"You can stay here, if you like, till a tenant is found. No more wood must be cut, however, and no more corn ground. All I have must be sold to pay the debts of the concern, as the responsibility is mine," was the cheering reply.

"Who is to pay us for what we have lost? I gave all I had—furniture, time, strength, six months of my children's lives—and all are wasted. Abel gave himself body and soul, and is almost wrecked by hard work and disappointment. Are we to have no return for this, but leave to starve and freeze in an old house, with winter at hand, no money, and hardly a friend left, for this wild scheme has alienated nearly all we had. You talk much about justice. Let us have a little, since there is nothing else left."

But the woman's appeal met with no reply but the old one: "It was an experiment. We all risked something, and must bear our losses as we can."

With this cold comfort, Timon departed with his son, and was absorbed into the Shaker brotherhood, where he soon found that the order of things was reversed, and it was all work and no play.

Then the tragedy began for the forsaken little family. Desolation and despair fell upon Abel. As his wife said, his new beliefs had alienated many friends. Some thought him mad, some unprincipled. Even the most kindly thought him a visionary, whom it was useless to help till he took more practical views of life. All stood aloof, saying: "Let him work out his own ideas, and see what they are worth."

He had tried, but it was a failure. The world was not ready for Utopia yet, and those who attempted to found it only got laughed at for their pains. In other days, men could sell all and give to the poor, lead lives devoted to holiness and high thought, and after the persecution was over, find themselves honored as saints or martyrs. But in modern times these things are out of fashion. To live for one's prinicples, at all costs, is a dangerous speculation; and the failure of an ideal, no matter how humane and noble, is harder for the world to forgive and forget than bank robbery or the grand swindles of corrupt politicians.

Deep waters now for Abel, and for a time there seemed no passage through. Strength and spirits were exhausted by hard work and too much thought. Courage failed when, looking about for help, he saw no sympathizing face, no hand outstretched to help him, no voice to say cheerily:

"We all make mistakes, and it takes many experiences to shape a life. Try again, and let us help you."

Every door was closed, every eye averted, every heart cold, and no way open whereby he might earn bread for his children. His principles would not permit him to do many things that others did; and in the few fields where conscience would allow him to work, who would employ a man who had flown in the face of society, as he had done?

Then this dreamer, whose dream was the life of his life, resolved to carry out his idea to the bitter end. There seemed no place for him here— no work, no friend. To go begging conditions was as ignoble as to go begging money. Better perish of want than sell one's soul for the sustenance of his body. Silently he lay down upon his bed, turned his face to the wall, and waited with pathetic patience for death to cut the knot which he could not untie. Days and nights went by, and neither food nor water passed his lips. Soul and body were dumbly struggling together, and no word of complaint betrayed what either suffered.

His wife, when tears and prayers were unavailing, sat down to wait the end with a mysterious awe and submission; for in this entire resignation of all things there was an eloquent significance to her who knew him as no other human being did.

"Leave all to God," was his belief; and in this crisis the loving soul clung to his faith, sure that the All-wise Father would not desert this child who tried to live so near to Him. Gathering her children about her, she waited the issue of the tragedy that was being enacted in that solitary room, while the first snow fell outside, untrodden by the footprints of a single friend.

But the strong angels who sustain and teach perplexed and troubled souls came and went, leaving no trace without, but working miracles within. For, when all other sentiments had faded into dimness, all other hopes died utterly; when the bitterness of death was nearly over, when the body was past any pang of hunger or thirst, and soul stood ready to depart, the love that outlives all else refused to die. Head had bowed to defeat, hand had grown weary with too heavy tasks, but heart could not grow cold to those who live in its tender depths, even when death touched it.

"My faithful wife, my little girls—they have not forsaken me, they are mine by ties that none can break. What right have I to leave them alone? What right to escape from the burden and the sorrow I have helped to bring? This duty remains to me, and I must do it manfully. For their sakes, the world will forgive me in time; for their sakes, God will sustain me now."

Too feeble to rise, Abel groped for the food that always lay within his reach, and in the darkness and solitude of that memorable night ate and drank what was to him the bread and wine of a new communion, a new dedication of heart and life to the duties that were left him when the dreams fled.

In the early dawn, when that sad wife crept fearfully to see what change had come to the patient face on the pillow, she found it smiling at her, saw a wasted hand outstretched to her, and heard a feeble voice cry bravely, "Hope!"

What passed in that little room is not to be recorded except in the hearts of those who suffered and endured much for love's sake. Enough for us to know that soon the wan shadow of a man came forth, leaning on the arm that never failed him, to be welcomed and cherished by the children, who never forgot the experiences of that time.

"Hope" was the watchword now; and, while the last logs blazed on the hearth, the last bread and apples covered the table, the new commander, with recovered courage, said to her husband:

"Leave all to God—and me. He has done his part; now I will do mine."

"But we have no money, dear."

"Yes, we have. I sold all we could spare, and have enough to take us away from this snowbank."

"Where can we go?"

"I have engaged four rooms at our good neighbor, Lovejoy's. There we can live cheaply till spring. Then for new plans and a home of our own, please God."

"But, Hope, your little store won't last long, and we have no friends."

"I can sew and you can chop wood. Lovejoy offers you the same pay as he gives his other men; my old friend, Mrs. Truman, will send me all the work I want; and my blessed brother stands by us to the end. Cheer up, dear heart, for while there is work and love in the world we shall not suffer."

"And while I have my good angel Hope, I shall not despair, even if I wait another thirty years before I step beyond the circle of the sacred little world in which I still have a place to fill."

So one bleak December day, with their few possessions piled on an ox-sled, the rosy children perched atop, and the parents trudging arm in arm behind, the exiles left their Eden and faced the world again.

"Ah, me! my happy dream. How much I leave behind that never can be mine again," said Abel, looking back at the lost Paradise, lying white and chill in its shroud of snow.

"Yes, dear; but how much we bring away," answered brave-hearted Hope, glancing from husband to children.

"Poor Fruitlands! The name was as great a failure as the rest!" continued Abel, with a sigh, as a frost-bitten apple fell from a leafless bough at his feet.

But the sigh changed to a smile as his wife added, in a half-tender, half-satirical tone:

"Don't you think Apple Slump would be a better name for it, dear?"

DIANA AND PERSIS

I

A PAIR OF FRIENDS

A TAP at the studio door broke the silence which had lasted for hours, and the busy worker looked up with an impatient, "Who is there?"

"Only Percy."

"Come in! Come in!" and throwing down her tools the young woman in the linen pinafore hastened to greet the newcomer with a sudden kindling of the absorbed face which showed how welcome she was.

"You have come to tell me something!" she exclaimed, the moment her eye fell upon that other face, more than ever unlike her own, for an unusually resolute expression made it both brilliant and intense.

"Yes, I have decided at last," and Percy threw her hat into one chair, herself into another with a somewhat tragical air.

"You have said yes?"

"I have said no."

"Thank heaven for that!" and Diana shook hands with an animation which was as sure as becoming.

"I knew *you* would be satisfied if no one else was," said Percy smothering a sigh, for she had a right womanly heart and it always ached when she was forced to utter that hard monosyllable to one of her many lovers.

"I am *never* satisfied and never expect to be, with myself at least," and the keen clear eyes glanced round the room as if seeking vainly for any

383

touch of perfection in the plaster, iron and marble figures that stood there as beautiful and calm as herself.

"For that reason it is both good and bad for me to have you for a bosom friend. You spur me on and you discourage me at the same time; for I must walk only in one path—and if I look to the right or left you frown upon me. I've told you one decision that pleases you, now I'll tell another that will displease you, though you ought to approve it since it is the right way: I am going abroad," announced Percy with something of the rapture which is always visible in the faces of art lovers when uttering those joyful words.

"Again?" asked Diana in surprise.

"Again. The first time I went to wonder, admire and discover what a conceited ignoramus I was to call myself an artist. Now I am going to begin more humbly and work hard for two or three years at least, content to call myself a student, nothing more."

"Humility is a good sign, especially when one has much to be proud of. But can you leave your Grandmother?"

"If we give ourselves entirely to Art we must trample on Nature occasionally; so in escaping from the lovers who annoy me to the work I prefer I must also turn my back on the last of my kindred and my dearest friend. Unless she will come too?" and Percy opened her arms with a look and gesture which would have made a sympathetic observer pity the unfortunate lovers whom she was eluding.

But Diana shook her head decidedly.

"No, dear, it is impossible. My time has not come yet and I have much to do before I am ready. But I am glad *you* are going though it leaves me forlorn, for in giving yourself wholly to work you will escape the temptations that beset you here. Now tell me all about it," and as if the thought of approaching separation melted away the native coldness that lay like a light frost upon her youth and beauty, she sat down beside her friend with a face full of affectionate interest.

"I am tired of everything! Especially of waiting for inspiration; I cannot find it here so I am going to look for it," began Percy, leaning back with her hands clasped over her head in a posture full of graceful abandon and an expression of ardent discontent which betrayed a liberty-loving nature trying to divine and obey instincts as unerring as the flower's love of light, the bird's impulse to sing.

"'Genius is infinite patience,' you remember," and Diana pointed to the motto of Michael Angelo inscribed above her door.

"Genius makes its own mood, talent needs much help and gets discouraged if there are too many obstacles to surmount."

"I'm afraid you will always have one sort of obstacle in your way because you cannot help being most attractive and lovable," said Diana, fondly smoothing the breezy brown locks which framed a face far less beautiful than her own but infinitely more lovely, being full of the color, light, and changefulness which makes a woman's countenance enchanting.

"Oh yes, I can! I intend to brush out my curls, wear that unbecoming sage green gown of mine and look as repulsively plain and artistically absorbed as possible," laughed Percy, holding back the rebellious waves that clustered about cheek and forehead as if they loved to keep youth there.

Diana smiled also but was not satisfied, for though the change added age, it also discovered the fine lines traced by five and twenty years of a very earnest life, making the face both sweet and noble.

"Unfortunately men have eyes all the world over and foreigners use them more freely than our courteous countrymen, so I shall still tremble for you, Percy."

"You need not, except in England. There I shall feel at home and maybe in danger. I so much admire color, strength and stature in both men and women. On the continent I will veil myself like a vestal virgin and keep the vow I make my chosen goddess, Diana."

"My vengeance will be heavy if you forget. But, seriously, are you bent on this, Percy, or is it only one of your impatient moods?"

"Seriously I am bent on this, and it is not a passing mood. I am impatient—because I feel power of some sort stirring in me, yet I cannot put it into any shape that satisfies me."

"It satisfies others and that is a great deal. How many women of your age have done so much, made so excellent a beginning, and won such genuine praise? Most people would be content to stop, for a time at least, to enjoy their success."

"I cannot! I have not *earned* my success, it came by accident. My work is not thoroughly good, only striking; for I aimed high and audacity always tells at first; but when the novelty of style wears off, the poverty of the material will show. I know I *can* do better if I can only get more criticism and less praise; find the right atmosphere, the right inspiration, and really do my best."

"And you hope to discover both in Rome?" asked Diana, looking as if the noble discontent of her friend woke some longings in her own ambitious soul.

"No, Rome will come later; Paris is the place to study in, and that is what I want. My eye for color is a gift that blinds me as well as others to my bad drawing, so I am going to sit on the low seats and learn. A year of hard work at it will do me good, for those Frenchmen *can* draw, though their coloring is often atrocious. I know this is what I need and I mean to have it at any price. Here there are too many pleasures to distract me, too many temptations to let my art go and do as other women do. Grandmamma says I should be happier if I did. Perhaps she is right—I certainly need motive of some sort if only I knew where to find it." Percy's face seemed to sharpen with the keen anxiety of a nature both impetuous and conscientious, longing to find and do the right.

"Don't look for it in marriage, that is too costly an experiment for us. Flee from temptation and do not dream of spoiling your life by any commonplace romance, I implore you," cried Diana earnestly, and this was not the first time she had given the same advice.

"Yet love is the great teacher they say. I want to learn of the best. I am half tempted to try sometimes, for I have a hungry heart as well as an ambitious spirit and art alone does not seem to satisfy me as it does you."

There was a touch of pathos in the girl's voice and a wistful look in the eyes that wandered around the large, bare room, coldly lighted from the north and peopled with many forms of classic beauty; a strong contrast to the sunshine, life and warmth that filled her own little studio and made it as charming as herself.

"Percy, you regret that last No, and this new plan is a flight because you doubt yourself?" and Diana took the clouded face in her two hands to read it with anxious scrutiny.

The frank eyes met her gaze freely though the sensitive lips trembled a little as they answered with a smile half proud, half sad.

"I regret nothing; but it is always hard to deny what most women delight to give and receive. If I had a marble heart like you, I should be much happier."

"You would lose your greatest charm which is your tender and sympathetic nature. You could not paint as you do without it, for warmth and color are your delight as clay and stone are mine, and we are both suited to our work."

Diana kissed the face and let it go reluctantly as if peculiarly conscious of the charm just then.

"That reminds me! I want your opinion of a little thing I have here; just a fancy; a thought rather," said Percy rising to untie the parcel she had thrown down with her hat.

Leaning it against the august knees of a Pallas on the bracket opposite, she resumed her seat and silently watched her friend as she examined it. Only an unframed canvas, high and narrow, with a mere suggestion of a grassy field below, all above was sky meeting from silvery morning mist through sunny blue to the palest gold, and midway between, a bird soaring and singing as if Heaven's gate was the goal of its desire.

A simple thing, but exquisitely painted, for one seemed to feel the cool breath of early day, to see the little bosom swell and quiver with its ecstatic music, and following the lark's flight to echo the immortal songs that make it an emblem of aspiration.

"Percy, it is *very* good! The rising mist is wonderful and that sky simply perfect. I never saw a lark go up but I know how it looks. You were not waiting for inspiration when you did this, I am sure," said Diana with conviction, her eye still on the picture, giving it the commendation of perceptive interest which artists value more than words of praise.

"Glad you like it. I have a superstitious sort of feeling about it because it was born of a mood, and I sometimes find when I follow such that they lead me to unexpected results. I was very dismal and discontented the other day, longing for something fresh and cheery to lift me out of the fog, and suddenly I found myself recalling a certain summer morning when I lay under a yellow gorse bush on Wimbledon Common and saw the larks go up while talking about ambition with my friend Vaughn. I *was* waiting for inspiration; it came in this form, I fell to work, and when my picture was done I had decided to go abroad."

"For another talk about ambition under the gorse bushes?" asked Diana, with a suspicious glance and a sudden recollection of Percy's words, "No danger except in England."

"Vaughn's wife and pretty boys were with us, so you need not smile in that satiric way. I am done with lovers and leave them all behind me, I devoutly hope," answered Percy, with a disdainful shrug. "Would you like it better if the foreground were more clearly defined?" she added, going back to her picture as if the other subject had lost all interest for her. "Grandmammma said it tired her to think the poor lark had no place to rest in, because no bird that flies is without a nest of some sort, and sings the sweeter for it."

"Pretty sentiment, but the picture is better without it. Anyone can paint a nest but few a sky like that and make us feel in looking at the lark, 'Bird thou never wert.'"

"Thanks. Grandma admired it very much but said, "If you mean a spirit paint one, my dear, but if you want that bird to be happy give her a comfortable nest full of little responsibilities, for the highest flyers need a home and that lark for all its twittering has got to drop sometime since it cannot live in the clouds."

"You certainly have one frank critic. Nevertheless I am glad you did not spoil your work. My lark does not stoop to fill gaping beaks with worms while her own is full of music that delights all ears, nor sit content among the daisies when she can fly above the clouds," said Diana, jealously covering with her slender hand the vague hint of a nest in the foreground.

"Yet the same instinct that sent her up brings her down, so I suppose she is wise to follow it, and Grandma may be right after all." And Percy stared thoughtfully at a dusty engraving of the Cotter's Saturday Night tucked behind the Minerva as of little worth.[1]

"Follow the instinct that takes you away from all sickly sentiment before you disgrace yourself. When do you go?" asked Diana, returning abruptly to the safer topic.

"Next week. Solitary confinement and hard work for one year at least is my sentence, so you see I am to atone for my errors and be a credit to you. It will have an excellent effect upon me, I am sure, and tone me down till I am as steadfast, calm and contented as my model. Art is a jealous mistress and now I give myself to her entirely."

Percy threw herself into the arms of her friend with a dramatic gesture, as if she personified the austere goddess henceforth to be served with perfect devotion.

"Now I am pleased with you and prophesy great things of you. Hold fast to your purpose and in a year or two I will come rejoice over you, and we will go to Rome together."

"We will!" and the friends sealed the bargain with a laughing embrace, both being heartily in earnest and both glad to sweeten the sorrow of separation by the thought of that happy reunion. "Now what can I do to help? If you sail in a week you leave yourself little time for preparation," said Diana, as Percy took up her hat.

"I need even less than I have because I leave all my finery behind me and go in light marching order as becomes a student who means work. I've nothing to do but buy a pea jacket, pack my paint box and a few old gowns, kiss Grandma and be off," answered Percy, assuming a brisk and breezy air pleasant to behold.

"You will write often? for I shall be so lonely and so interested in all you do I shall depend on long and frequent letters."

"That will be the one luxury I shall allow myself. But the letters will be dull, I warn you, for I shall keep out of society and have no gaiety to report. I intend to live like a hermit and toil like a slave, for it is possible to do both in dear delightful Paris, as many a hardworking student can tell you."

"Don't live alone. It is not good for a social girl like you, though it suits me excellently. Hunt up some of your old mates and make one of the busy little households we hear about over there. Now promise me you will?" and Diana anxiously urged her point, for the idea of this impulsive, attractive creature trying to live alone oppressed her as if she saw a child about to be shut into a prison cell.

"My dear soul, I'm going straight to Anna Becket and her cousin who have been there several years and are continually begging me to come and join them. That will be my refuge for a time, just while I look about me and settle my plans. The vastness and vagueness of the whole expedition is its charm. I feel like Columbus going to discover a new world, for when I went before, it was as a fine lady with all proper guards and guides; now I go alone with only my own common sense and courage to protect me."

"How did you ever bring your Grandmother to consent, and you the apple of her eye?" asked Diana looking with both wonder and admiration at this energetic friend of hers who, though some years her junior, was launching her little boat so bravely and blithely into the sea of experience and leaving so much behind her.

"The dear old lady is a wise woman who believes that we must each live out our own life in our own way and it is folly to try and shape us all in the same mold. She knows that I shall drift into matrimony with half a heart unless I break away and follow my heart till I am satisfied. So she lets me go with her blessing and not a word of complaint, like a Spartan mother as she is. A sacrifice for both of us, but she shall be proud of me and so I will repay her."

Percy's eyes shone eager, proud and tender through the sudden dew that rose to them and it was plain to see that her share of the sacrifice was not a light one.

"I know you will! And while you are gone I shall try to fill our place, and in rejoicing over you we shall comfort one another."

"I give you an order for a bust of her; it is too fine a head to be lost and in making it you will come to know and love one another better for my sake. Will you do this for me? Put the dear old face in marble since it cannot be immortal otherwise, and I may not find it here when I come back," added Percy with a sudden falter in her voice that made refusal impossible.

"I will, and put my heart into the work. It is so like you to do a kindness as if receiving a favor! You shall pay for the bust in letters; I will take no other coin," and Diana put both hands on her friend's shoulders to enforce her words with the gentle pride which no poverty could humble since affection and principle ennobled it.

"As you like; and I'll send you my first great picture in return," began Percy, privately resolving to circumvent her friend in some way.

"No, leave me this unless you value it too much," interrupted Diana, taking up the little canvas with a face full of fond covetousness. "Your Grandmother will not care for it since it tires her. I like it; I too have a superstitious feeling about it, and associate it with you, fancying I can watch your flight as I watch this bird with its spread wings and open beak just passing out of the mist into the blue above."

"Keep it then until I send a better, showing that ambitious fowl high up against the gale." For a moment the two stood looking silently at the dumb canvas which was as eloquent to their eyes as a chord of stirring music to a musician's ear, a key to the great symphony which in tone or color, thought or deed makes life harmonious for earnest livers.

"Now I must go. Come tomorrow and help me choose the pea jacket. I can't fly off so easily as the swallows on their journey south, more's the pity," said Percy, descending suddenly into the commonplace as a relief from too much feeling.

"Good bye, my lark, soar and sing and get above the clouds as soon as possible, and stay there as long as you can," answered Diana, with a gaiety that thinly veiled more serious significance.

"Good bye, my eagle; however high I go I shall find you before me, for you can look at the sun with unwinking eyes and your wings never tire; while I can only twitter up a little way and tumble down again all out of breath," answered Percy with equal meaning and went away humming to herself,

Higher still and higher
From the earth thou springest,
Like a cloud of fire;
The deep blue thou wingest,
And singing still dost soar, and soaring ever singest.[2]

These two had been friends from girlhood, the tie between them being artistic ambition and a sincere respect for each other's powers. Both were unusually gifted, not only with talent but with the courage and patience which are the wings of genius; and after ten years of steady upward climbing they were now ready for the flight out of the world of effort into the region of achievement, that promised land which so many sigh for and never see.

Diana stood alone now, a strong, self-reliant woman of twenty-eight; laboring always with calm persistence at the purpose of her life, to reach Rome and there do the great work which should unlock the golden future to her longing soul. No nun in her cell ever led a more austere and secluded life than this fine creature intent upon her self-appointed task.

Denying herself the pleasures of youth, the honors of sex and beauty, the joys of love, the solaces of home, she went on her steadfast way, unresting and unhasting as a star; as cold and brilliant and remote to all except the few who had discovered hidden fires in this fair planet. Bread and the right to work was all she asked of the world as yet. One friendship was the only luxury she allowed herself and in this she found not only the solace but the stimulant she needed, for it was a most sincere and sympathetic bond.

Percy had blossomed in a sunnier soil and from it gathered the warm, rich nature which makes some women among their kind what roses are among the flowers, thorny yet sweet, infinitely various but always lovely and beloved. A happy childhood, a free, fresh girlhood, and now a womanhood full of promise, because the wise and earnest culture of those years began to blossom into high thoughts, courageous action, noble purposes, which time alone could ripen.

What adversity had done for Diana, prosperity had done for Percy and each drew from the soil of life the nourishment she needed, growing toward the sun of their desire slowly and steadily as green things struggle up in spring. The same aim was theirs, success and happiness; but with Diana success came first, with Percy happiness; both being conscious at times of that secret warfare of thwarted instincts and imperious ambitions, the demands of temperament as well as of talent, the lessons Nature teaches all of us in ways more mysterious and masterful than any Art can give.

Diana was the stronger willed woman, Percy the deeper hearted, and each found in the other the attributes most needed to complete her own character. Not a sentimental but a most helpful and enduring affection which had lasted unbroken for years and might still live for many more unless the master passion which dissolves all lesser ties should come between them. As yet it had not, for Diana hid herself in her little studio, consecrating even her beauty to her art, and being her own model, since a better it would be hard to find, and Percy staunchly tried to follow her example in spite of many obstacles, her winsome self included.

That genial old gentlewoman Madam Lennox made a most attractive home for her granddaughter in whom was bound up her love and hope and pride, for she was the last of her line. Wisely leaving the girl to unfold as God willed, the tender soul hid her own doubts and desires, waiting for time to teach and love to tame the ardent, ambitious girl.

Percy could no more help having lovers than a clover can forbid the bees and butterflies from coming for its honey, and but for her dreams of art, she might soon have found her fate as many a young girl does, believing that women were born to be wives only, and finding out too late that every soul has its own life to live and cannot hastily ignore its duties to itself without bitter suffering and loss. Fortune she had not, being dependent on her kinswoman, but youth and the gift of attraction, more potent than beauty, she had in fullest measure, and the cordial grace of her frank manners, the enthusiasm which went into everything she did, the quick sympathy that was a key to all natures, made her a very winning woman, and there was no lack of suitors for so loyal a heart, so generous a hand.

But Percy's ideal was a high one, and with the arrogance of happy youth she would abate no item in the list of virtues which made up the perfect man who was her hero, so the enamoured gentlemen pleaded all in vain. Diana, devoutly believing that "Success is impossible, unless the passion for art overcomes all desultory passions," held Percy to her ideal with stern vigor, always hoping that the time would come when her friend would give all to art and let love go, as she herself had done. Therefore she trembled at every temptation, rejoiced at every fresh denial, and now although her heart sank at the thought of its great loneliness in losing Percy, she bade her go, sure that in work alone her salvation as an artist lay.

Hiding her pain with a heroic smile, she went to say farewell when the last hour came, and Percy, equally heavy hearted but not equally strong, clung to her with the remorseful tenderness of those who go toward those left behind. Both kept up bravely till the great steamer swung round into the stream, then both hearts swelled to overflowing and tears dimmed the eyes that sought and held each other across the widening gulf between them.

"In a year!" cried Percy, leaning down for one last hopeful word.

"Remember!" answered Diana, with a warning gesture toward the nosegay in her friend's hand, a farewell taken from the lover who dared not come to reutter what the roses sweetly said for him.

"I will!" and with a tearful laugh, an impulsive motion, Percy flung the poor flowers far away into the bitter waves that swept them out of sight among the foam.

Diana waved her hand, well pleased at this brave casting behind her of all dangerous sentiment, and dashing the rare drops from her own eyes watched till the receding figure could be no longer seen, then turned away, thinking with a desolate sort of resignation—"My work still remains, and that must satisfy me, for a year at least."

But Percy went below to hide her tears, saying with a sob in her throat as she tenderly removed a little spray of green which had blown back and clung to the rough bosom of her pea coat when she flung away the nosegay:

"Love won't be disowned, it seems; I'll keep this bit of sentiment to comfort me when I'm homesick all alone on the great, cold sea."

II

LETTERS

✡✡✡✡✡

SEP T.

"*DEAREST DI,*

My first letter telling of my voyage and safe arrival was to Grandmamma of course, but this shall be all yours, for in it I will unfold my projects and tell you how propitious the fates have been.

Straight to Paris and Anna Becket did I come, for London in the autumn does not tempt me, though I did take a peep at my beloved National Gallery the one day I passed there. I found Anna and her cousin Cordelia settled in a nice little apartment at the foot of Montmarte, with its picturesque old windmill to gladden our eyes when we look out from our sixth story windows, for like true artists we live up among the clouds. Not a fashionable but an eminently respectable Quartier, I beg to assure you, for Thiers lives just around the corner, as it were. Three tiny bedrooms, a pretty salon, and studio with a kitchen is our establishment and here we live, three merry spinsters, doing most everything for ourselves in the simple, free and easy way best suited to our professions and our purses.

My friends are capital girls and welcomed me so kindly that I felt at home at once, and thanked my fortunate stars that I had found so pleasant a refuge and such congenial comrades. By Anna's advice I went immediately to K's studio for women and entered my name as a pupil; for it gives us most of the advantages of J's great school for men and women. We pay more but we are spared many of the trials which

395

afflict us at the other place. We looked in at J's where most of the great painters have studied till they went to the Beaux Arts, and here we found a fine model posing to a crowd of men who whistled, sang and joked while drawing away in the most vigorous style. I could have borne it if there had been no other place for us, but felt very grateful that there *was*. At K's I find a good earnest set of women and our master is a most agreeable man and a fine teacher. Three of the best painters in France come twice a week to criticize and correct our work. There are fourteen pupils in the morning, all American or English, and as many more in the afternoon, but a younger set. By paying for both classes one can also draw in the evening as gaslight is considered excellent for the shadows.

I see that it will be best for me to work all day for six months at least, drawing the ensemble in the morning and painting in oils from the head only in the afternoon. I shall not try work in the evening as I need the rest and time to do other things. Working from life models is most exciting as you know, but, Di, *we* never had such grand ones as these, and I long for you every time I sit down before one of them.

Our model this week is Italian with a superb physique and the head of a god. His rich coloring distracts me because I can not paint it all day, and I try vainly to get a good copy of his great dark eyes, proudly dilating nostrils and picturesque head with its jovelike curls. The pose is perfect, and it is wonderful how he can keep it so long. Figure to yourself the difficulty; head thrown back, eyes raised, stepping forward with an air of rapid motion in every limb, and so he stands for an hour like a statue, and we draw like mad, for soon great drops come upon his forehead and every muscle shows, so great the effort and yet so perfect his control. He has been a model for years and is so proud of his posing that his indignation knew no bounds when one of the ladies suggested that he was not quite in position. With a glance of scorn he threw himself into a magnificent pose and did not deign us any further notice that lesson.

So much for school, which I find intensely interesting and work with all my soul, as it is impossible to help doing here, for nothing draws me away as at home and I never tire though I never toiled so hard. You may like a hasty sketch of our day, uneventful as it usually is. We are up early, light being precious, and in our wrappers, "fly round" each doing her share, for thus is housekeeping made easy. One steps into the little kitchen and puts a match to the few bits of charcoal needed to make our coffee or chocolate, another dusts the salon and studio, and the third runs out to do our dainty marketing and order dinner from the *restaurant* nearby. We take our coffee and rolls while dressing, talking and laughing all together, in the jolliest way. Isn't Grandma shocked? Then Anna makes ready for her sitters (she is a portrait painter, you know, and does wonders in that line). Cordy retires to her den to write the letters you must read in the American papers, and I hurry away to school, eager to be at work though I hate drawing in black and white and long for my colors. At twelve I run home for a hot breakfast, or lunch we should call it, cooked by the girls who make the most delicious messes out of nothing in the true French style. Then back to work till dusk which always comes too soon for me. We dine at six and in the evening sew, study, see friends and frolic in a mild artistic manner, going to bed early to sleep well and dream of immortality.

I told you my letters would be dull and you see how quiet life is likely to be. But I did not come to play and I am more than ever convinced that this is the best place in the world to study, though it takes the conceit out of one to see how these people work. Careful drawing from the life model to begin with, whether landscape or figure is to be the profession afterward; the same routine that Broyan, Dupais and Casâl went through with for years before their reputations were established. It must be hard study for a year or so at least and no "pot boilers" allowed, to help out expenses. But they are very small living in the cozy, simple way we do, and six or seven hundred a year is enough for women who take no thought for frippery and frivolity. A thousand is a fortune, so, thanks to the dearest old lady in the world, I am quite a millionaire.

Only here a fortnight and I already begin to dream of the Salon which alone makes a name for the happy soul who gets in.[3] There's audacity for you! I always did aim high, and in two years I will be far up the tree with every prospect of a perch in the topmost twig in time. It is impossible to help being sanguine and ambitious, for the earnestness I find here is most contagious and one cannot take hold of painting superficially when everybody is intent on doing his or her very best. Art pervades the air, everyone paints, all the talk is of pictures. Color, shapes surround us, studios are thicker than houses in this quarter, and at 8 a.m. the streets swarm with artists of all nationalities, paint box in hand, hurrying in every direction with absorbed faces. I am told there are forty thousand of these ambitious souls in France alone, all trying to go where glory awaits them, and Paris seems to be their headquarters; so you cannot wonder that the fever rages here and I am rapidly falling a victim to it, being a susceptible creature as you know.

Now, dear, I have told you my debut, so don't imagine me gamboling about this gay city with wild students, or leading a Bohemian life while pretending to study. Think of me always as in deadly earnest, for this is the place to meet one's fate, success or failure, and I am started on the exciting race, so wish me God speed, and write often to keep me up to the mark as you always can.

A thousand loves to dear Grandma. My next shall be to her, for you must take turns and so will get variety.

Ever yours,
P.L."

Nov.

"Dear Di,

All the gossip I could collect went to Grandmamma last week, so I can drop into Art for you this time, having nothing else to offer. It is Sunday, and after going to church like good girls, we sit in our little salon round the first fire of the season painting while Cordy reads aloud, for without a brush or crayon in our hands we feel like old ladies bereft of their knitting. I am at work on a still life study just for practice. A brass brazier standing on a dark polished table with a scarlet flower in it. Anna is putting the last touches to a splendid portrait of a handsome lady in black velvet, sitting on a yellow satin sofa, gorgeous to behold. Cordy is reading the newspaper letter of a Paris correspondent which she means to answer as we are all indignant about it. It is just such hastily written, one-sided things that do infinite harm at home by prejudicing people against aiding women in the art studies which they so much need; the obstacles being so great that only those in desperate earnest are able to surmount them at great cost of money, time and feeling. We should have had no fine pictures by Rosa Bonheur if with her tastes she had contented herself with flowers or still life, "the only things this writer considers delicate and proper for a lady's brush."[4]

As for "the women who unsex themselves by going to J's studio," where alone they could get the teaching they needed, we think it a thing to heartily respect them for, as one respects those who study anatomy in order to be surgeons. That little band of dignified and earnest women so far from unsexing themselves were treated with the utmost respect at J's, and very soon made by their mere presence a purer atmosphere about them. Courage is honored everywhere, and this terrible effort to get the same advantages as men in the same profession at any cost, won for them a place at once in the regard of all real art students. I had rather the French judged us by these brave, rightminded women than by the frivolous creatures who bring discredit on the name of American girls by their wild pranks and empty heads.

We are twitted with getting no medals at the Salon. How can we when hitherto we were not allowed to study at the life schools yet expected to do as well in a third of the time and with half the help men have? How few of them get prizes with all their chances. Wait a little, Messieurs, give us a few years of equal teaching, equal opportunities and see what we will do.

Now I feel better and will go on more calmly and only I beg you will read my protest to all our mates and tell them not to be daunted but to come on, and do their best for every success helps us up.

I have little to report at the studio for it has been a steady grind for me, yet I like it and get on, I am sure. The great M, our most dreaded critic, when our studies were given to him to examine the other day asked, "Who did that?" and lo, it was mine. He gave me a look, a nod said, "This flesh is luminous," and looked again at my work, a head in oils. No more, but I was much elated and my mates patted me on the head when we were alone. I tell you this as my first small success, for you will understand how it cheers one after weeks of dogged work and the despondency that will come to the most sanguine of us when thinking how endless is the lesson we artists have to learn.

We have been a little gay this last week, and as I have made a new friend I will tell you of her, for she is one after your own heart. Miss Cassal[5] comes to the studio to draw when we have a fine model and I liked her strong face the first time I saw it. She liked my work and came very kindly to tell me so one day when I was struggling with a hard lesson, for K would have me draw to the waist when I preferred only the head of our model. She asked me to come and see her and I went. She is a grand woman, full of real genius, I think, and but for her sex would have made a name before now, since all who know her acknowledge her power. She has the modesty of true talent and so is content to do fine things and let others get praised for mediocre work, she biding her time. Her pictures are handled in a masterly way and with a strength one seldom finds in a woman's fingers. I am told that men are jealous of her, and her "Joel" was refused at the last Salon merely because of its boldness and power. She smiles and paints on tranquilly, content to be felt if not seen. She has money and uses it nobly, not only in helping herself but others, and we have a plan in our heads to get up a school for women, a studio where we can club together and have the best models and masters and a chance to show what we can do with a clear track and fair judges. Her enthusiasm delights me and we shook hands like old friends after my long visit full of the most interesting talk.

This week we went to tea in her studio which is a charming place and the resort of many of the young artists, men as well as women; there last evening, we met fifteen or twenty of them and had a most enjoyable time sitting in antique chairs on Persian rugs with tapestry backgrounds, fine pictures on the walls, pretty things all about us, and the whole lighted by hanging lamps in the most artistic and effective manner. Some of the men sang and we sipped tea and ate ices, but the talk was the best, for it was art, still art. I was much interested in several of these people and in answering my questions Miss C told me some pretty little stories about them, which you will like as they show how kind these artists are to one another.

One young man, an American, shy, awkward and plain but with an eye that is full of fire and a resolute mouth, was the hero of one tale. He has been plugging along here for some years on almost nothing, slowly but surely overcoming poverty, ignorance and neglect and at last begins to see light, having done a good picture and received an order or two (thanks to Miss C, I suspect). He was just rejoicing over his luck when he hurt his right hand seriously and could not work for some time. He was in despair, for he earns his daily bread with this right hand of his, but his friends came to the rescue and, knowing he was too proud to accept alms, asked him to be their model, as he has a fine stalwart figure. So he stands to them and is well paid, for they not only paint him but cheer him with friendly talk and a little kindness instead of leaving him to eat his heart out alone. "Now I like that!" says dear Grandmamma. So do I.

Here is another. A portrait painter, a woman (not Anna, she has more than she can manage, thank Heaven!), wanted sitters but was unknown and too poor to fit up an attractive studio. A brother artist, with a name, offered to sit, knowing that she only needed a start to be appreciated. His portrait is a success; is exhibited in his own much frequented atelier and greatly admired; a good word is said for the painter and orders flow in. So the modest girl is led to the place she has earned by the kind hand of a comrade and puts all her heart into her work that she may prove her gratitude by being an honor to him.

These and many more like them did Miss C tell me, for she is a sort of refuge to the younger set, being forty and full of maternal sympathy and generosity which is so winning I don't wonder the poor fellows are glad to come to her with their hopes and plans, trials and defeats, and it is both comical and pathetic to hear about them.

We have our little society at home, for Anna and Cordy have a most interesting circle of friends, and in the evening they drop in to report progress and see how we are getting on. Our countrymen mostly, studying for dear life as we are, so our interests are the same and we can help one another in many ways. The little homes we women naturally make for ourselves are very attractive to these poor fellows, often homesick and lonely, longing for society after the day's work is done, and too poor or too wise to seek the sort easiest found in Paris. We can give them an innocent helpful kind of pleasure for which they are grateful, and they bring into our quiet lives the masculine element which stimulates us without harm, for we are all too busy for sentiment and are just good comrades, nothing more I assure you.

Clothes, my dear? In answer to your question regarding that usually all absorbing topic, I rely that I don't think of it. In fact, drawing such noble nude figures all day makes modern drapery seem impertiment and ugly and I long to dress with antique simplicity in a tunic and veil. The sage green serge is all I need for school, and the old wine-colored silk does well for evening when we receive. Indeed it is a success to my great amusement and I am glad I brought it to please Grandma, for Anna declares she will paint my portrait in it on the famous yellow sofa which comes into play continually. The effect will be Turneresque, and when it is done I'll send it to you labeled "The Fighting Seinereraise," or a "Symphony in Red and Yellow," à la Whistler.[6] No, Di, no new raiment even here in the Vanity Fair of the world. I want all my money for lessons and every hour of the time taken from dear Gran shall be spent in good honest work, not fun and feathers, for I mean to prove that some women do love art better than dress.

With which beautiful moral sentiment I will say adieu.

Ever your P."

Dec.

"My Dear,

I have neglected you shamefully of late, but I am so busy I really get only time for a hasty letter once a fortnight and my last two or three have been hardly worth sending. Work goes on apace, but the last week nothing interesting broke the daily routine, then the holy days were celebrated by two exciting events, for me at least. I have come to honor unexpectedly, and I must tell you about it like a vain peacock as I am. I was in the depths of discouragement on Monday and went to the Studio resolving to give it all up and sail in the next steamer. You know the state of mind, so I need not describe it. I found a new model, and sat down before him in despair for he was a grand figure and I felt that I was not in the mood to grapple with him. The lesson was a full length drawing of this Othello, as I at once named the handsome Moor, who was really a chief in his own country, has been decorated for bravery in the Crimean War, and is now a famous model here in Paris.

If I could have put the fine dark face and red drapery into color I should have been happy, but as it was only drawing I did not get on very well till a discussion arose about the man. Two of the class are Southerners and were rather scornful about the "negro" as they called him. He could understand little English but I know he *felt* what was said, for his eyes kindled and the brave breast with the scars on it (better than medals in my eyes), heaved now and then as if he longed to speak, while he looked what he is, every inch a soldier and a prince. I could not bear to have things said even in jest which might wound him since he could not resent them, and getting excited by the discussion I gave an antislavery lecture which would have delighted Grandma, who longs for the stirring times when she and her stout-hearted contemporaries sat out many a mob knitting with majestic composure up aloft while brick bats and hard words flew about below.

Well I fired all my big guns and silenced the enemy after a lively skirmish, for we all took sides as K was in his room with the great M. So busy was I defending my man that I drew without thinking what I was about and when the time was up was surprised to see how well I had wrought both spirited pose and expression. We did not dream that the gentlemen heard or understood us, but when M came out to look at our work we discovered that he at least had. When he reached that dashing haphazard sketch of mine, he gave the decided nod which makes our hearts leap, and said as he looked carefully at it, "With what passion and enthusiasm you draw this ensemble! It is very vigorous; it shows your knowledge, not your scorn of the race. Mademoiselle, I make you my compliment," and with a bow he marched away.

He spoke in French. Othello understood and flashed a smile at me as he vanished behind the screen, leaving me as red, with surprise and pleasure, as the drapery he flung over his shoulder with a superb gesture.

Then did I vaingloriously exalt myself and strut gaily home to recount my triumph. Really, Di, it *was* well done, and I feel as if I had got a good grip at last, for what was very hard three months ago now grows more easy with each day's efforts and now and then I seem to take a leap ahead. I am to paint my prince soon, I will send him home if I do well, for I want you to see this fine head. Tell Grandma I owe this success to her, for the principles she taught me inspired my pencil and so brought me to honor.

On the spur of the moment I proposed that we present M with a grand bouquet on New Year's Day and the vote was unanimously carried. We have had a little Christmas merry-making and I, going at one skip from the Slough of Despond to my present high state of spirits, enjoyed the fun with all my heart. Dumont, our friend who is sitting for Anna in cavalier costume, as I told you in my last, is a jolly soul and always doing kind things; so on Christmas Day among other gifts from other comrades came a great Christmas pie from him, for he lives like a luxurious bachelor in his own apartment with a first-class cook.

A truly noble pie was this, with his crest in the crust and a great red rose was laid atop with a French air. We feasted on this delectable pastry and a turkey cooked in our own oven which with difficulty contained his grand proportions. A merry dinner, though we drank "To the absent" with full eyes and talked much of home. In the eve we sent back D's dish full of bonbons and a note of thanks illustrated by Anna. Our chosen bird, the owl, was drawn sitting on the back of a chair with a lace handkerchief at her eyes, and great tears dropping into an empty dish on the table below, while from her beak came the mournful strain, "Joys we have tasted."

Jan. 2nd

"I left my letter open to add how nicely our little presentation went off. M was both surprised and pleased when our lovely great nosegay was presented, accompanied by a few grateful words. With the grace and address of a Frenchmen, he paid us a pretty compliment by likening us to the flowers, as he thanked us for the honor we did him in giving him our photographs on New Year's Day. So now we all feel very friendly and begin the year in the best of spirits. I am disappointed at not having my prince to paint at once, but he is elsewhere and I must wait. Meantime, with artistic versatility I go from heads to heels, for our model this week has not an interesting face so I take his legs, which are good. He wears leather breeches, worsted gaiters with tassles, and muddy shoes, as the rest only use his shaggy head. He naturally crossed these legs as he sat and I booked them, to the great amusement of the class, for they were done *con amore,* with big brushes and lots of paint, and do look as if they would get up and walk out of the canvas. K laughed when he saw it, but said, "That is good strong work," so I was satisfied and had a heavenly time daubing away with my "beloved paintpots" as Grandma and you irreverently call them. She would be scandalized at the state of my elbows, for I cannot spare time to darn, so go in rags, "picturesque but not tidy," as she used to say when I went about professionally disheveled. Yes, I do long for home, but must stay my time out, for I begin to feel as if I had the *right* to be here since I am really getting on, unless my master and mates deceive me. So you must prepare to join me in the autumn, and persuade the dear old lady to come along. You would find yourself a new world, and she would enjoy this life immensely. Tell her to remember how Mrs. G gallantly swung her bonnet on the Cheops at seventy-five and go and do likewise. Come, oh come to

Your P."

March

"Oh my dearest Di, we live in such exciting times just now! I hardly know where to begin to tell about them. It is such a sudden plunge out of the last two or three months of dull grind into all sorts of hopes and plans and possible glories. You remember my despair over the failure of my prince's head, and how I took to still life studies in a rage? Well, things never go as one expects and art is a continual surprise party. I did a stupid little affair one day; a bottle, jug and dish of fruit just as they happened to stand on our dining table with the oak wainscot for background. Anna praised it, but I, still smarting with my disappointment over the head, rather scoffed at it, calling it the "onions and copper kettle style," which I don't care for though it *is* good practice, I admit. I took it to school to be criticized and you

405

may judge my astonishment when M came round to look at my drawing, and dismissing it with a word, took up the study which I had forgotten, saying (hold on to something, Di, for I am about to knock you down, metaphorically speaking) "Ha, this is excellent, I could not do better myself. Send it to the Salon and I shall be proud to call you my *élève*."[8] K stood by beaming upon me much pleased at the Master's praise, and before I could get my breath to reply, M said, "Take that into the class and show those ladies what painting simply what you see without trying to *make a picture* will do for one, even without great practice." Then he looked again and repeated, "*Trés bien, trés bien, Mademoiselle;* you cannot do better than to go on in this way. Send that to the Salon."

With this astonishing advice he left me, and I am hardly recovered from the agreeable shock yet. A more amazed young woman did not exist than I, and you will believe that my wits are quite gone when I tell you that I am actually going to send that insignificant study to the Salon. I shall never believe it is good till I see it there, for in spite of all my master says I feel that if I ever do win fame it will be in painting heads and not pots and pans. Mark my prophetic words, uttered this day from the tripod of a shabby music stool, for I am in an uplifted state and feel oracular.

Anna is going to send her portrait of me if she can get it done in time. It is capital, and I have put my study into a cheap frame, and mean to send it along as the most stupendous joke of the season. If it *is* accepted (which I don't dream of) it will be a great honor as I am but a beginner, and a fine feather in my cap. If I am refused (which I fully expect) it will be no disgrace as I am a foreigner, a woman without a name, and six thousand were refused last year.

Everyone is in a frenzy now, for next Monday the 18th is the day for sending in the pictures and I have caught the fever since all the artists are hurrying madly to get done. As my great work is finished, I sit every day to Anna, who has had other things on hand and so let my portrait lie by; but it does not need much time to finish it if the light will only be good. Did I tell you that we gave up the red dress, and I am in peacock blue with all my curls out on a holy day and a muff and a hat, which turn the studious grub into a gay butterfly? It is a good likeness and I shall send it to Grandma who will value it whether it is accepted or not. I am wanted and must fly, for I write with all my borrowed gauds on while waiting for Anna to snatch her dinner.

Later

Such a scramble! but it is over now, and I can tell of it, for it was splendid fun. For the last two or three days Anna has been painting at a great pace, and I have hardly stirred except to eat a morsel and get what sleep I could. Miss Cassal came to help us along and we had gay suppers after the day's hurry was over. You would have laughed to see me rushing about in my swishing blue train and dashing hat while Anna tyrannized over me and Cordy brought us food, and friends kept dashing in to hear how we got on.

We finished in time and I was whisked into a fine frame and left to dry as fast as I could in a warm room till the man came for *both* our works. Glad to escape Miss C and I went off to see the pictures arrive at the Palais de l'Industrie where an immense crowd was assembled; mostly art students who, as the pictures were carried up the steps and dumped to be registered, sent up howls of derision or cries of admiration at the work of anyone known to them.[9]

It was intensely exciting, and we stood with a group of friends as anxious as ourselves; for as six o'clock drew near and wagon after wagon drove up to be unloaded, the painters got perfectly distracted and rushed the pictures up in desperate haste, the elegant frames flying in splinters sometimes, amid the jeers of the crowd and the groans of the poor artist who saw his treasured work thus sadly handled. We stood for three mortal hours and forgot weariness in our interest. Still our pictures did not arrive, and we set off down the long line of wagons to see if we could find them. Just driving up the last of six still waiting to be unloaded came our cart and Dumont hurried the men and out I came with my little study in its ten franc frame behind me. How we laughed as the pair were borne away to get in as they could, and did, thanks to D for the doors close at a certain hour and the judges are *inexorable,* so latecomers are lost.

Then we went home and fell into our beds exhausted. Now we wait to know our fate. I am prepared for mine since I am sure the poor thing won't get in.

Your P."

April 11

"Hurrah! wave your hats and reward the little grey postman who brings the good news from Ghent to Aix. My picture is accepted! Yes, truly! at the great Salon where out of 8,500 works sent in only 2,000 were accepted, and my small study was thought worthy of a place among them! I don't believe it, and I know you won't either; but I am going to see it hung among the rest and then I shall be able to grasp the amazing fact. Now aren't you glad you let me come, my dearest Grandma? Don't you rejoice over your willful P, Diana? Wasn't I wise to follow my instinct and go where glory waited me? I must soberly confess that I do not in the least understand why that ordinary little thing got in; but being in I will try to treat it with due respect and not mourn over the splendid heads that I tried to paint and couldn't.

My lucky star is certainly in the ascendant this year, for Anna's portrait is also accepted and you should have seen the joyful festival we had the day the glad news came. Everyone congratulated us, and it was beautiful to see the rejoicing over the successful ones among us, the sincere sympathy felt for those who failed, as of course many did. If you two could only be here to share all this pleasure with me on the spot, I should be too happy. My pass permits me to go as often as I like and take my friends, so I long for Grandma to see a certain lady in blue sitting in state to be surveyed by admiring nations, and Di to behold how small a candle makes a great light in this naughty world.

On Varnishing Day I went early, and there in the first salon stood face to face with my study, which looked very like a postage stamp, surrounded by the immense pictures whose gilded frames seemed to make a sort of glory, to my eyes at least, about this unpretending child of mine. I looked at it with new respect and saw that it *was* good, vigorous work; simple in subject and unaffectedly treated. I fancy this very simplicity is the secret of its success, for we too often attempt more than we are equal to, and so fail. It is a good lesson to me and teaches me both humility and a proper regard for patient thoroughness rather than effective haste.

Not only do its neighbors give it dignity but the hanging committee did me the honor to put it so low as to be nearly on the line, a place artists often pay large bribes to hangers to secure for their pictures. When I saw what fine specimens of still life are there, I was more than ever surprised that mine was accepted, for I have no friend at court and M is not among the judges. So I had another private jubilee as I stood before my old blue jug and the straw-covered wine bottle, then, after reading my name in the fat catalogue with a nice little notice after it, I went on to view thirty more rooms full of pictures, feeling that I too was an artist!

As soon as our works are restored to our proud arms, I will bundle them home to you, for I quite ache to have you see them both. Now I can fall to work again with a brave heart, for I mean to do great things this year, and have a superior head in the next Salon. You know there is nothing so successful as success.

Yours ever, P."

III

AT HOME

✢✢✢✢✢

"NOW I will go and see how well Percy's experiment succeeds. If she can combine art and domestic life harmoniously she will be a more remarkable woman than even *I* think her."

This resolved Diana on receiving the happy letter which told of the birth of Percy's little daughter in the early spring. She had been longing to go to her friend with a desire which sometimes was almost irresistible; but a certain proud yet sad conviction that she was no longer first and dearest restrained her till these last letters, full of such blissful content, such loving entreaties to come and see and rejoice over the one perfect and delicious baby in the world, proved too strong for her and she answered promptly.

"I will come, deluded dear, as soon as I can set my affairs in order and store away my children, for fortunately *I* am not a slave to them as you are to your latest work."

But even her marble offspring proved somewhat difficult to dispose of, and her small affairs took some time to settle, so it was several months before Diana sailed. She did not warn Percy of her approach but promised herself the pleasure of taking her by suprise, and discovering if this happy family was in truth all her friend's glowing pen had painted it.

Arriving in Paris in the evening, Diana was glad to go with some pleasant fellow travelers to a hotel for the night. Bewildered and excited by the novelty of all she saw and heard, she felt like one released from the quiet solitude of a prison cell and suddenly turned loose into the big, bustling world. Few guessed the inward perturbation, however, for her natural dignity and self control seemed undisturbed and stood her in good stead now.

Next morning she set bravely forth alone to find her friend, for by no word or message would she spoil the long contemplated surprise with which she hoped with a woman's tender sort of malice to avenge the years Percy had been happy without her. The gay city looked its best in the brilliant June weather, and as Diana glided away by sail to one of its most beautiful environs through blooming gardens and orchards, she felt as if passing out of the small, dull world of reality into the enchanting regions of romance, and gave herself up to the new charm with the wondering delight of a child turning for the first time the pages of a fairy story.

Holding Percy's description as a clue, she easily found her way to the little villa on the hillside, but even while her heart beat fast with the joy of the expected meeting, she was constrained to pause in the gateway and look about her at the lovely view which makes that spot famous. Down the terraced slope to the wide river winding down under the airy viaduct, through the green valley, up the opposite bank, and away over the billowy, blooming landscape swept the delighted eye to where afar off in a golden haze the great city shone against the landless azure of the sky. Spring fragrance filled the balmy air from the little garden behind her, white curtains fluttered from the windows above as if to welcome her, and like the sound of a brooding wood dove came a familiar voice, with a new tone of tenderness in it, cooing a lullaby in the room that opened on the balcony.

Holding her breath to enjoy this delicious moment to the uttermost, Diana looked up with eager eyes, hoping to catch a glimpse of the dear face, but saw only a man's dark head bent as if over a book, and as she turned to enter, the notes of a violin arrested her, so exquisitely fine and clear was the strain, so in keeping with the fair scene, the happy hour, the softened mood that filled her eyes with sudden tears and set wide the doors of her heart to let a new emotion in.

As the music ended, a voice cried "Now August, do put down the violin and let me have my will with you while I can." Percy's voice! and as if the sound drew her straightway in, Diana hastened up the white steps, through doors standing wide as if to let in the spring, to the threshold of a room which seemed familiar, she had so often studied the sketch of Percy's little home. A little home it looked indeed, as the newcomer took it all in with one comprehensive glance, for Percy's husband sat in the antique chair, his violin dropped to his knee, smiling with the silent satisfaction of a man whose eyes behold the treasures of his life; Percy's baby lay like a pink and white apple blossom blown in upon the Persian rug that half covered the polished floor, a tiny, three months creature, but full of life as it lay cooing in the sunshine with the soft, aimless motions that say so much to women's eyes; and Percy herself sat low beside her little daughter, busily sketching the face she loved best in the world.

Diana had time to see no more, for as her eye touched her friend she looked up, uttered a glad cry, and flew to meet her in the old impulsive way.

"My dearest girl! All this long journey alone and never let me know! August, it is Di, really come to us at last."

Down went violin and bow as quickly as drawing board and crayon and up rose Percy's husband to greet her friend with almost equal cordiality though fewer words.

"You are most welcome! Now Percy will be quite content."

"Indeed I shall, for now I have all I love safe in my own home. See, dear, this is August and this—my little Di, the champion baby of the world."

She certainly was a good baby, for she bore her mother's rapturous snatching up with great nerve, uttering no protest except a hiccough as she was held proudly forth to be admired, winking at her godmamma like a little owl.

"A dear baby, Heaven bless her!" and Diana was surprised at the warmth with which she kissed and embraced her small namesake, for children did not usually interest her.

"Now take her, Papa, while I make Di comfortable and show her all my kingdom. It won't take long," and with a blithe laugh Percy tucked the baby into the capacious cradle of her father's arms where she evidently felt as much at home as the violin.

"Here is my studio; just one peep and then leave it for by and by," continued Percy, showing a second salon which, judging from the dust upon the easel and the dried-up paint upon the palette, had not been very lately used.

Diana's quick eye saw it and Percy read the meaning in her look, but ignored it except by the haste with which she dropped the portière and hastened to open a door across the passage, saying as she flung wide the door, "This is the blue room especially prepared for you. Sly creature, if you had only let me know when you were coming it would have been less stuffy. Never mind, you are come and that is joy enough. Dear Di, you look so pale now, I'm afraid you have been pining for me, selfish woman that I am." exclaimed Percy, holding her close and then falling back to study her face with remorseful solicitude.

"I wanted you, but you were happy so I did not pine. I am only a little tired with my journey. Now I am safely here I shall soon be as rosy and gay as yourself. How well and glad and beautiful you look, my Percy," answered Diana, examining in turn with admiring surprise.

In truth she did look so, for the first happy year of married life that blesses many women had been an unusually serene and perfect one to Percy and its tender glow still beautified her face, as the morning red transfigures all things for one fresh and dewy hour. Not only was she lovelier but more noble, for she had passed through the deep experience which sanctifies forever in heart and memory the coming of the first-born. The touch of those baby hands had not only baptized her with a holy happiness but laid upon her sacred responsibilities, endless duties, higher aspirations, and she accepted them devoutly. But something of the youthful audacity was gone, and the eyes that had looked so fearlessly into the future for herself began to wear the tender anxiety that mother's eyes take on when peering hopefully, prayerfully into the unknown future of a child. This was a fleeting expression however, only seen at thoughtful moments on a face full of the supreme content, the happy energy of a woman living her most precious hours and eager to lose no instant of their sunshine.

"Now tell me all about your plans, for if I once begin my gossip I warn you it is a story without an end," said Percy, hovering about her guest, to put by hat and mantle, do the honors of the muslin-draped toilet table, and with her own affectionate hands smooth the pale gold braids that always crowned the stately head. "Come then and sit together on this pretty lounge in the window, so that I can feast my eyes on that enchanting view. It held me fast outside and I cannot keep away from it even now," said Diana, drawing her hostess down beside her, forgetting her story for a moment as she leaned to look again into the green abyss before her, to glance up at the ruined chateau above or let her eyes wander to the shining domes and spires in the distance.

"If that were not wicked Paris I should say it looked like the Celestial City [10] in this light," she added enthusiastically, yielding herself to the spell which draws so many to this woman-city of the world.

"It has been almost that to me," answered Percy, with sweet seriousness. "One can find Heaven anywhere when one loves and is beloved. Oh, Di, it has been such a rich and perfect year. I never knew how much a human being can enjoy, and only wonder how I ever lived so long alone," she added fervently.

"Early days yet, Percy; enjoy while you may but don't expect it to be midsummer always," Diana regarded her with the affectionate compassion which the uninitiated usually shows for those whom love's glamor blinds to the possibility of there ever being a rough side to life.

"I knew you'd say that, and take immense comfort in pitying my delusion. I'm ready to be scolded, and won't try to defend myself if you will only like August and admire the baby," said Percy, smiling down upon her from the serene heights of her indescribable and seemingly unassailable repose.

"I take them both on trust and promise to admire; especially the baby. I have often wanted one to model and now if you will let me I should like to try it while you paint your lord and master. Do you know, Percy, that to find you hard at work was an inexpressible comfort to me," and Diana's tone of intense satisfaction betrayed how her fear had been that these new obstacles would prove fatal to all progress.

Percy laughed in her sleeve, for half an hour earlier Diana would have caught her with a dust cap on, sweeping her little parlor while August rocked the baby and Fanchette scolded about the marketing. Her eyes twinkled mirthfully but she divulged no domestic secrets and answered with an air of demure conviction. "Then we could not have posed better if we had studied to please you? I am glad of that, for really, Di, I want you to see and acknowledge that it is possible to put my theory in practice. I have done a good deal of work this last year—how could I help it with August to inspire and criticize and rejoice over me. Even Baby is not much of an interruption, she is such a little angel. Papa says her artistic tastes are already developing. I really think she notices colors and I know he can always quiet her with music."

"Then the angel does occasionally cry?" said Diana, with a provoking readiness to spy out a thorn upon the rose.

"My dear, she is a mortal child and must have her little ailments; though why the innocent should be so plagued with wind I cannot see. August jokes about it in the most unfeeling way, and says she shall play the flute when he is first violin, she can hold her breath so long in a crying spell," and Percy's face was a droll mixture of maternal piety and girlish fun, as she recalled some of the musical nights the family had spent together.

Diana looked a little scandalized, but seemed to enjoy watching her friend in this new role, very much as the chaste goddess might have looked down upon some shepherd's happy wife before she found her own Endymion and kissed him in his sleep.

"You always did love your dolls, and were never happier than when all six were dangerously ill, I remember. Your experience will be of use to you now, I'm sure," she said, with her soft, sarcastic smile as she glanced at a tiny bottle labelled "Chamomilla" thrust into one of Percy's buttonholes as if ready for emergencies.

"I think it is, seriously, Di, for I am learning to manage my baby nicely and she is a healthy creature, thank heaven. Among the books you sent me from home was an old one of Grandma's, 'A Young Mother's Friend,' full of receipts, directions, and notes in her own hand, and it has been such a help to me. Dear Grandma! Though she is gone her loving care still seems to follow and surround me. How I wish I could lay my baby on her lap where my mother left her little girl and both of us be folded in her arms together once."

A few bright drops fell from Percy's eyes in memory of her loss, proving that the new love had not dimmed the old, although its balm had taken all the bitterness from sorrow. The beloved name was a key to unlock the hearts of both, and for an hour they sat together giving and receiving with tears and tender talk the sacred legacy of those last peaceful words and days, forgetting the present joy to live again the grief that drew them closer and bridged across the years of absence. They were just passing on to Diana's plans when a little impatient cry, which had been smothered more than once, burst out imperiously and arrested further confidences, for at the sound Percy sprung up, saying as she hurried away full of maternal compunction, "I must go to Baby! Rest and refresh yourself, Di, then come to us and have lunch; I won't insult your Puritan ears by calling it *déjeuner.*"

Stretching herself upon the couch, Diana nested luxuriously, examining the pretty chamber as she lay, and listening to the sounds from the adjoining room which interested, amused and enlightened her.

"Poor little girl! was she neglected by her bad, forgetful mother? Come now and go to byelow in her own nest like a drowsy darling as she is." And Percy's voice began again the pretty German Sleep Song as contented murmurs from Di expressed her pardon.

But the lullaby was frequently interrupted by directions and remarks in a sing-song tone that neither lunch nor deluded Baby's nap might be retarded.

"Papa, dear, would you just step into the garden and get a handful of flowers for the table? I was so busy this morning that I had not time, and I want things to be nice for Di. As you go out, please tell Fanchette to be very careful about the salad dressing, and since you have your hat on, you might run around the corner and get fresh oil—yes and some strawberries, they are so effective whether sweet or sour. Only, dearest man, don't, I beg of you, march in and give your bundles to me before company, as you did when the fine Hammonds were here. I don't mind Di so much, but you must be trained, my love. How do you like her: a handsome creature, isn't she?"

"Doubtless, but I have scarcely seen her, she was swept away so soon," answered the man's voice, deep and strong above the low chant of the woman.

"You will like her, I am sure of it, because she is your sort, silent, brave and self-reliant; proud too and with a will of her own. Ah, you may regret that you did not see her before you wasted yourself on a poor thing like me," said Percy, in a stifled tone suggestive of a little hand held against her lips.

"No fear, the same unlikeness which makes her thy friend makes *me* thy happy husband. Shall I order a sweet dish at the *pâtissier's* when I get the fruit? We must do honor to this guest of ours."

"We will save that for Sunday. Fanchette will make an omelette-soufflé, and with coffee it will be enough. There, Baby is off already, little dear! While I go to lay her down, will you pull out the big portfolio and the heads from the high shelf. Di was pleased to find me at work and I never told her what a lazy woman I have been lately."

"Lazy! I often think I let thee do too much, my busy little housemother."

Here Diana felt herself in honor bound to cough aloud that her hosts might be reminded of her proximity, though by so doing she deprived herself of any further domestic revelations. Steps departed, doors closed, and silence reigned, but Diana could not resist peeping from behind the blue curtains for a glimpse of this unknown August who had usurped her place in Percy's life. She had been too shy to look at him before, except one glance as he took her hand, receiving only an impression that he *was* a far manlier man than any pictures she had ever seen of Shelley. A tall, slender gentleman moving about the little garden, careless alike of the wind that blew his hair into his eyes or the thorns that pricked his fingers as he hastily pulled roses from the trellis and threw them into his hat, looking as if the oil and strawberries, sketches and salad dressing laid a little heavy on his mind and memory. A fine head it seemed, with clustering dark hair, and a face full of that indescribable something which is better than beauty in a man, a certain nobility of expression, the sure index of a character in which rectitude and resolution reign. With an artist's eye Diana scorned the outward semblance of the man, with a friend's solicitude she tried to guess the inward nature, and with a woman's quick yet inexplicable instinct she felt that she should like him, rival though he was.

Just as this feeling came to her and she involuntarily leaned out from her ambush to see him pass below, he looked up suddenly, smiled, bowed and paused to say, with a swift comprehension of the thought in her face, which would have been rather startling but for the playfulness of the question—"Well, Mademoiselle, am I to be forgiven?"

"For what?" asked Diana, coloring with surprise yet looking down with a glance almost as steadfast as that which met her own in what she now saw were "the blue and constant eyes of the North."

"For robbing you of Percy, I know what it is; I too have had friends taken from me and found it so hard to bear that I was tempted to console myself in like manner."

"Since she is happy I forgive you," answered Diana, smiling back at him, for the look said far more than the words and touched a sympathetic chord in her lonely heart.

"You are magnanimous. In her name I thank you and reward you." And he threw up a great red rose which lit on Diana's breast and seemed to warm the cool grey of her dress as pleasantly as these new interests gave color to her life.

She nodded and set the flower in her buttonhole, feeling that the ice was broken by the little compact between them, then watched August as he came out again and went away to do his errands with a good will that lent romance even to prosaic marketing.

Curious to see Percy at work, she went presently to look for her, but stopped on the way to examine the studies set forth in the pretty little salon. These absorbed her while Percy came in to lay the table, giving glimpses of a tiny kitchen where a white-capped *bonne* was beating eggs with vigor, for they only occupied an apartment in the villa and kept but a single maid. The dining room had been sacrificed to the studio, and the salon did double duty, so art-gossip and table-setting went on harmoniously together, though the cream pot was inadvertently upset into the stream of chat, and Fanchette did not achieve a perfect omelette, being distracted by her efforts to observe the distinguished stranger through the keyhole.

August soon returned; but discreetly shut himself into a pantry which with difficulty held him while he concealed the guilty parcels and then strolled into the parlor with the satisfied expression of a man who has executed a delicate maneuver with skill and been rewarded for it. Diana enjoyed the innocent little farce immensely, and was found smiling in the face of a grim Medusa when her host came to do the honors of the big portfolio, while her hostess set forth her small store of silver, glass and china in festival array, proudly brought in salad and fruit, hot coffee and cold chicken with delectable rolls and a pot of butter still in its grape leaf fresh from the dairy, saying gaily as she placed flowers in the midst— "Now if I could serve Baby among the roses my feast would be complete. As I cannot, admire if you please my fine jar of old Delft, and let August fill your glass with the wine we keep for red letter days like this."

So they ate and drank gaily together, with all the loveliness of spring outside, and the greater loveliness of love itself inside, touching everything with its peculiar charm. The sense of having stepped into a romance grew upon Diana every moment, and she kept saying to herself, "I shall wake presently in the old studio at home." But she had no wish to wake, for she heartily enjoyed this glimpse of the sweet old story forever being told the wide world over, and forever full of enchantment for those who read as for those who write it.

Percy talked most and with all her accustomed enthusiasm, whether it was of Rome or railroads, ancient history or modern baby blankets, and into everything she said and did, she put such fun and fancy that the little salon rang with innocent merriment and Fanchette smiled involuntarily among her casseroles in the kitchen. August did his share with spirit and skill, proving himself to Diana's delight an art lover and art critic of no mean order. With feminine tact the women ignored a past in which he had no part and discussed topics of general interest; but allusions and reminiscences, old hopes and projects insensibly slipped into their conversation, enlightening him as to many things he had never known or vaguely guessed before. Presently he fell silent and sat watching Percy while she listened to Diana's plans with a growing ardor in her face, an unconscious tone of regret now and then in her eager voice, an entire absorption in the subject which for the first time in her married life made her forgetful of his presence. His eye went from one face to the other, resting longest upon Diana's which he scrutinized with intense but covert interest as if trying to read the character of this friend whose influence he already saw was much stronger than he had imagined.

No jealousy mingled with the very natural anxiety which grew upon him, lest the new element should disturb the peace of home, very precious to a man so long homeless. The generous desire that Percy should have all the happiness life could give her, even if he were not the donor, struggled with a fear that, by this rousing the old ambitions, something of the old unrest and discontent might mar the beautiful repose which had possessed her for a year. He knew by sad experience how hard the effort is to bind a passionate desire and hold it captive at the feet of duty, yet he also knew what rich compensations such sacrifices sometimes bring, since mastery of self is nobler than mastery of the world. He was more ambitious for this young wife of his, both as woman and artist, than she was herself, but man-like he loved the woman best, and yearned to keep her for a little longer all his own. Time enough for glory by and by, just now he did not want his Paradise invaded even by admiring angels, and a shadow crept into the eyes that watched Diana, as if she were the fair serpent who was beguiling his impetuous Eve to taste the ruddy apple she had nibbled at already.

He drank the last drops in his neglected coffee cup, finishing them both cold and bitter since Percy had forgotten to replenish it, and at the next pause in the lively conversation he rose, saying with gay and friendly air which seemed native to him, "My half holyday has been so unexpect-edly celebrated that I am tempted to make a whole one of it. I will leave you to your coffee-gossip while I go to town for an hour or two and be back again by the time your projected works rival those of Raphael and Michael Angelo."

"Yes, dear, and don't forget to see that Di's luggage comes out safely. I gave you the list of things for Baby this morning. Oh, and get, please, a canvas 18 by 20, I shall go to work at once upon your portrait in oils. And don't be late, August, because we must show Di the old chateau at sunset," added Percy, holding her husband by both lapels of his coat to impress her directions upon his mind.

"My friend, I shall remember."

"He really will, for he is one of the few men who have a memory for women's commissions," said Percy, looking around with a face full of wifely pride in this unusual accomplishment.

"One woman's commissions, would be a closer statement, Madame," began August with masculine accuracy, but Percy stopped him with a kiss, and he departed, only saying with a grave sort of tenderness, which Diana liked better than any gush of sentiment, "Do not tire thyself, else thee can not walk at sunset."

He made the "hour or two" as long as possible, yet when he returned they were still hard at it. He found them in the studio where there had evidently been a great resurrection of the past two or three years' work, for there was a mild confusion of studies and sketches, panels and portraits in every sort of style. He also found them both drawing from the nude, their model being his cherished daughter set forth in the costume of a Cupid on a red cushion in the sunshine, where she lay decidely enjoying her little self, for the pink legs, freed from petticoats, kicked delightedly and a pair of dimpled arms moved like wings making ready for a flight.

Both women were intent upon this task, working as rapidly as they talked, with frequent bursts of laughter at the impossibility of catching the pretty poses of their lively model. There was a brilliant color in Percy's cheeks, her eyes shone with unusual fire, and she wore what her husband called her "painting frenzy" look, an excited, absorbed expression which he had not seen since she used to come in after a successful day at the Gallery in London. The shadow flitted across his face again, but was gone in a moment as he joined involuntarily in their merriment when Baby, staring vaguely at nothing, hit her own minute nose with a soft fist and gasped like a little gold fish with surprise at the exploit.

"Unnatural mother! Would you sacrifice your child at the altar of your insatiable art?" he demanded, pointing tragically at the placid squirmer as he joined them.

Diana looked rather conscience-stricken, for she had proposed the immolation; but Percy promptly whipped Baby into her blue blanket—as she said, nothing daunted—"She always has a sun bath and can't take cold for the windows are all shut. But we must wait, Di, till she is asleep; one might as well try to draw an eel awake. Kiss your stern father, child, and tell him you are to be immortalized in marble by and by."

She held up the blue bundle with such loving pride and looked so happy that August gladly listened and agreed to all she told him, promising to order clay tomorrow and expressing great interest in the work but wisely keeping to himself the opinion that no living artist could do justice to the exquisite little piece of sculpture in his arms.

Percy was very quiet through dinner and lest the evening walk should be spoilt, took her turn at listening while Diana and August talked. She was proud of her husband then, for he had read much and of the best; his English was excellent, and only an occasional phrase or accent betrayed him and when interested he talked fluently and well. Diana's reserve soon melted in this genial atmosphere, and she was insensibly won to do her best, proving that her seclusion had not been a narrow one, since high thoughts make a world for themselves, and a purposeful life enriches itself from every attainable source. So Percy listened well pleased, and left them still discussing Ruskin while she went to put Baby to bed, leaving Fanchette to guard the treasure while she was away.

As the lovely day waned toward its still lovelier close, the three set forth to watch the pageant of the western sky from the ruins of the old chateau. Diana looked with surprise at Percy who with garden hat upon her head, a piece of knitting in her gloveless hands, walked beside her husband, nodding to white-capped women and blue-bloused men, artists loitering home after a hard day's work, trying to paint the unpaintable, or families supping on their doorsteps in the social French fashion.

"Don't look shocked, dear piece of propriety; you will come to it in time and enjoy the freedom as I do. It is a charming way to live, so simple, friendly and picturesque. I never can go back to the old cumbersome dull fashion again," said Percy, strolling along with her fingers busily shaping a tiny sock while her eyes were reveling in the tender nuances of color fading from the sky.

"I was only wondering what some of our friends at home would say to see the elegant Miss Lennox now. I'm afraid they would not enjoy it as I do, for it suits you, excellently and I like it," answered Diana, pocketing her own gloves and yielding to the carefree influences all about her.

"We used to take our books and work and supper and camp where we pleased, getting as hearty, brown and gay as these good neighbors of ours. As soon as my daughter is old enough, I shall pack her on my back like a gypsy mother, let her tumble on the wholesome grass while I sketch and Papa improves my mind."

"The pleasant times you used to tell of in your letters? You must not let me interrupt them. Everything is so new to me I cannot fail to enjoy whatever comes," said Diana, looking about her with wide eyes, and drawing in long breaths of the balmy air like a thirsty traveler who has found the much desired spring at last.

"A summer here with us, if you do not tire of our quiet ways, will prepare you for the still greater freedom of artistic life in Italy," said M. Müller, quite unconscious that he added much to the picturesqueness of their group by wearing a slouched hat and carrying Percy's red shawl flung carelessly over a black velvet shoulder.

"Not a summer, thank you; I must have a glimpse of Switzerland before I cross the Alps, for I may never come back and must snatch all I can as I go. Some friends who I met in London invited me to join them in July and I could not deny myself the pleasure."

"Only a month? I will not hear of it, Di! Go to Switzerland for the hot season, I want you to see August's wonderful country, but come back to us in September, and let us start you safely off to Rome a month or two later," cried Percy, feeling as if this sight of her friend only made it the harder to give her up again.

"I promise if you want me; but I fear I may be an intruder in this happy little home of yours, for the honeymoon does not seem to be over yet," answered Diana, below her breath, as M. Müller lingered behind to gather some blossoming grasses by the wayside.

"Many people would be but not you," said honest Percy, adding with a backward glance, "I want you two to be friends. He will like you, I am sure, and you him if you wait a little, he does not wear his heart on his sleeve as I do, but oh, he is far better worth the knowing."

"We shall see. Do you ever regret the old life, Percy?"

"Never!" she uttered the word with such energy that her husband heard it and looked the question which he did not ask. Percy laughed at her own warmth and explained, taking his arm as if to make herself a tie between the two.

"It will be a very bitter hour to me when I discover that she finds her loss greater than her gain." M. Müller looked from under the wide hat brim with something like reproach in the eyes which were always a surprise to Diana, having in them nothing of the Southern fire and softness which would have matched his warm coloring and dark hair.

He directed his reply to her, and in it she fancied there lurked a warning or an appeal, and felt a little guilty that her question had been asked. Both were already conscious of the affectionate jealousy, the spirit of rivalry with which they could not help regarding the richly endowed woman who stood between them, since they represented the two strong passions which divided her heart and ruled her life.

"To me also, since the choice is so happily made. But you know the wiseacres say we women cannot have all, and must decide between love and fame, so I am curious to see which of us will fare the best," said Diana lightly, hoping to slip away from the dangerous subject with a jest.

But Müller answered with an earnestness which impressed her then and was remembered long afterward, as he laid his hand upon his wife's as if bestowing all he asked for her.

"Pardon, I believe a woman can and ought to have both if she has the power and courage to win them. A man expects them, achieves them, why is not a woman's life to be as full and free as his? The road may be different, but the end is the same and the prizes should be justly given. Love alone is not enough for any large and hungry soul, it should have all it can hold, else it has thwarted the purpose of its Maker." Surprise kept Diana silent, but her face betrayed her and Percy exulted over her with delight.

"There, Di! Could the most liberal-minded American say more than that? I did not convert him, he came to it himself through his own love of liberty, being a free Switzer with as great a hatred for tyrants as our glorious William Tell himself."

"Yes, truly! I not only cherish this belief but I hope to see it beautifully realized by the success of this splendid wife of mine, who is to be the greater artist for being a happy woman, please God!" And Müller lifted his hat as if registering a vow, with a flash of the eyes that showed he meant it.

Diana bowed gravely, charmed with his warmth but not one whit convinced by it, for her opinion on this point was as firmly fixed as Mont Blanc.

"You see, I have someone to fight my battles for me now, and I find it very comfortable. You and August can argue that vexed question as often and as fiercely as you like and I'll sit by enjoying it. Meantime I propose a truce while you admire the view." And Percy waved a little sock like a white flag before the contending parties as she led them to the platform whence one could look far and wide.

Diana enjoyed it vastly, and they sat there till twilight fell, and with it the dew. Then Müller wrapped Percy in her shawl and took her home with a gentle sort of authority which she seemed to like, while Di secretly resented it, preferring to wait for moonrise. As if she guessed her friend's mood, Percy, having obediently laid herself upon the sofa, proposed music, sure that such playing as August's would have charms to soothe a far more savage breast than dear old Di's.

Glad to be allowed to spend the evening in the way which best atoned to him for a day of absence and irksome duty, Müller gave them some exquisite things from the Midsummer Night's Dream,[11] with the fitting accompaniment of wandering wind, soft dusk and the rustle of leaves eager for the coming of the elves.

Diana, sitting beside the couch with Percy's hand often stealing into hers full of mute eloquence, listened thirstily, for the artistic temperament keenly enjoys all forms of beauty, and her ear drank in the music which fed her soul as did the loveliness on which her eye dwelt. Nor was it sensuous pleasure only, for finer influences were at work, and though no word was spoken, music and moonlight made the strangers friends.

As August played he seemed to make the little instrument speak for him, and its truthful tones expressed the man better than any picture painted even by the loving artist near him. The mingled strength and lightness of the touch, the sweet whispering notes, the sad undertones that crept in here and there, the thrilling chords, full of passionate pathos, the fine clear echo of the climbing harmony melted into silence with no fall to mar the strain that seemed to lift and leave the listener at Heaven's gate.

Diana felt all this, and found herself saying, "He is worthy of her, and will work the miracle if man can."

But while she listened with closed eyes, the moonlight stole into the room and shone upon her face, never more beautiful than now when hope and happiness were leading her across the hills she had climbed so patiently into the land of promise for such as she. Percy did not see it, for she was thinking what they should have for breakfast, since morning would inevitably bring that dreadful question. But August, playing on, looked out from his shadowy corner at the figure bathed in light, finding it not only fair but winning, for the keen eyes were shut now, the firm lips smiled, the proud head leaned like a drowsy flower, and the whole face was softened wonderfully, not only by the magic of the moon but by the unwonted mood which unlocked her heart, and for an hour showed how much unsuspected tenderness it held.

"She is not all the artist but a woman to be loved as well as admired. I will not be afraid, but trust her as Percy does," he said within himself, and as if relieved from some unacknowledged fear he passed suddenly from a melancholy Nocturne to such gay dance music that it startled both listeners wide awake, leaving Percy undecided between fish or cutlets, and Diana wondering if she could be happy with a musical husband in a home like this.

So they went merrily to bed, and the rivals shook hands with new cordiality as they said "Good Night!"

IV

PUCK

✺✺✺✺✺✺

ONE February afternoon Diana went to the Pincio[12] to watch the sunset, see her fellow creatures, and enjoy the ever new surprise of spring, coming so early, and with such a wealth of beauty here. All the world was there as usual; the band playing deliciously, the sky a blaze of gold and purple, and the air full of a soft stir, not only of human enjoyment but the more delicate life of awakening Nature. Contenting herself with a passing glance at the gay throng, the circling train of brilliant equipages, and the picturesque figures continually crossing her path, Diana glided away to the quieter recesses of the Pincio, where distance lent enchantment to the sweet clamor of the music, and softened the blended colors to hues as fine as those in the blooming terraces below.

Leaning on the low parapet, she refreshed her weary eyes by looking down into the Borghese Gardens with their avenues, stone pines "like green islands in the air," dancing fountains and ruined altars whence seemed to rise, like incense, the rich breath of hidden violets. In the blue distance shone Soracte[13] clear against the sky; the dome of St. Peter's soared like a golden bubble above the city bathed in rosy light and from the campanile came the chime of bells ringing the Ave Maria.

The tender mood that comes to most of us in such hours was upon Diana then, full of a pleasant weariness, of voiceless longings, and vague sweet expectations stirring softly like imprisoned butterflies when spring sunshine call them from the chrysalis. She thought of Percy, feeling soli-

427

tary now her day's work was done, and tenderly imagined her happy in the nest that filled so fast the mother bird had little time for friendship. She thought of her own life, so high and lonely, its ever growing ambition, and the sense of power that strengthened every year. Yet at times she was conscious of a deeper want, an unconquerable yearning, a bittersweet regret for something lost or never found; as if a timid hand was put forth and meeting no responsive grasp withdrew again into the soft gloom which wrapt that recess of her heart, even from herself.

As this rare emotion came and lingered for a moment, a sudden mist passed before her eyes, eyes grown spiritual with much gazing at fair ideals, but all the lovelier for the unwanted dew that softened their clear brightness. "I am homesick," she said smiling at herself, unconscious that she spoke aloud. "So am I," replied a child's voice and a small hand slipped into hers as it hung beside her. She turned quickly to find a little creature looking up at her with a pathetic expression in its lovely face. "A golden boy," as the Germans would have called him for he seemed made up of sunshine, so profuse was the bright hair that lay upon the shoulders and made a sort of glory about the head. A round and rosy face, eyes like violets, and a red mouth shaped for kissing gave one the impression of a cherub; but the frill of rich lace, encircling the throat like the cloud which often finishes off these bodiless babies, was in this case supplemented by a velvet tunic, and ended in a pair of sturdy legs, brave in purple hose and two muddy little shoes, making up a very winsome mortal child of five or six.

"Are you? poor baby!" and conscious only of the sympathy the sweet face expressed, Diana stooped and kissed it involuntarily.

As if the touch of a woman's lips, the caress of a woman's hand was what he wanted, the boy rubbed his soft cheek against that softer one and nestled to her with a little sigh of pleasure, evidently hungry for the fostering tenderness mothers alone can give.

"I thought you were Aunt Alice and I want to see her, much, oh, very much," he said, stroking her hand and wrapping the folds of her dress about him like an unfledged bird anxious to be hidden under a sheltering wing.

"I wish I were. But I am very glad you came to me. I want a little friend and we can comfort one another," began Diana, full of interest in the small stranger and feeling as if she owed him some atonement for the disappointment.

But the kiss seemed to have satisfied him for the moment, sentiment gave place to curiosity and, taking advantage of the offer with childish promptitude, he released himself and beat upon the wall saying imperiously, "Lift me up. I wish to look over, Papa lets me."

Glad to keep her welcome playmate, Diana obeyed, and holding him fast, let him look abroad and shout to his heart's content, finding for herself a new pleasure in the mere touch of this chubby elf, so velvet soft, so full of life and warmth that thrilled her sensitive hands chilled by long contact with cold marble and damp clay. That innocent kiss had been like the stroke upon the sack, and all the pent-up tenderness of her nature seemed to gush out, sprinkling the dust of what for a moment at least looked like a desert path along which she was following a mirage. She was amazed to feel how thirstily she drank of the sweet water so unexpectedly brought to her dry lips and laughed at herself even while she prolonged the drought, "for the child's sake," she thought.

"Dear little thing I must hold you fast or you will fly away as suddenly as you came," she said, wrapping him close in both arms as he danced upon the wall and flapped his arms with all the bright hair blowing in the wind.

He turned about to answer seriously, while he peeped under her hat brim and stroked her cheeks with innocent freedom. "I cannot fly. I like to stay, for you hold me nicely; Nanna shakes me so I run away. Papa's face is rough but yours is soft like Aunt Alice and so I love to kiss you," which he did impetuously, hugging close the new friend whose face and figure recalled the only mother he had ever known.

"I am glad of that. Now tell me your little name. I think it must be Angelino," said Diana, receiving with an almost shy delight the embraces of this small lover.

"It is an ugly name, but Papa makes it pretty. He calls me Nino. Do you like Antony Stafford more than that?" asked the boy with a grimace as if the rough name hurt his rosy little mouth.

"Yes! then Papa is a sculptor?" cried Diana quickly, for with the utterance of that name her eyes shone, and a hope sprung up in her heart that these childish hands might open a door before which she had often stood, longing yet not daring to knock.

"Oh yes, he makes marble things but I do not care for them. I like the nice, soft clay and I make birds and lambs, and once I made a lion!" said the boy, trying to mold his own blooming face into an expression of leonine ferocity.

The rolling eyes and puffed out cheeks were so droll that Diana laughed as she had not done for months, and the child laughed also with a gleeful prance.

"The lambs are best for such small fingers. I too work in the nice clay, and I shall love to make this face full of dimples if I can. Would not you like to see it in pretty white marble by and by, that will never break nor grow old?"

But Nino shook his head till all the curls flew widely about, and sitting suddenly down he crossed the purple legs, took up the sketch book lying there and changed the subject by saying with immense decision, "No, I will not be pounded out of stone. It makes me ache to see the men do it. I will be only Nino and I will see these pictures. Tell me all about them."

Leaning beside him Diana obediently turned the pages best suited to his taste; telling where she saw the little goat that stood upon its hind legs to crop the grass among the crevices of the ruins; and how the boyish St. John was a bigger lad who stood as a model, and being cold with nothing on but his sheepskin, wrapped it round him and danced about the studio as one saw him there, a very jolly saint indeed. Coming to a priest Nino looked up to say, as he pointed with a chubby finger toward a procession of students winding like a scarlet thread along the paths below.

"Those are little ones, and when they grow up they will all wear black. Papa calls them lobsters." But just in the act of going off into another fit of merriment Nino saw his nurse approaching with anger in her black eyes, and a threatening gesture of a brown forefinger.

"No! No. I will not go, Nanna," he cried rebelliously, and dropping from the wall fled as fast as the sturdy legs would go, carrying his prize with him.

Pausing only to beg the Signorina's pardon for the spoiled bambino, Nanna hastened after him, scolding as she went while Diana awaited the capture with some anxiety as to the fate of her sketch book, rich in the fugitive fancies and helpful hints of an artist's brain and eye. But she had something better now to engross her thoughts than daydreams or the vague melancholy born of solitude and springtime.

Stafford was a well-known sculptor whose fame was already made, whose maturity was already crowned with success, but whose life had been eclipsed at noonday by the darkness of a great sorrow which seemed to have paralyzed the cunning hand and chilled the ambitious spirit just when both were ready to achieve their best. Diana knew the story well, the short sad romance that many had mourned over both for the man's and the artist's sake. The youth of brave struggle, the well-earned reward of fame and fortune at forty, then in the mid-summer of his life the happy love without which no success is perfect. One year of bliss and then the lovely English wife died, leaving a child to be an innocent reminder of the dearer because lost so soon. In the first anguish of this bitter disappointment Stafford could not bear the sight of the poor baby and, leaving it to the care of the mother's sister, went away to bury himself for five years. The world waited for him patiently, touched by such faithful grief. He worked no more; and though to mortal ear he uttered no complaint but hid the sorrow in a sacred silence, this carelessness of fame, this abandonment of the beloved art proved how deep the wound had been, how useless the balm which has power to heal most sorrows in a man's life. The death of the child's tender guardian recalled Stafford to his duty, and seeing the lovely boy now grown so like the lost mother, seemed to reawaken the father's heart and to fill it with a love both passionate and remorseful.

He took the little creature to himself, and devoted his life to it with a tenderness as entire as his neglect had been, finding unexpected solace in the childish affection that clung to him, the innocent face that recalled the sweet one turned to dust. For the boy's sake a spark of the old ambition kindled slowly under the ashes of a burnt-out despair, and in the spring-time new hopes began to cast a faint glow over the barren features, as the rosy bloom budded on the bare boughs of the peach trees along the grey hill sides.

Back to Rome he came with the child in his arms, opened the long disused studio and villa and seemed waiting only for new inspiration to take form and bear fruit for the beloved boy. As yet he had begun nothing, and the wide circle of friends and admirers that welcomed him back with a satisfaction both proud and tender looked anxiously to see the rich fancy and gifted hand at work. But Stafford seemed in no haste to feel fresh laurels on a head too early grey, and was content for a time at least to handle only the soft limbs of the little, living statue given him to mold into a man.

Diana was thinking of this with an interest which few persons would have had the power to inspire in her mind, for she had looked upon Stafford as the man who did most honor to her chosen profession, had longed to see him, and when she did so at last in the streets of Rome, had watched him eagerly, never daring to make herself known, though in him she felt that she might find the help and counsel she was too proud to ask.

She had never chanced to see the boy or had not observed him, for hers were eyes that looked straight forward above the level of the little heads of children. Now and then when wearied of that steady gaze into the golden mist of the future, or the upward glance into the still more golden and distant world of an artist's highest heaven, she was glad to rest her eyes on the green grass and smell the wholesome earth from which so much beauty grows. In such a moment this human crocus thrusting itself up sunny and bold from the snows of death and sorrow looked into her face and wooed her touch, seeming all the fairer, the more attractive for the pain and passion of the romance out of which it sprang.

"I wish he would come back," she said to herself, when many minutes passed and no repentant truant appeared. The book bore her name and she felt sure of its return in time, but had she seen what messenger was bringing it, she would not have stood so tranquilly dreaming in the sunset.

The touch of that rosy mouth seemed to have unsealed the closely folded lips and left a smile there; the eyes that looked down upon the children playing on the terraces below were full of a new expression, wistful yet tender, and in her whole figure was something womanly and winning, as if the last clasp of childish arms had warmed the fair statue into still fairer flesh and blood. Her attitude was full of the unconscious grace of harmonious proportions, and as she leaned there, a slender yet stately figure in pale grey with no touch of color but the knot of crimson carnations in her bosom and the evening glow full on the face, half folds of a veil shrouded in folds of silvery gauze, she was a more attractive object than any marble nymph among the shrubs behind her.

Stafford, approaching with the book in one hand, the little rebel in the other, saw and recognized this beautiful woman as one whom he had observed with a sculptor's pleasure, passing through the streets like a grey nun unfolded in her own sweet thoughts and high purposes as in a veil that shut out the admiration of man's eyes. He was glad to find that the "pretty lady" Nino spoke of was this attractive person whose name he had discovered from the book, which likewise showed her talent and betrayed that she was the artist of whom he had heard, for on one page was a colorful drawing of the Saul. He would gladly have lingered a little as he went, to study her before she was conscious of his presence and confused by it as most women were, eager to show the sympathy and admiration alike distasteful to him. But Nino had no scruples about disturbing her, and quite unabashed by the mild rebuke he had received, ran gaily forward, crying in a shrill small voice, "Here is Papa; please tell him all about St. John and the pretty goat as you did me."

With the delightful freedom of a tenderly cherished child unused to repulse, he threw his arms about Diana, sure that his request would be granted. A little startled by the sudden onset she looked up to see a grey uncovered head bending above the yellow one, and heard a man's voice saying quietly, "I have to ask pardon for this imp's rudeness and restore his theft. I find it easy to forgive him since a glance at its pages shows me that I have found a comrade whom it is a pleasure to know, if I may ask the honor?"

What she answered Diana never knew, for she was absorbed in one of those swift comprehensive glances with which a trained eye seizes a look for the significance of the countenance it rests on. "A rugged face steeped in genius": as someone has described a greater man, were the words which would best have described Stafford just then. Hair and head still dark below but white above as if with a sudden snow fall; eyes that would have been melancholy but for the fire of a courage nobler than pride, and aquiline features bronzed by the ardor of Spanish skies. Straight and tall, he reminded her of the stone pines yonder, stately yet somber, their strong trunks defying the storm yet their green recesses full of a sad murmur, lifted high above the world as if the sigh that haunted them was too sacred to be heard below.

"Tell us what that one is? Papa looked at it longest and liked it best. I did not because the man seems in pain," broke in the boy, possessing himself of the book and eagerly showing the page that held the figure of Saul.

Feeling as if "the imp" were in truth a spirit of good who was serving her in the sweetest way, Diana glanced with new pride as well as doubt at her work, and in a few expressive words explained the sketch. "I have heard of it, and hoping to meet you at some friend's house, I have delayed asking permission to come and see this fine piece of work," said Stafford, with a growing sense of pleasure in looking at the face that neither blushed nor smiled, nor avoided his commanding eyes, but met them with a clear and candid look while an expression of heartfelt satisfaction shone in every feature. He liked too the frank simplicity of her manner, for in it was both the gentle reserve of a woman accustomed to admiration and the glad humility of a pupil saluting a much honored master.

"You need not have waited, sir, since your name is a passport to any studio; and it is I who ask a favor in asking you to see my work," she said, laying the book upon the wall as Nino skipped away to chase a bird.

"How long have you been about this? Such things take time and patience to reach perfection," asked Stafford, glancing from the strong sketch to the slender hands which had remained ungloved since they turned the pictured pages for the boy.

"Four years, it is not in marble yet."

He liked that brief answer unfollowed by any complaint, for it showed that the woman could not only work but wait, crowning power with patience; and his own successful hand held back the fluttering leaves with new respect and interest as he asked further questions in a tone that made it both easy and delightful to reply. Each felt the charm of this propitious hour, and the conversation was soon as frank and fluent as a mutual interest made the strangers friends by the freemasonry of their craft. The music died away, the sunset pageant faded, and the crowd thinned fast, but still they leaned there talking rapidly, conscious at first that Nino played about them, then forgetting him till he startled both by creeping along the parapet unperceived till he reached and caught his father round the neck. An involuntary motion of the man's swung the boy over the wall and but for Diana's quick gesture and strong grasp the precious little body would have rolled down the steep bank to fall broken on the stones far below. In the act of lifting him to safety, Stafford snatched him from her hold and clasped him tightly as if the mere thought of such a loss bereft him of self-control for a moment. But Nino caught his breath and cried out lustily as he bent back his head with cheeks reddened by the passionate carresses his father gave them.

"I am not hurt! Your face is rough! I love to kiss the signorina best. Let me go to her and I will be good."

"Go then, naughty child, and thank her for saving you from destruction. You make a woman of me with your reckless pranks."

Stafford pushed the boy toward Diana and half turned away as if ashamed of the emotion he had betrayed. But Nino got no kisses, for Diana, with the wisdom few mothers would have found it possible to show just then, took the engaging torment by the chin, saying in a tone of soft severity which must impress the spoilt child by its novelty.

"You may thank me by promising not to do that dangerous thing again. Then I shall love to call on my little friend, and trust you not to frighten your father any more."

Grateful for the diversion, Stafford watched the boy with a smile that covered his own emotion and reassured the culprit, who looked perplexed at the unexpected penance demanded of his Highness.

"Now then, little marplot, repent and receive absolution as soon as possible for we must go before the mist rises," said the father anxious to house the child and fearing new mischief was brewing in that busy brain.

There was, for Nino had no thought of submission, and with an audacious laugh he snatched the carnations from Diana's bosom and scampered away impenitent and unforgiven.

"We will settle the account at bedtime and he shall thank you later. I will not try to do so now, but hope the time may come when I can prove how much I owe you."

He took off his hat and offered his hand with a look and gesture which said infinitely more than the moved tone in which he spoke, then hastened after the boy, leaving Diana to follow slowly, feeling as if almost anything were possible now.

435

"When will he come?" she said to herself many times during the next few days with more of the artist's than the woman's impatience. She pined to learn his opinion of her statue, for if *he* praised it she would be satisfied. *She* knew its faults, she also knew its power, and felt that few women had dared, or if daring had succeeded in doing such bold work as this. Strength had been her aim, not sentiment nor beauty. These women can and have expressed in many shapes with varying success. But power in visible form and undeniable truth is rare from men's hands, almost unknown from women's, and she thirsted to hear from his lips whose praise was success the three words, "It is good."

The masculine fibre in her nature demanded recognition as it does in all strong natures, and having won it she could permit the softer side of her character to assert itself without fearing the accusation of weakness, which she hated like a man.

Eagerly she set her studio in order, brushed off the dust that had laid undisturbed so long upon her statue, and spent several of her carefully hoarded dollars for deep red drapery to hang behind it, feeling acutely how inadequate the dead plaster was to express what only marble could fitly embody and transfigure. Flowers she set about in graceful vases, and brought out her small store of art treasures to embellish the bare walls. She had never cared before, but now an honored guest was coming and she longed to make her domain beautiful not for her own sake but for that of the work it held.

Day after day went by, however, and still the desired guest did not come. But Diana had learned patience in a hard school and while she waited, fell to modeling a head of Nino, more because she found it impossible to settle to any other task than because she hoped for any great success. The pretty boy had brought her good fortune and a certain sense of gratitude seemed to constrain her to celebrate the event by an enduring memorial of the Puck whose spiriting had already done so much for her.

A week passed and Diana began to think with the sad resignation taught by many disappointments, "He will not come. He has forgotten like all the rest." On the seventh day she covered up the little head, wetting the damp cloth with a few quiet tears as if a hope as beautiful and innocent was dying fast, and went out into the garden to gather flowers for the vases seven times filled in vain.

Sitting on the fallen pillar by the fountain, she fell to dreaming with her lap full of trailing greenery and hands that forgot to tie up the last of her snowdrops and violets. So absent were her thoughts that she heard nothing till the sound of little feet on the path recalled her, and she looked up to see Nino dancing toward her with a great bunch of purple and yellow crocuses and anemones, crying as he came:

"*Buon giorno, Signorina!* I gathered these all for you myself in the Pamphili Donia gardens, and Papa sent me to ask if he may come in."

Dispatching her permission by Maniuccia, who followed to announce *"Sua Eccellenza,"* Diana paused a moment to welcome the child who breathlessly explained that he had been ill, and wanted to see her very much, but Papa would not go for her. Now he had come to see her himself, and where were the lizards she told him about?

When Stafford entered the studio he saw nothing but the pretty group framed by the open door that led into the garden; for to his eyes it was more beautiful than any other in all Rome. Nino was holding Diana fast, pleading with her to stay and tickle the lizards as she promised; and she was trying to escape with gentle eagerness. They looked like a mother and child at play, for the boy had caught her in a loop of ivy; she was caressing the small hands as she tried to force herself from their hold, and in the struggle the great nosegay had fallen apart deluging the pair with flowers. Both laughed, both golden heads were close together, and both faces were full of an innocent gaiety that made them lovely. Diana's cheeks were almost as rosy as Nino's, and her eyes shone and she was so happy that the long desired moment had come at last she willingly delayed that other meeting for a moment.

A pigeon alighting on the fountain's brim to drink attracted the boy and freed the captive who hastened to find her guest examining the rough sketches on the walls, from which he turned with such an expression of almost tender interest that she involuntarily glanced at the familiar scrawls to see what caused it.

"I sent Nino to explain the reason of our delay and make his peace. I was as impatient as he, so let me see at once. I have not even stolen a look, though much tempted."

With no answer but a grateful smile, Diana went straight to the curtain which hid her work and pushing it aside waited for the verdict.

Stafford lifted his brows and stepped back a little as if surprised at the size of the statue. Then he stood looking silently, and as his eyes dwelt on it, they kindled, first with interest, then pleasure, then the satisfaction a master takes in recognizing excellence; and presently with a sudden illumination of the whole face he said slowly—"I am glad a woman did that."

"Because it's so weak?" Diana held her breath to hear the answer, doubting what she saw.

"Because it is so strong! There is virile force in this, accuracy as well as passion—in short, genius."

"Few men would say that to a woman." And Diana's voice shook with the irrepressible emotion which showed how intense her own anxiety had been, how exquisite was her joy at such commendation.

"Few women give us the chance to say it. We have had sentiment enough. Power conquers the proudest, and wrings the truth from the meanest. This is noble work, let me study it."

There was a pleasant sort of roughness in Stafford's manner, and he turned his back to look again. Diana liked this infinitely better than if he had overwhelmed her with compliments. It suited her to be forgotten in her work, and she stood mutely watching him as he walked about the statue, talking more to himself than to her, saying things that humbled by their sincere approval, and made her proud by their just criticism. This was what she wanted, and coming as it did was of immense value since the honest opinion of such a man was more to her than any medal she might hereafter win.

Presently he seemed to remember her, and turning, looked at her with the piercing glance which nothing appeared to escape. Keen but kind, and in it she saw a new respect dearer to her than any other homage. She bore the long gaze tranquilly, meeting it eye to eye with a fine mixture of honest pride and satisfaction in her own, much as a pupil might show a master over a hard lesson faithfully learned and justly praised. It seemed a fresh surprise and pleasure to find this sturdy sort of spirit in such a shape, and a sudden smile warmed his austere face as he offered his hand, giving hers the cordial grasp one man gives another when he says heartily, "Comrade, well done!"

"This must be hidden here no longer, but put in marble at once. Can you let it go?"

"I can; but ought I?" answered Diana quickly, feeling as if all her long cherished dreams were becoming beautiful realities at last. Her face showed her desire but the woman's dignity checked the artist's ardor, and she added slowly, "I have longed to see it done for years, yet I am slow to receive so great a favor even from so generous a hand."

"But not to grant one? Let me pay the debt I owe you and save your child from oblivion as you saved mine from harm. Obligation burdens me also, and I claim the right to fulfill the desire of your life, as you preserved the treasure of mine. So we are quits. You will consent?"

Asked in that way, how could she refuse? With most men she would have shrunk from such a service, but here she seemed to have earned it, for he not only thanked her as a woman but greeted her as an artist worthy of the name. The sculptor's satisfaction in her work was more to her than the father's gratitude, for such recognition was very precious to her sensitive pride, her love of justice, and the independence she cherished as she did her life. Her face grew soft and bright with confidence and happiness as she looked up after that instant's hesitation, yet there were tears in the eyes that were more eloquent than her few words.

"I do consent, and I thank you from my heart."

"It is I who am to be grateful; I who am glad to be the instrument which puts this fine creature before the world; I who will find the task a godsend. It shall be put in hand at once. My atelier is empty, my men wait for employment; I will give it to them, and when I hear the old music of the mallets I may find inspiration as well as occupation."

"Do you ever need it?" Diana asked involuntarily, struck by the air of mingled desire and despondency with which he spoke.

"Always, *now* for the power has gone out of me. My friend, may you never know the awful weariness that comes when the golden apples one has struggled for turn to ashes on the lips."

The words seemed to break from him against his will, and were so full of bitter sadness, while over the strong face there swept such a tragic shadow that for one instant Diana felt as if her Saul had spoken.

A woman's instinct prompted the happy answer to that involuntary betrayal of the disappointment which but for one tie would have deepened to a fixed despair.

"You have the boy to live and work for. Is not that an aim and a consolation?" she asked, with a gentle frankness that made its undertone of sympathy the sweeter.

"It shall be! Pardon the complaint; it was wrung from me by the memory of the time when I saw *my* first success and rejoiced in it as you do now. I thought the cup was full then, but one bitter drop turned the wine to wormwood, and I have not learned yet to drink it patiently."

The room was very still for a moment, and nothing broke the silence but the soft babble of the fountain and the boy's voice cooing with the doves. As if the music of this little David soothed the troubled soul of the man, Stafford turned to the sunny doorway and stood there asking himself why this woman unconsciously allured such confidence from him, unless it was that in her he saw curiously blended an image of his own ambitious youth and a faint likeness to the wife he mourned.

Full of pity and anxious to divert his thoughts, Diana dropped the curtain before her great work with one glance of exultation, and busied herself in unwrapping the little head of Nino, sure that only pleasant fancies could be stirred by the pretty thing.

"See what I have dared to do without permission. He is so beautiful I could not resist the desire to keep him. I am often tired of attempting grand impossibilities and find repose and delight in work like this."

"That is charming! My very Nino, imp and angel all in one. Lift the hair just here, and curl the corners of the mouth more. He has his mother's perfect lips, poor baby!"

If Diana had sought for comfort suited to his mood, she could have found nothing better than this, for both man and sculptor felt the tender tact with which she touched the one happy note that made music for him, and he thanked her for it by the air of relief and pleasure he wore as he watched her at work. It was as if he saw a woman giving the motherless boy the gentle caress he needed, for she used no tool, but with her own deft fingers twined the little curls back from the brow, caressed the soft contour of the cheek in smoothing it, and moulded the pouting lips to Nino's own naughty smile as if remembering the kisses they had given her unasked.

"That is my bambino, and I am truly glad you did it. I have often begun but could never finish, yet I should have done it, these frail little lives are so easily blown out," he said, making one effective dent in the round chin which gave Nino's dimple to the life and he smiled as if his fingers felt the charm of their old mastery as they hovered above the small ear, and touched the fine arch of the baby head.

"I shall take great satisfaction in finishing it for you sir, if I may," said Diana, infinitely gratified to have found a way to lighten, even a little, the favor which she knew could oppress her in spite of the grace of its bestowing.

"I shall accept it with sincere delight. It pleases me to find that the hand which grappled so bravely with the difficulties of that Saul can also put such tender truth into a baby's face. I bereave you of your giant but I will lend you the pretty pigmy as often as you like in return."

As if to make good his father's promise, Nino appeared at the moment, announcing that he was hungry. Gladly Diana brought forth her little store of sugar biscuits and dates hanging like great amber drops from the stem they grew upon, and fed the child, who leaned against her knee, contentedly smearing his lip with honey and scattering crumbs over the purple lap that held his plate. Stafford meantime was roving about the studio, apparently seeing only evidences of hopeful work everywhere and commending it heartily; yet in reality reading the story of the woman's life in that solitary room, and admiring her genius the more for the hard soil out of which the rare flower had sprung.

Entirely forgetful of herself, Diana talked eagerly and well on the topics most dear to her, inspired to do so by the cordial interest her guest expressed, and the rich experience out of which he spoke. To him there was something piquant in listening to the boldest opinions from this handsome creature's lips, uttered with a certain calm conviction and unsparing truthfulness which contrasted curiously with the patient care with which she put one sweet morsel after another into the rosy mouth held up so persistently, and the tender zeal with which she washed a pair of dirty little hands after the feast was over.

"One feels as if there was a fine man and a fine woman working there together, and one scarcely knows which to admire most," he thought to himself as he went away, leaving Diana to work with enthusiasm on the arched head of the boy, to which she added a pair of winged shoulders and called it Puck.

JO'S LAST SCRAPE

THE March family had enjoyed a great many surprises in the course of their varied career, but the greatest of all was when the Ugly Duckling turned out to be, not a swan, but a golden goose, whose literary eggs found such an unexpected market that in ten years Jo's wildest and most cherished dream actually came true. How or why it happened she never clearly understood, but all of a sudden she found herself famous in a small way, and, better still, with a snug little fortune in her pocket to clear away the obstacles of the present and assure the future of her boys.

It began during a bad year when everything went wrong at Plumfield; times were hard, the school dwindled, Jo overworked herself and had a long illness; Laurie and Amy were abroad, and the Bhaers too proud to ask help even of those as near and dear as this generous pair. Confined to her room, Jo got desperate over the state of affairs, till she fell back upon the long-disused pen as the only thing she could do to help fill up the gaps in the income. A book for girls being wanted by a certain publisher, she hastily scribbled a little story describing a few scenes and adventures in the lives of herself and sisters,—though boys were more in her line,—and with very slight hopes of success sent it out to seek its fortune.

Things always went by contraries with Jo. Her first book, labored over for years, and launched full of the high hopes and ambitious dreams of youth, foundered on its voyage, though the wreck continued to float long afterward, to the profit of the publisher at least. The hastily written story, sent away with no thought beyond the few dollars it might bring, sailed with a fair wind and a wise pilot at the helm straight into public favor, and came home heavily laden with an unexpected cargo of gold and glory.

A more astonished woman probably never existed than Josephine Bhaer when her little ship came into port with flags flying, cannon that had been silent before now booming gayly, and, better than all, many kind faces rejoicing with her, many friendly hands grasping hers with cordial congratulations. After that it was plain sailing, and she merely had to load her ships and send them off on prosperous trips, to bring home stores of comfort for all she loved and labored for.

The fame she never did quite accept; for it takes very little fire to make a great deal of smoke nowadays, and notoriety is not real glory. The fortune she could not doubt, and gratefully received; though it was not half so large a one as a generous world reported it to be. The tide having turned continued to rise, and floated the family comfortably into a snug harbor where the older members could rest secure from storms, and whence the younger ones could launch their boats for the voyage of life.

All manner of happiness, peace, and plenty came in those years to bless the patient waiters, hopeful workers, and devout believers in the wisdom and justice of Him who sends disappointment, poverty, and sorrow to try the love of human hearts and make success the sweeter when it comes. The world saw the prosperity, and kind souls rejoiced over the improved fortunes of the family; but the success Jo valued most, the happiness that nothing could change or take away, few knew much about.

It was the power of making her mother's last years happy and serene; to see the burden of care laid down forever, the weary hands at rest, the dear face untroubled by any anxiety, and the tender heart free to pour itself out in the wise charity which was its delight. As a girl, Jo's favorite plan had been a room where Marmee could sit in peace and enjoy herself after her hard, heroic life. Now the dream had become a happy fact, and Marmee sat in her pleasant chamber with every comfort and luxury about her, loving daughters to wait on her as infirmities increased, a faithful mate to lean upon, and grandchildren to brighten the twilight of life with their dutiful affection. A very precious time to all, for she rejoiced as only mothers can in the good fortunes of their children. She had lived to reap the harvest she sowed; had seen prayers answered, hopes blossom, good gifts bear fruit, peace and prosperity bless the home she had made; and then, like some brave, patient angel, whose work was done, turned her face heavenward, glad to rest.

This was the sweet and sacred side of the change; but it had its droll and thorny one, as all things have in this curious world of ours. After the first surprise, incredulity, and joy, which came to Jo, with the ingratitude of human nature, she soon tired of renown, and began to resent her loss of liberty. For suddenly the admiring public took possession of her and all her affairs, past, present, and to come. Strangers demanded to look at her, question, advise, warn, congratulate, and drive her out of her wits by well-meant but very wearisome attentions. If she declined to open her heart to them, they reproached her; if she refused to endow pet charities, relieve private wants, or sympathize with every ill and trial known to humanity, she was called hard-hearted, selfish, and haughty; if she found it impossible to answer the piles of letters sent her, she was neglectful of her duty to the admiring public; and if she preferred the privacy of home to the pedestal upon which she was requested to pose, "the airs of literary people" were freely criticised.

She did her best for the children, they being the public for whom whe wrote, and labored stoutly to supply the demand always in the mouths of voracious youth,—"More stories; more right away!" Her family objected to this devotion at their expense, and her health suffered; but for a time she gratefully offered herself up on the altar of juvenile literature, feeling that she owed a good deal to the little friends in whose sight she had found favor after twenty years of effort.

But a time came when her patience gave out; and wearying of being a lion, she became a bear in nature as in name, and retiring to her den, growled awfully when ordered out. Her family enjoyed the fun, and had small sympathy with her trials, but Jo came to consider it the worst scrape of her life; for liberty had always been her dearest possession, and it seemed to be fast going from her. Living in a lantern soon loses its charms, and she was too old, too tired, and too busy to like it. She felt that she had done all that could reasonably be required of her when autographs, photographs, and autobiographical sketches had been sown broadcast over the land; when artists had taken her home in all its aspects, and reporters had taken her in the grim one she always assumed on these trying occasions; when a

series of enthusiastic boarding-schools had ravaged her grounds for trophies, and a steady stream of amiable pilgrims had worn her doorsteps
with their respectful feet; when servants left after a week's trial of the bell
that rang all day; when her husband was forced to guard her at meals,
and the boys to cover her retreat out of back windows on certain occasions when enterprising guests walked in unannounced at unfortunate
moments.

A sketch of one day may perhaps explain the state of things, offer
some excuse for the unhappy woman, and give a hint to the autograph-
fiend now rampant in the land; for it is a true tale.

"There ought to be a law to protect unfortunate authors," said Mrs.
Jo one morning soon after Emil's arrival, when the mail brought to her an
unusually large and varied assortment of letters. "To me it is a more vital
subject than international copyright; for time is money, peace is health,
and I lose both with no return but less respect for my fellow-creatures and
a wild desire to fly into the wilderness, since I cannot shut my doors even
in free America."

"Lion-hunters are awful when in search of their prey. If they could
change places for a while it would do them good; and they'd see what bores
they were when they 'do themselves the honor of calling to express their
admiration of our charming work,'" quoted Ted, with a bow to his parent,
now frowning over twelve requests for autographs.

"I have made up my mind on one point," said Mrs. Jo with great
firmness. "I will *not* answer this kind of letter. I've sent at least six to this
boy, and he probably sells them. This girl writes from a seminary, and if I
send her one all the other girls will at once write for more. All begin by
saying they know they intrude, and that I am of course annoyed by these
requests; but they venture to ask because I like boys, or they like the books,
or it is only one. Emerson and Whittier put these things in the waste-paper
basket; and though only a literary nursery-maid who provides moral pap
for the young, I will follow their illustrious example; for I shall have no
time to eat or sleep if I try to satisfy these dear unreasonable children;" and
Mrs. Jo swept away the entire batch with a sigh of relief.

"I'll open the others and let you eat your breakfast in peace, *liebe
Mutter,*" said Rob, who often acted as her secretary. "Here's one from the
South;" and breaking an imposing seal, he read:—

Madam,—As it has pleased Heaven to bless your efforts with a large fortune, I feel no hesitation in asking you to supply funds to purchase a new communion-service for our church. To whatever denomination you belong, you will of course respond with liberality to such a request.

Respectfully yours,   Mrs. X. Y. Zavier.

"Send a civil refusal, dear. All I have to give must go to feed and clothe the poor at my gates. That is my thank-offering for success. Go on," answered his mother, with a grateful glance about her happy home.

"A literary youth of eighteen proposes that you put your name to a novel he has written; and after the first edition your name is to be taken off and his put on. There's a cool proposal for you. I guess you won't agree to that, in spite of your soft-heartedness towards most of the young scribblers."

"Could n't be done. Tell him so kindly, and don't let him send the manuscript. I have seven on hand now, and barely time to read my own," said Mrs. Jo, pensively fishing a small letter out of the slop-bowl and opening it with care, because the down-hill address suggested that a child wrote it.

"I will answer this myself. A little sick girl wants a book, and she shall have it, but I can't write sequels to all the rest to please her. I should never come to an end if I tried to suit these voracious little Oliver Twists, clamoring for more. What next, Robin?"

"This is short and sweet."

Dear Mrs. Bhaer,—I am now going to give you my opinion of your works. I have read them all many times, and call them first-rate. Please go ahead.

Your admirer,   Billy Babcock.

"Now that is what I like. Billy is a man of sense and a critic worth having, since he has read my works many times before expressing his opinion. He asks for no answer, so send my thanks and regards."

"Here's a lady in England with seven girls, and she wishes to know your views upon education. Also what careers they shall follow,—the oldest being twelve. Don't wonder she's worried," laughed Rob.

"I'll try to answer it. But as I have no girls, my opinion is n't worth much and will probably shock her, as I shall tell her to let them run and play and build up good, stout bodies before she talks about careers. They will soon show what they want, if they are let alone, and not all run in the same mould."

"Here's a fellow who wants to know what sort of a girl he shall marry, and if you know of any like those in your stories."

"Give him Nan's address, and see what he'll get," proposed Ted, privately resolving to do it himself if possible.

"This is from a lady who wants you to adopt her child and lend her money to study art abroad for a few years. Better take it, and try your hand at a girl, mother."

"No, thank you, I will keep to my own line of business. What is that blotted one? It looks rather awful, to judge by the ink," asked Mrs. Jo, who beguiled her daily task trying to guess from the outside what was inside her many letters. This proved to be a poem from an insane admirer, to judge by its incoherent style.

To J. M. B.

"Oh, were I a heliotrope,
    I would play poet,
And blow a breeze of fragrance
    To you; and none should know it.

"Your form like the stately elm
    When Phœbus gilds the morning ray;
Your cheeks like the ocean bed
    That blooms a rose in May.

"Your words are wise and bright,
    I bequeath them to you a legacy given;
And when your spirit takes its flight,
    May it bloom a flower in heaven.

"My tongue in flattering language spoke,
And sweeter silence never broke

In busiest street or loneliest glen.
I take you with the flashes of any pen.

"Consider the lilies, how they grow;
    They toil not, yet are fair,
Gems and flowers and Solomon's seal.
    The geranium of the world is J. M. Bhaer.

"JAMES."

While the boys shouted over this effusion,—which is a true one,—their mother read several liberal offers from budding magazines for her to edit them gratis; one long letter from a young girl inconsolable because her favorite hero died, and "would dear Mrs. Bhaer rewrite the tale, and make it end good?" another from an irate boy denied an autograph, who darkly foretold financial ruin and loss of favor if she did not send him and all other fellows who asked autographs, photographs, and autobiographical sketches; a minister wished to know her religion; and an undecided maiden asked which of her two lovers she should marry. These samples will suffice to show a few of the claims made on a busy woman's time, and make my readers pardon Mrs. Jo if she did not carefully reply to all.

"That job is done. Now I will dust a bit, and then go to my work. I'm all behindhand, and serials can't wait; so deny me to everybody, Mary. I won't see Queen Victoria if she comes to-day." And Mrs. Bhaer threw down her napkin as if defying all creation.

"I hope the day will go well with thee, my dearest," answered her husband, who had been busy with his own voluminous correspondence. "I will dine at college with Professor Plock, who is to visit us to-day. The *Jünglings* can lunch on Parnassus; so thou shalt have a quiet time." And smoothing the worried lines out of her forehead with his good-by kiss, the excellent man marched away, both pockets full of books, an old umbrella in one hand, and a bag of stones for the geology class in the other.

"If all literary women had such thoughtful angels for husbands, they would live longer and write more. Perhaps that would n't be a blessing to the world though, as most of us write too much now," said Mrs. Jo, waving her feather duster to her spouse, who responded with flourishes of the umbrella as he went down the avenue.

Rob started for school at the same time, looking so much like him with his books and bag and square shoulders and steady air that his mother laughed as she turned away, saying heartily, "Bless both my dear professors, for better creatures never lived!"

Emil was already gone to his ship in the city; but Ted lingered to steal the address he wanted, ravage the sugar-bowl, and talk with "Mum;" for the two had great larks together.

Mrs. Jo always arranged her own parlor, refilled her vases, and gave the little touches that left it cool and neat for the day. Going to draw down the curtain, she beheld an artist sketching on the lawn, and groaned as she hastily retired to the back window to shake her duster.

At that moment the bell rang and the sound of wheels was heard in the road.

"I'll go; Mary lets 'em in;" and Ted smoothed his hair as he made for the hall.

"Can't see any one. Give me a chance to fly upstairs," whispered Mrs. Jo, preparing to escape. But before she could do so, a man appeared at the door with a card in his hand. Ted met him with a stern air, and his mother dodged behind the window-curtain to bide her time for escape.

"I am doing a series of articles for the 'Saturday Tattler,' and I called Mrs. Bhaer the first of all," began the new-comer in the insinuating tone of his tribe, while his quick eyes were taking in all they could, experience having taught him to make the most of his time, as his visits were usually short ones.

"Mrs. Bhaer never sees reporters, sir,"

"But a few moments will be all I ask," said the man, edging his way further in.

"You can't see her, for she is out," replied Teddy, as a backward glance showed him that his unhappy parent had vanished,—through the window, he supposed, as she sometimes did when hard bestead.

"Very sorry. I'll call again. Is this her study? Charming room!" And the intruder fell back on the parlor, bound to see something and bag a fact if he died in the attempt.

"It is not," said Teddy, gently but firmly backing him down the hall, devoutly hoping that his mother had escaped round the corner of the house.

"If you could tell me Mrs. Bhaer's age and birthplace, date of marriage, and number of children, I should be much obliged," continued the unabashed visitor as he tripped over the door-mat.

"She is about sixty, born in Nova Zembla, married just forty years ago to-day, and has eleven daughters. Anything else, sir?" And Ted's sober face was such a funny contrast to his ridiculous reply that the reporter owned himself routed, and retired laughing just as a lady followed by three beaming girls came up the steps.

"We are all the way from Oshkosh, and couldn't go home without seein' dear Aunt Jo. My girls just admire her works, and lot on gettin' a sight of her. I know it's early; but we are goin' to see Holmes and Longfeller, and the rest of the celebrities, so we ran out here fust thing. Mrs. Erastus Kingsbury Parmalee, of Oshkosh, tell her. We don't mind waitin'; we can look round a spell if she ain't ready to see folks yet."

All this was uttered with such rapidity that Ted could only stand gazing at the buxom damsels, who fixed their six blue eyes upon him so beseechingly that his native gallantry made it impossible to deny them a civil reply at least.

"Mrs. Bhaer is not visible to-day,—out just now, I believe; but you can see the house and grounds if you like," he murmured, falling back as the four pressed in gazing rapturously about them.

"Oh, thank you! Sweet, pretty place I'm sure! That's where she writes, ain't it? Do tell me if that's her picture! Looks just as I imagined her!"

With these remarks the ladies paused before a fine engraving of the Hon. Mrs. Norton, with a pen in her hand and a rapt expression of countenance, likewise a diadem and pearl necklace.

Keeping his gravity with an effort, Teddy pointed to a very bad portrait of Mrs. Jo, which hung behind the door, and afforded her much amusement, it was so dismal, in spite of a curious effect of light upon the end of the nose and cheeks as red as the chair she sat in.

"This was taken for my mother; but it is not very good," he said, enjoying the struggles of the girls not to look dismayed at the sad difference between the real and the ideal. The youngest, aged twelve, could not conceal her disappointment, and turned away, feeling as so many of us have felt when we discover that our idols are very ordinary men and women.

"I thought she'd be about sixteen and have her hair braided in two tails down her back. I don't care about seeing her now," said the honest child walking off to the hall door, leaving her mother to apologize, and her sisters to declare that the bad portrait was "perfectly lovely, so speaking and poetic, you know, 'specially about the brow."

"Come, girls, we must be goin', if we want to get through to-day. You can leave your albums and have them sent when Mrs. Bhaer has written a sentiment in 'em. We are a thousand times obliged. Give our best love to your ma, and tell her we are so sorry not to see her."

Just as Mrs. Erastus Kingsbury Parmalee uttered the words her eye fell upon a middle-aged woman in a large checked apron, with a handkerchief tied over her head, busily dusting an end room which looked like a study.

"One peep at her sanctum since she is out," cried the enthusiastic lady, and swept across the hall with her flock before Teddy could warn his mother, whose retreat had been cut off by the artist in front, the reporter at the back part of the house,—for he had n't gone,—and the ladies in the hall.

"They've got her!" thought Teddy, in comical dismay. "No use for her to play housemaid since they've seen the portrait."

Mrs. Jo did her best, and being a good actress, would have escaped if the fatal picture had not betrayed her. Mrs. Parmalee paused at the desk, and regardless of the meerschaum that lay there, the man's slippers close by, and a pile of letters directed to "Prof. F. Bhaer," she clasped her hands, exclaiming impressively, "Girls, this is the spot where she wrote those sweet, those moral tales which have thrilled us to the soul! Could I—ah, could I take one morsel of paper, an old pen, a postage stamp even, as a memento of this gifted woman?"

"Yes'm, help yourselves," replied the maid, moving away with a glance at the boy whose eyes were now full of the merriment he could not suppress.

The oldest girl saw it, guessed the truth, and a quick look at the woman in the apron confirmed her suspicion. Touching her mother, she whispered, "Ma, it's Mrs. Bhaer herself. I know it is."

"No? yes? it is! Well, I do declare, how nice that is!" And hastily

pursuing the unhappy woman, who was making for the door, Mrs. Parmalee cried eagerly, "Don't mind us! I know you're busy, but just let me
take your hand and then we'll go."

Giving herself up for lost, Mrs. Jo turned and presented her hand like
a tea-tray, submitting to have it heartily shaken, as the matron said, with
somewhat alarming hospitality,—

"If ever you come to Oshkosh, your feet won't be allowed to touch
the pavement; for you'll be borne in the arms of the populace, we shall be
so dreadful glad to see you."

Mentally resolving never to visit that effusive town, Jo responded as
cordially as she could; and having written her name in the albums, provided each visitor with a memento, and kissed them all round, they at last
departed, to call on "Longfeller, Holmes, and the rest,"—who were all
out, it is devoutly to be hoped.

"You villain, why did n't you give me a chance to whip away? Oh, my
dear, what fibs you told that man! I hope we shall be forgiven our sins in
this line, but I don't know what *is* to become of us if we don't dodge. So
many against one is n't fair play." And Mrs. Jo hung up her apron in the hall
closet, with a groan at the trials of her lot.

"More people coming up the avenue! Better dodge while the coast is
clear! I'll head them off!" cried Teddy, looking back from the steps, as he
was departing to school.

Mrs. Jo flew upstairs, having locked her door, calmly viewed a young
ladies' seminary camp on the lawn, and being denied the house, proceed to
enjoy themselves by picking the flowers, doing up their hair, eating lunch,
and freely expressing their opinion of the place and its possessors before
they went.

A few hours of quiet followed, and she was just settling down to a
long afternoon of hard work, when Rob came home to tell her that the
Young Men's Christian Union would visit the college, and two or three of
the fellows whom she knew wanted to pay their respects to her on the way.

"It is going to rain, so they won't come, I dare say; but father thought
you'd like to be ready, in case they do call. You always see the boys, you
know, though you harden your heart to the poor girls," said Rob, who had
heard from his brother about the morning visitations.

"Boys don't gush, so I can stand it. The last time I let in a party of girls, one fell into my arms and said, 'Darling, love me!' I wanted to shake her," answered Mrs. Jo, wiping her pen with energy.

"You may be sure the fellows won't do it, but they *will* want autographs, so you'd better be prepared with a few dozen," said Rob, laying out a quire of note-paper, being a hospitable youth and sympathizing with those who admired his mother.

"They can't outdo the girls. At X College I really believe I wrote three hundred during the day I was there, and I left a pile of cards and albums on my table when I came away. It is one of the most absurd and tiresome manias that ever afflicted the world."

Nevertheless Mrs. Jo wrote her name a dozen times, put on her black silk, and resigned herself to the impending call, praying for rain, however, as she returned to her work.

The shower came, and feeling quite secure, she rumpled up her hair, took off her cuffs, and hurried to finish her chapter; for thirty pages a day was her task, and she liked to have it well done before evening. Josie had brought some flowers for the vases, and was just putting the last touches when she saw several umbrellas bobbing down the hill.

"They are coming, Aunty! I see uncle hurrying across the field to receive them," she called at the stairfoot.

"Keep an eye on them, and let me know when they enter the avenue. It will take but a minute to tidy up and run down," answered Mrs. Jo, scribbling away for dear life, because serials wait for no man, not even the whole Christian Union *en masse.*

"There are more than two or three. I see half a dozen at least," called sister Ann from the hall door. "No! a dozen, I do believe; Aunty, look out; they are all coming! What *shall* we do?" And Josie quailed at the idea of facing the black throng rapidly approaching.

"Mercy on us, there are hundreds! Run and put a tub in the back entry for their umbrellas to drip into. Tell them to go down the hall and leave them, and pile their hats on the table; the tree won't hold them all. No use to get mats; my poor carpets!" And down went Mrs. Jo to prepare for the invasion, while Josie and the maids flew about dismayed at the prospect of so many muddy boots.

On they came, a long line of umbrellas, with splashed legs and flushed faces underneath; for the gentlemen had been having a good time all over the town, undisturbed by the rain. Professor Bhaer met them at the gate, and was making a little speech of welcome, when Mrs. Jo, touched by their bedraggled state, appeared at the door, beckoning them. Leaving their host to orate bareheaded in the wet, the young men hastened up the steps, merry, warm, and eager, clutching off their hats as they came, and struggling with their umbrellas, as the order was passed to march in and stack arms.

Tramp, tramp, tramp, down the hall went seventy-five pairs of boots; soon seventy-five umbrellas dripped sociably in the hospitable tub, while their owners swarmed all over the lower part of the house; and seventy-five hearty hands were shaken by the hostess without a murmur, though some were wet, some very warm, and nearly all bore trophies of the day's ramble. One impetuous party flourished a small turtle as he made his compliments; another had a load of sticks cut from noted spots; and all begged for some memento of Plumfield. A pile of cards mysteriously appeared on the table, with a written request for autographs; and despite her morning vow, Mrs. Jo wrote every one, while her husband and the boys did the honors of the house.

Josie fled to the back parlor, but was discovered by exploring youths, and mortally insulted by one of them, who innocently inquired if she was Mr. Bhaer. The reception did not last long, and the end was better than the beginning; for the rain ceased, and a rainbow shone beautifully over them as the good fellows stood upon the lawn singing sweetly for a farewell. A happy omen, that bow of promise arched over the young heads, as if Heaven smiled upon their union, and showed them that above the muddy earth and rainy skies the blessed sun still shone for all.

Three cheers, and then away they went, leaving a pleasant recollection of their visit to amuse the family as they scraped the mud off the carpets with shovels and emptied the tub half-full of water.

"Nice, honest, hard-working fellows, and I don't begrudge my half-hour at all; but I *must* finish, so don't let any one disturb me till tea-time," said Mrs. Jo, leaving Mary to shut up the house; for papa and the boys had gone off with the guests, and Josie had run home to tell her mother about the fun at Aunt Jo's.

Peace reigned for an hour, then the bell rang and Mary came giggling up to say, "A queer kind of a lady wants to know if she can catch a grasshopper in the garden."

"A what?" cried Mrs. Jo, dropping her pen with a blot; for of all the odd requests ever made, this was the oddest.

"A grasshopper ma'am. I said you was busy, and asked what she wanted, and she says she, 'I've got grasshoppers from the grounds of several famous folks, and I want one from Plumfield to add to my collection. Did you ever?" And Mary giggled again at the idea.

"Tell her to take all there are and welcome. I shall be glad to get rid of them; always bouncing in my face and getting in my dress," laughed Mrs. Jo.

Mary retired, to return in a moment nearly speechless with merriment.

"She's much obliged, ma'am, and she'd like an old gown or a pair of stockings of yours to put in a rug she's making. Got a vest of Emerson's she says, and a pair of Mr. Holmes's trousers, and a dress of Mrs. Stowe's. She must be crazy!"

"Give her that old red shawl, then I shall make a gay show among the great ones in that astonishing rug. Yes, they are all lunatics, these lion-hunters; but this seems to be a harmless maniac, for she does n't take my time and gives me a good laugh," said Mrs. Jo, returning to her work after a glance from the window, which showed her a tall, thin lady in rusty black, skipping wildly to and fro on the lawn in pursuit of the lively insect she wanted.

EXPLANATORY NOTES

HOSPITAL SKETCHES

1. Miss General S. was Hannah Stevenson, a well-known Boston reformer for whose projects Alcott had done sewing. *Hospital Sketches* is dedicated to her.

2. Dr. H. is William Alexander Hammond, surgeon-general of the Union forces.

3. Alcott refers to Harriet Prescott's "In a Cellar," *Atlantic Monthly* 3 (Feb. 1859): 151–72, which describes diamonds as a "mass of white magnificence" (Jones xix).

4. where the riot took place: on April 16, 1861, on its way to protect Washington, the Sixth Massachusetts Regiment was attacked by a Baltimore mob, representative of the pro-Southern sentiments held by many in the city. Disorders lasted several days, but the regiment eventually reached Washington.

5. Randolph's expression probably refers to the American statesman John Randolph (1773–1833), but the description of Washington is in fact attributed to Pierre Charles L'Enfant, the architect who planned the "city of magnificent vistas."

6. Tribulation is describing the statue of Andrew Jackson in Lafayette Square.

7. my friend, Sairy: Sairey Gamp, the drunken and talkative midwife in Dickens's *Martin Chuzzlewit*. She was one of Alcott's favorite literary characters; also her name was one of the family nicknames for Alcott.

8. Burnside's blunder refers to the disastrous Union defeat at Fredericks-

burg in December 1862. Union General Ambrose E. Burnside, after a series of failed preparations, decided to advance nonetheless, and faced well-positioned Confederate forces who turned the Union attack into a slaughter. The bloody defeat aroused Northern public sentiment against the Lincoln cabinet.

9. *vi et armis:* by force of arms.

10. "Ensign Spooney" is a character in Thackeray's *Vanity Fair,* I.i.xxiv.

11. Betsey Prig is the companion of Sairey Gamp in *Martin Chuzzlewit.*

12. rigolette: a wool scarf worn as a head covering.

13. the celebrated Seven: the Seven Sleepers were early Christian youths who fled from Ephesus in the third century A.D. to escape persecution and miraculously slept for several hundred years until Christianity became the accepted religion of the empire.

14. Grandma Rigglesty is a character in an antislavery novel, *Neighbor Jackwood* (1856), by J. T. Trowbridge.

15. Charles Sumner (1811–74) was senator from Massachusetts and Preston Brooks (1819–57), a South Carolina congressman; in 1856 Brooks severely injured Sumner in the Senate chamber in response to the latter's fierce antislavery speeches attacking Andrew Butler, the senator from South Carolina. Senator Henry Wilson of Massachusetts was later vice-president under Ulysses S. Grant.

16. The dome of the Capitol was uncompleted, and the Rotunda was decorated with patriotic sculptures and panels by Turnbull, Brumidi, and Costaggini.

17. Alcott refers to the bronze statue of Armed Liberty by Thomas Crawford, later placed on the dome.

18. D. D. is Dorothea Dix, supervisor of nurses.

19. Mark Tapley is the irrepressibly cheerful servant in *Martin Chuzzlewit.*

20. Mrs. Perrybingle is a character in Dickens's Christmas story, *The Cricket on the Hearth.*

21. The irrepressible Folsom refers to Abby Folsom (1792–1867), abolitionist, reformer, free-speech advocate.

22. old Aunt Chloe is Uncle Tom's wife in Harriet Beecher Stowe's *Uncle Tom's Cabin* (1852).

23. On January 1, 1863, the Emancipation Proclamation went into effect.

24. another Shepherd: William Henry Channing (1810–84), then chaplain for the House of Representatives in 1863–64.

25. a certain faithful pastor: Theodore Parker, who had died in Florence in May 1859.

26. Mrs. Cluppins, Chadband, and Sam Weller are comic characters in *The*

Pickwick Papers and *Bleak House*. Alcott added the comment about Dickens's jewelry in the 1870 edition. On her trip abroad in 1866 she had met Dickens and had disapproved of his diamond stickpin, ring, and studs (Saxton 319).

27. Dr. Z. was Dr. John Winslow, a Quaker who befriended Alcott, invited her to dinner and to hear Channing preach.

MY CONTRABAND

1. The "F.F.V.s" were the First Families of Virginia, or the Virginia social elite.

2. The attack on Fort Wagner was part of the July 1862 siege of Charleston, culminating in the victory of the offensive side, the Union. Governor John Albion Andrew (1818–67) was the abolitionist governor of Massachusetts during the Civil War. He organized the 54th Massachusetts, the first all-black army regiment on the Union side.

PSYCHE'S ART

1. John Flaxman, English draftsman and sculptor (1775–1826). Among the other artists mentioned in the first part of the story are Joseph Turner (1775–1851), British landscape artist; Bartoleme Murillo (c. 1617–82), Spanish painter of mainly religious subjects; Michelangelo (1465–1564), Italian painter, sculptor, poet, and architect; Rembrandt van Rijn (1607–1669), Dutch painter and foremost of the Dutch masters; Raphael (1483–1520), leading Italian Renaissance painter; Peter Paul Rubens (1577–1640), Flemish painter of religious and historical subjects, landscapes, and portraits; and Sir Joshua Reynolds (1723–1792), English portrait painter.

2. The Peerybingle's baby appears in Dickens's *The Cricket on the Hearth*.

3. These lines are from "Life a Duty," attributed to Ellen Sturgis Hooper (1816–41).

Explanatory Notes

THE SUNNY SIDE

1. In a famous passage in her novel *Cranford* (1851), Elizabeth Gaskell describes the exquisite prudery of the elderly spinsters who do not want to be seen eating oranges in public: "Miss Jenkyns did not like to cut the fruit; for, as she observed, the juice all ran out nobody knew where; sucking (only I think she used some more recondite word) was in fact the only way of enjoying oranges; but then there was the unpleasant association with a ceremony frequently gone through by little babies; and so, after dessert, in orange season, Miss Jenkyns and Miss Matty used to rise up, possess themselves each of an orange in silence, and withdraw to the privacy of their own rooms, to indulge in sucking oranges."

WORK: A STORY OF EXPERIENCE

1. Elizabeth Fry (1780–1845) was an English advocate of prison reform.

2. Zenobia (d. 274 A.D.), the powerful and strong-willed queen of Palmyra during the Roman Empire. Her defiance of Rome led to the defeat of her armies and the siege of Palmyra. After her capture by the emperor Aurelian, she was given an estate and pension.

Aspasia was the consort and wife of the Athenian orator Pericles, and the heroine of Lydia Maria Child's novel *Pilothea*.

3. *The Abbot* (1820) is a novel by Sir Walter Scott about Mary Stuart, told from the points of view of the men surrounding her.

4. Mr. Micawber is an improvident character in Dickens's *David Copperfield*.

5. Boadicea was an early British queen (d. 62 A.D.) who killed herself when Britain fell into the hands of the Romans.

6. Britomart is the woman knight intended to represent militant chastity in Edmund Spenser's Renaissance allegory, *The Faerie Queene* (1590).

7. Rachel was the stage name of the great French actress Elisabeth Rachel Félix (1820–58).

8. Tilly Slowboy is Mrs. Peerybingle's clumsy nurse in *The Cricket on the Hearth* by Dickens.

9. Miss Miggs is a character in Dickens's *Barnaby Rudge* (1841), whose career includes a stint as an especially censorious female turnkey.

10. *Masks and Faces* is an 1852 play written by Charles Reade and Tom Taylor based on the life of the eighteenth-century actress Peg Woffington.

11. *The Rival Queens* is a Restoration tragedy (1677) by Nathaniel Lee.

12. John Halifax is the rags-to-riches hero of Dinah Mulock Craik's popular novel *John Halifax, Gentleman* (1857). Phineas Fletcher is a major character in the novel.

13. Peg Woffington (1714–60) was an Irish actress famous for playing male characters, and the subject of *Masks and Faces,* mentioned in Chapter 3 (n. 10).

14. Plato (c. 426–346 B.C.), Greek philosopher; Pericles (499–29 B.C.), Athenian orator and statesman, and patron of the arts; Hypatia (late 4th and early 5th centuries), neoplatonic philosopher celebrated for her beauty, reviled for her paganism, and ultimately murdered and dismembered by a band of monks.

15. Madame de Staël (1655–1817) was an early Romantic French novelist and hostess of a celebrated literary salon.

16. Mr. Greatheart is the pilgrim's guide in the second part of John Bunyan's *Pilgrim's Progress.* He slays an array of allegorical giants (Grim, Maul, Slaygo, and Despair) to protect the pilgrim Christiana and her party, and finally brings them to salvation. The City of Destruction is Christian's original home in *The Pilgrim's Progress,* which he believes will be destroyed by God's wrath.

17. John Brown (1800–59), was a militant abolitionist executed for his part in an 1859 slave revolt during which he led twenty-one followers to the capture of a United States arsenal. Colonel Shaw was Union leader of the 54th Massachusetts, the first regiment of black soldiers from a free state.

HOW I WENT OUT TO SERVICE

1. This reference means that from aspiring to be like the great actress Mrs. Siddons, she will now become Cinderella.

DIANA AND PERSIS

1. "The Cotter's Saturday Night" was an illustration of Robert Burns's poem (1786) about Scottish domestic life.

2. Percy goes off to the second stanza of "To a Skylark," the famous poem by Percy Bysshe Shelley (1792–1822) on which her painting is modelled.

3. The salon was the annual exhibition organized by the Société des Artistes Français.

Explanatory Notes

4. Rosa Bonheur (1822–99) was a French painter of landscapes and animal life who often dressed in men's clothing.

5. Miss Cassal is the American artist Mary Cassatt (1845–1926), who strongly supported and exhibited with the Impressionists.

6. "The Fighting Seinereraise" is a takeoff on Turner's celebrated painting, *The Fighting Temeraire being Towed to Her Last Berth* (1938); "Symphony in Red and Yellow" parodies one of Whistler's many 1868 "symphony" paintings, such as *Symphony in Blue and Pink*, or *Symphony in Green and Violet*, depicting women and the sea.

7. The Slough of Despond is one place in the allegorical landscape of *The Pilgrim's Progress*; Pilgrim is rescued by Help after floundering in the spiritual doubt the Slough represents.

8. élève: pupil.

9. The Palais de l'Industrie was the location of the Salon.

10. The Celestial City is Heaven, in *The Pilgrim's Progress*.

11. Felix Mendelssohn's music for *Midsummer Night's Dream* was written in 1836.

12. The Pincio is at the western end of the Borghese gardens, a park on the Pincian hill in Rome, fashionable as a tourist spot in the nineteenth century as it is today.

13. Socrate is a mountain north of Rome.